DNA REPLICATION & REPAIR; EUKARYOTIC CHROMOSOMES

Biology Lecture I

OBJECTIVES

- DNA Replication
  - Review: Nucleotides, the phosphodiester bond, and DNA structure
  - Characteristics of DNA replication
  - Enzymes and steps of DNA replication
  - Prokaryotic vs. eukaryotic replication
  - Telomeres
- Types of DNA Mutations
- Mechanisms of DNA Repair
- Eukaryotic Chromosomes
  - Structure and Organization: histones, nucleosomes, chromatin
  - Heterochromatin and euchromatin
  - Centromeres; p and q arms
  - Repetitive DNA

Review: Nucleotides and DNA Structure

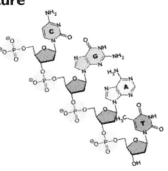

Nucleic acid = macromolecule composed of nucleotide monomers
- DNA and RNA (mRNA, tRNA, rRNA, snRNA, etc.)
- Structure: linear strand of nucleotides joined by phosphodiester bonds
- May be single stranded or double stranded

Nucleotide = nitrogenous base + sugar + 1-3 phosphates

- **Nucleic acid "backbone"**: sugar and phosphate group of each nucleotide linked by phosphodiester bonds

- **Glycosidic bond** between sugar and the base; **Hydrogen bonds** between the bases if double stranded

- DNA and RNA differ in the 2' carbon of the sugar: RNA (ribose) has an OH; DNA (deoxyribose) has H

- Base linked to the 1' C of sugar, phosphate linked to 5' C

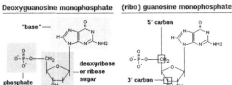

Nitrogenous Bases:

Purines: Adenine and Guanine
- Double ring

Pyrimidines: Cytosine, Uracil, and Thymine
- Single ring
- Thymine = DNA, Uracil = RNA
- U and T differ in a methyl group

adenine   guanine

uracil   cytosine

thymine

Base Pairing:

- Adenine always base pairs with Thymine (with Uracil in RNA → 2 H-bonds

- Cytosine always pairs with Guanine → 3 H-bonds (stronger base pair)

DNA Structure:

- **Double helix** = 2 nucleic acid strands linked by H-bonds between nitrogenous bases The linked strands are twisted into a **right-handed helix**
- Strands are **"anti-parallel"**: 5' end of one strand is aligned with the 3' end of the other
    - **5' end** of strand is where phosphate group (linked to 5' C) is the last group
    - **3' end** is where OH (linked to 3' C) marks the end of the strand
    - DNA sequences read/written 5' → 3'
- DNA is built by adding the 5' end of incoming nucleotide to 3' OH of existing strand
    - Pyrophosphate (two phosphates) lost when built from nucleotide triphosphates

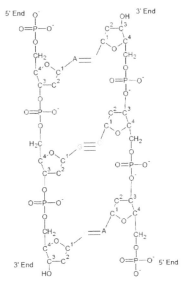

What **DNA** sequence will be complimentary to the following?:

5' ATGCGCT 3'

Answer: 5' AGCGCAT 3'

$$
\begin{array}{|c|}
A=T \\
T=A \\
G\equiv C \\
C\equiv G \\
\end{array}
$$

5' – ATGCGCTAGCTCATTT –3'
3' – TACGCGATCGAGTAAA –5'

DNA Replication: Overview

Overall: one DNA molecule replicated → two identical copies
- Occurs during the S phase (synthesis phase) of the cell cycle
- Cell division requires DNA replication to occur

Semi-Conservative nature of DNA Replication:
- When the mechanism of DNA replication was first discovered, there were three different methods proposed; semi-conservative was found to be correct
- The strands of the original DNA molecule separate and serve as templates for the synthesis of new, complementary strand

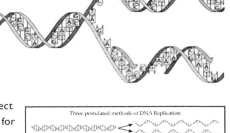

- The synthesis of the new "daughter strand" occurs on top of the "parent strand" through the addition of free floating nucleotides

- DNA replication requires a template (the parent DNA strand), as well as a primer to jumpstart the synthesis (RNA primer)

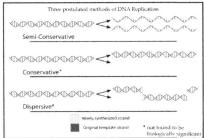

- DNA is built in the 5' → 3' direction of both daughter strands

Enzymes involved in DNA replication:

DNA Helicase- unwinds the parent DNA strands

Topoisomerase- relaxes DNA supercoils that accumulate due to the unwinding
- **DNA Gyrase** is a type of topoisomerase

Single Strand Binding (SSB) Proteins - stabilize the single parent strands of DNA once unwound

Primase- lays down the RNA primer (a type of RNA Polymerase)

DNA Polymerase- builds the daughter strand of the DNA; proofreads and corrects errors; replaces the RNA primer

Ligase- links the Okazaki fragments of DNA daughter strand

Steps:
- Beginning at a specific region of the DNA (the "ORI"/origin of replication), helicase binds to DNA and begins to unwind it by breaking H-bonds between bases → forms a replication bubble with replication forks on either end
  - ORI found by other helper proteins
- Topoisomerase relaxes supercoils that occur upstream of the replication bubble due to the unwinding of the strands
  - Cuts DNA and unwinds the excess coils
- SSBPs stabilize the newly separated parent strands, making sure they don't reanneal

- Primase lays down a few RNA bases that are complementary to the parent strand and serve as a primer, from which DNA Polymerase can build off of
  - DNA Pol can only extend, cannot initiate
  - These RNA primers must later be removed and replaced with DNA
- DNA Polymerase elongates from the primer, adding nucleotides one by one and using the parent strand as a template
  - Free floating dNTPs are added (triphosphate) and the release of two phosphate groups from the molecule provides the energy for this reaction
  - 3' hydroxyl group on the last nucleotide of the daughter strand performs nucleophilic attack onto phosphate (at 5' end) of the incoming nucleotide

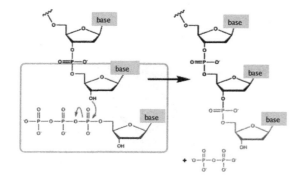

- At each replication fork there is a **leading strand** and a **lagging strand** of the daughter molecules, due to the requirement that the new strands are built in a 5'→3' direction of elongation
- Leading strand is synthesized in the same direction as the extending replication fork and is a single continuous strand
- Lagging strand is not continuous and made up of multiple **Okazaki fragments** that are soon after joined together by DNA ligase
- Synthesis is **bidirectional** because it extends in both directions from the replication bubble
- RNA primers are eventually replaced with DNA using DNA Polymerase

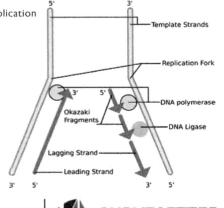

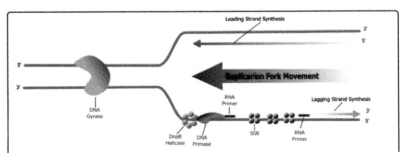

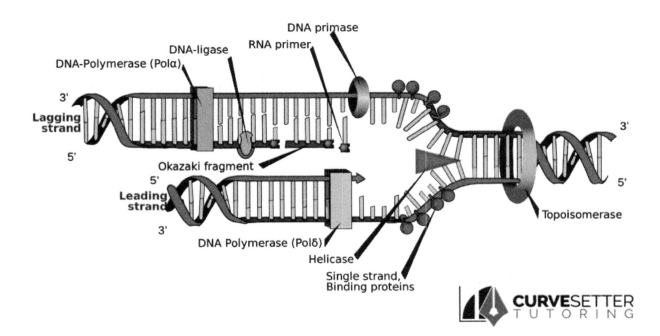

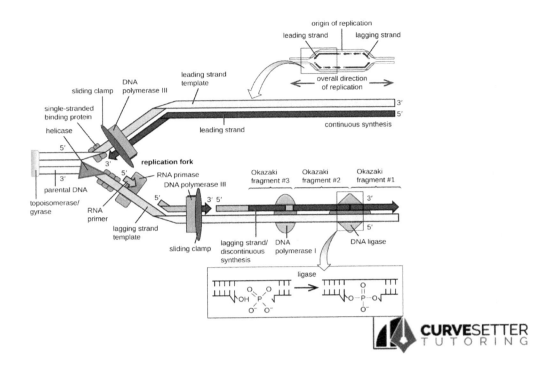

Eukaryotes vs. Prokaryotes

Eukaryotes:
- The process occurs in the nucleus
- Many origins of replication per DNA molecule (linear DNA) → multiple replication bubbles at once; ultimately the bubbles meet each other and the newly formed DNA molecules separate
  - Many simultaneous replication bubbles enables fast replication
- 5 DNA Polymerases
- Only eukaryotes have telomeres

Prokaryotes:
- The process occurs in the cytosol
- One ORI per DNA molecule (circular DNA) → theta replication
- 3 DNA Polymerases
  - DNA Pol III: the main DNA Pol that extends the daughter strands
  - DNA Pol I: slower than Pol III; exonuclease activity enables it to remove RNA primer and replace with DNA; also plays role in DNA error repair

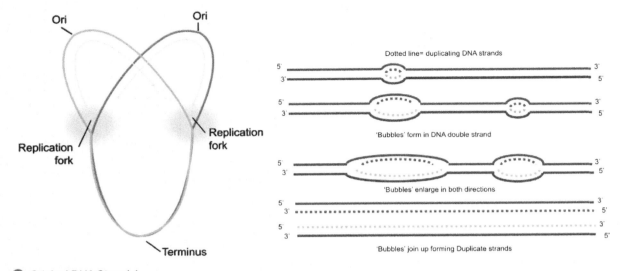

Original DNA Strand 1
Original DNA Strand 2
New DNA

Telomeres

- At the very end of each eukaryotic DNA molecule, on the newly synthesized lagging strand, there is an RNA primer that cannot be replaced once removed
- As a result, chromosomes shorten at each round of replication
- To prevent this shortening from affecting coding DNA regions, non-coding repeats called telomeres are added to the ends of DNA
  - Telomeres are a form of protection
  - Telomeres shorten at each cell division
- If telomere is too short the cell will stop dividing and functioning properly (**senscence** = biological aging)
- Length of telomere associated with age of cell → biological clock

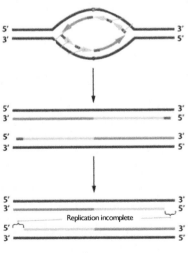

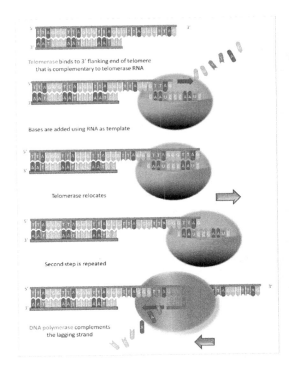

Telomerase binds to 3' flanking end of telomere that is complementary to telomerase RNA

Bases are added using RNA as template

Telomerase relocates

Second step is repeated

DNA polymerase complements the lagging strand

Telomerase is an enzyme that catalyzes the lengthening of telomeres

- Adds to the ends of telomere a specific repeated base sequence
- Uses its built-in RNA strand as a template to add this DNA
- RNA-dependent DNA Polymerase (makes DNA but must use complementary RNA as the template) → reverse transcriptase
- Telomerase is found in germ line, stem cells, and often in cancerous cells

Types of DNA Mutations

DNA Polymerase occasionally makes errors during replication, and mutations may occur as a result:

Point Mutations (Substitution)- characterized by their effect on the transcribed mRNA/translated polypeptide
1. **Silent mutation:** same amino acid will be translated despite a base pair error
2. **Missense mutation:** base pair change results in a change in the amino acid that is translated
    - Conservative: New amino acid has similar biochemical properties to the original one
    - Impact of this type of mutation depends on the specific change in the amino acid (D → E unlikely to have a huge effect; D → G more likely to have an effect)
3. **Nonsense mutation:** base pair change causes the DNA and transcribed mRNA to encode a stop signal so that transcription and translation terminate prematurely

Insertions and Deletions- insertions occur when one or more additional base pairs are inserted and deletions occur when one or more base pairs are deleted
- Insertions or deletions may result in a frameshift, meaning that the reading frame of the gene is changed so that all of downstream region of the gene will also be affected
- the cat ran → tuh eca tra
    - Occurs if the insertion/deletion is not in a multiple of 3 base pairs

It is important to remember that mutations are the basis of genetic variation in organisms and therefore enable species to evolve. So, although most mutations have a deleterious effect, not all are bad and they are essential for natural selection to occur.

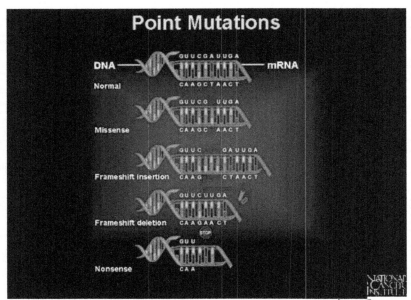

	No mutation	Silent	Nonsense	Missense	
				conservative	non-conservative
DNA level	TTC	TTT	ATC	TCC	TGC
mRNA level	AAG	AAA	UAG	AGG	ACG
protein level	**Lys**	**Lys**	**STOP**	**Arg**	**Thr**

Point mutations

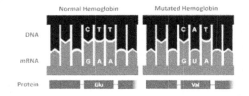

Other forms of DNA damage occur due to some **endogenous** agent (reactive metabolites, free radicals, ROS, etc.) or due to an **exogenous** trigger (UV radiation, X-rays, chemical exposure, etc.). A mutagen is any agent that causes damage to and changes in DNA.

- **Hydrolysis of DNA**

- **Chromosomal translocations**

- UV radiation → **Pyrimidine dimers**

- **Cross-linking of bases**

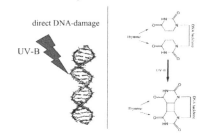

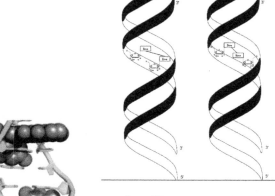

- **Chemical intercalation:** a chemical (usually aromatic ring) inserts itself between the bases of DNA

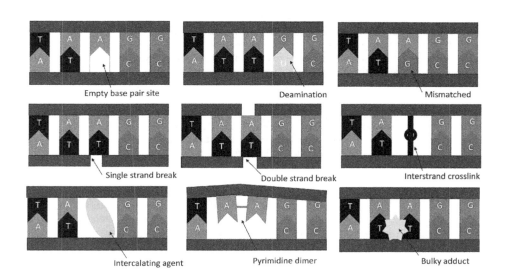

Transposon/Transposable Element (TE): regions of DNA that can move around in the genome and often cause structural changes and mutations in DNA

- Found in both prokaryotes and eukaryotes; make up over 40% of human DNA
- Part of the TE encodes for enzymes that copy and paste the DNA segment into a different place in the genome (or cut and paste) → transposase
- May cause insertions, inversions, deletions, duplications
- Can result in the disabling of a gene, and are implicated in many diseases

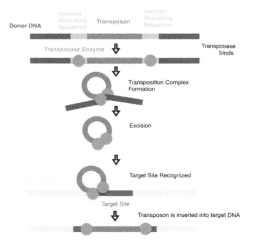

Mechanisms of DNA Repair

DNA Polymerase has proofreading and editing capabilities so that errors detected during replication can be immediately fixed (nuclease activity enables it to remove the incorrect base, like a backspace button, and then it adds the correct one). If the mutation is not initially detected, then **DNA mismatch repair (MMR)** can detect a mismatch in the base pairs, figure out which strand is the new daughter strand, and correct it. After that, there are many other mechanisms that also fix different types mutations. If the mutation cannot be fixed, the cell often undergoes apoptosis.

Mismatch Repair Pathway
- DNA Polymerase errors may result in a base mismatch (A with C, G with T, etc.)
- Via MMR, the daughter strand is recognized and the mismatched base of that strand is removed then replaced
  - Bacteria → new strand recognized by lack of methylation

Nucleotide and Base Excision Repair

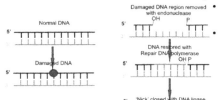

- Remove bulky DNA legions that are caused by UV radiation, chemicals, and other mutagens → prevent future error in the next DNA replication
- Small region of DNA surrounding the error is removed, DNA polymerase replaces the region, and DNA ligase joins the fragments

Homologous End Joining

- Fix double strand breaks and removals of DNA regions
- Must be done after DNA replication because requires a sister chromatid (another copy of that DNA region)
- Homologous DNA serves as a template for removed region to be synthesized → requires DNA Pol and ligase

Non-Homologous End Joining

- Fix double strand breaks and removals of regions of DNA when homologous DNA is not available
- Cleaved ends of DNA are ligated together → mutagenic

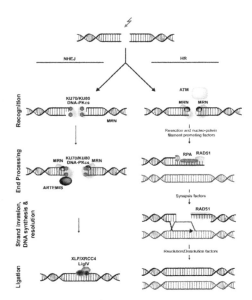

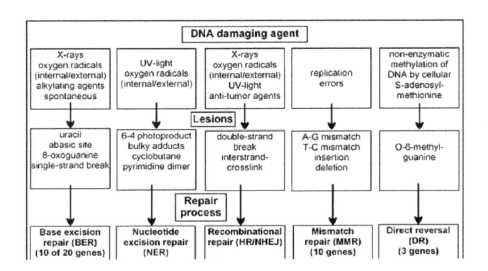

Eukaryotic Chromosomes

- Eukaryotic chromosomes are composed of doubled stranded DNA molecules and associated proteins that are folded and bundled into a rod-like shape (unduplicated) or an x-like shape (duplicated)
  - Following DNA replication and during metaphase of mitosis, the X shaped chromosome is visible. It is composed of 2 identical **sister chromatids** linked by a **centromere**

Human chromosomes:

- 46 total chromosomes into 23 pairs → each pair composed of one maternal and one paternal chromosome
- 22 pairs of autosomal chromosomes and 1 pair of sex chromosomes (XX = female, XY = male)
- Autosomes are numbered 1 – 22

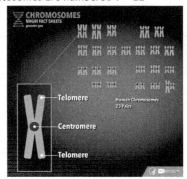

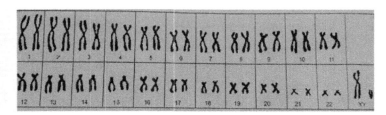

- **Telomeric DNA** caps the ends of the chromosomes
- When centromere is slightly off-center one arm of each chromatid will be longer than the other arm
  - Shorter arm: **p arm**; longer arm: **q arm**

Structure:
- **Nucleosome:** region of DNA wrapped around a **histone octamer** (8 histone proteins) → histones have + charge to attract – DNA
- **Chromatin** = DNA + histone proteins → "Beads on a string"
- Chromatin bundles up and condenses into long rods
- Centromere (binding proteins and specific DNA sequences) links two DNA molecules (sister chromatids)

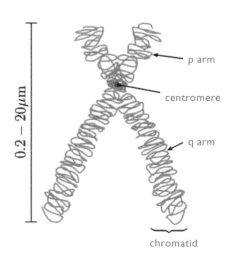

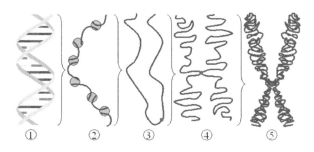

- Chromatin is classified as heterochromatin and euchromatin, indicating structural properties and transcriptional activity

- **Heterochromatin:** chromatin is densely packed and not accessible to enzymes of transcription → transcriptionally "silent"

- **Euchromatin:** chromatin is loosely packed, making it accessible to transcriptional enzymes → transcriptionally active

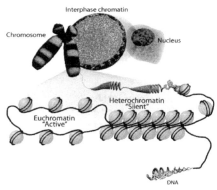

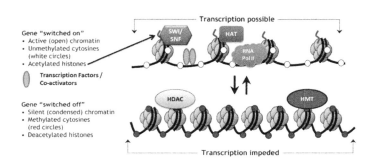

Chromosomal Abnormalities: may or may not be deleterious; often fatal and many associated with disease

- Large-scale structural changes: deletion, duplication, inversion, insertion, translocation, etc.
- **Aneuploidy:** organism has an abnormal number of chromosomes (humans: more or less than 46 chromosomes)
- **Polysomy:** organism has one or more additional copies of a chromosome
  - Ex. Trisomy 21 (Down Syndrome), Triple X Syndrome, Kleinfelter's Syndrome, Turner Syndrome

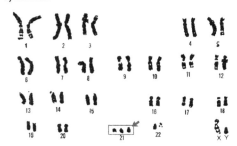

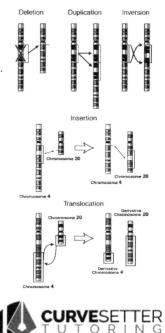

Repetitive DNA:

- A large proportion of eukaryotic and prokaryotic DNA is comprised of highly repetitive sequences (2/3 in humans)
- Non-coding and not translated
- Many different types: tandem repeats (satellite and microsatellite DNA), transposons, etc.
- Highly variable between individuals

Single Copy DNA:

- Most translated genes
- Highly conserved (low mutation rate)

Variable Nucleotide Repeat Sequences

Individual 1

GGT	AGTCGGTAAG	AGTCGGTAAG	AGTCGGTAAG	AGTCGGTAAG	AGTCGGTAAG	AGTCGGTAAG	CGGTAAGTAGCSA

Individual 2

GGT	AGTCGGTAAG	AGTCGGTAAG	AGTCGGTAAG	AGTCGGTAAG	AGTCGGTAAG	AGTCGGTAAG	AGTCGGTAAG	AGTCGGTAAG	CGTT

- Type of Minisatellite because
  - The repeat sequence is 10-100 nucleotides
  - The sequence repeats 5-50 times
- Number of repeats differs between two different individuals, but the repeating sequence does not

THE CENTRAL DOGMA: TRANSCRIPTION & TRANSLATION

Biology Lecture 2

OBJECTIVES

- Overview of The Central Dogma
  - Codons and anti-codons
  - Characteristics of the triplet code
  - Start and stop codons
  - Properties and role of mRNA
- Transcription: DNA → RNA
  - The process of transcription
  - Eukaryotic mRNA processing
  - Introns and exons
  - Macromolecules involving in RNA processing
- Translation: RNA → protein
  - The functions and properties of rRNA and tRNA
  - Ribosomes: structure and function
  - The process of translation
  - Protein modification

Overview of The Central Dogma

- **The Central Dogma** describes the processes by which proteins are synthesized from the genetic code
    - DNA → RNA → protein

- **Transcription** (DNA → RNA): mRNA is synthesized by RNA Polymerase using DNA (gene) as a template
    - Occurs in the nucleus for eukaryotes, cytoplasm for prokaryotes
    - Template strand of DNA is complementary to the transcribed RNA

- **Translation** (RNA → protein): polypeptides are made by ribosomes and tRNA using the instructions encoded by mRNA
    - Occurs in the cytoplasm

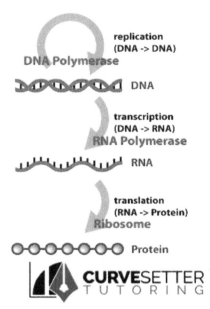

The Triplet Code

- The "code": 3 base pairs code for a specific amino acid of the polypeptide

- **Codon:** 3 nucleotides of the mRNA; complementary to the DNA template strand
    - 1 RNA molecule has many codons and each nucleotide triplet codes for a single amino acid of the synthesized polypeptide

- **Anti-codon:** 3 nucleotides of the tRNA; complementary to the mRNA codon
    - Anticodon in at the tip of the tRNA molecule and base pairs with mRNA; this complementary relationship is how the mRNA codon calls for a specific tRNA to bring over the correct amino acid

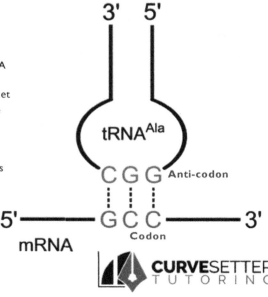

Properties of the triplet code

- The codons are continuous and don't overlap; they encode the correct primary structure of the protein

- **Degenerate:** the code is degenerate (redundant) because multiple codons often code for the same amino acid

- **Wobble Pairing:** when base pairing doesn't follow the Watson-Crick rules (A with U/T, C with G)
  - Occurs often between codons and anticodons
  - The third nucleotide of the mRNA codon (when read 5' → 3') pairs very loosely with the tRNA
  - Wobble pairing allows > 1 mRNA codon to pair with the same tRNA and therefore code for the same amino acid
  - Most tRNA molecules pair with more than one codon → less tRNA's needed
  - Ex. GUU, GUC, GUA, GUG → all code for valine

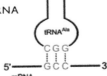

- Start and stop codons:
  - **Initiation/start codon** = AUG → signals the start of translation and is the first amino acid; always methionine
  - **Termination/stop codon** = UAA, UGA, UAG → signals for translation to end; no tRNA involved

- There are 64 total codons, three of which are stop signals → 61 codons for only 20 amino acids
  - 45 or less tRNA's

ORF = Open Reading Frame → continuous stretch of nucleotides that has the possibility of being translated; usually starts with start codon and ends with stop codon

Prokaryotes:
- Polycistronic mRNA → 1 RNA molecule can code for more than 1 polypeptide
  - Usually more than 1 ORF's within one mRNA molecule (each coding for a different polypeptide)
- No RNA processing
- Transcription and translation take place in the cytosol; can occur simultaneously with newly made mRNA being translated before it is finished being transcribed from DNA
- mRNA rapidly degraded so only used for a short period of time
- 1 main RNA Polymerase

Eukaryotes:
- Monocistronic mRNA → 1 mRNA molecule codes for polypeptide
  - "one gene, one protein"
- Transcription occurs in the nucleus and makes hnRNA; hnRNA processed to make mRNA (RNA processing)
  - DNA → hnRNA → mRNA
- Translation occurs in the cytoplasm
- 3 main RNA Polymerases: RNA Pol I makes rRNA; RNA Pol II makes hnRNA/mRNA; RNA Pol III makes tRNA

Transcription: DNA → RNA

- DNA acts as template for making RNA, but only one of the strands can act as the template

    - Template = "template strand", "anti-sense strand"; other (non-template) strand = "coding strand", "sense strand"

- Sequence of transcribed RNA will be the same as the coding strand, but with U instead of T

- RNA made by RNA Polymerase in a 5' → 3' direction (template strand read 3' → 5')

- Unlike DNA Pol, RNA Pol does not require a primer

- RNA Pol cannot proofread the synthesized RNA, so transcription errors are more frequent than replication errors

- RNA Pol moves "downstream"; DNA nucleotides numbered: 0 at start site, - #s upstream, + #s downstream

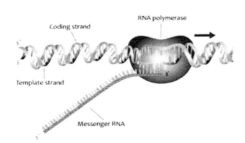

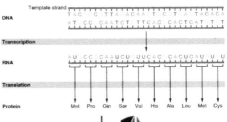

Steps of Transcription-
Initiation:

- **RNA Polymerase** enzyme plus **factor sigma** (helper molecule) form the holoenzyme and bind to **promoter** region of the DNA, just upstream from the start site → closed complex formed

    - Prokaryotic promoters have specific sequences at -10 and -35, which bind to specific regions of RNA Pol
    - Eukaryotes: other helper proteins (transcription factors/TFs) find the promoter and recruit RNA Pol; promoter has a "TATA Box" with many T and A bases

- RNA unwinds this region of DNA → open complex formed

Elongation:

- RNA Pol adds free-floating nucleotide triphosphates to synthesize the RNA strand; they are complementary to the DNA template strand
- RNA moves downstream along the DNA, elongating the RNA in a 5' → 3' direction

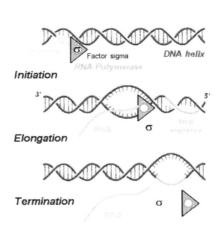

Termination:
- (Prokaryotic) **Intrinsic Termination**: specific sequence of the DNA results in RNA folding back on itself into a "stem-loop" shape, which ultimately knocks RNA Pol off of the RNA

- (Prokaryotic) **Rho-dependent Termination**: Rho protein recognizes a specific RNA sequence and latches onto the RNA molecule, knocking off RNA Pol

- Eukaryotic Termination: depends on the gene; not important for you to know

Regulation of Transcription:
- The strength of the association between RNA Pol and the promoter affects the transcription rate
    - RNA Pol has stronger affinity for the promoter → higher transcription rate

- **Repressors**- proteins that bind to the promoter region or the **silencer** regions of DNA and decrease the rate of transcription

- **Enhancers**- region of DNA that **activator** proteins can bind to; this association increases the rate of transcription
    - Usually at a position on the DNA molecule that is distant from the gene

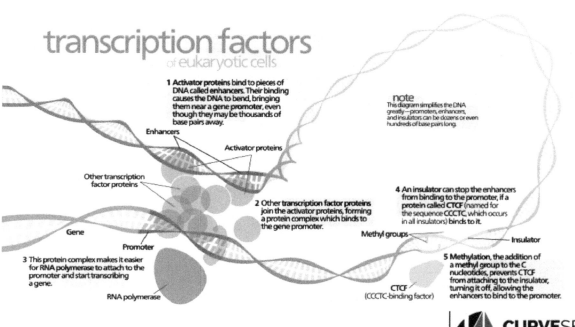

transcription factors
of eukaryotic cells

1 Activator proteins bind to pieces of DNA called enhancers. Their binding causes the DNA to bend, bringing them near a gene promoter, even though they may be thousands of base pairs away.

Enhancers

Activator proteins

note
This diagram simplifies the DNA greatly—promoters, enhancers, and insulators can be dozens or even hundreds of base pairs long.

Other transcription factor proteins

2 Other transcription factor proteins join the activator proteins, forming a protein complex which binds to the gene promoter.

4 An insulator can stop the enhancers from binding to the promoter, if a protein called CTCF (named for the sequence CCCTC, which occurs in all insulators) binds to it.

Gene

Methyl groups

Insulator

Promoter

3 This protein complex makes it easier for RNA polymerase to attach to the promoter and start transcribing a gene.

5 Methylation, the addition of a methyl group to the C nucleotides, prevents CTCF from attaching to the insulator, turning it off, allowing the enhancers to bind to the promoter.

CTCF
(CCCTC-binding factor)

RNA polymerase

RNA Processing

- In eukaroytes, transcription produces hnRNA, which must be further processes to form mRNA
- RNA processing occurs in nucleus; mature mRNA exits the nucleus to be translated

Splicing: introns removed and exons joined together
- Performed by spliceosome complex: snRNA (small nuclear RNA) plus proteins
- **Exons:** regions of a gene that encode the protein sequence (EXons as Expressed)
- **Introns:** regions of a gene that are transcribed but not translated; don't encode the protein
- **Alternative Splicing:** enables more than 1 different mRNA molecules to be made from the same hnRNA
    - Some exons skipped/spliced out so that differing combinations of exons can be used to make the mRNA

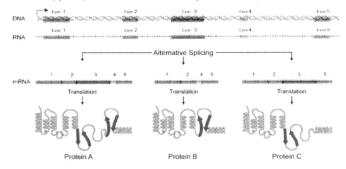

Cap and Tail:
- A "5' cap" consisting of a methylated guanine is added
- A "3' poly-A tail" consisting of multiple adenine nucleotides is added
- Both modifications increase the mRNA's stability and protect it from degradation in cytoplasm

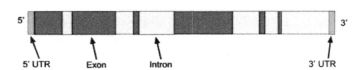

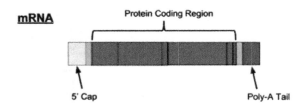

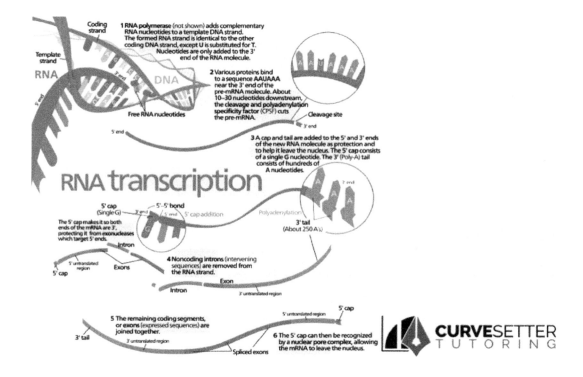

RNA transcription

Importance of Introns:
- A "gene" is composed of both introns and exons, but only exons make it into mRNA and are translated
- May become functional non-coding RNA molecules after being spliced out
- Enable alternative splicing to occur, which allows more than one different proteins to be made from the same mRNA transcript
  - Break the gene up into distinct exons and contain sequences ("splice sites") that are recognized by the spliceosome

Ribozymes:
- RNA molecules with catalytic activity (like "RNA enzymes")
- Found in ribosomes (which catalyze translation)
- Also required for splicing

snRNPs:
- Small nuclear ribonucleoproteins
- RNA-protein complexes (snRNP = RNA + proteins)
- Form the spliceosome

Translation

- Mature eukaryotic mRNA contains a coding region, which is the region that gets translated, as well as a 5' and 3' UTR (untranslated region)

- 5' UTR regulates translation; contains the ribosome binding sequences

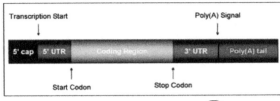

Roles of rRNA and tRNA:

- **rRNA (ribosomal RNA)-** makes up ribosomes (along with associated proteins), which catalyze the synthesis of polypeptides

- **tRNA (transfer RNA)-** contains anti-codon complementary to mRNA codon; brings the correct amino acid to the growing polypeptide chain due to this codon-anti-codon interaction
  - Forms a stem and loop structure (intramolecular H-bonds)- anti-codon on one end and associated with its corresponding an amino acid on the other end
  - Inosine – modified A base; often at the wobble position of the anti-codon
  - Inosine can base pair with A, U, and C

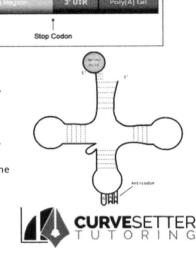

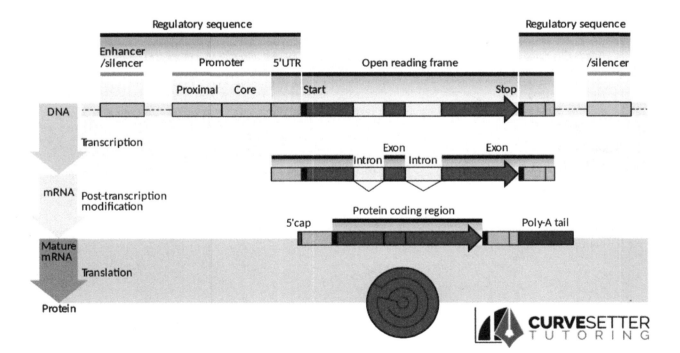

Ribosomes

Function:
- Catalyzes protein synthesis in the cytosol

Structure:
- Made of rRNA and other proteins
- Contains a small and a large subunit
  - Large subunit- catalyzes the peptidyl transfer
  - Small subunit- recognizes and binds to the correct region of the mRNA (eukaryotes: **Kozak sequence**; prokaryotes: **Shine-Dalgarno sequence**)
- Large and small subunits associate during translation, with the mRNA between them
- Ribosomes are names based on their sedimentation coefficients (how quickly they sediment)

- Prokaryotes:

- Eukaryotes: 40S + 60S → 80S   *NOT a numerical addition*

Ribosome sites- regions of the ribosomal large subunit; tRNA moves from A → P → E site during protein synthesis

A site: amino acyl-tRNA site → where the tRNA molecule enters the ribosome and delivers the a.a.

P site: peptidyl-tRNA site → where the tRNA carrying the growing polypeptide chain is held most of the time

E site: exit site → the tRNA has transferred the growing peptide to the tRNA in the P site, and exits the ribosome

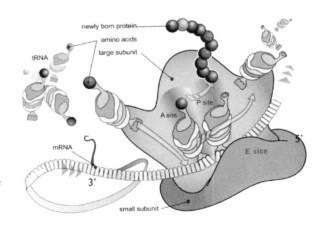

Translation Properties:
- mRNA read 5' → 3'; polypeptide made N-terminus → C-terminus
- ORF translated from start codon (AUG) to stop codon
- Prokaryotes: polycistronic mRNA and lack of RNA processing → transcription and translation may be simultaneous; often multiple ribosomes associated with 1 mRNA molecule (polysome/polyribosome)
- Energy input required at every step (tRNA loading, initiation, translocation, termination)

Amino acid activation/tRNA loading: the process by which an amino acid is attached to its tRNA (with the correct anti-codon for that amino acid)

- Non-spontaneous tRNA loading coupled to ATP hydrolysis
  - Requires 2 "equivalents" of ATP per a.a. because ATP → AMP
- Catalyzed by **aminoacyl tRNA synthetase**- attaches the correct a.a. to the correct tRNA with very high specificity (low error rate)
  - Many different types of this enzyme, one for each a.a.

1. **a.a. + ATP → aminoacyl-AMP + PPi**

2. **aminoacyl-AMP + tRNA → aminoacyl-tRNA + AMP**

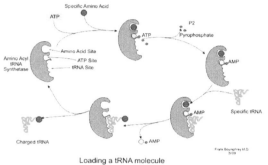

Loading a tRNA molecule

Initiation: formation of the initiation complex

- Initiation complex = mRNA + tRNAfMet + ribosome large & small subunits + initiation factor (IF) proteins
- Prokaryotes: small ribosomal subunit plus initiation factors bind to mRNA at Shine-Dalgarno sequence → initiator tRNA (tRNAfMet) joins (bonding to AUG start codon) with another IF → large subunit joins
  - Initiator tRNA has a slightly modified methionine (fMet)
- Eukaryotes: tRNAMet , small ribosomal subunit and other initiator proteins (eIF) associate at the 5' end of mRNA (Kozak sequence recognized) →   scan for start codon (AUG) → large ribosomal subunit joins
- tRNAMet is in the P site at the end of initiation and start of elongation

Initiation

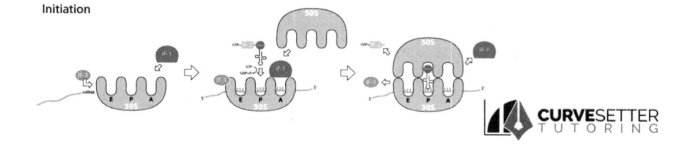

Elongation:

- Incoming aa-tRNA enters the A site (requires GTP and elongation factors)
- Large ribosomal subunit catalyzes the formation of a peptide bond between the a.a. in P site (linked to growing peptide chain) and the new a.a. of A site
- Growing peptide chain has been transferred to the tRNA of the A site
- tRNA at P site moves to the E site, then exits, as the tRNA at A site (with the peptide chain) moves into P site
- mRNA dragged along when tRNA moves A → P
- Elongation factor and GTP are required

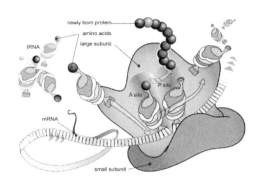

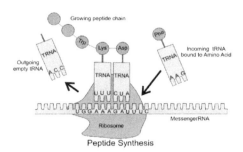

Peptide Synthesis

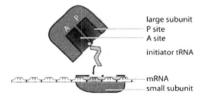

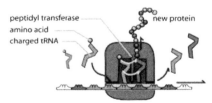

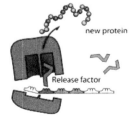

Termination

- Stop codon (UAA, UGA, UAG) enters the A site causing release factor (RF) proteins to join the complex at P site
- Bond between the last tRNA and the peptide chain is cleaved, releasing the protein
- GTP and other proteins allow the entire complex to dissociate

Energy Requirement: #aa x 4 = # ATP needed

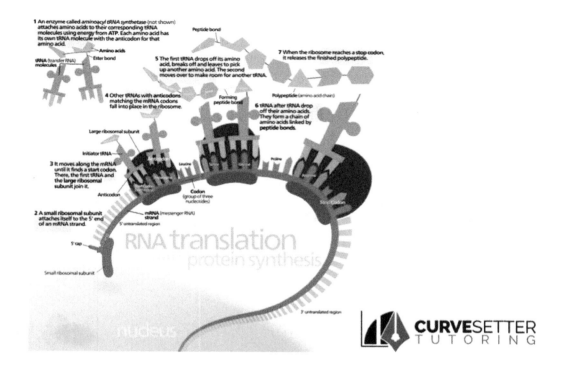

Post-Translational Protein Modification

- After translation, some proteins immediately fold into their native conformation, while others may require a chaperone protein
  - Chaperone protein = helps proteins fold into their native conformation by isolating them and preventing aggregation

- Proteins undergo a variety of different modifications-
  - Cleavage of a region of the polypeptide (zymogens)
  - Glycosylation: addition of sugars
  - Lipidation: addition of lipids (often tags a protein to be part of the cell membrane)
  - Acetylation and methylation
  - Formation of disulfide bonds

- Proteins often contain a sequence that targets them to go to the ER or the Golgi apparatus for further modification and/or proper folding

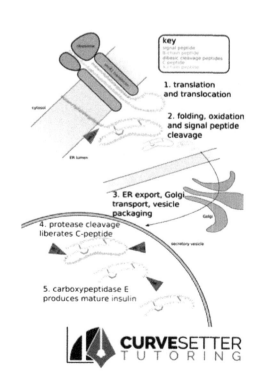

CONTROL OF GENE EXPRESSION; BIOTECHNOLOGY

Biology Lecture 3

OBJECTIVES

- Prokaryotic control of gene expression
  - Operons and control of the lac operon
  - Bacteria: gene repression and activation
- Eukaryotic control of gene expression
  - Regulation at the level of transcription: TFs, DNA binding proteins, etc.
  - Changes in gene number
  - Regulation following transcription
  - Failures of control → Cancer: proto-oncogene, oncogene, and tumor suppressor gene
  - DNA and chromatin: structural modifications
- Biotechnology
  - Gene cloning, restriction sites, and restriction enzymes
  - Genomic library vs. cDNA library: function and process
  - Fluorescent in situ hybridization (FISH)
  - Polymerase Chain Reaction (PCR)
  - RT-PCR and qPCR to assess gene expression
  - Gel electrophoresis
  - Southern Blot, Northern Blot, and Western Blot
  - DNA Sequencing
  - Uses of stem cells in research and medicine
  - DNA technology: real-world applications

The Operon Concept

Operon = a group of genes controlled by a single promoter

- All genes of the operon transcribed onto 1 mRNA → all transcribed together → therefore all genes of the operon are expressed together (or none expressed)
- Operons that result in multiple genes per mRNA molecule (polycistronic mRNA) only exist in prokaryotes
- Contain an **operator**, which enables regulation of the genes of the operon
  - Operator = region of DNA to which **repressor** protein binds, decreasing transcriptional activity
- Operons also regulated by **activator** proteins (increase rate of transcription)

Well-known operons include the **lac operon** and the **trp operon**:

- Lac operon = catabolic role → transcription induced by presence of the substrate (lac) that the operon's enzymes break down
- Trp operon = anabolic role → transcription repressed by the presence of the product (trp) of the operon's enzymes

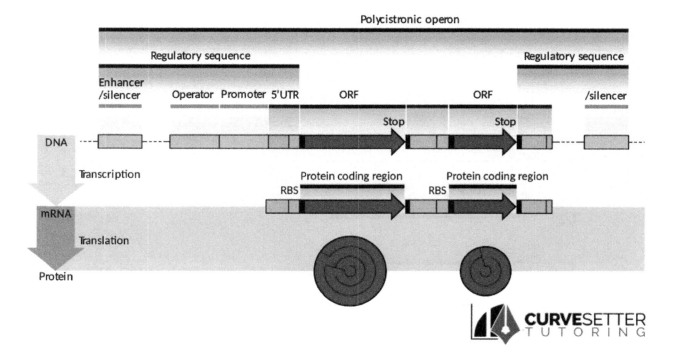

The Lac Operon

- Lac operon is required for the metabolism of lactose in bacteria
- Glucose is their primary energy source but lactose must be used when glucose low
  - Transcription of operon induced when glucose low and lactose high

Parts of lac operon:
- **P region** = promoter; RNA pol binds to begin transcription
- **O region** = operator; repressor binds to decrease transcription
- Structural genes: **lac Z, lac Y, lac A**

Other genes (not part of lac operon) that regulate the operon:
- **Lac I gene** = codes for lac repressor which inhibits transcription (repressor bound to operator when lactose absent; not bound when lactose present)
- **crp gene** = codes for **CAP** which activated transcription (CAP binds upstream of promoter when glucose absent → induces transcription by activating RNA Pol)

The *lac* Operon and its Control Elements

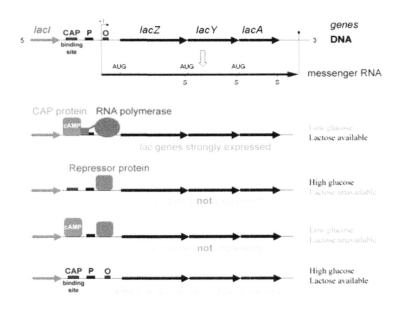

Trp Operon

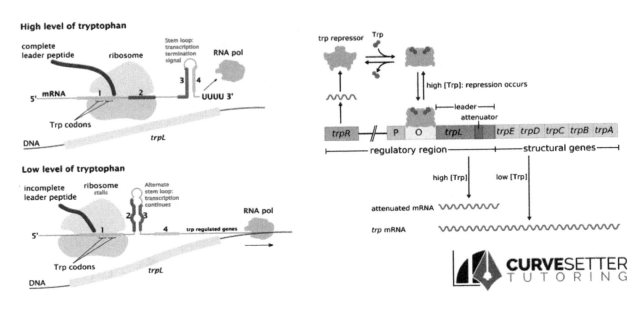

Bacteria: gene repression and activation

- In prokaryotes, gene regulation occurs primarily at the level of transcription, due to the fact that transcription and translation are often simultaneous (translation starting just shortly after transcription)

- The strength of the association between RNA Pol and the promoter affects the transcription rate
  - RNA Pol has stronger affinity for the promoter → higher transcription rate

- **Repressors**- proteins that bind to the **operator** regions of DNA and decrease the rate of transcription

- **Enhancers**- region of DNA that **activator** proteins can bind to; this association increases the rate of transcription
  - Usually at a position on the DNA molecule that is distant from the gene

Eukaryotic control of gene expression

- **Transcription Factor (TF)** = protein that controls the rate of transcription by binding directly to DNA
  - Turn genes "ON" and "OFF" by activating or repressing the activity of RNA Polymerase
  - Vital to controlling cell differentiation, cell function, and cell life cycle (growth, division, death)
  - TFs all contain a **DNA binding domain**
- TFs bind to regions of DNA called **enhancers** (increase transcription) or **silencers** (decrease transcription)
  - Often distant (upstream) from the gene
  - **Activator** proteins binds to enhancers
  - **Repressor** proteins bind to silencers

- The strength of the association between RNA Pol and the promoter affects the transcription rate
  - RNA Pol has stronger affinity for the promoter → higher transcription rate
  - TFs often modulate the interaction between RNA Pol and the promoter

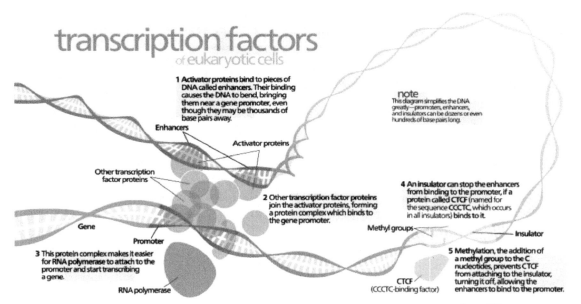

Gene regulation following transcription:

- **RNA Processing:** the addition of a 5' cap and 3' tail is a modification that increases the stability of the RNA, making it last longer in the cytosol and therefore enabling it to be translated an increased number of times

- **Alternative Splicing:** enables different proteins to be translated from the same gene depending on the immediate needs of the cell

- **RNA Interference:** RNA molecules reduce translation by resulting in the degradation of specific mRNA molecules
  - **miRNA:** single stranded RNA molecules that are complementary to the mRNA molecule, bind to it, and result in its degradation
  - **siRNA:** double stranded RNA that forms a complex with a protein, then binds to a specific mRNA molecule, cleaving it

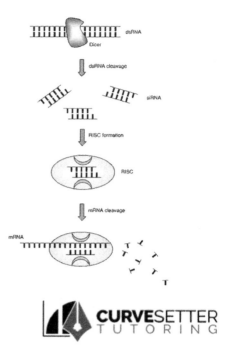

Changes in gene number-

- **Gene amplification (gene duplication):** the duplication of a region of DNA resulting in an increase in the number of copies of a gene
  - Usually caused by errors in DNA replication, meiosis, or mitosis; also can be caused by transposons
  - One of the most common forms of mutation
  - Duplicated gene often acquires mutations at a higher rate because it isn't under as strong selection
  - Still, having an extra copy of the gene can negatively impact the organism

- **Anueploidy:** having an abnormal # of chromosomes (an entire chromosome has been duplicated or lost)
  - Usually negatively impacts the organism

- **Cancer cells:** duplication of oncogenes is a common cause of cancer

Failures of Control → Cancer

- Cancer cells grow and divide uncontrollably; fail to respond to normal controls that regulate growth, division, and apoptosis
  - Normal cells undergo apoptosis when DNA mutations accumulate, but cancer cells don't (avoid apoptosis; seemingly immortal)
  - Cancerous tissue invades and damages surrounding organs
  - Cancer cells stimulate angiogenesis → grow their own supply of blood vessels → fuels tumor growth

- **Oncogenes:** genes that regulate cell growth, differentiation, and the process of apoptosis, and can potentially cause cells to become cancerous
  - Mutated or highly expressed in cancerous cells
  - Usually begin as **proto-oncogenes** (normal genes involved in cell growth/division) that get mutated

- **Tumor Suppressor genes:** genes that have the potential to prevent cancer; decrease cell growth/division, involved in DNA repair, or trigger apoptosis
  - The mutation of tumor suppressor genes enables a cell to grow and divide uncontrollably, possibly becoming cancerous

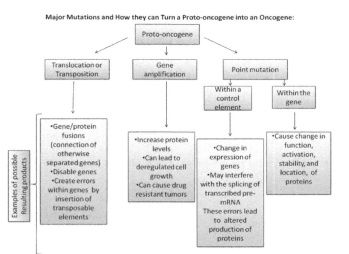

Major Mutations and How they can Turn a Proto-oncogene into an Oncogene:

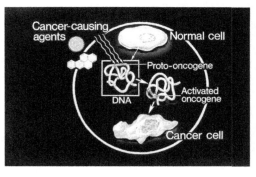

Chromatin Modifications

- **Epigenetics** = changes in gene expression and function not due to a change in DNA sequence
  - Chromatin remodeling (eukaryotes only)

- **Chromatin remodeling:** changing the arrangement of chromatin between a densely-packed, transcriptionally silenced state (**heterochromatin**) and a loosely packed, transcriptionally active state (**euchromatin**)
  - Packing of chromatin affects its accessibility to the machinery required for transcription → changes in gene expression

- Chromatin remodeling often occurs due to covalent modifications of histone proteins
  - **Acetylation/deacetylation:** the addition of an acetyl group to histone proteins causes the DNA to be more transcriptionally active
  - **Methylation/demethylation:** the addition of a methyl group to histone proteins can result in the repression OR activation of transcription, depending on the location of methylation
  - **Phosphorylation:** associated with increased transcriptional activity

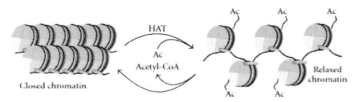

DNA Methylation:

- Methyl group added to cytosine base by DNA methyl transferase (DNMT)

- Represses transcription when methylated at the promoter

- Differentiated cells must have some level of DNA methylation

- Excess or insufficient methylation can causes disease (such as cancer)

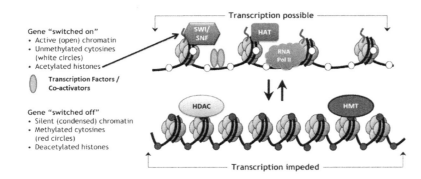

Biotechnology

Recombinant DNA (rDNA): DNA molecule made from combining DNA from 2 or more different sources

Restriction enzymes: endonucleases that recognize and cleave at a specific DNA sequence
- Cleavage often produces "sticky ends" → matching sticky ends from 2 different
  DNA sources can be annealed together, producing rDNA

Gene cloning: making many copies of a gene
- Procedure: gene of interest inserted into a bacterial plasmid using **restriction enzymes** followed by **DNA ligase**→ rDNA formed
  - rDNA plasmid then put into bacteria (**transformation**) → bacteria must be made **competent** (able to take up the rDNA), which is done with heat shock or electroporation
  - Bacterial colony grown on a medium that selects for cells that have the plasmid
    - If plasmid has antibiotic resistance gene, grow it on that antibiotic
      - As colony grows (bacteria dividing), more copies of the gene are being produced
        - Isolate the gene of interest by lysing the bacteria followed by purification

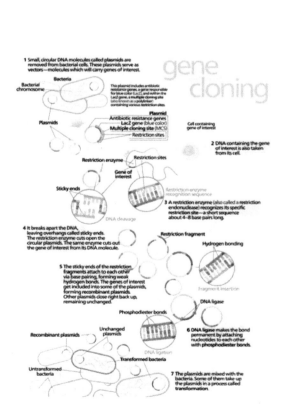

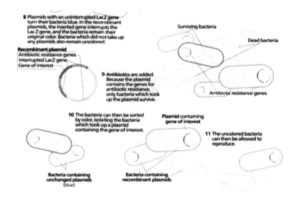

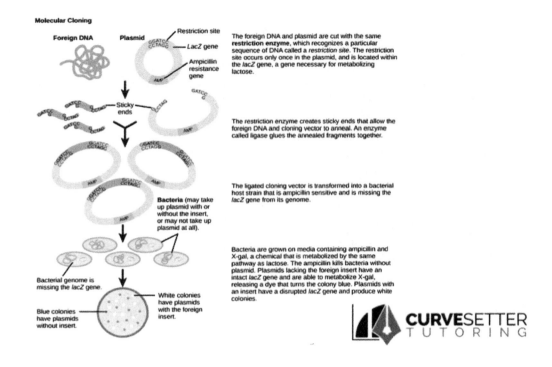

Molecular Cloning

The foreign DNA and plasmid are cut with the same **restriction enzyme**, which recognizes a particular sequence of DNA called a *restriction site*. The restriction site occurs only once in the plasmid, and is located within the *lacZ* gene, a gene necessary for metabolizing lactose.

The restriction enzyme creates sticky ends that allow the foreign DNA and cloning vector to anneal. An enzyme called ligase glues the annealed fragments together.

The ligated cloning vector is transformed into a bacterial host strain that is ampicillin sensitive and is missing the *lacZ* gene from its genome.

Bacteria are grown on media containing ampicillin and X-gal, a chemical that is metabolized by the same pathway as lactose. The ampicillin kills bacteria without plasmid. Plasmids lacking the foreign insert have an intact *lacZ* gene and are able to metabolize X-gal, releasing a dye that turns the colony blue. Plasmids with an insert have a disrupted *lacZ* gene and produce white colonies.

Genomic and cDNA Libraries

Genomic Library: a collection of all the DNA of an organism
- Represents the organism's entire genome (coding and non-coding DNA)
- **Procedure:** genome is broken into fragments using a restriction enzyme → all fragments inserted into the same type of vector (usually a plasmid) so that each vector contains one part of the genome → plasmids inserted into a host, such as bacteria, for storage and/or cloning
- **Function:** usually used to determine or analyze the sequence an organism's entire genome

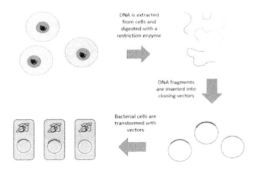

cDNA Library: library of genetic material made from full transcribed and spliced eukaryotic mRNA

- **Procedure:** Requires reverse transcriptase to make the cDNA using mRNA molecules as a template
- cDNA molecules then inserted into vectors (usually plasmid) that are then put into host cells, just like a genomic library
- Unlike genomic library: lack non-coding DNA, introns, and other regulatory regions (promoters, enhancers, etc.)

- **Function:** Assess the genetic material being actively expressed in that cell/tissue at that time the sample was collected
- Can also use to insert and express a eukaryotic gene in a prokaryotic organism (cDNA lacks introns and eukaryote-specific regulatory regions)

Formation of a cDNA Library

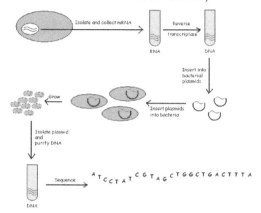

Fluorescent in situ hybridization (FISH)

- Use to determine gene expression in a specific tissue/region of an organism
    - Is a certain gene expressed? If so, how much and in what regions of the tissue?
- Procedure: Slice of tissue is put on a slide and cell membranes lysed → Labelled (fluorescent) DNA probe added to the sample → probe DNA and sample DNA denatured → probe hybridizes to regions where there is complementary DNA → Amount and location of fluorescence on slide is detected

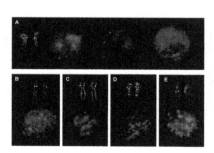

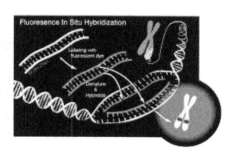

Polymerase Chain Reaction (PCR)

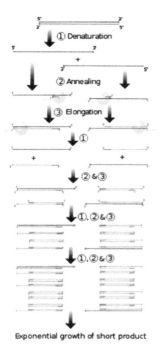

Exponential growth of short product

- PCR is used to amplify a region of DNA; exponential growth occurs → can get millions of copies

- Requires heat resistant DNA Pol (called Taq Polymerase) and primers complementary to the target region of DNA

- Repeated cycles of heating and cooling occur: denaturation→ annealing → extension

- qPCR (quantitative PCR): assess the amount of the amplified PCR product in real time, and quantify the amount that was initially present

- RT-PCR (reverse transcriptase-PCR): similar to qPCR, but quantifying and amplifying mRNA molecules → can assess gene expression

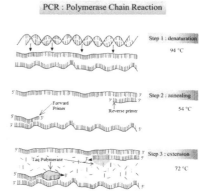

Gel electrophoresis

- Technique used to separate macromolecules, such as DNA and proteins, by size and charge
  - Usually **agarose** or **polyacrylamide** gel used
- Sample placed in wells at one end of the gel → gel has pores through which macromolecules can migrate → larger ones held back more and take longer to migrate (closer to start wells)
- Electrical field applied to the gel and buffer apparatus so that negatively charged molecules (such as DNA/RNA) migrate towards the other, positively charged, end
  - **Cathode** = - end; **anode** = + end → DNA start at cathode and run to anode

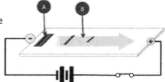

- **SDS-PAGE**: separate denatured proteins by their molecular weight
  - SDS (Sodium dodecyl sulfate) denatures the proteins and gives them a uniform mass to charge ratio

- **Native-PAGE**: proteins separated by size in their native conformation
  - Ex. Assess enzyme-substrate binding or lack there-of

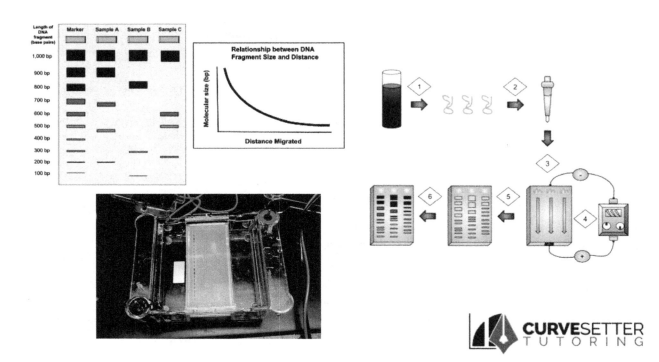

Southern Blot, Northern Blot, and Western Blot

Southern Blot: used to detect a certain fragment of **DNA** from a sample
- DNA molecules separated by gel electrophoresis
- Separated fragments transferred to a nitrocellulose membrane
- Membrane exposed to labelled probes, which hybridize to segment of interest
- Location of probe visualized

Northern Blot: used to detect a certain fragment of **RNA** from a sample

Western Blot: used to detect a specific **protein** from a sample

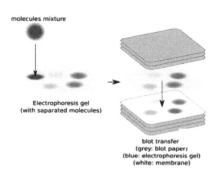

molecules mixture

Electrophoresis gel
(with separated molecules)

blot transfer
(grey: blot paper)
(blue: electrophoresis gel)
(white: membrane)

Western Blot:

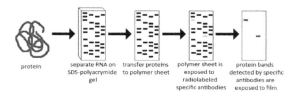

protein → separate RNA on SDS-polyacrymide gel → transfer proteins to polymer sheet → polymer sheet is exposed to radiolabeled specific antibodies → protein bands detected by specific antibodies are exposed to film

Northern Blot:

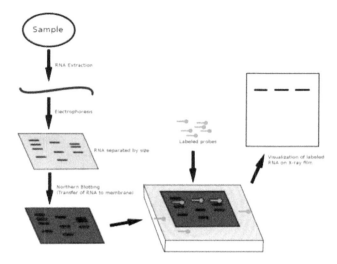

DNA Sequencing

- Determining the nucleotide sequence of a DNA sample
  - Has enabled us to sequence the entire genome of many organisms, including humans
- There are numerous different methods of DNA sequencing, which have improved dramatically in their ease and efficiency over the past few decades
- One of the most popular methods in the 80's, 90's, and early 2000's was Sanger Sequencing

- **Sanger Sequencing** (Chain-termination method):
  - Uses modified nucleotide without a 3' OH group (ddNTP) → DNA cannot be extended anymore once ddNTP is added → generate multiple fragments that all vary in length based on when the ddNTP (as opposed to normal dNTPs) was added

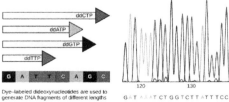

Dye–labeled dideoxynucleotides are used to generate DNA fragments of different lengths

G A T A A A T C T G G T C T T A T T T C C

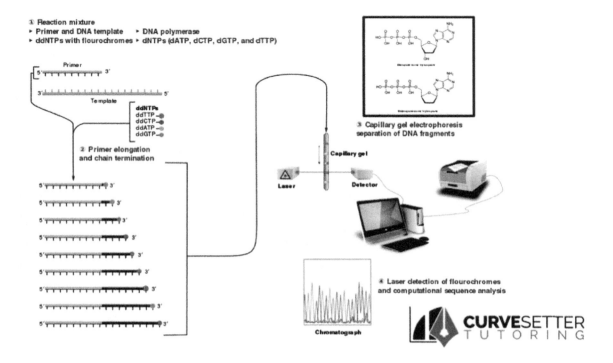

① Reaction mixture
▸ Primer and DNA template ▸ DNA polymerase
▸ ddNTPs with flourochromes ▸ dNTPs (dATP, dCTP, dGTP, and dTTP)

③ Capillary gel electrophoresis separation of DNA fragments

② Primer elongation and chain termination

④ Laser detection of flourochromes and computational sequence analysis

Chromatograph

Uses of stem cells in medicine:

- Stem cells can be induced to differentiate into various specialized cells and are often used in medical therapies

- **Stem cell therapy:** the use of stem cells to treat a disease

- Stem cells harvested, grown, differentiated, and injected into individual with a deficiency in or damage to a specific cell type

- Bone marrow transplant: bone marrow contains multipotent hematopoietic stem cells; bone marrow from healthy donor given to individual with bone marrow damaged by cancer, chemotherapy, or other disease

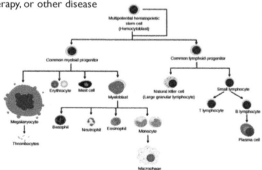

Potential uses of
Stem cells

Stroke — Baldness
Traumatic brain injury — Blindness
Learning defects — Deafness
Alzheimer's disease
Parkinson's disease — Amyotrophic lateral-sclerosis
Missing teeth
Wound healing — Myocardial infarction
Bone marrow transplantation (currently established) — Muscular dystrophy
Spinal cord injury — Diabetes
Osteoarthritis — Multiple sites:
Rheumatoid arthritis — Crohn's disease — Cancers

DNA technology: real-world applications

Medicine/Pharmaceuticals:

- Diagnosis of disease; prenatal diagnosis of diseases
    - Cystic fibrosis, chromosomal abnormalities, sickle cell anemia, etc.
- Understanding the pathophysiology of diseases
- Human Genome Project
- Creation of recombinant products (insulin, HRT)
- Vaccines
- Gene therapy
- Anti-viral therapy

Forensics:

- DNA fingerprinting to ID criminals
- Paternity tests

Environmental:

- Usage of microbes in sewage plants to metabolize toxic chemicals
- Using bioluminescent organisms to detect the presence/levels of hazardous chemicals

Agriculture:

- Improving crop yield (pest-resistance etc.)
- Improving the nutritional value of plants (more protein-rich, inserting gene for beta-carotene into rice)

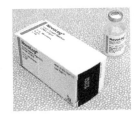

DNA Profiling
RFLP (Restriction Fragment Length Polymorphism) Analysis

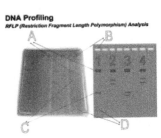

MENDELIAN GENETICS, MEIOSIS, AND GENETIC DIVERSITY

Biology Lecture 4

OBJECTIVES

- Genetics: The Basics
  - DNA as the genetic material
  - Basic terms and concepts
  - Diploid and haploid genomes
  - Homozygosity vs. heterozygosity; wild-type vs. recessive
  - Other types of inheritance: complete dominance, incomplete dominance, co-dominance
  - Penetrance and Expressivity
  - Genetic hybridization
- Meiosis and Genetic Diversity
  - Overview of meiosis
  - Differences between meiosis and mitosis
  - The process of meiosis
  - Recombination and the role of crossing over in genetic diversity
  - Non-disjunction (NDJ)
  - Segregation of genes: Law of Independent Assortment
  - Sex determination and sex-linked traits
  - Cytoplasmic inheritance; mitochondrial DNA

DNA as the Genetic Material

The following researchers' experiments contributed to the conclusion that DNA (and not proteins, as first expected) was the genetic material.

Griffith: Transformation

- Working with 2 strains of Strep bacteria:
  - R Strain (rough) = non-lethal
  - S Strain (smooth) = lethal
- Expose rat to S strain → rat dies;   expose rat to R strain → rat lives
- Expose rat to heat-killed S strain → rat lives
- Expose rat to R strain + heat-killed S strain → rat dies

Conclusion: S strain somehow conferred the virulence to the R strain

→ R strain was **transformed**

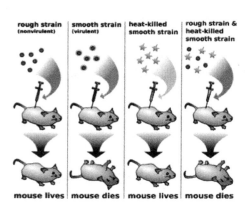

But is it DNA or protein that is the transforming agent?

Avery, McCarty and MacLeod:

Wanted to assess what macromolecule of the heat killed S strain enables virulence to be conferred-

- Heat-killed S strain + protease → transformation occurs; rat dies

- Heat-killed S strain + RNAase → transformation occurs; rat dies

- Heat-killed S strain + DNAase → NO transformation occurs; rat lives

Conclusion: DNA most likely to be the transforming agent

Hershey Chase:

- Wanted to verify that DNA is the transforming agent that confers virulence

    - Known: Bacteriophage T2 virus latches onto the bacteria and inserts some heritable macromolecule into it,

      "hijacking" the bacteria's molecular machinery, causing it to produce virus progeny → Is it DNA or protein?

- Phage grown in ^{35}S → protein labelled → centrifuge phage + bacteria → label found in supernatant (not in bacteria)

- Phage grown in ^{32}P → DNA labelled → centrifuge phage + bacteria → label found in bottom pellet (inside bacteria)

Conclusion: DNA is the genetic material of the phage

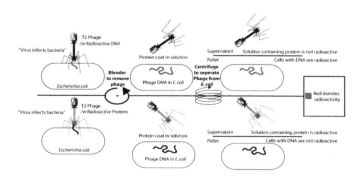

Genetics: Terms

- **Genotype:** The genetic makeup of an organism (with respect to one or more traits, or the entire organism)
  - DNA sequence only; composed of different genes

- **Phenotype:** The observable trait(s)/characteristic(s) of an organism
  - Ex. green eyes, blonde hair, tall
  - The expression of the genotype
  - Affected by genes and the environment

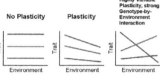

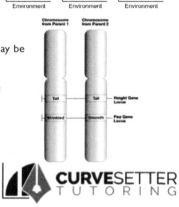

- **Gene:** sequence of DNA that encodes for a certain protein or function in the cell (may be more than one product for prokaryotes); the basic unit of heredity

- **Locus:** certain position on a chromosome, usually representing the location of a gene

- **Allele:** different versions of a gene (but located at the same locus)
  - Different alleles arise by mutations
  - Humans (diploid) have 2 alleles per gene
  - But, there may be more than 2 different alleles *possible* for a given gene
    - Ex. Blood type: 3 alleles → I^A, I^B, and i

- **Diploid (2n):** organism has two sets of chromosomes (one from each parent), called homologous chromosomes
  - Homologous chromosomes: one maternal and one paternal; have the same set of genes
  - For one gene an individual has 2 alleles, one on each homologous chromosome
  - The alleles may be the same (**homozygous**) or different (**heterozygous**)

- Homozygous: AA
- Heterozygous: Aa; AB

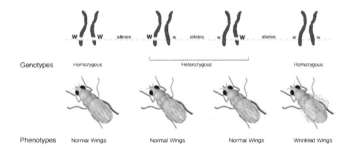

- **Haploid (1n):** organism has one set of chromosomes
  - Each gene encoded by one allele (no dominant or recessive; all alleles "dominant" because expressed)

- **Polygenic trait:** A trait that is controlled by 2 or more different genes
  - Ex. height

- In diploid organism- if heterozygous for a given trait (AB) and the phenotype of A is expressed, then A is **dominant** and B is **recessive**
  - Usually, dominant allele indicated with capital letter and recessive with lowercase letter
  - Recessive phenotype only shown if organism has two copies of recessive allele

- **Complete dominance:** AA and Aa organisms both show the dominant phenotype

- **"Wild-type":** the most common form of a trait (may be the recessive allele)
  - Other form is usually called **"mutant"**

- **Co-dominance:** both alleles of the gene are expressed
  - Ex. AB blood type → both A and B

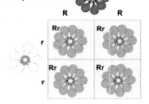

- **Incomplete dominance:** an intermediate phenotype is expressed
  - Ex. If R = red and r = white, then Rr = pink

- **Penetrance:** percent of individuals with a given genotype that show the expected phenotype
  - Ex. If 9/10 people with a certain disease-causing mutation have the disease, then the penetrance of that disease is 90%
  - **Incomplete penetrance:** penetrance less than 100%

- **Expressivity:** the amount that the genotype affects an individuals' phenotype
  - Of individuals with a certain genotype, the phenotype is more dramatic in some and less dramatic in other
  - Ex. Of all individuals with a certain disease (and the same genotype), some people will have more symptoms of the disease and/or an increased severity of them

- **Gene pool:** all of the possible alleles in a given population

- **Hybridization:** two individuals from distinct populations (or species) breed; may or may not produce a viable offspring
  - Ex. Horse + donkey = mule → viable offspring but sterile

Meiosis

- **Meiosis:** Cell division that results in the formation of 4 haploid daughter cells, all of which are genetically distinct from the parent cell
    - DNA replication → meiosis I → meiosis II
    - Daughter cells = germ cells → meiosis occurs in sexually reproducing organisms

- Meiosis is an important **source of genetic diversity** because it involves **recombination / cross-over** of homologous chromosomes as well as **independent assortment** of the parent chromosomes
    - Homologs exchange some genetic material before being partitioned into different daughter cells
    - Resultant chromosomes are distinct from those of the parent cell → same genes represented but different combination of alleles

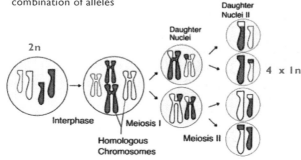

Main sources of genetic diversity:
- Independent Assortment
- Crossover/Recombination
- New alleles arising due to genetic mutation

Mitosis:
- Produces 2 diploid (2n) daughter cells, genetically identical to the parent cell
- 1 round of division
- Somatic cells produced
- NO recombination

We will review mitosis again later

Meiosis:
- Produces 4 haploid (1n) daughter cells, genetically distinct from the parent cell
- 2 rounds of division (meiosis I and II)
- Germ cells produced
- Recombination between homologous chromosomes (tetrad formed)

Meiosis and Mitosis:
S phase (DNA replication) precedes both meiosis and mitosis
- **P (prophase)-** chromosomes condense, nuclear membrane breaks down
- **M (metaphase)-** chromosomes attached to spindle fibers and line up in the middle of the cell
- **A (anaphase)-** chromosomes (or chromatids) pulled away from each other to opposite poles
- **T (telophase)-** nuclear membrane reforms, chromosomes de-condense back into chromatin, cytokinesis occurs
    - **Cytokinesis:** division of the cytoplasm of the two cells; actin and myosin filament ring contracts (forming the cleavage furrow) and splits the cell into two

Binary fission · Mitosis · Meiosis

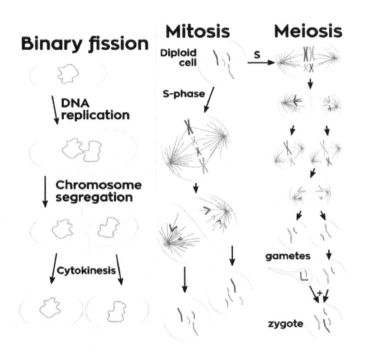

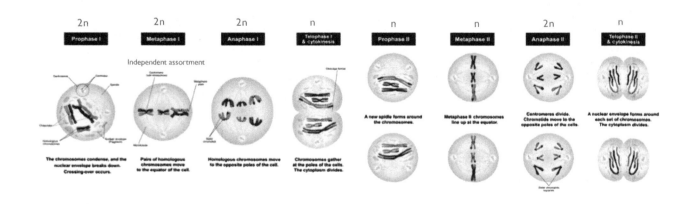

- During Prophase I of meiosis, homologous chromosomes pair up in **synapsis**, forming a **tetrad**
  - **Synapsis:** the pairing of homologous chromosomes
  - **Tetrad:** 2 chromosomes, each with 2 sister chromatids → 4 total chromatids

- Then, they exchange genetic material (**crossing over / recombination**)
  - Single crossover: crossover occurs at one point in the tetrad
  - Double crossover: crossover occurs at two points in the tetrad → some genes end up on the same original chromosomes

- **Chiasma:** physical link between the chromatids of homologous chromosomes during recombination

- **Synaptonemal complex:** protein complex that enables synapsis to occur

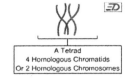

A Tetrad
4 Homologous Chromatids
Or 2 Homologous Chromosomes

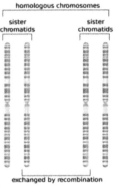

homologous chromosomes

sister chromatids   sister chromatids

exchanged by recombination

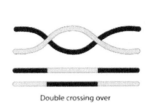

Double crossing over

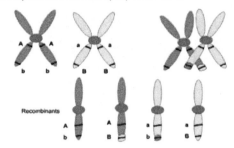

Recombinants

CURVESETTER
TUTORING

Non-Disjunction

Non-Disjunction (NDJ): when homologous chromosomes or sister chromatids do not separate correctly during meiosis or mitosis
- Meiosis I: homologous chromosomes fail to separate
- Meiosis II and mitosis: sister chromatids fail to separate

- NDJ results in the daughters cells of division having either too many or too few chromosomes (aneuploidy)

- If NDJ occurs during meiosis and the germ cell produced by the faulty division becomes the egg/sperm of a zygote, then the aneuploidy impacts every cell of that offspring and the organism may not be viable

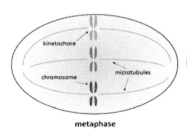

kinetochore

chromosome   microtubules

metaphase

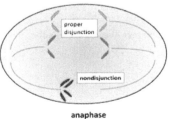

proper disjunction

nondisjunction

anaphase

CURVESETTER
TUTORING

- Normal disjunction → n, n, n, n
- NDJ in meiosis I → n+I, n+I, n-I, n-I
- NDJ in meiosis II → n+I, n-I, n, n

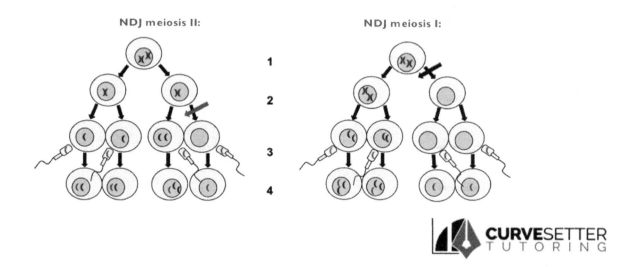

Law of Segregation: a parent has 2 alleles per gene but only passes one allele onto the next generation; those two alleles of the parent cell segregate into daughter cells (gametes) randomly, resulting in gametes that have one allele for a given gene

Law of Independent Assortment: the alleles of one gene separate into daughter cells independently of the alleles for another gene → traits are inherited randomly and independently
- Ex. parent: gene I = Aa; gene 2 = Bb → offspring is equally likely to be… Ab, aB, ab, AB → gene I and 2 segregate independently
- Stipulates that genes are not linked… i.e. based on genes being on different chromosomes

Exception to the Law of Independent Assortment-

Linkage: genes that are close to each other on a chromosome are more likely to be inherited together (linked). Why? Because the closer they are to each other on a chromosomes, the lower likelihood of them being separated onto different chromosomes in a crossover event.
- Closer genes are more tightly linked and less likely to independently assort

Recombination frequency (Rf) is a quantification of genetic linkage → measured in units of **cM** (centimorgan)

- Rf = likelihood of two genes being involved in a crossover event

- Rf is proportional to the physical distance between those genes on the chromosomes (larger Rf = further apart

    = more likely to crossover and therefore independently assort)

- Calculate: Rf = # of recombinant offspring / total # offspring

- Interpret: Rf = 1 cM → 1% chance that those genes will crossover

    - Rf value ≥ 50% → independent assortment occurs

- Ex. Parental: AABB x aabb
    offspring (F1): AB + ab → AaBb
    possible F1 gametes (F2): AB, ab, Ab, aB → recombinant gametes
    Q: If F1 is crossed with aabb and the resultant F2 generation is 30% Aabb or aaBb, then what is the Rf?

Sex Determination

- One sex chromosome inherited from each parent
- Biological sex: XX → female, XY → male
- Egg always donates X chromosome, sperm donates X or Y
- Y chromosome has the **SRY gene** (sex-determining region)

    - SRY gene in males encodes for the SRY protein, which is a TF that causes the undifferentiated gonads to develop into testes instead of ovaries

    - no SRY protein → gonads develop into ovaries so female is often called the "default sex"

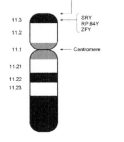

Sex-linked genes:

- "sex-linked gene" = gene found on the X or Y chromsomes
- The Y chromosome is very small and, other than SRY, carries very few other genes of importance
- Males always express genes found on the X chromosome (whether dominant or recessive allele)

- X-linked recessive disorders are much more common in men than women because men only need one copy of the recessive allele to have the disorder, but women need 2 copies

- Ex. Female carrier (X^AX^a) x normal male (X^AY)
  - Male offspring: will get the Y chromosomes from their father and the X from their mother. So males have a 50% chance of having the disorder (50% likelihood of receiving X^a from their mother)
  - Female offspring: receive X^A from their father, so have a 50% chance of being a carrier but 0% chance of expressing the disorder

- **X-linked recessive disorders:** color blindness, hemophilia, muscular dystrophy

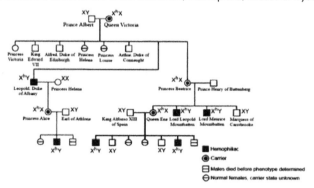

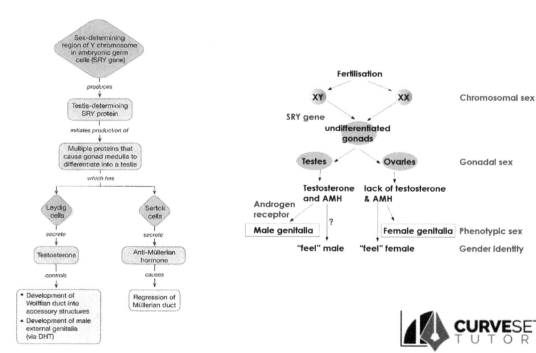

Cytoplasmic Inheritance:

- Cytoplasmic inheritance: inheritance of gene found outside of nuclear DNA

  - Mitochondria and chloroplasts carry their own DNA

- Mitochondria and all other cellular organelles are inherited from the **mother**

- Mitochondrial traits are **hemizygous** → diploid has only 1 copy of a given gene

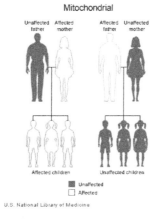

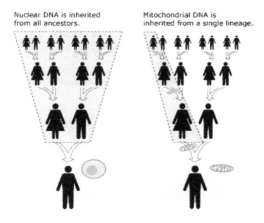

GENETIC ANALYSES, EVOLUTION, AND NATURAL SELECTION

Biology Lecture 5

OBJECTIVES

- Genetics: Methods of Analysis
  - Punnett squares; Pedigree charts
  - Biometry: Statistical methods in genetics
  - Gene interactions
  - Expected genotype ratios
  - Testcross and backcross
- Evolution, Natural Selection, and Speciation
  - Overview of evolution; Mechanisms of evolution
  - Concepts: Genetic drift, gene flow, bottleneck
  - Convergent evolution, divergent evolution
  - Hardy Weinberg Equilibrium
  - Natural selection and the concept of "fitness"
  - Stabilizing, directional, and divergent selection on a trait
  - Sexual selection, artificial selection, and kin selection
  - Species concept, reproductive isolation, and speciation
  - Inbreeding and outbreeding

Genetics: Methods of Analysis

Punnett Square: diagram used to predict the probability of each possible genotype outcome for the offspring of a given cross
- Determine the alleles of the parents
- Write each possible gamete (1 allele if 1 trait or 2 alleles if 2 traits) from parent 1 along the top of the chart and parent 2 along the side of the chart
- Fill in the chart with every possible gamete combination, then determine the ratios

For 1 gene-

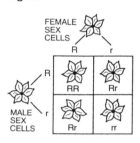

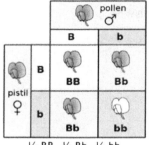

¼ BB, ½ Bb, ¼ bb
BB: Bb: bb = 1: 2: 1

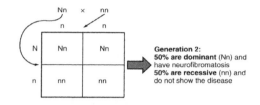

Generation 2:
50% are dominant (Nn) and have neurofibromatosis
50% are recessive (nn) and do not show the disease

For 2 genes-

Parent 1 = AaBb

	AB	Ab	aB	ab
AB	AABB	AABb	AaBB	AaBb
Ab	AABb	AAbb	AaBb	Aabb
aB	AaBB	AaBb	aaBB	aaBb
ab	AaBb	Aabb	aaBb	aabb

Parent 2 = AaBb

Offspring:

A-B-: A-bb: aaB-: aabb = 9: 3: 3: 1

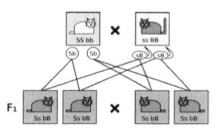

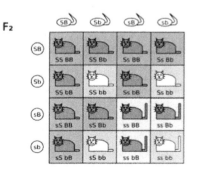

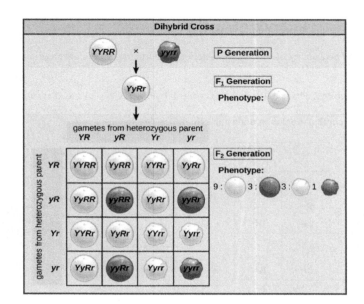

Parental generation (parents)

F1 generation (children)

F2 generation (grandchildren)

The "tree method":

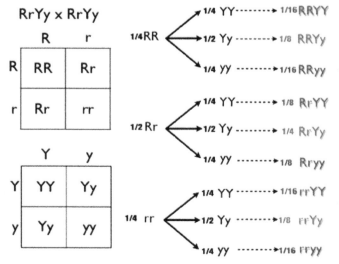

You don't have to write out the entire punnett square! Use **biometry** (statistical methods in biology)-

P (A and B) = P(A) x P(B)
A and B must be independent events (genes not linked)

P (A or B) = P(A) + P(B)

Ex. P(RR and YY) = P(RR) x P(YY) = ¼ x ¼ = 1/16
P(RRYY or rryy) = P(RRYY) + P(rryy) = 1/16 + 1/16

Pedigree Charts:

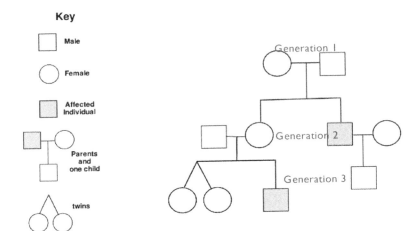

Key

- Male
- Female
- Affected Individual
- Parents and one child
- twins

Autosomal dominant:

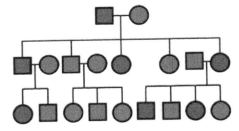

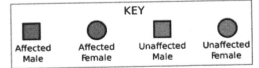

KEY

- Affected Male
- Affected Female
- Unaffected Male
- Unaffected Female

- Every affected individual must have an affected parent
- Often appears in almost every generation

Autosomal recessive:

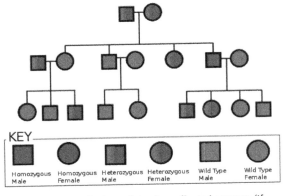

KEY

- Homozygous Male
- Homozygous Female
- Heterozygous Male
- Heterozygous Female
- Wild Type Male
- Wild Type Female

- Affected individual may have 2 unaffected parents (if both parents carriers)
- 2 affected parents produce all affected offspring

X-linked recessive:

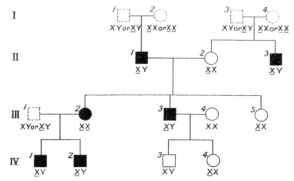

COLOUR-BLINDNESS.

Numerous pedigrees of colour-blindness are now on record. Red-green colour-blindness is generally inherited as a typical male-sex-linked character, recessive in the female, due to a gene in the X chromosome.

FIG. 21.—PEDIGREE CHART OF COLOUR-BLINDNESS.

Testcross:

- Use to determine if an individual that shows the dominant phenotype is homozygous (**AA**) or heterozygous (**Aa**)
- Cross the individual in question with a homozygous recessive individual (aa) → assess offspring
- If any recessive individuals are in the offspring (aa), then individual in question must be heterozygous (Aa)

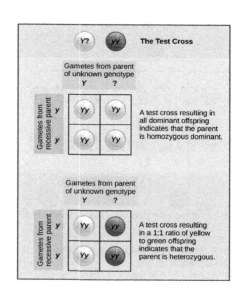

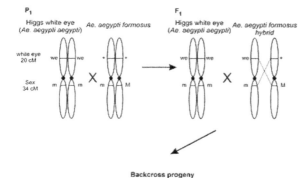

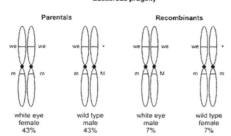

Backcross: Hybrid individual crossed with one of its parents (or an individual with the same genotype as its parents)

$R_f = 14\%$ → genes are 14 cM apart

Other genetics terms-

Epistasis: the expression of alleles for 1 gene is dependent on the alleles for another ("modifier") gene
- The presence of one gene (either dominant or recessive) completely masks the presence of another gene
- Ex. Mouse coat color:
  - Gene 1- B = black coat, b = brown coat
  - Gene 2- C = colored coat, c = no pigment (albino)
  - Any mouse with cc will be albino, regardless of the alleles of gene 1
  - BbCc x BbCc → ¼ cc therefore ¼ albino

Pleiotropy: 1 gene that affects multiple different traits
- Ex. PKU (phenylketonuria) = inborn error of metabolism caused by mutation of a single gene
  - Effects range from seizures to mental disorder to cognitive disability to changes in skin color and more…

Allelic Series: multiple different alleles for a gene with varying degrees of dominance. One allele may be dominant when paired with a certain allele and recessive when paired with another
- Ex. Blood type: $I^A = I^B > i$
- Ex. Rabbit coat color: $C > c^{ch} > c^h > c$
    - C = full coat color, c^{ch} = chinchilla (partially colored), c^h = colored feet and nose only, c = albino
        - $Cc^{ch} \times cc \rightarrow$ ½ full color, ½ chinchilla

Complementation test:
- Use to assess if a mutation in two different genes can give rise to the same mutant phenotype
- If two pure-breeding mutants are mated and produce a WT offspring, then they are said to complement
    - Each original strain was homozygous recessive in a different gene that produced the mutant phenotype
- Occurs when more than one gene product are required for the same function

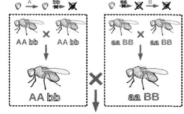

Polygenetic: traits that are influenced by multiple different genes
- genes interact *additively* to produce the phenotype
- Ex. Human skin color

Gene Interactions and Expected Ratios

Expected phenotype ratios from the cross between two heterozygotes (assessing **1 gene**):

Aa x Aa → ?

- Complete dominance: 3 : 1

- Lethal recessive allele: 2 : 1 (aa is lethal)

- Codominance or incomplete dominance: 1 : 2 : 1

Expected phenotype ratios from the cross between two double heterozygotes (assessing **2 genes**):

AaBb x AaBb → ?

- Complete dominance - 9 : 3 : 3 : 1 (A-B-: A-bb: aaB-: aabb)

- Recessive epistasis - 9 : 3 : 4 (aa for gene 1 is dominant over gene 2)

- Dominant epistasis - 12 : 3 : 1 (A- for gene 1 is dominant over gene 2)

Evolution

Definition: a change in the heritable traits of a population/species across multiple generations

Driving forces of evolution-
1. Natural selection
2. Random genetic drift
3. Mutation
4. Gene flow
5. Bottleneck effect

Genetic Drift: sudden change in allele frequencies due to chance alone
- Usually because some individuals leave a population/die in a random chance event
- Bottleneck effect and founder effect are examples

Gene Flow: the movement of genes/alleles between populations → migration

Bottleneck Effect: population size is dramatically reduced → subsequent population doesn't resemble the population before it (genetic drift occurs)
- Usually caused by a random disaster/event that kills off some individuals by chance
  - Nothing to do with fitness

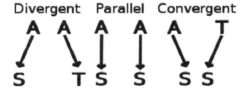

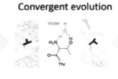

Convergent evolution

Archean proteasome

ornithine acetyltransferase

Ancestral PA clan protease

Divergent Evolution

Convergent evolution: different species without a common ancestor evolve similar traits; due to adaptation to a similar environment

Divergent evolution: species with a common ancestor diverge away from each other over time (accumulate differences)

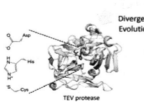

TEV protease

Chymotrypsin

Analogous structures- similar traits not due to common ancestry but due to adaptation to a similar environment; structures usually serve similar purpose

- Ex. Wings of birds and wings of insects
- Often a result of convergent evolution

Homologous structures- structures that appear in different animals due to shared common ancestry; has often been adapted to a different purpose

- Ex. Forelimb bone structure of numerous different species
- Differences in homologous structure often due to divergent evolution

Human   Dog   Bird   Whale

Hardy Weinberg Equilibrium

Allele frequencies in a gene pool will stay constant if there is…

1. **No mutation**
2. **No migration**
3. **No natural selection**
4. **Random mating**
5. **Large population**

All are evolutionary forces. If all are absent, there is no evolution therefore no changes in allele frequencies

- Used a null hypothesis → if allele frequencies are changing then one of the above rules must have been violated
  - Always violated in nature

Hardy Weinberg Equation:
- For a single gene with two alleles: If **p = frequency dominant allele** and **q = frequency recessive allele**, then:
  - **p + q = 1**
  - **$p^2 + 2pq + q^2 = 1$** → p^2 = frq AA, $2pq$ = frq Aa, q^2 = frq aa
    - Can use to convert between genotype and phenotype frequencies; if you know the amount of homozygous recessive individuals in a population (q^2), you can determine the amount of heterozygous or homozygous dominant individuals

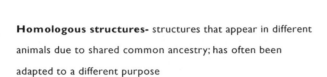

- To determine if a population is in H-W equilibrium, observe at least 2 generations and compare the allele frequencies of those 2 generations
    - If no change → it is in H-W equilibrium
    - If change → it is not in H-W equilibrium; it is evolving and one or more of the H-W rules is being violated

- Going from genotype frequencies → allele frequencies
    - $p = AA + \frac{1}{2}Aa$
    - $q = aa + \frac{1}{2}Aa$

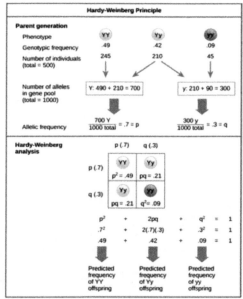

Natural Selection

Natural selection is one of the main forces of evolution.

- There is **variation** and traits are **heritable** in a population
- **Differential reproduction** → different traits confer differing abilities to survive and reproduce; not all individuals survive and reproduce to their full capacity
- Individuals with that phenotypes that enable them to leave more offspring (**higher fitness**) will **pass down their genes more** to the next generation
- **Result:** alleles associated with advantageous traits become more abundant in subsequent generations of the population

Fitness: how successful an animal is at passing down its genes to the next generation
- Measured by how many offspring they have, which depends on survival, mate-finding, and reproductive success
- Fitness depends on the specific environment an organism is in (it's a relative term)

- Natural selection acts on **phenotypes**, which may be influenced by both the genotype and the environment, to differing degrees depending on the trait
  - Even when dominant allele is more fit, heterozygotes and homozygotes will have the same phenotype (if trait completely dominant) so heterozygotes won't be selected against → recessive allele will remain in the population

- Mutations (if in the germ line) and crossing over introduce more genetic diversity into a population → this is the raw material that natural selection can act upon

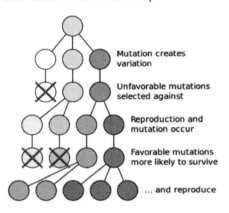

(a) Stabilizing selection

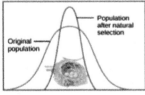

Robins typically lay four eggs, an example of stabilizing selection. Larger clutches may result in malnourished chicks, while smaller clutches may result in no viable offspring.

(b) Directional selection

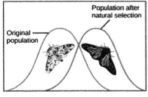

Light-colored peppered moths are better camouflaged against a pristine environment; likewise, dark-colored peppered moths are better camouflaged against a sooty environment. Thus, as the Industrial Revolution progressed in nineteenth-century England, the color of the moth population shifted from light to dark, an example of directional selection.

(c) Diversifying selection

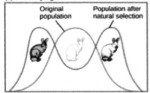

In a hyphothetical population, gray and Himalayan (gray and white) rabbits are better able to blend with a rocky environment than white rabbits, resulting in diversifying selection.

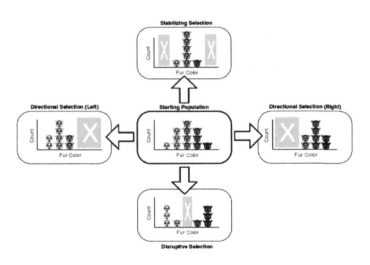

Sexual Selection: a form of natural selection that occurs due to the preferences of one sex for a particular trait in the other sex, and due to competition between members of the same sex for mates

- Certain desirable forms of a trait will enable some individuals to have more offspring and therefore that form of the trait is more highly represented in the next generation
- Desired trait may not be inherently beneficial to health/survival (could even be detrimental), but it enables higher fitness due to increased reproductive success

Artificial Selection: human intervention results in breeding between certain individuals with desired traits

- Human have been doing this with animals and plants for centuries, making them better fit to our preferences/desired uses

Kin Selection: organisms will often behave in ways that benefit individuals closely related to themselves → increasing their genetic representation in the population

- Kin altruism- sacrificing self for a closely related kin

Domain: bacteria, archaea, eukarya

Human: domain = eukarya, kingdom = animalia, phylum = chordata, class = mammalia, etc.

Species: a group of genetically similar organisms that are able to interbreed, producing viable and fertile offspring

Population: a group of organisms of the same species that live in the same general region and naturally interbreed with each other

Symbioses: 2 organisms interacting closely

- **Mutualism = +,+**

- **Commensalism = +,0**

- **Parasitism = +,-**

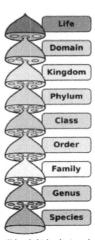

"dumb kids playing chase on the freeway get squished"

How do new species form?

Speciation: the creation of a new species (that branches off from a preexisting species)

- Usually occurs when one group of organisms enters a new and isolated niche, or when a geographical barrier is erected, dividing the species into 2 or more isolated groups

- The separated groups (geographical isolation) do not interbreed and they begin to diverge genetically from each other → after many generations they are so different that they can no longer produce viable offspring (reproductive isolation)

Reproductive isolation: keeps distinct species separate; prevents hybridization

- **Prezygotic barriers-** prevents the act of mating/the process of fertilization (geographic separation, temporal isolation, behavioral isolation, mechanical differences, etc.)

- **Postzygotic barriers-** hybrid offspring is inviable or sterile

Inbreeding: when closely related organisms reproduce

- Deleterious because closely related organisms are likely to carry similar recessive alleles for certain diseases → more likely to produce homozygous recessive offspring

- Often results from a dramatic and sudden decrease in the size of a population (such as a bottleneck)

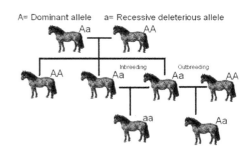

Inbreeding depression: excessive inbreeding within a population leads to decreased fitness of that population (and decreased genetic diversity)

- In general, the higher genetic diversity that there is within a population, the more fit it is

Outbreeding: mating between individuals that are not closely related

Specialization: traits become more specialized as the organisms occupy a particular environment/niche

- If too many organisms occupy a similar niche, competition will be high → drives organisms to become more specialized

CURVESETTER
TUTORING

EUKARYOTIC CELLS: PLASMA MEMBRANE AND CYTOSKELETON

Biology Lecture 6

OBJECTIVES

- The Plasma Membrane
  - Function and general structure (Fluid Mosaic Model)
  - Phospholipid bilayer
  - Membrane components and fluidity
  - The rearrangement of phospholipids and proteins
- Movement of solutes across the membrane
  - Osmosis, osmotic pressure, and colligative properties
  - Passive vs. active transport
  - Channel proteins, carrier proteins, aquaporins
  - Ion concentrations across the membrane
  - Exocytosis and endocytosis
  - Cell surface receptors
  - Intercellular junctions
- Cytoskeleton
  - Functions
  - Microtubules, intermediate filaments, microfilaments
  - Cilia and Flagella; MTOC and centrioles

The Plasma Membrane

Functions:

- Contain cellular components
- Control which solutes enter and exit the cell through a variety of methods
- Dictate ion concentrations across the membrane and therefore control membrane potential
  - **Membrane potential** between -40 → -80 mV (depends on cell type)

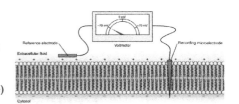

General Structure:

- All plasma membranes are composed of a **phospholipid bilayer**
  - Double layer of phospholipids; hydrophobic tails facing each other on the interior of the membrane, hydrophilic head groups face the aqueous exterior environment and cytoplasm
  - Formation of bilayer from free floating phospholipids is spontaneous (-ΔG)

- **Fluid Mosaic Model:** describes the cell membrane as a dynamic structure with different proteins and other molecules (such as cholesterol) embedded throughout it

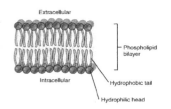

The Components and Functions of the Plasma Membrane	
Component	Location
Phospholipid	Main fabric of the membrane
Cholesterol	Attached between phospholipids and between the two phospholipid layers
Integral proteins (for example, integrins)	Embedded within the phospholipid layer(s). May or may not penetrate through both layers
Peripheral proteins	On the inner or outer surface of the phospholipid bilayer; not embedded within the phospholipids
Carbohydrates (components of glycoproteins and glycolipids)	Generally attached to proteins on the outside membrane layer

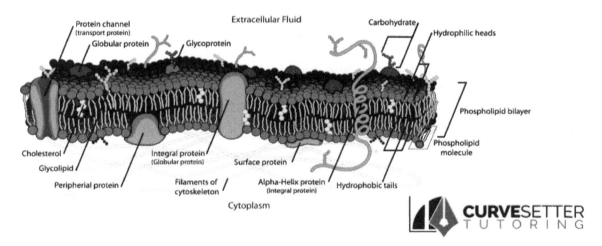

Components of the Plasma Membrane

Phospholipids: comprise the phospholipid bilayer; flexible and dynamic
- Allow small non-polar molecules to pass through (due to hydrophobic interior): O_2, CO_2, steroid hormones, etc.
- Water passes through special protein channels; ions and other large, polar molecules pass through channel proteins
- Phospholipids **rearrange**: flip-flop and move laterally; may occur spontaneously or with catalysis and/or energy input
- **Unsaturated** fatty acids (more kinks so less LDF) and **shorter** fatty acids (less LDF) = **more fluid** bilayer

Glycolipids:
- Carbohydrate attached to a lipid
- Found on the exterior surface of eukaryotic cell membranes
- Enable cell-cell communication, recognition, binding, interaction
  - Ex. Immune system inflammation response; blood type is determined by the oligosaccharide on red blood cells

Cholesterol:
- Large component of cell membranes
- Maintains fluidity **and** firmness of the membrane (prevents it from becoming too fluid or too stiff)
- Rings of cholesterol interact with fatty acid tails of phospholipids

Peripheral protein: located on the outer surface of the plasma membrane; rooted by polar and ionic interactions between the protein residues and polar phospholipid head group

Integral protein: embedded to some degree into the plasma membrane; non-polar interactions between region of the protein that is embedded in membrane and hydrophobic lipid tails

Transmembrane protein: type of integral protein that spans the entire length of the plasma membrane
- Usually have a pore through the middle and act as a channel/carrier protein
- Connect cytoplasm to extracellular environment

Movement: proteins can move throughout the membrane laterally, but cannot flip-flip

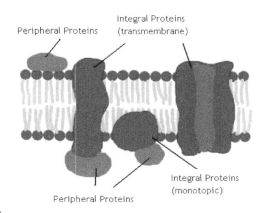

Osmosis: movement of water across a semi-permeable membrane from an area of low solute concentration (**hypotonic**) to an area of higher solute concentration (**hypertonic**)
- Water wants to move to the hypertonic side of the membrane
- Effect is to equalize the solute concentrations on either side of the membrane
- Cell membranes are semi-permeable; osmosis is the primary method by which water moves across membrane
- Water passes through **aquaporin** proteins in the membrane
- Concentration of solute particles in solution relative to the intracellular environment impacts cell volume

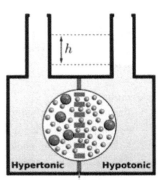

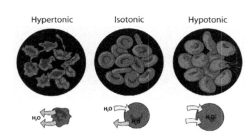

Osmotic Pressure:

- The external pressure that would need to be applied in order to prevent water movement by osmosis
- Greater difference in concentration across the membrane → more water movement occurs → higher osmotic pressure

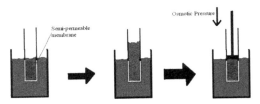

Calculation- $\pi = iMRT$

π = osmotic pressure

i = van't Hoff factor → # of ions/particles the molecule dissolves into

$C_6H_{12}O_6$ → i = 1; $CaCl_2$ → i = 3

M = molar concentration of solution

R = ideal gas constant

T = temperature

Colligative Properties:

- Depend only on the ratio of solute particles to solvent particles, not on the identity of the solute
- Osmotic pressure is a colligative property
- **Boiling point elevation:** solute particles act like an anchor on the water molecules, making it more difficult for them to be vaporized (more solute particles = higher BP)
- **Vapor pressure lowering:** solution with more solute particles boils at higher temperature so at any given temp has a lower vapor pressure
- **Freezing point depression:** solute particles interrupt the crystalline lattice structure of ice (more solute particles = lower freezing point)

Solute Transport across the Membrane

Passive Transport: no energy input required; solute particle moves down its gradient into an area of lower concentration (spontaneous movement)

- **Simple diffusion:** solute particle diffuses across the membrane without requiring a helper protein
  - Solute is small and hydrophobic

- **Facilitated Diffusion:** molecule requires a helper protein to cross the membrane (moving *down its gradient*); selectively permeability because proteins only allow certain solutes to diffuse through

  - **Channel protein-** transmembrane proteins with a tunnel through the middle that selectively allows solute particles to pass through based on size/charge
    - **Ion channels** allow ions through
    - **Gated channels** open in response to a change in voltage (**voltage-gated channels**) or to the binding of a specific ligand, such as a neurotransmitter (**ligand-gated channels**)

  - **Carrier protein-** not a tunnel; bind to the molecule that needs to be transported → conformational change → molecule released to the other side
    - **Uniport, symport, antiport**

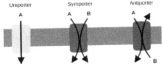

Facilitated vs. simple diffusion: the rate of simple diffusion increases linearly as the driving force increases (but limited by surface area); facilitated diffusion reaches a max rate and levels off when all of the transport proteins are saturated with solute particles

Active Transport: energy input required because particles transported against their gradient (from a region of low concentration to a region of higher concentration → non-spontaneous movement); requires ATP and a protein

- **Primary active transport:** transport of the molecule is directly coupled to ATP hydrolysis

- **Secondary active transport:** ATP used to create an electrochemical gradient (a form of stored potential energy) → energy of releasing that gradient is harnessed to pump a different solute particle against its gradient

Sodium-potassium pump (Na⁺/K⁺-ATPase): actively transports 3 Na⁺ ions out of the cell and 2 K⁺ ions in
- Maintains an excess of sodium outside of the cell and an excess of potassium inside of the cell

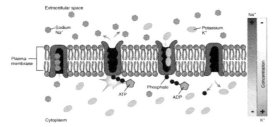

- **Membrane potential:** The Na⁺/K⁺-ATPase pump transports 3 + ions out of the cell and only brings 2 + ions back in → net loss of 1+ charge per pump results in a charge difference across the membrane → inside of the cell is more negative than the outside
    - The **resting** membrane potential is usually approximately **-70 mV**
    - Some potassium comes out of cell via potassium leak channels (even more loss of + ions adds to the negative membrane potential)
    - This is what enables action potentials to occur in neurons (depolarization → spike in the membrane potential)

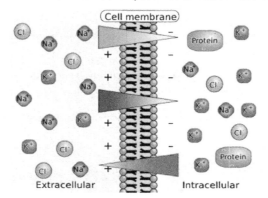

Ion concentrations across the membrane:

- Na⁺, Ca⁺², and Cl⁻ → higher outside the cell

- Proteins, K⁺ → higher inside the cell

Exocytosis:

- Membrane-bound vesicle (endosome) fuses with the plasma membrane, releasing its contents to the extracellular environment
  - Requires energy input
  - Neurotransmitters being released into the synaptic cleft
  - Exocytosis may also be used to insert compounds (proteins, phospholipid, etc.) into the membrane → vesicle fuses with the membrane- phospholipids of the vesicle and contents of vesicle become part of membrane

Endocytosis:

- Substances taken into the cell when part of the plasma membrane invaginates, forming a vesicle that is then released into the cell
  - Also requires energy input
  - Like endocytosis, this is used to transport large (and usually polar) molecules, such as proteins, that cannot use passive or active transport methods
- **Phagocytosis:** "cell eating" → solid particles taken in
- **Pinocytosis:** "cell drinking" → liquids taken in
  - Phagocytosis and pinocytosis are relatively nonspecific

- **Receptor-mediated endocytosis:** highly specific uptake of molecules
  - Clathrin (protein) on the intracellular surface of the membrane and specific receptor on extracellular surface
  - Receptor recognizes and binds to the molecule of choice → clathrin-coated pit forms around the molecule
  - Can be used to uptake specific molecules (such as cholesterol), viruses, proteins, etc.

Endocytosis

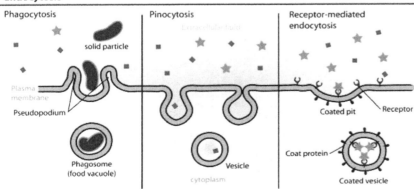

Cell Surface Receptors

- Cell surface receptors are integral membrane proteins that bind to molecules in the extracellular environment (hormones, neurotransmitters, ligands/solutes, etc.) and relay a signal to the cell
  - Communication- enables cells to alter their structure and function in response to signals
- Signal may be physical contact, a specific chemical/ligand, or a change in membrane potential

- **Signal transduction:** ligand binds to membrane receptor and signal is transmitted to the inside of the via a cascade of changes, often involving protein phosphorylation
  - Protein kinases involved in phosphorylation of molecules and/or other proteins during the cascade
  - Often the end result is changes in transcription and/or translation of specific genes
  - Ligand that triggers the cascade = primary messenger
  - **Secondary messengers** are molecules within the cell and are involving in transducing and amplifying the signal (cAMP, cGMP, etc.)

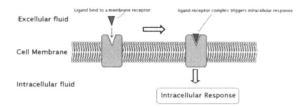

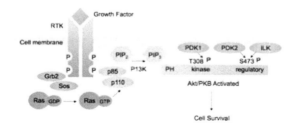

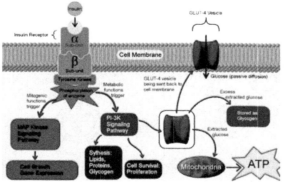

Types of membrane receptors-

- **Ion channel-linked receptor (ligand-gated ion channel):** the binding of a neurotransmitter triggers an ion channel to open → ion exits or enters the cell → cell depolarizes (excitatory) or hyperpolarizes (inhibitory)
  - Ex. Acetylcholine binds → Na^+ enters the cell → cell depolarizes → action potential fired

- **Enzyme-linked receptor:** membrane protein is associated with another enzyme (usually a kinase); or the cytoplasmic side of the membrane protein itself acts as a kinase

- **G-protein coupled receptor:** membrane protein is linked to a G-protein which activates a signal cascade via secondary messengers

  - Membrane protein detects a signal in environment (ligand, protein, light, hormone, etc.) → G-protein becomes activated when GDP exchanged for GTP → G-protein alpha subunit bound to GTP dissociates from the complex and moves to activate an effector protein → signal cascade occurs

  - Ex. Activated G protein activates adenylyl cyclase → adenylyl cyclase makes cAMP from ATP → different enzymes get phosphorylated by kinases → signal cascade occurs

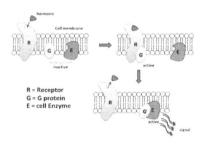

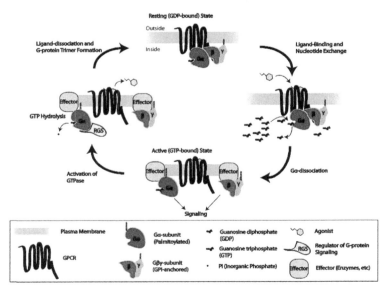

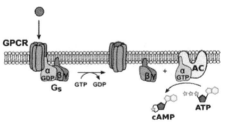

Intercellular Junctions

Gap junction:

- Pore-like connection between two cells that directly connects their intracellular environments
- Enable solutes and electrical impulses to pass between the adjacent cells
- Junction is regulated – may be open or closed
- Composed of connexon proteins
- Found in animal cells (similar to plasmodesmata of plant cells)
- Ex. Muscle- gap junctions enable the action potential to be transmitted directly from cell to cell

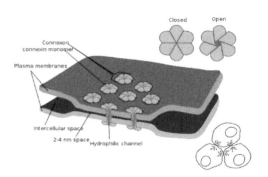

Tight junction:

- Stitched two cells together by forming a tight seal between them
- Prevents substances from passing between the connected cells
- Rows of tight junctions form an impermeable barrier
- Required in many tissues to seal off a region (epithelial cells of GI tract, bladder, etc.)
- Seal off the basolateral side of an organ/tissue from the apical side

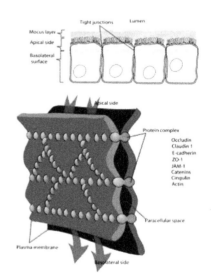

Desmosome:

- Connect cells at certain spots by linking their cytoskeletons; "spot welds"
- Fibers of the desmosome span the connected plasma membranes and radiate into the cell, connecting to both cells' cytoskeleton via intermediate filaments
- Structural role – provide mechanical strength to a tissue
- Cadherin and keratin proteins used

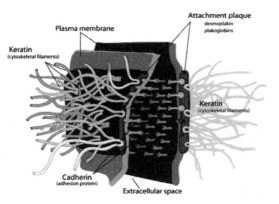

- Tight junctions, gap junctions, and desmosomes are found in animals cells

- Plant cells junctions are called **plasmodesmata**
    - Transverse through the cell walls of adjacent plant cells like a tunnel
    - Connect adjacent cells enabling communication and exchange

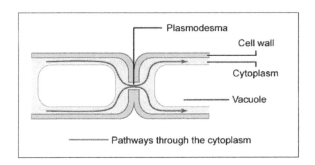

Cytoskeleton

The components of the cytoskeleton are large protein complexes with multiple associated subunits
- Eukaryotes (animalia): microtubules, intermediate filaments, and microfilaments

Roles:
- Structural support- organizing the organelles in the cytosol and the overall cell shape
- Cell movement- cilia and flagella; amoeboid movement (movement of eukaryotic cells involving extension of pseudopodia; endo- and exocytosis
- Transport- enable the transportation of vesicles and other substances throughout the cell

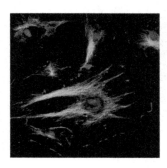 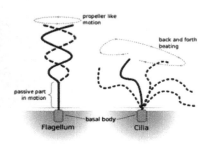 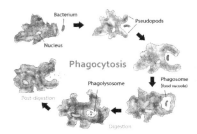

Microfilaments

Structure:
- Polymers of **actin protein** – double helix of actin polymer chains
- Dynamic- constantly being polymerized and depolymerized

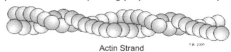

Actin Strand

Function:
- Cytokinesis – cell division contractile ring of actin and myosin (cleavage furrow)
- Amoeboid movement – large scale cell movement
- Muscle contractions – actin filaments associate with myosin head group
- Endocytosis and exocytosis

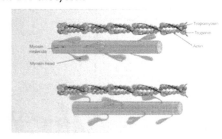 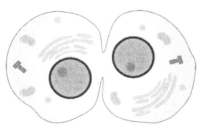

Intermediate Filaments

Structure:
- Polymer of many different associated proteins (not a homogenous structure)

Function:
- Supports overall cell shape and structure; bears tension- generally more permanent than microtubules/microfilaments
- Cell-to-cell adhesion- keratin intermediate filaments as a component of desmosomes

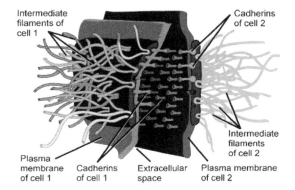

Microtubules

Structure:
- Hollow rob of tubulin proteins (alpha and beta tubulin dimers)

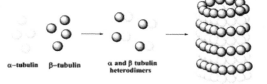

Function:
- Create tracks in the cells upon which substances and vesicles can be transported by motor proteins (like a cellular highway)
- Cell division - the mitotic spindle enables separation of sister chromatids and homologous chromosomes
- Microtubules organizing center (MTOC)- structure that organizes microtubules
  - Curates the spindle apparatus for division and microtubules in cilia/flagella
- Cilia and flagella- appendages that extend out of eukaryotic cells
  - Enable extensive cells movement
  - Flagella longer than cillia

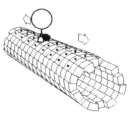

Spindle Apparatus (Meiotic/Mitotic Spindle)-

- Various associated proteins- mainly microtubules and some motor proteins

- **Centrioles** go to opposite ends of the dividing cell during early meiosis/mitosis → microtubules fibers (spindle fibers) elongate outward from the centrioles and attach to centromeres at the **kinetochore**
    - Centriole: hollow ring of 9 microtubules triplets
    - **Centrosome**: 2 centrioles and other associated proteins; prepared to curate cell division

- The dynamic shortening and elongating of the spindle fibers facilitates cell division and pulls the homologous chromosomes/chromatids to opposite ends of the cell

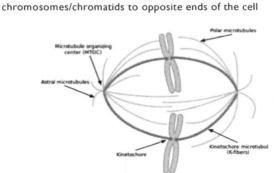

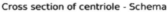

Cross section of centriole - Schema

Cilia and Flagella (eukaryotic)

- Cilia smaller and shorter than flagella
- Generally many cilia per cell and only one or a few flagella
    - Ex. Sperm cell has a single flagellum
- Cilia beat back and forth, moving fluid over the surface of the tissue

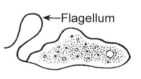

Structure:

- Appendage is attached to the plasma membrane at the **basal body**
- **"9 + 2"** arrangement of microtubules- 9 in a ring, 2 in center
- Dynein connects the microtubules and contracts so tubule dimers slide past each other

Ultrastructure of Cilia and Flagella

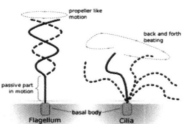

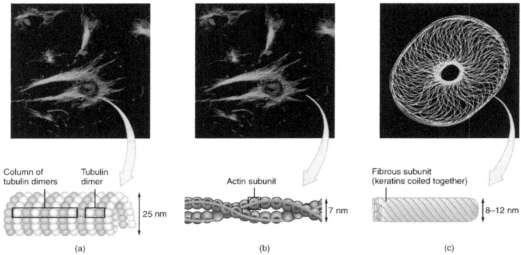

Column of tubulin dimers   Tubulin dimer

25 nm

(a)

Actin subunit

7 nm

(b)

Fibrous subunit (keratins coiled together)

8–12 nm

(c)

EUKARYOTIC CELLS: ORGANELLES AND THE CELL CYCLE

Biology Lecture 7

OBJECTIVES

- Hallmarks of Eukaryotic Cells
  - Differences between prokaryotes and eukaryotes; the Endosymbiotic Theory
- Nucleus
  - Overall structure and function
  - The nucleolus, nuclear membrane, and nuclear pores
- Mitochondria
  - Function and structure: inner and outer membranes, IMS
  - Mitochondrial DNA and inheritance
- Lysosome
- Rough Endoplasmic Reticulum
- Smooth Endoplasmic Reticulum
- Golgi Apparatus
- Peroxisome
- The cell cycle
  - Stages of the cell cycle
  - Mitosis: stages and structures required
  - Control of the cell cycle and growth arrest

Hallmarks of Eukaryotic Cells

Eukaryotic Cells	Prokaryotic Cells
Domain: eukarya	Domain: bacteria or archaea
Many different membrane bound organelles (rough/smooth ER, mitochondria, Golgi, lysosome, peroxisome, etc.)	No membrane bound organelles (doesn't include ribosomes, which aren't membrane bound)
Majority of the genetic material enclosed in the nucleus (excluding mitochondrial/chloroplast DNA)	No nucleus; DNA found in a central region called the nucleoid
DNA is wrapped up into chromatin (associated with histone proteins); multiple linear chromosomes	No histone proteins ("naked DNA"); usually genome is a single circular chromosomes
Asexual division by mitosis; sexual division by meiosis	Division by binary fission
Cell wall: none in animals (but have ECM for additional structural support); primarily chitin in fungi and cellulose/some polysaccharide in plants	Bacteria have cells walls of peptidoglycan (peptide plus polysaccharide)
Flagella is made of 9 + 2 microtubules arrangement plus dynein proteins	Flagella is made of flagellin protein

Eukarya: includes protists (generally unicellular, often mobile), plants, fungi, and animals

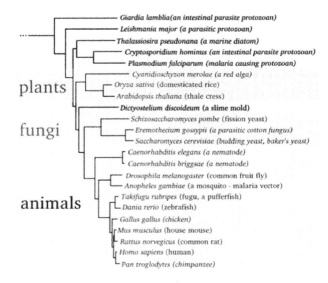

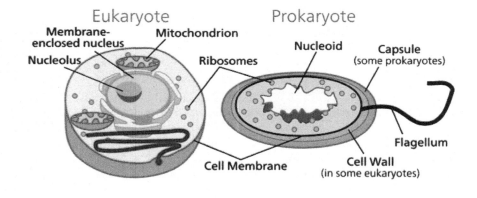

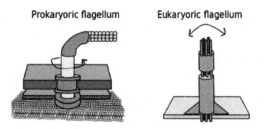

The Endosymbiotic Theory describes how, long ago in evolutionary history, an ancestral eukaryotic species engulfed another prokaryotic cell → the engulfed prokaryote and the host cell lived in symbiosis → engulfed species became an organelle (mitochondria, chloroplast) in the newly formed eukaryotic cell

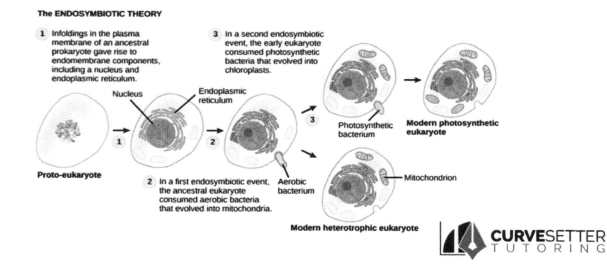

Animal Cell:

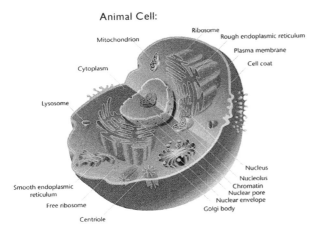

Plant Cell:

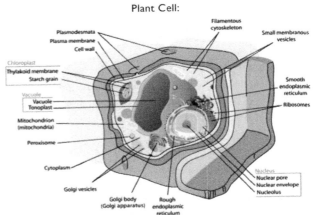

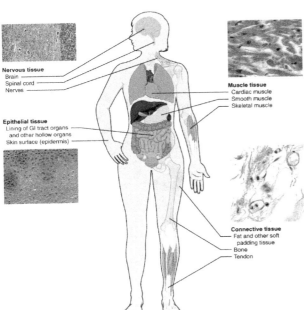

Epithelial Tissue:
- Squamous cells, cuboidal cells, and columnar cells
- Simple or stratified

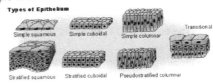

- Lines the surface of body cavities; surrounds organs and blood vessels- provides structural support, protection/barrier, organization of body plan, etc.

Connective Tissue:
- Bone, tendons, ligaments, cartilage, adipose tissue, and blood
- Cells have an extensive ECM (extracellular matrix)- grounds the cells and gives them support/strength
  - Not necessarily fibrous (ex. blood matrix = plasma fluid)
- Loose and dense connective tissue
- Fibers: collagen fibers, reticular fibers, elastic fibers

The Nucleus

Function: contain and protect the cells' genetic information
- Contain chromatin (DNA and associated histone proteins)
- Where DNA replication, RNA processing, and transcription occur

Nucleolus-
- Dense center of the nucleus composed of proteins, DNA, and RNA
- Site of ribosomes synthesis → rRNA transcribed in the nucleolus then associated with proteins

Nuclear membrane/envelope-
- Composed of two plasma membranes (outer and inner)

Nuclear pores-
- Large channel proteins that allow substances into and out of the nucleus (selectivity based on size)

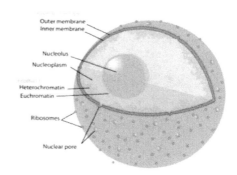

Mitochondria

- The site of the majority of ATP production
  - Creates the bulk of ATP for the cell → TCA cycle, oxidative phosphorylation
  - Proton motive force of H^+ gradient harnessed by ATP synthase

- Composed of two membranes (**inner membrane** and **outer membrane**), with the **intermembrane space** (IMS) between them
  - Inner membrane is extensively folded into **cristae** structures - large surface area

- **Matrix:** space within the inner membrane that houses many different enzymes of metabolism, as well as **mitochondrial DNA**

- Mitochondria are self-replicating (replicates independently from the cell) and contain all the machinery required for self-replication

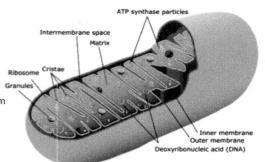

- Mitochondrial DNA (mtDNA)- small circular DNA that codes for various proteins of the TCA cycle and oxidative phosphorylation as well as the machinery for transcription/translation

- mtDNA is thought to have been derived from the prokaryotic cells that were engulfed far back in evolutionary history
  - Evidence for the endosymbiotic theory

- Transcription and translation machinery used by mitochondria differ from that of the rest of the cell
  - Mitochondria has its own (70S) ribosomes → evidence for the endosymbiotic theory

- mtDNA shows entirely maternal inheritance (cytoplasm of the ovum becomes cytoplasm of the zygote)

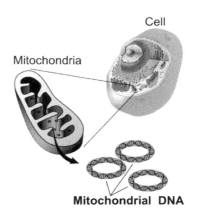

The Endomembrane System: collection of vesicles, membranes, and organelles that collectively modify, sort, transport, and export macromolecules
- Includes the nuclear envelope, endoplasmic reticulum, Golgi, lysosomes, vesicles, and the plasma membrane

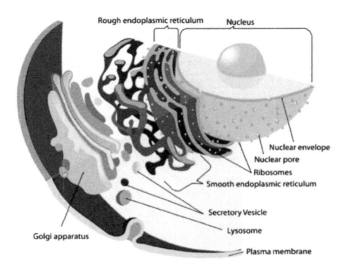

Lysosome

- Organelles that house the enzymes required to break down polymers such as lipids, proteins, DNA, and carbohydrates
  - **Acid hydrolases:** enzymes that degrade molecules by hydrolysis and function at low pH
  - Enzymes made in the RER and tagged for transport to lysosomes

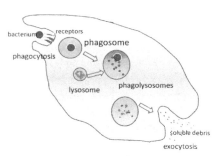

- Low pH of lysosome (around 4.5) is optimal for the enzymes but lower than the pH of the cytoplasm (7.2)
  - If the lysosomes lyses and its enzymes are released into the cell, they won't do too much damage

- "Trash and recycle receptacles of the cell" → degrade polymers from within the cell (**autophagy**) and particles taken in from the external environment (via endocytosis)
  - Autophagy – self-degradation of damaged or defunct cell parts
  - Vesicle formed by endocytosis fuses with the lysosome, dumping the contents into it

Endoplasmic Reticulum

Structure: continuous membrane-enclosed system composed of multiple flattened sacs (**cisternae**)

- Membrane of ER buds out from nuclear outer membrane
- Rough ER: membrane has ribosomes associated with its membrane, giving it a "rough" appearance
- Smooth ER: lacks ribosomes

Smooth ER (SER):

- Makes lipids (such as phospholipids and steroids), which are used by the cell or are secreted

- Metabolizes carbohydrates (such as glycogen, especially in the liver), steroids, and some toxins

- Sarcosplasmic reticulum: SER of myocytes (muscle cells) → stores and secretes Ca^{+2}

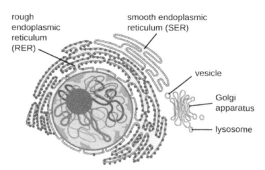

Rough Endoplasmic Reticulum (RER):

- Translation and post-translational protein modification occur in both the cytoplasm (cytoplasmic ribosomes) and in the RER (ribosomes temporarily docked on membrane of the RER)
    - Ribosomes synthesize the growing polypeptide into the ER lumen

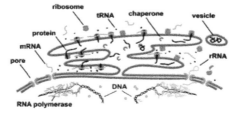

- Proteins made in the RER will be …
    - Secreted by the cell
    - Become part of the plasma membrane (transmembrane proteins)
    - Be used in the endomembrane system (ER, Golgi, lysosomes)

- Translation starts in the cytoplasm → N-terminus signal sequence is translated → sequence recognized by SRP (signal recognition particle) causing translation to pause and the ribosomes to become docked on the RER membrane → protein translated into the lumen of the RER → chaperone protein or other enzymes may modify it and signal peptide usually removed → RER works with Golgi to send protein to the proper location

Golgi Apparatus

- Modifies, sorts, packages, and sends out proteins and lipids (for use in the cell or for exocytosis)
    - Post-translational modification of proteins: adds oligosaccharide chains (glycosylation), phosphorylates them, tags them for their final destination, etc.

- **Structure:** stack of multiple flattened disks called **cisternae**
    - **Cis** region: receives proteins (packaged in vesicles) from the RER
    - **Trans** region: where proteins and other molecules are sent out from the Golgi to their proper destination

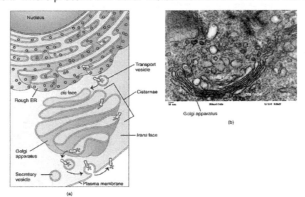

Peroxisome

Function:

- Breakdown of long chain fatty acids into shorter chain fatty acids (via beta oxidation)

- Metabolize drugs and other toxins (especially in the liver and kidneys)

- Carry out redox reactions with a variety of substrates, often producing H_2O_2 as a byproduct
    - H_2O_2 is damaging to the cell and therefore must be broken down in the peroxisome using **catalase**

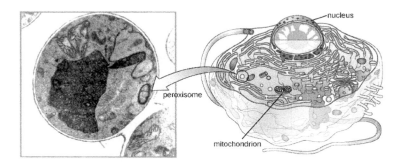

The Cell Cycle

- The cell cycle of eukaryotes is divided into interphase (G1 → S → G2) and the mitotic phase (mitosis and cytokinesis)

- Interphase: cells grows, prepares for cell division, and duplicates its DNA (DNA replication)

- G0 = cell not replicating or dividing; temporarily or permanently
    - Ex. majority of neurons are in a **quiescent state** (always in G0, never divide)

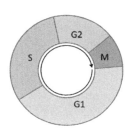

G1 - Growth

S - DNA synthesis

G2 - Growth and preparation for mitosis

M - Mitosis (cell division)

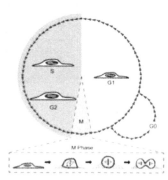

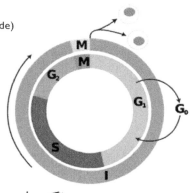

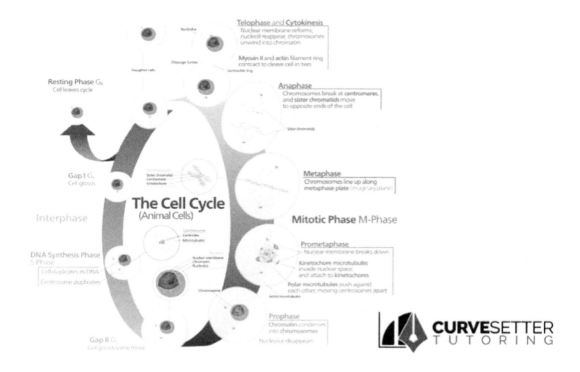

The Cell Cycle
(Animal Cells)

Interphase

Mitotic Phase M-Phase

Mitosis

- Cell division that produces two genetically identical diploid daughter cells
- Four sequential phases of mitosis (prophase, metaphase, anaphase, telophase) plus cytokinesis

P = Prophase → chromatin condenses into chromosomes; nuclear membrane breaks down; mitotic spindle is assembled and centrioles prepare to send out spindle fibers

M = Metaphase → condensed and duplicated chromosomes line up along the center of the cell (metaphase plate)

A = Anaphase → spindle fibers linked to the centromere of the chromosomes (via kinetochore protein complex) shorten, separating the sister chromatids and pulling them to opposite ends of the cell; other microtubules push against each other, elongating the dividing cell

T = Telophase → nuclear envelope reforms and chromosomes de-condense inside nucleus

Cytokinesis → division of the cytoplasm and organelles; cleavage furrow of actin and myosin filaments contracts to pinch the cells apart; occurs throughout A and T

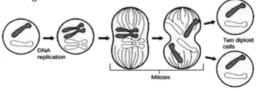

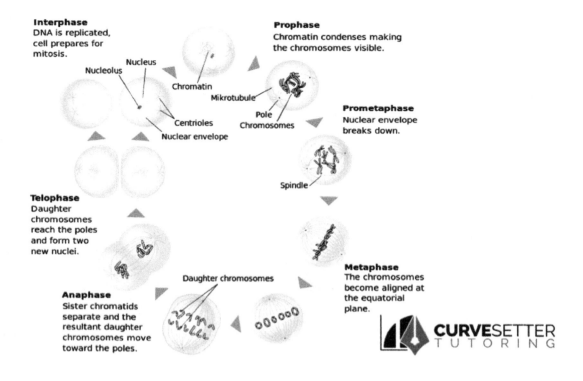

Interphase
DNA is replicated, cell prepares for mitosis.

Prophase
Chromatin condenses making the chromosomes visible.

Prometaphase
Nuclear envelope breaks down.

Metaphase
The chromosomes become aligned at the equatorial plane.

Anaphase
Sister chromatids separate and the resultant daughter chromosomes move toward the poles.

Telophase
Daughter chromosomes reach the poles and form two new nuclei.

Nucleus
Nucleolus
Chromatin
Mikrotubule
Pole
Chromosomes
Centrioles
Nuclear envelope
Spindle
Daughter chromosomes

Growth Arrest: cell doesn't proceed through the cell cycle; stays in G0

- Can occur due to a variety of reasons-
  - Accumulation of mutations
  - Specific cell types that divide minimally or not at all in their lifetime (neurons, cardiac myocytes)
  - Lack of nutrients

Control of the Cell Cycle:

- **Checkpoints** (G1, G2, M) → cell "pauses" and checks for certain conditions before proceeding - proper DNA replication, DNA damage/mutations, nutrient availability, proper growth, correct attachment of spindle fibers
  - If conditions are not met, cell cycle doesn't continue until issues are corrected
- Cancer cells- failure of these control mechanisms results in uncontrolled cell growth and division, and the evasion of apoptosis

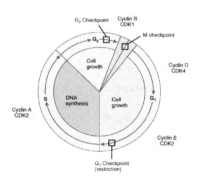

Apoptosis

- Apoptosis = programmed cell death (healthy and supposed to occur)
  - Necrosis = premature and un-programmed cell death due to cellular injury/trauma

- The cell breaks up into small blebs that are disassembled from within → later remains digested by other cells
  - Process is highly controlled and clean; doesn't damage nearby cells

- Triggered by extrinsic signal or intrinsic signal (cellular stress, irreparable DNA damage, etc.)
  - **P53** = common intrinsic trigger of apoptosis; tumor suppressor gene

- Apoptosis involves **caspases** → class of protease enzymes
  - Initiator caspases trigger effector caspases, which carry out apoptosis

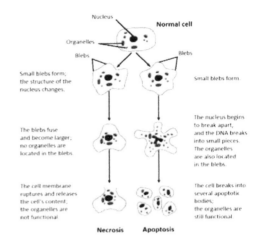

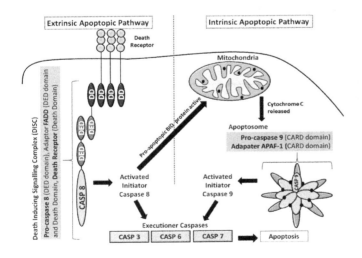

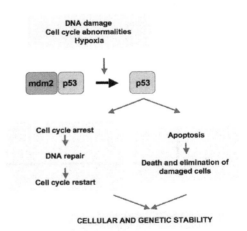

PROKARYOTIC CELLS AND VIRUSES

Biology Lecture 8

OBJECTIVES

- The Cell Theory
- Prokaryotic Cells
  - Defining characteristics of prokaryotes
  - Bacteria- characteristics and main classifications
  - Genome properties and genetics
  - Metabolic variation
  - Reproduction by fission
  - Conjugation; transformation; transduction
- Viruses
  - Defining properties
  - Contents and structural characteristics
  - General virus life cycle
  - Lytic and lysogenic viruses
  - Retroviruses
  - HIV; prions; viroids

The Cell Theory

Scientific theory proposed in mid 1800s:

- All living organisms (unicellular or multicellular) are composed of cells
- Cells are the basic unit of life and reproduction
- New cells can only arise from preexisting cells

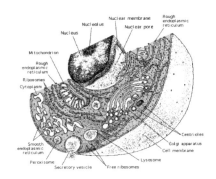

Prokaryotic Cells

Eukaryotic Cells	Prokaryotic Cells
Domain: eukarya	Domain: bacteria or archaea
Many different membrane bound organelles (rough/smooth ER, mitochondria, Golgi, lysosome, peroxisome, etc.)	No membrane bound organelles (doesn't include ribosomes, which aren't membrane bound)
Majority of the genetic material enclosed in the nucleus (excluding mitochondrial/chloroplast DNA)	No nucleus; DNA found in a central region called the nucleoid
DNA is wrapped up into chromatin (associated with histone proteins); multiple linear chromosomes	No histone proteins ("naked DNA"); usually genome is a single circular chromosomes
Asexual division by mitosis; sexual division by meiosis	Division by binary fission
Cell wall: none in animals (but ECM for additional structural support); primarily chitin in fungi and cellulose/some polysaccharide in plants	Bacterial cells walls usually peptidoglycan (peptide + polysaccharide)
Flagella made of 9 + 2 microtubules arrangement + dynein protein	Flagella made of flagellin protein

- Bacteria and archaea share many similarities (the hallmarks of prokaryotic cells), but branched away from their common ancestor long ago in evolutionary history

- Archaea differ from bacteria in their metabolic pathways, genetics, reliance on energy sources, etc.
  - Often live in extreme environments (extremophiles)

Prokaryotic Living Conditions - Terms:

Parasitic: harm the host → pathogens

Symbiotic: live in harmony with the host → mutually beneficial
- Huge diversity of bacteria living in and on the human body – necessary for our survival (the human microbiome)

Thermophile: live in extremely high temperatures (extremophile)

Mesophile: live in moderate temperatures

Psychrophile: live in very low temperatures

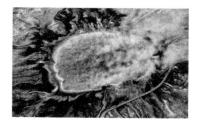

Bacteria- Characteristics and Classifications

- **Size:** smaller than eukaryotic cells; approximately the same size as eukaryotic organelles

- **Genome:** 1 circular DNA molecule (chromosomal DNA) + any number of plasmids

  - **Plasmid =** small circular extra-genomic DNA molecule; can provide advantages such an antibiotic resistance
    - o Shared between bacteria via **conjugation**
    - o Chromosomal DNA contains all the genes necessary for life and reproduction; plasmids contain genes that may benefit the organism such as antibiotic resistance, living in an specific niche, etc.
    - o Can replicate independently from the chromosomal DNA

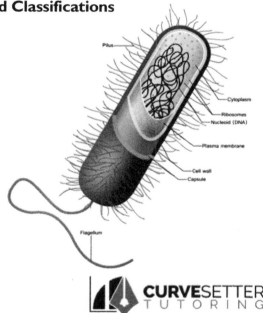

Flagella: enables propulsion/motility of the cell
- Composed of flagellin protein; basal unit, hook, rod, filament, etc.

Pili: small protrusions from the cell
- Enable bacterial conjugation → two cells attach to each other and form a bridge to transfer genetic material

Capsule: sticky later of gelatin surrounding the bacterial cell
- Virulence factor because it prevents host eukaryotic cells from engulfing bacteria

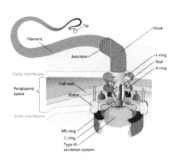

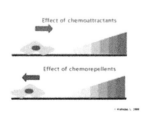

Chemotaxis- organism moves in response to gradient of a chemical stimulus (towards or away from increasing concentrations the substance)

Gram Staining:

- **Gram Negative-** possess two lipid bilayers with a cell wall (peptidoglycan) between them; staining color → pink
    - More resistant to antibiotics
    - Produce mainly endotoxins → only released when cell lyses
- **Gram Positive-** single lipid bilayer surrounded by a cell wall; staining color → violet (dye sticks to cell)
    - Produce mainly exotoxins → diffuse into surroundings

Bacteria shapes:

- **Coccus-** sphere-shaped
    - Ex. Streptococcus (strep throat infections), MRSA
- **Baccilus-** rod-shaped
    - Generally very dangerous to human health
    - Ex. Anthrax, E. Coli
- **Spirilla-** spiral-shaped
    - Generally harmless
    - Ex. H. pylori

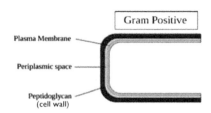

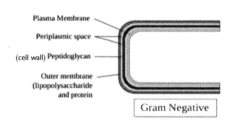

Bacili   Cocci   Spirilli

Bacterial Metabolism

Autotroph: produces its own nutrients (carbs, fats, proteins, etc.) using light and/or chemical energy
- Producer; "fixes carbon"
- Ex. Plants use photosynthesis (CO_2 as carbon source) to produce glucose

Heterotroph: relies on organic nutrients made by autotrophs → must ingest a carbon source
- Consumer

Chemotroph: Energy obtained from chemicals (oxidation)

Phototroph: Energy obtained from light

Auxotroph: mutant organism that cannot synthesize a particular substance required for growth or cannot metabolize a particular nutrient
- Ex. trp⁻ → trp must be added to the growth medium for them to survive; lac⁻ → can't use lactose as energy source

Simple comparison of an Auxotroph and Prototroph

Arginine Auxotroph
(Needs Arginine to grow)

Minimal media (MM)   MM + Arginine   MM + Lysine

Prototroph

Minimal media (MM)   MM + Arginine   MM + Lysine

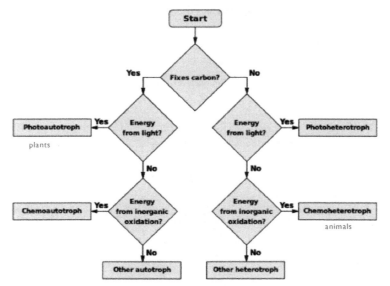

Oxygen Use-

Aerobe: use the TCA cycle + oxidative phosphorylation (O_2 is the final e- acceptor) to produce the bulk of their ATP
→ *require* oxygen to survive

Anaerobe: can grow and produce ATP without sufficient O_2 in the environment (fermentation or anaerobic respiration)
- **Obligate anaerobe-** are poisoned by oxygen
- **Facultative anaerobe-** can grow with or without O_2; uses O_2 when present, uses fermentation when not present
- **Aero-tolerant anaerobe-** don't ever use O_2 but can survive in its presence

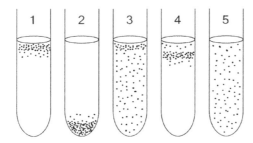

Binary Fission

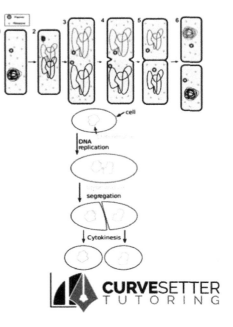

- "Asexual" reproduction of bacteria → produces 2 identical daughter cells
- Parent cell grows, replicates DNA, and undergoes cytokinesis
- No recombination (therefore no inherent increase in genetic diversity)

Bacterial Population Growth-

- Under ideal conditions (growth medium provided) the growth of a bacterial colony is **exponential**
- **Lag phase**: bacteria prepare the cellular parts required for the initial rounds of duplication
- **Exponential growth phase**
- **Stationary phase**: nutrients are limited (space, energy source, etc.) → population reaches carrying capacity

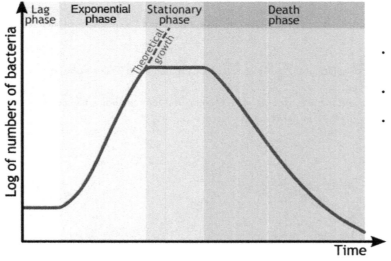

- Taking the log of an exponential growth curve results in a linear function
- log(# bacteria) → linear
- 10^1 → 10^2 → 10^3

Conjugation

- Bacteria exchange genetic material through direct cell-to-cell contact *(horizontal gene transfer)*
  - *Unidirectional* transfer – one cell donated and one cell receives

- Increase in genetic diversity of the bacterial population

- Conjugation requires a **pilus** to connect the cells in a **sex/conjugation/mating bridge** → copy of the plasmid passes directly from donor cell to recipient cell via the conjugation bridge

- One strand of the donor's DNA is transferred → both donor and recipient synthesize a new complementary strand

- **F (fertility) factor** is required for conjugation to occur – region of *extrachromosomal* DNA that encodes the genes required for conjugation to occur
  - Pilus attachment and formation of the conjugation bridge, etc.

- **Donor cell = F⁺ cell** → possesses the F-factor

- **Recipient cell = F⁻ cell** → receives the plasmid in addition to the F-factor genes

- **Hfr (high frequency recombination) cell** = has the F-factor incorporated into its chromosomal DNA
  - Can initiate conjugation; does so very efficiently

- Normally, conjugation between a F⁺ cell and an F⁻ results in the F⁻ cell receiving the F-factor and becoming an F⁺ cell
  - Not the case for conjugation between F⁻ and Hfr

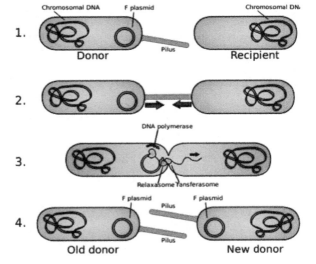

Transformation

- Bacteria take up foreign DNA from the surroundings

- Bacteria must be **competent** - able to directly uptake the exogenous DNA

- Competence may occur naturally or may be induced in the lab (electroporation, heat shock, etc.)

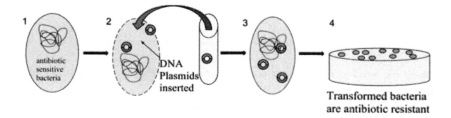

Transduction

- Virus (bacteriophage) latches onto bacteria and injects its genetic material into the cell
  - Genetic material may be indirectly transferred from one bacteria cell to another, with the virus being the agent of transfer

- Three ways of inserting new genetic material into a bacteria cell = conjugation (cell-to-cell), transformation (environment-to-cell) and transduction (virus-to-cell):

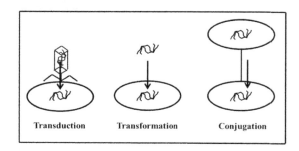

Defining Characteristics of Viruses

- Virus = genetic material enclosed in protein coat (**capsid**)

- **Viral genome:** ssDNA, dsDNA, ssRNA, **or** dsRNA; linear or circular

    - Often contain more than 1 ORF → more genes in a smaller amount of genetic material

- Not considered a living organism

    - Must replicate within a living host cell → use the host cell's machinery (enzymes, ATP, etc.) for replication, transcription, and translation

    - Lack a nucleus and possess no organelles

- **Size-** viruses are hundreds of times smaller than prokaryotic and eukaryotic cells

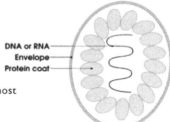

- **Enveloped:** possess an envelope (lipid bilayer) derived from budding out of the host and taking some of the hosts' membrane; envelope fuses with newly infected host

    - Enveloped viruses infect animal cells (plant cells and bacteria have cell wall)

- **Non-enveloped:** don't possess an envelope; "naked virus"

Bacteriophage (phage): virus that infects bacteria

- Must puncture through bacterial cell wall

- Not enveloped

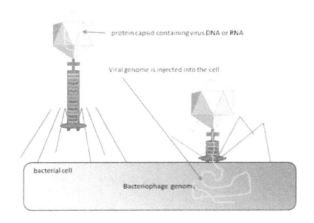

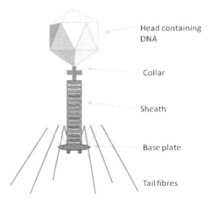

General Viral Life Cycle

- Virus attaches to cell (**adsorption**) and penetrates cell wall if present
  - Viral-host cell attachment is specific

- Virus enters cell by endocytosis or **injects** its viral genome into cell, leaving capsid outside

- Virus uses the host cell's machinery (ribosomes, polymerases), building blocks (dNTPs, amino acids), and energy to **replicate the viral genome** and **synthesize viral proteins** (such as capsid)

- Proteins and viral genetic material associate, forming many viral progeny

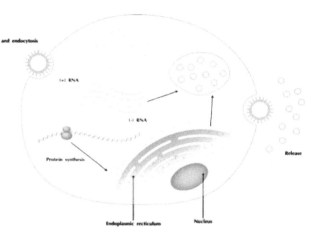

Lytic and Lysogenic Life Cycle

Lytic Life Cycle:
- Host cell infected and viral genome injected → viral genome replicated and proteins synthesized → host cell is lysed by viruses → viral progeny released
  - Host cell always destroyed
  - If cell wall present (host cell is a bacterium)- specific enzyme, such as lysozyme, required to destroy cell wall
  - RNA virus- must encode for RNA-dependent RNA polymerase in order to replicate its genome

Lysogenic Life Cycle:
- Host cell infected by virus and viral genome injected → viral genome incorporated into host genome (genome now called prophage) → prophage genes silent (not expressed; lay dormant) → Host carries out its normal activities; reproduces itself normally → prophage replicated and passed onto daughter cells → eventually environmental signal triggers the lytic phase to be entered
  - "Lysogen" = bacterium with viral genome integrated into its own chromosome but lying dormant

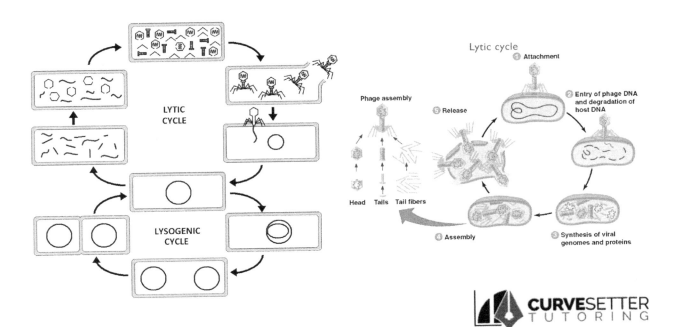

Lytic cycle

1 Attachment

2 Entry of phage DNA and degradation of host DNA

3 Synthesis of viral genomes and proteins

4 Assembly

5 Release

Phage assembly

Head   Tails   Tail fibers

Retroviruses

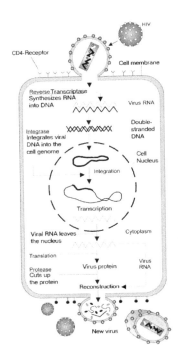

- RNA virus that uses a DNA intermediate in the lysogenic life cycle

- Viral genome encodes for **reverse transcriptase** (RNA-dependent DNA polymerase), which uses RNA genome to make DNA
  - No proofreading mechanism → high mutation rate → rapid evolution of virus

- DNA then incorporated into host cell genome and transcribed and translated to produce the viral proteins; transcription also produces copies of RNA viral genome to be assembled into viral progeny

- **HIV** is a retrovirus:

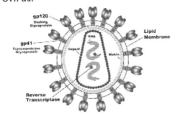

Prion

- **Prion:** an infectious protein molecule (no genetic material involved)
- Prions induce other, correctly folded proteins to mis-fold → prion is the template for its own propagation (self-replicating)
  - Misfolded proteins **polymerize/aggregate** into extremely **stable** structures → results in cell death and damages tissues
- Prion diseases have a very **long incubation period**
- Prions cause **TSEs** (transmissible spongiform encephalopathies)
  - Cause deterioration of the brain; progressive and eventually fatal
  - Creutzfeldt-Jakob disease in humans; mad cow's disease
- Prion may occur via mutation, inheritance, or ingestion (consumed in food)

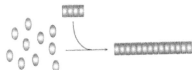

Viroid

- **Viroid:** infectious pathogen composed solely of a piece of circular ssRNA
  - Many self-complementary regions results in the RNA folding on itself and appearing double stranded
- No proteins involved; RNA doesn't code for proteins
- **Replication** – require RNA polymerase; rolling circle replication mechanism
- **Transmission** – plant to plant contact or indirect transmission through insect
- Cause disease in plants → primarily via **RNA silencing** (siRNA); also via ribozymal properties

NERVOUS SYSTEM AND ENDOCRINE SYSTEM

Biology Lecture 9

OBJECTIVES

- The Neuron
  - Structure: cell body, dendrites, axon, myelin sheath
  - Resting potential, depolarization, and hyperpolarization
  - Action potential
  - The synapse and neurotransmitters
  - Excitatory and inhibitory nerve fibers
  - Glial cells: oligodendrocytes, Schwann cells, astrocytes, microglia
- The Nervous System
  - Major functions and organization of the nervous system
  - Central and Peripheral Nervous Systems
  - Sympathetic and Parasympathetic Nervous Systems
  - Reflex Arc
- The Endocrine System
  - Mechanisms of hormone transport and action
  - Major types of hormones
  - Functions of endocrine system
  - Major glands and their hormones and effects
  - Nervous system and endocrine system
  - Feedback control

Neurons

Neuron (nerve cell): specialized cell of the nervous system that can receive and send messages via electrical impulses
- **Afferent neuron –** send information from the body to the brain/spinal cord (CNS)
- **Efferent neuron –** send information from the CNS to the rest of the body
- **Interneuron –** form connections between neurons (reflex arc)

Function: neurons send and receive signals and interact with each other in neural networks to coordinate how the body functions (movement, consciousness, memory, sensation, reflexes, etc.) and regulate the internal environment

Structure:

Soma/cell body- contains the nucleus and organelles

Axon hillock- region of the soma where the action potential is initiated

Dendrite- extensions from the soma that receive input

Axon- action potential is propagated down the axon in order to send information to other neurons, muscles, or tissues

Myelin sheath- fatty substance that covers the axon intermittently (gaps between called **Nodes of Ranvier**); insulates the axon to speed up conduction

Axon terminal- release neurotransmitter into the synapse when action potential reaches the end of the axon

Synapse- junction between neurons; small gap across which neurotransmitters are sent from one cell to the other to transmit a signal

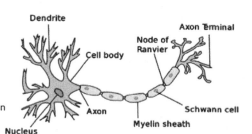

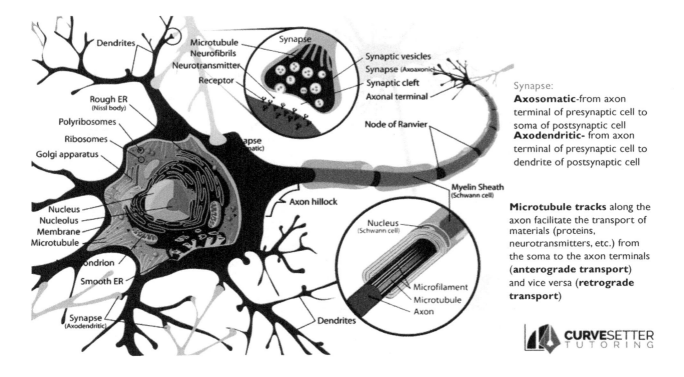

Synapse:

Axosomatic-from axon terminal of presynaptic cell to soma of postsynaptic cell

Axodendritic- from axon terminal of presynaptic cell to dendrite of postsynaptic cell

Microtubule tracks along the axon facilitate the transport of materials (proteins, neurotransmitters, etc.) from the soma to the axon terminals (**anterograde transport**) and vice versa (**retrograde transport**)

Resting Potential:
- Resting potential is approximately -70mV, largely due to Na^+/K^+-ATPase pump and K^+ leak channels
- **Electrochemical gradient-** chemical gradient is the difference in ion concentrations across a membrane; electrical gradient if the difference in charge across a membrane
- Deviations from the resting potential signify excitation or inhibition of the neuron

Depolarization: inside of the neuron becomes less negative (more positive)
- Can be mediated by an influx of cations or an efflux of anions
- Generally caused by **influx of Na^+ ions** → $[Na^+]$ higher outside the neuron; when voltage-gated Na^+ channels open, Na^+ ions rush into the cell and increase the membrane potential
- Depolarization = **excitation** → if the cell depolarizes enough (reaches a threshold) then action potential will fire

Excitation: Depolarization

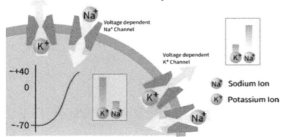

Hyperpolarization: inside of the neuron becomes more negative (below the resting potential)

- Can be mediated by an influx of anions or an efflux of cations
- Generally caused by an **efflux of K⁺ ions** → [K⁺] higher inside the neuron; when voltage-gated K⁺ channels open, K⁺ ions rush out of the cell and decrease the membrane potential
- Occurs in response to **inhibitory** stimuli and makes it more difficult for that neuron to fire a new action potential because a larger negative voltage must be overcome to reach the threshold

Overall:

- Stimuli (chemical, electrical, or mechanical) are received at the dendrites of a neuron and result in either excitation (EPSP) or inhibition (IPSP)
- The effects of multiple concurrent inputs are summed together in the soma (axon hillock) and result in a net depolarization or hyperpolarization that determines the cell's response → cell responds by firing an action potential if threshold is reached or is temporarily inhibited from firing
- **Temporal Summation:** repeated inputs sent from a single neuron are summed
- **Spatial Summation:** inputs sent from multiple different neurons (arriving at different areas) are summed

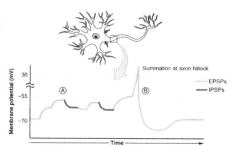

Action Potential

- **Resting potential:** Na⁺/K⁺ ATPase pumps working to achieve high [K⁺] inside the neuron and low [Na⁺] inside the neuron → ~ -70 mV

- **Depolarization:** depolarizing inputs from other (presynaptic) neurons are summed at the axon hillock and lead to the opening of *some* voltage-gated Na⁺ channels → Na⁺ comes into the cell and membrane potential rises to the threshold → ~ -55 mV

- Once the threshold voltage is reached, all of the voltage-gated Na⁺ channels open (via positive feedback loop) and an **action potential** will fire down the length of the axon, starting at the axon hillock

- After a region of the axon depolarizes to ~40 mV, the sodium channels close while voltage-gated K⁺ are activated → K⁺ flows out of the cell and the cell potential drops back down

- **Undershoot** (after-hyperpolarization): K⁺ channels stay open a little too long and the membrane potential drops below resting potential → referred to as a **refractory period** because it is much more difficult for a cell to initiate a new action potential at this time

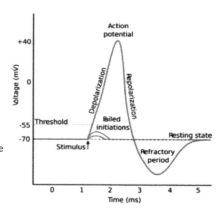

Nodes of Ranvier- gaps between the myelin sheath along the length of the axon
- Myelin sheath insulates the axon and prevents the exchange of ions, so only at the Nodes of Ranvier can ions exit and enter the axon (how the action potential is propagated)
- **Saltatory conduction:** Action potential (AP) "jumps" from node to node down the length of the axon
  - Na^+ ions diffuse down the axon from one node to the next one → depolarization triggers the next node to open all the Na^+ channels
- At node that is depolarizing during an AP, the nodes behind it have already begun to hyperpolarize → ensures that the action potential only moves in one direction down the axon (from soma to axon terminals)

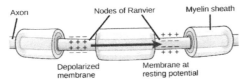

All-or-none- action potential is all or none; if the threshold is reached then an AP fires, if not, then it doesn't
- Once AP has been initiated it will continue to completion; all APs are of the same magnitude

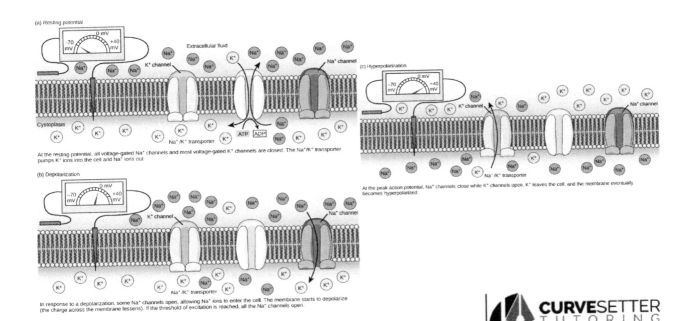

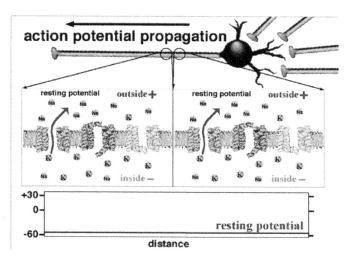

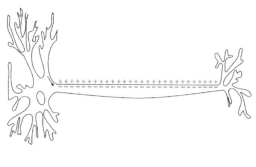

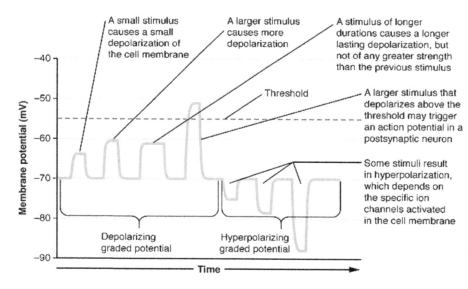

Synaptic Activity

- Once an action potential reaches the end of the axon, it causes voltage-gated Ca^{+2} channels to open → Ca^{+2} rushes into the axon terminal

- **Ca^{+2} influx** triggers neurotransmitter-containing vesicles to fuse with the membrane of the axon terminal → neurotransmitters (NT) are released into the **synaptic cleft**
  - **SNARE proteins** mediate vesicle fusion

- NT binds to receptors on the membrane of the postsynaptic cell (usually at a dendritic spine)
  - Some of the NT diffuses away or remains in the cleft until it is cleared away by **reuptake** mechanisms (then broken down or recycled)

- NT receptor on postsynaptic cell is usually a ligand-gated ion channel (or linked to an ion channel) → binding of the NT results in ion influx or efflux → **EPSP** or **IPSP**

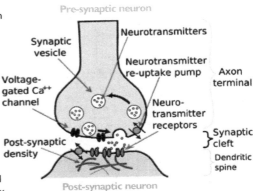

Glial Cells (Neuroglia)

Glial cells = non-neuronal "helper cells" of the nervous system; provide structural support, nutrition, insulation, waste cleanup, and protection

Oligodendrocytes: produce the myelin sheath that surround and insulates the axons of neurons in the **CNS**
- One oligodendrocyte can myelinate multiple axons

Astrocytes: star-shaped glial cell
- Support of the blood brain barrier
- Repair and scarring of injured CNS tissue
- Regulate ion concentrations in the extracellular fluid
- Provide structural support and nutrition to neurons

Microglia: immune defense in the CNS (serve as macrophages)
- Recognize foreign bodies, destroy infectious agents and other debris, control inflammation

Schwann cells: produce the myelin sheath that surround and insulates the axons of neurons in the **PNS**
- Wrap around a region of a single axon

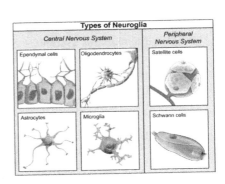

The Vertebrate Nervous System

Main Functions:
- Integrate and coordinate the organ systems of the body
- Interpret and adapt to changing conditions in the external environment and to cues from within the body
- Consciousness, learning, memory, sensory capabilities, control of bodily functions, motivation, etc.

Organization:

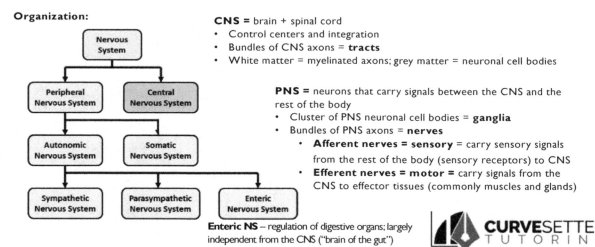

CNS = brain + spinal cord
- Control centers and integration
- Bundles of CNS axons = **tracts**
- White matter = myelinated axons; grey matter = neuronal cell bodies

PNS = neurons that carry signals between the CNS and the rest of the body
- Cluster of PNS neuronal cell bodies = **ganglia**
- Bundles of PNS axons = **nerves**
  - **Afferent nerves = sensory** = carry sensory signals from the rest of the body (sensory receptors) to CNS
  - **Efferent nerves = motor =** carry signals from the CNS to effector tissues (commonly muscles and glands)

Enteric NS – regulation of digestive organs; largely independent from the CNS ("brain of the gut")

Peripheral Nervous System Divisions

Somatic Nervous System:
- Voluntary control of the skeletal muscles of the body
- Acetylcholine used as the neurotransmitter

Autonomic Nervous System:
- Involuntary control of visceral motor functions
  - Effectors = smooth and cardiac muscles; glands
- Regulation of the internal environment - homeostasis
- Has 2 major subdivisions (pus the enteric NS)-
  Sympathetic Nervous System: "fight-or-flight"
  - Response to stress and dangerous situations → arouses the body and prepares it for action
  - Increases blood flow to skeletal muscles and decreases flow to GI tract
  - Increases HR, BP, and breathing rate; dilates pupils; mobilizes fuel (glycogenolysis)

  Parasympathetic Nervous System: "rest and digest"
  - Conserves energy during restful state and promotes "house-keeping" activities
  - Increase blood flow to digestive and excretory systems
  - Decreases HR, BP, and breathing rate

- **Sensory (afferent)** neurons enter the spinal cord at the **dorsal** root

- **Motor (efferent)** neurons exit the spinal cord at the **ventral** root

"DAVE"

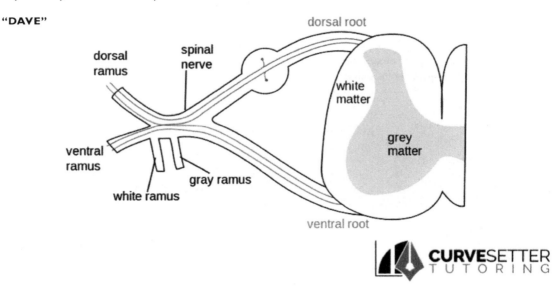

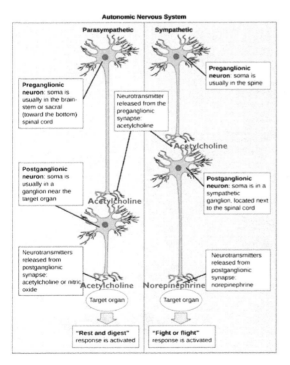

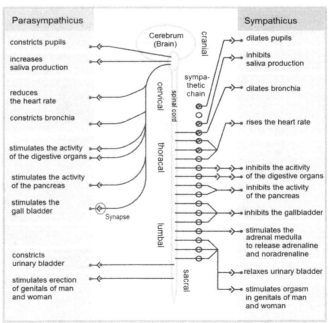

Reflexes

Reflex Arc: nerve pathway controlling a reflex (no conscious control of the response to a specific stimulus)

- Stimulus registered by a sensory receptor in the body (muscles, skin, etc.)
- Afferent nerve fiber synapses in spinal cord or brain stem
- Interneuron may or may not be involved
- Efferent nerve fiber carries signal to an effector, where the response is carried out
    - **Monosynaptic reflex:** sensory neuron → motor neuron
    - **Polysynaptic reflex:** sensory neuron → interneuron(s) → motor neuron

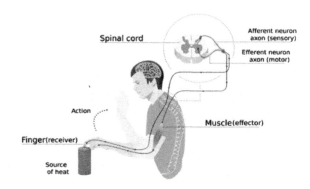

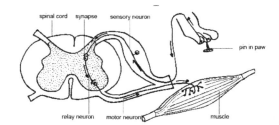

Feedback Loop:

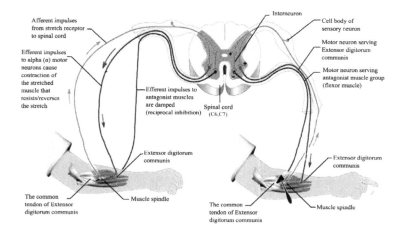

Intro to the Endocrine System: Terms

Types of signaling –

Autocrine: signal affects the same cell type (or same cell) as the one that secreted it

Paracrine: signal affects a cell nearby the cell that secreted it

Exocrine: signals produced in glands and released into ducts

• Ducts in GI tract or ducts in skin (sweat glands)

Endocrine: signals (hormones) produced in glands and released into bloodstream

Hormone: signaling molecule **travels in the blood** to reach a **distant target organ**, where it causes response

• **Tropic hormone:** regulate the release of other hormones

Hypothalamus → pituitary → endocrine gland

Hormones

• Constant and cyclic blood circulation enables **the endocrine system** to be in constant communication with the rest of the body, itself, and the nervous system (feedback loops)

• Produced by **glands** → in response to: levels of specific chemicals in the blood, neural signals, and other hormones (tropic hormone)

• Regulate metabolism, behavior, growth, mood, digestion, sleep, etc.

• Hormones (endocrine system) are slower to act but longer-acting than neurotransmitters (nervous system)

• Hormones have **high specificity** for their target organ (due to **receptor** for hormone in/on target cells)

• Hormones often trigger signal cascade in the cell

  • GPCRs; secondary messengers such as cAMP, cGMP, and DAG + IP3 (cleaved from lipids)

• Main types of hormones: **hydrophilic hormones** and **hydrophobic hormones**

Hydrophobic hormones

- **Steroid** hormones
  - Ex. Hormones that regulate sexual development and behavior + reproduction; adrenal cortex steroids
- Made from cholesterol in the smooth ER
- General effects: regulate **gene expression** (transcription, mRNA levels, etc.)
  - Therefore slower but longer acting than most hydrophilic hormones
- Steroids can **diffuse** through plasma membranes – once synthesized, they pass directly out of the cell for immediate use in the body
  - Transported on carrier molecules in the blood
- Pass through membrane of target cell and bind in **cytoplasm or nucleus** to regulate gene expression

Hormones: cortisol, aldosterone, testosterone, progesterone, estrogen

Hydrophilic Hormones

- **Peptides** and **amino acid derivatives**
  - The **majority** of hormones
  - Tyrosine derivatives common (catecholamines such as epinephrine)
- Made and modified by rough ER + Golgi
- General effects: result in secondary messenger-involved signal cascades that alter **enzyme activity**
  - Exception: Thyroid hormones enter cell and bind to DNA to alter transcription
- Peptide hormones cannot diffuse through plasma membrane- once synthesized, they're packaged in **vesicles** for release only when needed (via **exocytosis**)
  - Can travel freely in blood
- Bind to specific receptor on **membrane** of target cell (can't pass through membrane)

Hormones: all others that aren't hydrophobic hormones

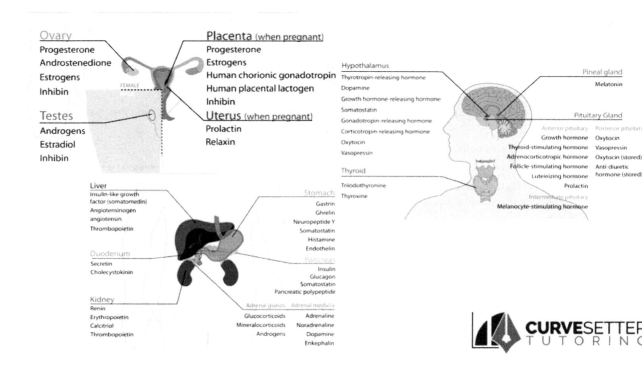

The Hypothalamus and the Pituitary Glands

Hypothalamus- brain region that is the "control center" of the endocrine system → directly controls the pituitary gland via tropic hormones (releasing/inhibiting factors)

- Provides a link between the nervous system and endocrine system (neuroendocrinology)
- Receives neural information about conditions in the body and constantly monitors levels of certain compounds in the blood; this information used to direct release of tropic hormones
- Located below the thalamus in the brain
- In general, controls the "four F's" → fighting, feeding, fleeing, and sexual functioning

Pituitary gland- "master gland of the endocrine system" → regulates endocrine glands throughout the body via the release of tropic hormones

- Composed of anterior pituitary and posterior pituitary
- Located below the hypothalamus and linked to it via portal system and neural connection (hypothalamic-pituitary control axis)
- **Portal system =** 2 capillary beds in sequence used for communication and transport

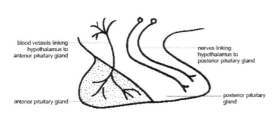

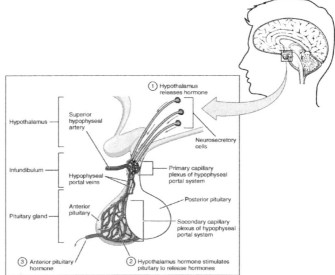

- Anterior pituitary linked to hypothalamus via portal system
  - Receives hormones from hypothalamus, which are secreted into the blood of the portal system

- Posterior pituitary has neural link to hypothalamus (neuroendocrine cells)
  - Somas in hypothalamus, axons extend into posterior pituitary where axon terminals are

Hormones of the hypothalamus and pituitary glands:

Hypothalamus
CRF (corticotropin releasing factor)- triggers anterior pituitary to secrete ACTH
TRH (thyroid releasing hormone)- triggers anterior pituitary to secrete TSH
GnRH (gonadotropin releasing hormone)- triggers anterior pituitary to secrete FSH and LH
Produces **oxytocin and ADH (anti-diuretic hormone/vasopressin)-** made in the soma of neuroendocrine cells whose axon terminals are located in the posterior pituitary; therefore *released by posterior pituitary*

Anterior Pituitary – "FLAT PiG"
FSH (follicle stimulating hormone)- facilitates production of eggs/sperm; facilitates puberty and reproductive processes
LH (luteinizing hormone)- Females- triggers formation of corpus luteum and ovulation (via increased estrogen and progesterone); Males- triggers production of testosterone in Leydig cells of the testes
ACTH (adrenocorticotropic hormone)- triggers adrenal cortex to release cortisol
TSH (thyroid stimulating hormone)- triggers release of TH from thyroid glands
Prolactin- facilitates production of milk in mammary glands
Growth Hormone- stimulates cell growth and division

Posterior Pituitary
ADH/vasopressin- stimulates water reabsorption in kidneys to increase blood volume and therefore increase BP
Oxytocin- roles in social bonding ("cuddle hormone") and sexual behavior

Main glands, their hormones, and the effects on target tissues:

Pineal
- **Melatonin-** makes one feel tired

Thyroid
- **Thyroid hormone** (thyroxine, T3/T4)- important for growth; increase metabolism and raise body temperature
- **Calcitonin-** lowers $[Ca^{+2}]$ in the blood by stimulating osteoblasts to use Ca^{+2} in the production of new bone and kidneys to secrete excess Ca^{+2} in urine
    Hyperthyroidism: too much thyroid hormone; excessively rapid metabolic rate
    Hypothyroidism: not enough thyroid hormone; low metabolic rate

Parathyroid
- **Parathyroid hormone-** increases $[Ca^{+2}]$ in the blood by stimulating osteoclasts to breakdown bone and release Ca^{+2}; reabsorption of Ca^{+2} in the kidneys and GI tract

Thymus
- **Thymus hormones-** stimulate T cell development

Heart
- **Atrial Natriuretic Factor (ANF)-** stimulates the kidney to secrete more dilute urine to decrease blood pressure

Adrenal Cortex → glucocorticoids (cortisol) and mineralocorticoids (aldosterone)
- **Cortisol-** response to stress – increase BGL, weakened immune response, etc.
- **Aldosterone-** stimulates kidney to reabsorb Na^{+2} so that more water is retained (less water secreted in urine; more concentrated urine) → raises blood pressure

Adrenal Medulla
- **Epinephrine/norepinephrine-** role in activating the sympathetic nervous system (can act at NTs, but here act as a hormone because travel in the blood)

Pancreas → islet of Langerhans cells: alpha cells- insulin; beta cells- glucagon; gamma cells- somatostatin
- **Insulin-** stimulates cells to uptake glucose and store it as fat or glycogen to decrease BGL
    Diabetes: insulin not secreted or cells are resistant to insulin
- **Glucagon-** stimulates glycogenolysis, gluconeogenesis, and less glucose uptake by cells to increase BGL
- **Somatostatin-** decreases secretion of growth hormone, insulin, and glucagon; decreases digestion

Testes
- **Testosterone-** stimulates the development of male sexual characteristics and behavior; stimulates spermatogenesis

Ovaries
- **Estrogen-** stimulates the development of female sexual characteristics and behavior; builds up endometrium
- **Progesterone-** maintains secretory endometrium

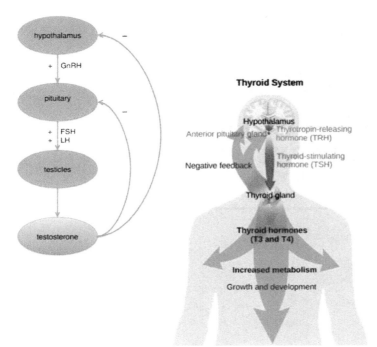

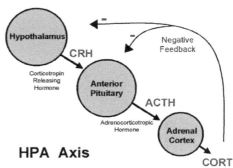

RESPIRATORY SYSTEM AND CIRCULATORY SYSTEM

Biology Lecture 10

OBJECTIVES

- Respiratory System
  - Functions
  - pH control, thermoregulation, particle filtration
  - Organs and structural composition of the system
  - Breathing: inspiration and expiration
  - Lungs and alveoli
  - Gas exchange in the alveoli
- Circulatory System
  - Functions
  - Role in thermoregulation
  - Pulmonary and systemic circulation
  - Heart: structure, valves, nodes, and cardiac muscle
  - Endothelial Cells
  - Blood vessels- structures and functions; key differences
  - Blood pressure- definition, maintenance, and regulation
  - Capillaries and capillary beds
  - Heat, gas, and solute exchange

The Respiratory System

Functions-

- **Gas exchange** – O2 inhaled into the lungs diffuses into the blood and then diffuses into cells of your body; CO2 (by-product of cellular respiration) diffuses out of tissues, into blood, then exhaled out of lungs

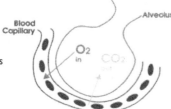

- **Thermoregulation:** breathing enables us to lose excess heat
  - Furry animals are limited in their ability to sweat (evaporative heat loss) so rely largely on the respiratory system to cool themselves down- evaporation occurs from the moist surfaces of the respiratory system and rapidly breathing out warm moist air (by panting) enables them to lose heat quickly
- **Protection:** Particulate matter filtered out via organs/tissues of respiratory system
  - Nostril hairs and mucus that lines respiratory tissues trap small particles to prevent them from getting into body; cilia line the airway to sweep mucus layer along to be swallowed and digested in the stomach
  - Alveoli lack mucus and cilia but have macrophages that line them for protection – locate, attack (if living), and digest any particulate matter than makes it to alveoli

pH regulation

- pH of the blood can be regulated via the blood bicarbonate buffer system

- In aqueous environments such as in the blood, CO_2 combines with H_2O to form H_2CO_3 (carbonic acid)

- Carbonic acid dissociated to form bicarbonate (HCO_3^-) plus a hydrogen ion (H^+) → lowers the pH

- Carbonic acid and bicarbonate (weak acid and its conjugate base) from a **buffer system,** that resists changes in the pH of the blood by absorbing excess OH^- or H^+

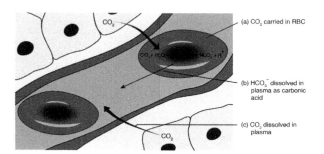

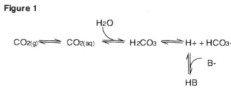

Figure 1

$$CO_{2(g)} \rightleftharpoons CO_{2(aq)} \overset{H_2O}{\rightleftharpoons} H_2CO_3 \rightleftharpoons H^+ + HCO_3^-$$

$$\downarrow B^-$$
$$HB$$

- Blood pH must be kept within a tightly controlled range: between 7.35 – 7.45

- **Respiratory acidosis:** excess CO_2 causes a drop in the blood pH because carbonic acid produces H^+ ions

  - Caused by **hypoventilation** – individual is not breathing enough so CO_2 is accumulating in the blood

  - Drop in blood pH recognized by chemoreceptors of the pons and medulla in the brain → send signals to increase the breathing rate and get rid of excess CO_2 in order to raise the pH

  - Renal compensation: excess carbonic acid is excreted and bicarbonate is reabsorbed (Le Chatelier's Principle)

- **Respiratory alkalosis:** reduced levels of CO_2 in the blood results in elevated pH

  - Less CO_2 = less H_2CO_3 → equilibrium shifts to the left and H^+ ion combine with HCO_3^- → increased pH

  - Caused by **hyperventilation**

Figure 1

$$CO_{2(g)} \rightleftharpoons CO_{2(aq)} \overset{H_2O}{\rightleftharpoons} H_2CO_3 \rightleftharpoons H^+ + HCO_3^-$$

Carbonic anhydrase

$$\downarrow B^-$$
$$HB$$

Structure:

- **Nasal cavity** - filters and warms incoming air; traps particulate matter
- **Trachea ("windpipe")** – brings air from the nose into the lungs
  - Reinforced by rings of cartilage
  - Branches into two bronchi
- **Lungs** – the main organ of gas exchange
  - Surrounded by **pleura** (two thin membranes)
- **Bronchi (2)** – supply each lung with air
  - Branch repeatedly into smaller tubes called **bronchioles**
  - Bronchioles terminate in alveoli
- **Respiratory bronchiole** – bronchioles that have some alveoli along their walls and can therefore directly participate in gas exchange
- **Alveoli** – sacs where the gas exchange occurs; O_2 diffuses from the air into the blood (of capillaries that surround the alveoli) and CO_2 diffuses from the blood into the air to be exhaled
  - Walls are 1 cell layer thick
- **Diaphragm** – muscle that facilitates inhalation and exhalation by changing the volume of the thoracic cavity

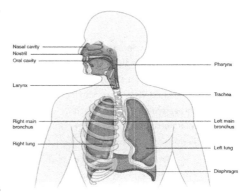

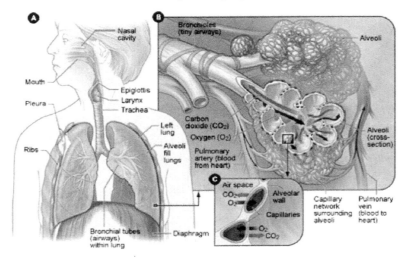

The Respiratory System

Breathing Mechanism

Inspiration:

- Diaphragm contracts (pulls downward), intercostal muscles contract pulling ribs outward → thoracic cavity expands → pressure inside the cavity decreases → air rushes into the lungs
  - P and V are inversely related (PV = nRT)
- "Negative-pressure breathing": pressure inside lungs is negative relative to the outside environment (atmospheric pressure) – air moves into areas of lower pressure
  - "Differential pressure" is the difference in pressure between two regions

Exhalation:

- Diaphragm relaxes (moves upward), intercostal muscles relax, and ribs pull in slightly → volume of thoracic cavity decreases → pressure inside cavity increases → air forced out of lungs

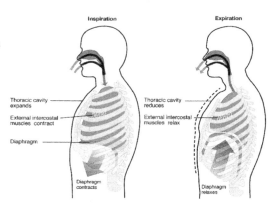

Elastic recoil: after inhalation, the lung naturally rebounds
- Connective tissue in lungs has **elastin fibers**
- **Surface tension** of fluid that lines alveoli enables the alveoli to rebound after being expanded during inhalation
- Elastic recoil decreased in **emphysema**

Intra-pleural pressure
- There are two pleural membranes and between them is the pleural cavity, filled with thin fluid layer; one layer is attached to the lungs and one is attached to the walls of the thoracic cavity
- Intra-pleural pressure (pressure within cavity) is usually less than atmospheric pressure → negative pressure keeps these two pleura stuck to each other and keeps the lungs from collapsing inward, as they naturally would
- Puncture of pleura destroys this negative intra-pleural pressure and lungs collapse

Surfactant: substance that decreases the surface tension of a liquid
- Alveolar cells produce surfactant to decreases surface tension of fluid layer that surrounds the alveoli
- Surfactant prevents alveoli from collapsing during exhalation

Trachea
(windpipe) ———————————

Pleura ———————
(lung lining)

Lung ———————

Pleural space ———————

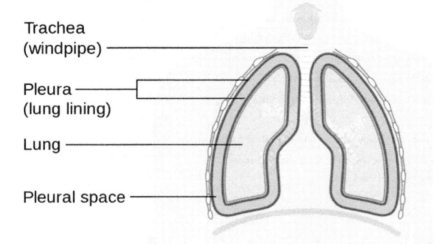

Pulmonary function test	Instrument	Measures	Function
Spirometry	Spirometer	Forced vital capacity (FVC)	Volume of air that is exhaled after maximum inhalation
		Forced expiratory volume (FEV)	Volume of air exhaled in one breath
		Forced expiratory flow, 25–75 percent	Air flow in the middle of exhalation
		Peak expiratory flow (PEF)	Rate of exhalation
		Maximum voluntary ventilation (MVV)	Volume of air that can be inspired and expired in 1 minute
		Slow vital capacity (SVC)	Volume of air that can be slowly exhaled after inhaling past the tidal volume
		Total lung capacity (TLC)	Volume of air in the lungs after maximum inhalation
		Functional residual capacity (FRC)	Volume of air left in the lungs after normal expiration
		Residual volume (RV)	Volume of air in the lungs after maximum exhalation
		Total lung capacity (TLC)	Maximum volume of air that the lungs can hold
		Expiratory reserve volume (ERV)	The volume of air that can be exhaled beyond normal exhalation
Gas diffusion	Blood gas analyzer	Arterial blood gases	Concentration of oxygen and carbon dioxide in the blood

Alveolar Gas Exchange

- **Capillaries** are the site of gas exchange in the body

- **Diffusion:** molecules naturally move into an area of lower concentration
    - In the capillaries surrounding the alveoli – deoxygenated blood returning to the lungs has a high concentration of CO_2 (picked up CO_2 from the tissues) and a low concentration of O_2
    - Air inside the alveoli has a high concentration of O_2 and low concentration CO_2
    - Exchange: CO_2 moves out of the capillaries and into the alveoli; O_2 moves from the alveoli into the capillaries → CO_2 exhaled from lungs and O_2 is delivered to the tissues

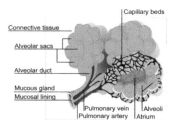

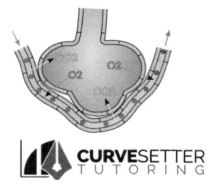

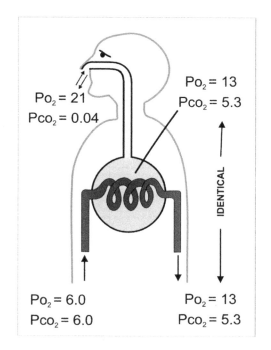

Henry's Law: the amount of gas that can dissolve into a liquid is directly proportional to the partial pressure of the gas and the solubility of the gas
- Higher partial pressure O_2 (P_{O_2}) in the alveoli = more O_2 that dissolves into the capillaries

The Circulatory System

Functions:

- Deliver oxygen to tissues: inhaled O_2 on the alveoli diffuse into the capillaries and then travel through the vessels of the body to be delivered to tissues

  - O_2 required for cellular respiration

- Nutrients, hormones, solutes, and fluids travel in the blood and can be picked up by tissues – diffuse out of capillary into tissues (down their gradient) or picked up via active transport

  - Hormones travel in blood to reach a distant target organ

- Carbon dioxide removed from tissues and carried in blood as carbonic acid/bicarbonate

  - Blood buffer system facilitates pH homeostasis

- Other metabolic wastes (such as urea) travel in the blood to reach the kidneys where waste is excreted in urine

System	Role of Circulatory System
Digestive	Absorbs nutrients and water; delivers nutrients (except most lipids) to liver for processing by hepatic portal vein; provides nutrients essential for hematopoiesis and building hemoglobin
Endocrine	Delivers hormones: atrial natriuretic hormone (peptide) secreted by the heart atrial cells to help regulate blood volumes and pressures; epinephrine, ANH, angiotensin II, ADH, and thyroxine to help regulate blood pressure; estrogen to promote vascular health in women and men
Integumentary	Carries clotting factors, platelets, and white blood cells for hemostasis, fighting infection, and repairing damage; regulates temperature by controlling blood flow to the surface, where heat can be dissipated; provides some coloration of integument; acts as a blood reservoir
Lymphatic	Transports various white blood cells, including those produced by lymphatic tissue, and immunoglobulins (antibodies) throughout the body to maintain health; carries excess tissue fluid not able to be reabsorbed by the vascular capillaries back to the lymphatic system for processing
Muscular	Provides nutrients and oxygen for contraction; removes lactic acid and distributes heat generated by contraction; muscular pumps aid in venous return; exercise contributes to cardiovascular health and helps to prevent atherosclerosis
Nervous	Produces cerebrospinal fluid (CSF) within choroid plexuses; contributes to blood–brain barrier; cardiac and vasomotor centers regulate cardiac output and blood flow through vessels via autonomic system
Reproductive	Aids in erection of genitalia in both sexes during sexual arousal; transports gonadotropic hormones that regulate reproductive functions
Respiratory	Provides blood for critical exchange of gases to carry oxygen needed for metabolic reactions and carbon dioxide generated as byproducts of these processes
Skeletal	Provides calcium, phosphate, and other minerals critical for bone matrix; transports hormones regulating buildup and absorption of matrix including growth hormone (somatotropin), thyroid hormone, calcitonins, and parathyroid hormone; erythropoietin stimulates myeloid cell hematopoiesis; some level of protection for select vessels by bony structures
Urinary	Delivers 20% of resting circulation to kidneys for filtering, reabsorption of useful products, and secretion of excesses; regulates blood volume and pressure by regulating fluid loss in the form of urine and by releasing the enzyme renin that is essential in the renin-angiotensin-aldosterone mechanism

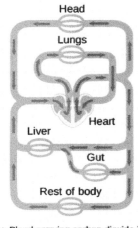

=> Blood carrying carbon dioxide in veins
=> Blood carrying oxygen in arteries

Anatomy & Physiology, Connexions Web site. http://cnx.org/cone ent/col11496/1.6/, Jun 19, 2013.

Thermoregulation:

- Vasoconstriction of vessels near the skin when cold to avoid heat loss

- Vasodilation of vessels near the skin when hot to get rid of excess heat

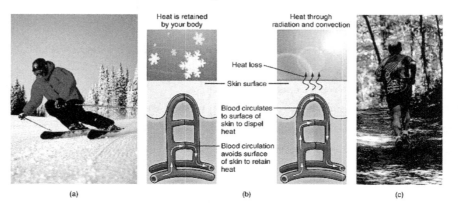

(a)   (b)   (c)

Terms-

Pulmonary Circulation: through lungs

Systemic Circulation: through entire body and brain

- Blood passes through the pulmonary circulation then through one capillary bed of systemic circulation

- Exception: Portal systems = 2 consecutive capillary beds
  - Hypothalamus-pituitary and hepatic* portal systems

Perfusion: flow of blood through a tissue

Ischemia: not enough blood flow through a tissue → tissue starved of oxygen and nutrients, dangerous wastes and metabolites build up

- Ischemic stroke

Hypoxia: lack of oxygen in a tissue

Angiogenesis: the formation of new blood vessels

- Occurs during development and during tumor growth

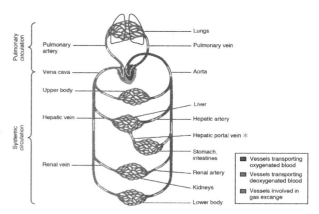

The Heart

Heart has **4 chambers**: R atrium, R ventricle, L atrium, L ventricle
- When looking at diagram of the heart, R/L directionality is reversed
- R atrium collects deoxygenated blood returning from the body
- Blood flows from R atrium into R ventricle
- Blood sent from R ventricle to lungs to exchange gases
- Blood flows from lungs into L atrium
- Blood sent from L atrium to L ventricle
- L ventricle sends blood out to the rest of the body

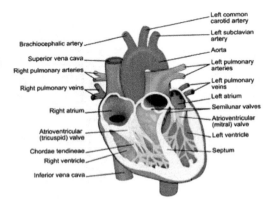

Main vessels:
- Superior/inferior vena cava: brings blood returning from the upper and lower body (respectively)
- Pulmonary artery brings blood from R ventricle to lungs
- Pulmonary veins brings blood from lungs to L atrium
- Aorta brings blood from L ventricle to rest of body

Ventricle = thicker and more muscular than the heart – must send blood through pulmonary or systemic circulation at high pressure
- Ventricular pressure higher than arterial
- L ventricle is thicker/more muscular than R

Valves:
- Tricuspid valve – between R atrium and R ventricle
- Pulmonary valve – flow from R ventricle into pulmonary artery
- Bicuspid/mitral valve – between L atrium and L ventricle
- Aortic valve - flow from L ventricle to aorta

Heart blood supply:
- The heart has its own blood supply from specific vessels
- Coronary arteries branch from the aorta to supply cardiac muscle with blood
- Coronary veins bring blood into the R atrium
- "heart attack" = myocardial infarction (MI) = blockage of one of these 3 coronary arteries → ischemia of cardiac muscle → cardiac muscle begins to die

Systole: when ventricles contract to push blood into the lungs and into the aorta to go to the rest of the body; blood from vena cava and pulmonary veins enters the atria at this time; atria contract in late systole

Diastole: when heart refills with blood after the ventricles have contracted

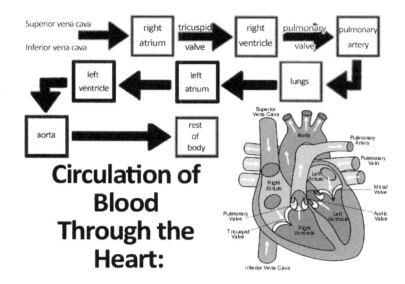

Circulation of Blood Through the Heart:

Cardiac Conduction:

Cardiac muscle cells = **functional syncytia** → cells interconnected via gap junctions

- Enables rapid spread of the action potential so that all cardiac cells of a certain region are synchronized (contract at approximately the same time)
- Cells of the R and L atria and connected but atria and separate from ventricles

Cardiac myocytes have 2 types of voltage-gated channels – fast sodium and slow calcium

- Slow voltage-gated calcium channels result in action potential lasting longer than usual

Node = specialized cardiac muscle cells that can generate electrical impulse (act like a neuron and myocyte)

- **Sinoatrial node (SA node) =** "pace maker of the heart" → region of cells found within the R atrium; spontaneously and regularly depolarizes causing the atria to contract and the signal to spread to the next node
    - Self-depolarizing due to huge amount of Na^+ leak channels
- **AV node =** propagates an action potential to the ventricles via the **Bundle of His** and **Purkinje fibers**
    - Signal slightly delayed so that ventricle contraction follows atria contraction

Action potential starts in SA node → spreads throughout atria and atria contract → signal spreads to AV node after slight delay → signal spreads from AV nose to Bundle of His and Purkinje fibers causing ventricles to contract

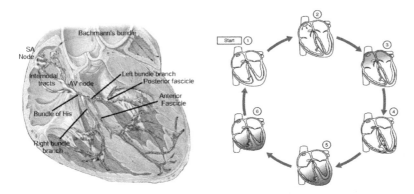

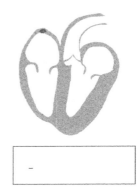

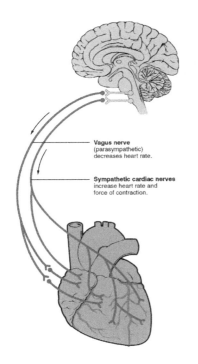

Parasympathetic: Acetylcholine inhibits/delays the SA node to slow down its firing → always occurring (vagal tone) to keep the heart rate down from its max to a normal rate of 60 – 70 BPM

Sympathetic: norepinephrine and epinephrine increase rate and force of contraction

Endothelial Cells (Endothelium): line the entire circulatory system - heart and all vessels; simple squamous cells

- Single layer sheet of flat cells
- Produces factors (such as NO) that regulate the contraction of smooth muscle cells surrounding the blood vessels – regulate vasodilation and vasoconstriction
- During inflammation, endothelium allows white blood cells to adhere and enter the tissue
- Regulate thrombosis (clotting) by preventing it when unnecessary and promoting when necessary
- Semi-permeable barrier – can be excessively leaky such as during extreme and prolonged inflammation
    - Edema = excess fluid flowing into tissues from blood because leaking through endothelium

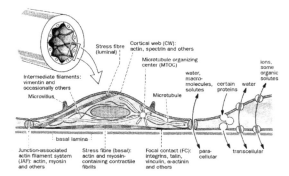

Blood Vessels

Blood Flow: arteries → arterioles → capillaries → venules → veins → the heart

Artery: carry blood away from the heart
- Consists of endothelium, smooth muscle and connective tissue
- Very elastic because must with stand high pressure and large pressure fluctuations
- Largest artery = aorta; other branch from the aorta
- Carry oxygenated blood except for pulmonary artery

Arteriole: smaller version of an artery
- Highly involved in vasoconstriction – control blood flow into capillary beds through contraction of smooth muscle (and precapillary sphincters)

Capillary: where solute and gas exchange occurs
- Smallest diameter vessels and thinnest (single cell layer thick)
- No smooth muscle

Venule: smaller version of a vein
- Capillaries merge into venules which merge into veins

Vein: carry blood back to the heart
- Carry deoxygenated blood except for pulmonary vein
- Consists of endothelium, smooth muscle and connective tissue
- Have valves to prevent backflow of blood
- Carry blood at low pressure – smooth and surrounding skeletal muscle contraction aid in the return of blood to the heart

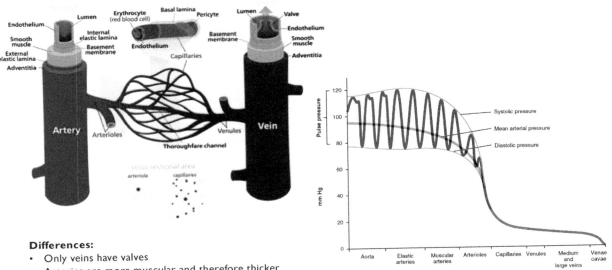

Differences:
- Only veins have valves
- Arteries are more muscular and therefore thicker
- Vasoconstriction largely carried out by arterioles
- Pressure differences (see above)

Blood Pressure

Systolic pressure: pressure exerted by the heart (specifically, contraction of the ventricles) on the vessels of the body as blood is being pumped throughout the body

Diastolic pressure: pressure in vessels when heart is momentarily resting (between heart beats)

Normal BP = Less than 120/80 (arterial pressure)

"Pulse pressure" = systolic P – diastolic P

Increased peripheral resistance to blood flow and/or **increased cardiac output** = increased blood pressure
- **Cardiac output** (CO) is the amount of blood flowing through your vessels per unit of time (L/min)
    - CO = SV x HR
    - SV = stroke volume (L/beat); HR = heart rate (beats/min)
- Increased **peripheral resistance** is caused by global vasoconstriction of arteries (smooth muscle contraction) or increased blood viscosity
- Large-scale vasodilation results in decreased BP
- Increased water retention in kidneys (ADH and aldosterone) = increased blood volume = increased blood pressure

Capillary Microcirculation

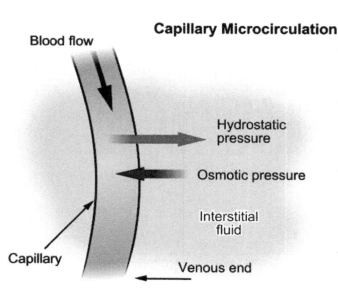

- **Hydrostatic pressure:** due to the fact that blood is pumped at high pressure by the heart
    - Tends to force fluid out of capillaries

- **Osmotic pressure:** blood is hypertonic to surrounding fluids due to high concentration of solutes/proteins → surrounding fluid tends to want to move into capillaries by osmosis

- *Net* balance usually achieved between hydrostatic and osmotic pressure
    - At arterial end of capillary, hydrostatic pressure slightly higher and ay venous end osmotic pressure slightly higher

- If hydrostatic pressure higher and/or capillaries are leaky (inflammation) → fluid leaks into tissues (edema)

BLOOD, LYMPHATIC SYSTEM, AND IMMUNE SYSTEM

Biology Lecture 11

OBJECTIVES

- Blood Composition
  - Solutes, cellular components, and plasma
  - Blood volume regulation
  - Red blood cells: characteristics and production
- Hemostasis and the coagulation cascade
- Gas transport in blood
  - Oxygen and hemoglobin
  - Oxygen affinity and cooperativity; Bohr's Curve and curve shifts
- Lymphatic System
  - Main functions
  - Overall structure; lymphatic vessels
- Immune System
  - Types of immunity
  - Innate immune system
  - Adaptive immune system: B cells and T cells
  - Recognition of self and auto-immune diseases
  - Antigen and antibody
  - Tissues of the immune system and their roles

Blood: Composition

Plasma = water + solutes + proteins
- **Albumin** = most abundant blood protein
- Other proteins include fibrinogen (clotting) and immunglobulins (immunity)
- Solutes include: dissolved gases, glucose, hormones, ions, bicarbonate, nitrogenous waste (urea), other metabolic wastes to be excreted by the kidneys

Hematocrit = red blood cells (erythrocytes)

Leukocytes = white blood cells; found in the circulatory and lymphatic system
- Involved in the immune response – identify and attack pathogens/foreign substances; and dispose of wastes; many different types:
  - **Basophil and eosinophil** – involved in the allergic response; basophil releases histamine; eosinophils attack parasites
  - **Neutrophil** – most abundant type; defend against fungi and bacteria
  - **B cell** – release antibodies
  - **T cell** – activate macrophages and other immune cells; destroy virus-infected and cancerous body cells; central to cell-mediated immunity
  - **Monocyte** – resident macrophages

Platelets: fragments of cells that originated in bone marrow
- Crucial to the clottinh response (hemostasis) – form a platelet plug

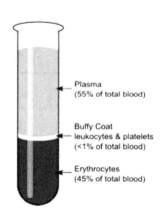

Plasma
(55% of total blood)

Buffy Coat
leukocytes & platelets
(<1% of total blood)

Erythrocytes
(45% of total blood)

Component and % of blood	Subcomponent and % of component	Type and % (where appropriate)	Site of production	Major function(s)
Plasma 46–63 percent	Water 92 percent	Fluid	Absorbed by intestinal tract or produced by metabolism	Transport medium
	Plasma proteins 7 percent	Albumin 54–60 percent	Liver	Maintain osmotic concentration, transport lipid molecules
		Alpha globulins— liver		Transport, maintain osmotic concentration
		Globulins 35–38 percent	Beta globulins— liver	Transport, maintain osmotic concentration
			Gamma globulins (immunoglobulins) —plasma cells	Immune responses
		Fibrinogen 4–7 percent	Liver	Blood clotting in hemostasis
	Regulatory proteins <1 percent	Hormones and enzymes	Various sources	Regulate various body functions
	Other solutes 1 percent	Nutrients, gases, and wastes	Absorbed by intestinal tract, exchanged in respiratory system, or produced by cells	Numerous and varied
Formed elements 37–54 percent	Erythrocytes 99 percent	Erythrocytes	Red bone marrow	Transport gases, primarily oxygen and some carbon dioxide
	Leukocytes <1 percent Platelets <1 percent	Granular leukocytes: neutrophils eosinophils basophils	Red bone marrow	Nonspecific immunity
		Agranular leukocytes: lymphocytes monocytes	Lymphocytes: bone marrow and lymphatic tissue	Lymphocytes: specific immunity
			Monocytes: red bone marrow	Monocytes: nonspecific immunity
	Platelets <1 percent		Megakaryocytes: red bone marrow	Hemostasis

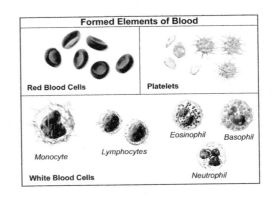

Formed Elements of Blood

Red Blood Cells   Platelets

Monocyte   Lymphocytes   Eosinophil   Basophil   Neutrophil

White Blood Cells

Version 8.25 from the Textbook
OpenStax Anatomy and Physiology
Published May 18, 2016

Blood Volume Regulation

- **Blood osmolality** affects erythrocyte volume (see diagram below)
  - Increased volume of blood due to increased water retention or over-hydration = decreased solute concentration = decreased osmolality → water moves into RBCs by osmosis
- **ADH:** released when osmolality is too high
  - Results in increased water retention in the kidneys (produce more concentrated urine) therefore increased plasma volume and decreased blood osmolality
- **Aldosterone:** causes sodium reabsorption in kidneys → increased water retention
  - Results in increased blood volume therefore increased blood pressure

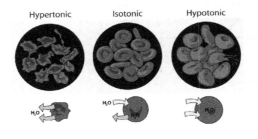

Hypertonic   Isotonic   Hypotonic

Erythrocytes (Red Blood Cells)

Function: pick up O_2 in the lungs then carry and deliver it to tissues

- Can trigger vasodilation by producing nitric oxide
- Contain carbonic anhydrase: enzyme that converts gaseous CO_2 into carbonic acid/bicarbonate to be easily carried in the blood and to promote the blood buffer system

Structure:

- Mature RBCs contain no nuclei or cellular organelles
    - Lack of mitochondria – rely on glycolysis and lactic acid fermentation to make ATP
    - No nucleus = no DNA → no protein synthesis and cannot divide or repair themselves
- Biconcave disk shape – enables high surface area for efficient gas transport and flexibility enables tem to squeeze through narrow capillaries
- Cytoplasm has an extensive amount of hemoglobin (protein that carries O_2)

Blood Type: depends on the antigen expressed on the surface of erythrocytes and on the antibodies present in one's blood (individual expresses antibodies to antigens not found on his/her own RBCs)

- **A/B/O blood type:** presence of A, B, or neither antigen
    - Alleles: I^A, I^B, i; $I^A = I^B > i$
    - Can be type A, B, AB, or O
- **Rh factor:** group of 50 different blood antigens; most common = Rh positive and Rh negative
- AB+ individual has all three of the most common antigens and therefore makes no antibodies to those
- O- individual has none of the three most common antigens and therefore is a universal donor

	Group A	Group B	Group AB	Group O
Red blood cell type	A	B	AB	O
Antibodies in Plasma	Anti-B	Anti-A	None	Anti-A and Anti-B
Antigens in Red Blood Cell	A antigen	B antigen	A and B antigens	None

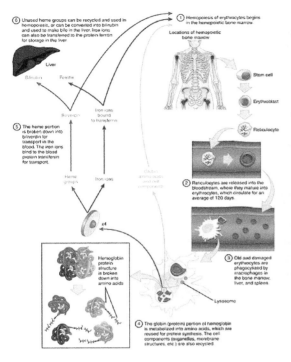

- All cells in blood (RBCs, platelets, WBCs) are made in **bone marrow** from stem cell precursor
- **Erythropoietin** = kidney hormone that stimulates RBC production in bone marrow
- RBCs have an average lifespan of 120 days → then are degraded/recycled in the bone marrow, liver, and spleen (by macrophages)

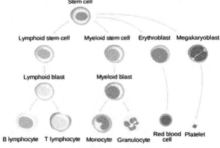

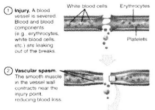

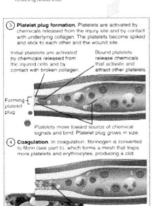

Hemostasis

- **Hemostasis** = blood clotting; stops extensive blood loss from damaged vessels
- Hemostasis involves **coagulation** – blood turning from liquid to solid form ("scabbing")
- Requires **clotting factors**, which are primarily made in the liver
  - Factors I – XIII; such as fibrinogen, prothrombin, etc.

Steps:

- **Vasoconstriction** of smooth muscle surrounding vessel – reduces blood flow through damaged vessel
- Platelets aggregate together and from a **platelet plug**
- **Coagulation cascade –** clotting factors become activated in a cascade, ultimately resulting in fibrinogen becoming fibrin and forming a **fibrin mesh**

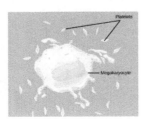

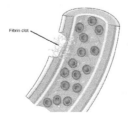

Transport in the Blood

- **CO2:** the majority of CO_2 is transported in the blood as carbonic acid and bicarbonate (equilibrium between them); requires the RBC enzyme carbonic anhydrase
  - Blood buffer system enables pH to be maintained within narrow range (7.35 – 7.45)
  - Small amount of CO_2 is carried on hemoglobin (on globin protien) and some travels freely as $CO_{2(g)}$
- **O2:** the majority of O_2 is carried by hemoglobin protein; small amount travels freely in plasma
  - **Hemoglobin (Hb):** protein composed of 4 subunits (2 alpha and 2 beta)
  - Each subunit has 1 **heme group** with an Fe^{+2} in the center and each subunit can carry 1 O_2 molecule → 1 Hb protein carries 4 O_2 molecules max

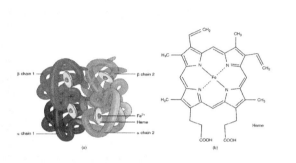 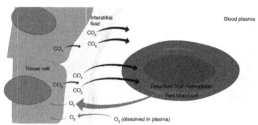

Capillary exchange of gases, solutes, and fluids:

- O_2, CO_2, and lipophilic molecules can diffuse from blood into tissues through endothelial cells of capillary
- Glucose, ions, and amino acids either undergo facilitated diffusion via specific protein transporters or squeeze through intercellular clefts of endothelium
- Large proteins may require vesicle transport (endo- and exocytosis)
- WBCs can squeeze through intercellular clefts
- The balance between osmotic and hydrostatic pressure affects the flow of fluid into or out of capillaries

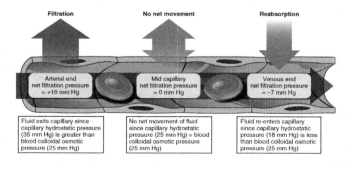

Hemoglobin and Oxygen Affinity

- Hb picks up O_2 in the capillaries surrounding alveoli, where $[O_2]$ is high and $[CO_2]$ is low → forms **oxyHb**
- Hb drops O_2 off in the tissues, where $[O_2]$ is low and $[CO_2]$ is high → forms **deoxyHb**
- Hb shows **cooperativity** – when one O_2 molecule binds, it becomes easier for others to bind

T/R states:

- Hb exists in 2 states: **T (tense state)** and R (relaxed) state
- T state has a low affinity for oxygen and R state has a high affinity for oxygen
- **R state is favored** at high pO_2, such as in the **lungs** → facilitates high efficiency of O_2 pick-up in the lungs
- **T state is favored** at low pO_2, such as in the **tissues** → facilitates O_2 drop-off in the tissues
- Other factors that **favor the T state**: high CO_2, low pH, high temperature, and high 2,3-BPG
    - Occurs in active muscles and at high altitudes → more O_2 dropped off in the tissues

hemoglobin
Oxygen affinity and cooperativity; Bohr's Curve and curve shifts

Oxygen dissociation curve:

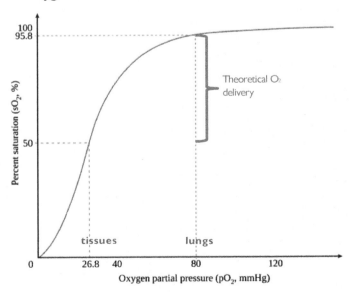

- pO_2 is high in the lungs → high oxygen saturation of Hb → O_2 picked up

- pO_2 is low in the tissues → low oxygen saturation of Hb → oxygen dropped off

- Nearly 50% of the O_2 that's picked up ca be delivered → highly efficient

- **Bohr shift:** efficiency of O_2 delivery can be improved by **right-ward shift** of the curve (aka overall lessened O_2 affinity) → slightly less O_2 picked up in lungs but much more dropped off in the tissues

- **Fetal Hb** has a **left-ward shift** (overall increased O_2 affinity) → enables it to take O_2 from mother

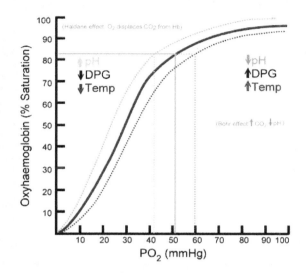

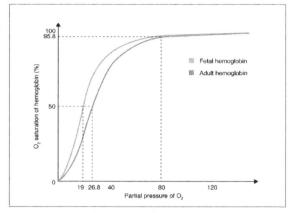

Lymphatic System

- The lymphatic system is part of the circulatory system composed of a network of vessels into which **lymph** drains from the tissues and is eventually returned to the blood
- Filtration of blood through capillaries results in plasma fluid being squeezed out of blood vessels; most is returned through direct capillary reabsorption but the remaining fluid (lymph) is collected in the lymphatic vessels and returned to the heart
  - One way flow of lymph through **lymphatic capillaries** and **lymphatic vessels**, which eventually empty into the vena cava; filtration through lymph nodes along the way
  - Lymphatic vessels have thin walls and valves to prevent back flow
- **Lymph nodes:** found throughout the body and function to filter the lymph
  - Contain many WBCs such as B and T cells → vital to immune response
- T cells produced in the **thymus**
- **Spleen** filters damaged cells from the blood and other debris

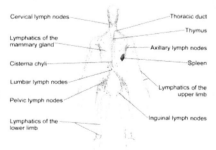

Functions of lymphatic system:

- Collect and filter plasma fluid that's been lost by capillary filtration to return it to the blood

- Proteins from the blood that leak out of capillaries are returned to the blood

- Fats reabsorbed from food in our intestines get transported in lacteals (lymphatic capillaries)

- Immune response – lymphoid cells (such as B cells and T cells) are found in the organs of the lymphatic system, such as the spleen and lymph nodes

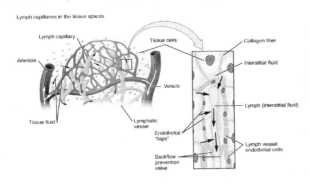

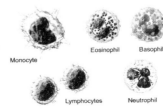

White Blood Cells

Immune System

Innate (non-specific) immunity-
- First line of defense against anything foreign/abnormal
- General protection, not specific to any pathogen
- **Skin, hair, mucus membrane, cilia** in the trachea
- **Saliva** and **tears** contain anti-microbial properties (lysozyme)
- **Phagocytes (macrophages, neutrophils)** phagocytize foreign particles, pathogens, and dead cells
  - Scavenge for foreign substances and then engulf and degrade them; may be attracted to an area by chemical signals such as cytokines (chemotaxis)
    - **Macrophages** = phagocytic WBCs; can move out of circulatory system by squeezing through capillary walls into the tissue; most efficient phagocyte
- **NK Cells:** recognize and kill tumor cells and virus infected cells; recognize the stress of these cells but don't use specific markers
  - Analogous to T cells of the adaptive immune system

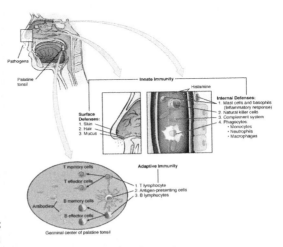

- **Complement System:** blood proteins become activated in a chemical cascade, resulting in stimulation of inflammatory response and the activation of phagocytic cells

- **Inflammatory response:** histamines and cytokines (among other factors) released; results in recruiting phagocytic and other immune cells to the area, swelling of the area, redness, etc.

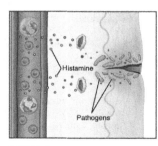

① Mast cells detect injury to nearby cells and release histamine, initiating inflammatory response.

Complement

Substance

Function: "Complement" describes a group of over 30 different kinds of proteins that work together and with other components of the immune system to attack pathogens. When activated by other immune processes, these proteins can create damaging holes in the membranes of pathogens.

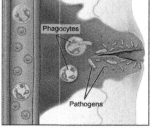

② Histamine increases blood flow to the wound sites, bringing in phagocytes and other immune cells that neutralize pathogens. The blood influx causes the wound to swell, redden, and become warm and painful.

Adaptive Immune System

Adaptive (specific) immunity-
- Highly specialized elimination of pathogens involving the creation of immunological memory
- **Immunological memory:** after the initial exposure to a pathogen, the immune system is more efficient at recognizing and eliminating that pathogen at subsequent exposures
- Main players are T cells and B cells

T Cells:
- **Cytoxic (Killer) T Cells –** kill abnormal host cells; pathogen-infected cells, cancer cells, and other damaged/dysfunctional host cells
  - Detection: T-cell receptor protein interacts with a specific **antigen** (bound to MHC class I proteins) displayed on the surface of the abnormal host cell
  - Each T cell is specific to a particular antigen/MHC complex
  - **Major Histocompatibility Complex (MHC):** proteins found on the surface of host cells that sample and display proteins (antigens) found within that cell; this antigen/MHC complex enables cells of the immune system to detect self versus foreign cells
    - ○ **Class I MHC:** found on all host cells (except RBCs); used to detect intracellular infection
    - ○ **Class II MHC:** only found on antigen presenting cells (APCs), like B cells and macrophages, which phagocytize a foreign cell and display its antigens

- **Helper T Cells** – central mediator of the adaptive immune system; don't kill abnormal cells/pathogens but organize other immune cells to manage their destruction
  - Signal to and activate cytoxic T cells, B cells, and other immune cells using specific signals
  - Recognize antigens presented on APCs (class II MHC)
  - These are the cells that are attacked by HIV

B Cells:
- Create **antibody (immunoglobulin) proteins** that travel in the blood, bind to specific **antigens** of foreign substances/pathogens, and result in the attack of that foreign substance via a variety of mechanisms
  - Mechanisms include: complement cascade, activation of NK cells and macrophages, prevent adhesion of pathogens to hosts' body surfaces, etc.
- Each B cell has a unique antibody bound to their membrane that recognizes and binds to a specific antigen
  - Huge variety of antigens due to extensive **genetic recombination** of antibody genes during B cell development

- When a foreign substance that displays the antigen is encountered, the B cell proliferates and differentiates further into a **plasma cell**
  - Plasma cells create and secrete more of the antibody, which bind to the pathogen and tag it for destruction
- Some of the plasma cells become **memory cells**
  - Memory cells remain in circulation as dormant but primed B cells that become activated and quickly respond if the same pathogen is encountered again ("acquired immunity" to a pathogen)

Recognition of self vs. non-self
- B cells and T cells express receptors/antibodies that recognize many different antigens; antibodies are very diverse and randomly generated
- Certain B and T cells may recognize antigens expressed on health host cells; this is dangerous as it would promote destruction of healthy host cells (**auto-immune disease**)
  - Auto immune diseases = type I diabetes, arthritis, celiac diseases, Parkinson's, etc.
- To prevent this, B and T cells expressing receptors for self-antigens will become inactivated, destroyed, or never het released into the blood

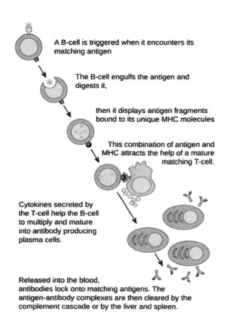

A B-cell is triggered when it encounters its matching antigen

The B-cell engulfs the antigen and digests it,

then it displays antigen fragments bound to its unique MHC molecules

This combination of antigen and MHC attracts the help of a mature matching T-cell.

Cytokines secreted by the T-cell help the B-cell to multiply and mature into antibody producing plasma cells.

Released into the blood, antibodies lock onto matching antigens. The antigen-antibody complexes are then cleared by the complement cascade or by the liver and spleen.

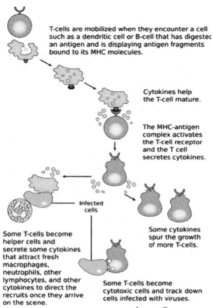

T-cells are mobilized when they encounter a cell such as a dendritic cell or B-cell that has digested an antigen and is displaying antigen fragments bound to its MHC molecules.

Cytokines help the T-cell mature.

The MHC-antigen complex activates the T-cell receptor and the T cell secretes cytokines.

Infected cells

Some T-cells become helper cells and secrete some cytokines that attract fresh macrophages, neutrophils, other lymphocytes, and other cytokines to direct the recruits once they arrive on the scene.

Some cytokines spur the growth of more T-cells.

Some T-cells become cytotoxic cells and track down cells infected with viruses.

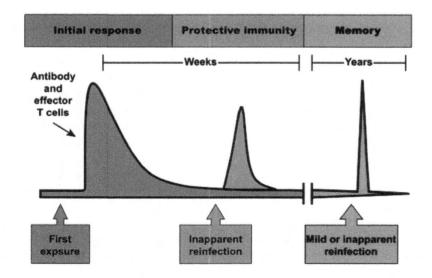

| Initial response | Protective immunity | Memory |

Weeks — Years

Antibody and effector T cells

First exposure

Inapparent reinfection

Mild or inapparent reinfection

Antigen and Antibody

- **Antibody/immunoglobulin** (Ig) is a protein found in the blood that binds to **antigens** on a foreign particle/cell and leads to its destruction (via phagocytosis, complement system, direct inactivation, etc.)
  - Antibodies are soluble in plasma and travel freely in the blood; they are produced by B cells
- **Antigen** is a toxin or any foreign substance; often a molecule found on the surface of a virus or bacterial cell
- The interaction between an antigen and antibody is **highly specific,** like a "lock-and-key" mechanism
- **APCs** (antigen presenting cells) such as B cells phagocytize a foreign cell and display its antigens
  - Antigen/class II MHC complex of B cell is then recognized by T cell
- Memory B cells enable much more efficient/strong response to subsequent exposures to the same pathogen via rapid production of antibodies

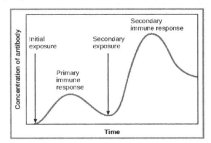

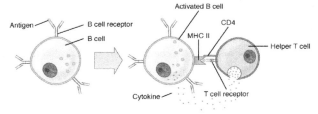

Clonal Selection: after initial exposure to a pathogen, many clones are produced of the B and T cells specific to that pathogen

Antibody Structure: protein is composed of 2 light chains and 2 heavy chains associated in a "Y" shape
- **Variable region** at the tips bind to the antigen with high specificity (epitope = region where antigen binds)

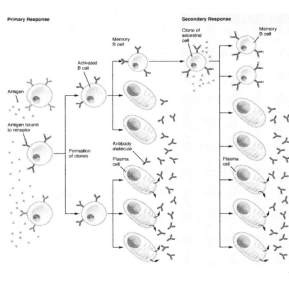

Tissues of the Immune System

Spleen: filter bloods, destroys/recycles old RBCs, and provides a place for platelets and WBCs to mature and reside

Thymus: location of T cell maturation

Lymph Nodes: filter through lymph, contain many WBCs, and serve as key immune response center

Appendix and Tonsils: contain lymph tissue and have immune roles but are not required

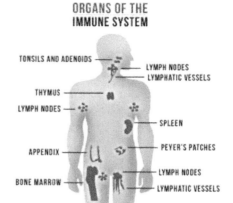

Bone Marrow: where all RBCs, platelets, and white blood cells (cells of the immune system) are produced; all types differentiate from hematopoietic stem cell found in red bone marrow

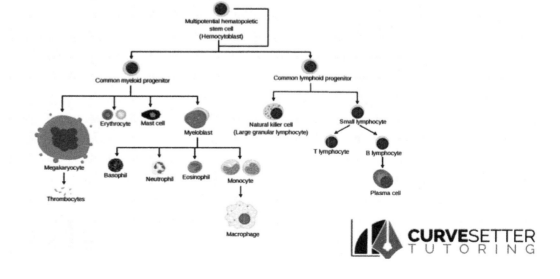

THE DIGESTIVE SYSTEM

Biology Lecture 12

- Overview of digestion and the organs involved (the path of food)
- Ingestion
  - Organs/tissues involved
  - The functions of chewing and saliva
- Structure, function and mechanisms of the following:
  - Stomach
  - Liver (and the role of bile)
  - Pancreas
  - Small intestine
  - Large Intestine
  - Rectum
- Peristalsis and muscles of the GI tract
- Endocrine and nervous control of digestion

The Digestive System

Food is metabolized in the following steps:
- Ingestion
- Digestion and nutrient absorption
- Secretion

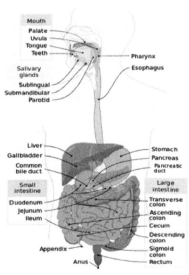

Path of food: food enters the **mouth** where it is chewed (mechanically broken down) and mixed with saliva (some chemical breakdown) → passes through the **pharynx** and into the **esophagus** where it is pushed down by muscular peristalsis → passes through a **sphincter** and enters the **stomach** where more breakdown and mixing of the **chyme** occurs → goes through the **pyloric sphincter** and enters the **duodenum** of the small intestine where it is mixed in with **bile** and other **digestive enzymes** → nutrient absorption occurs in the small intestine as it passes from the duodenum to the **jejunum** to the **ileum** → passes through the **ileocecal valve** and into the **large intestine** where water reabsorption occurs → passes through the **rectum** and excreted out the **anus**

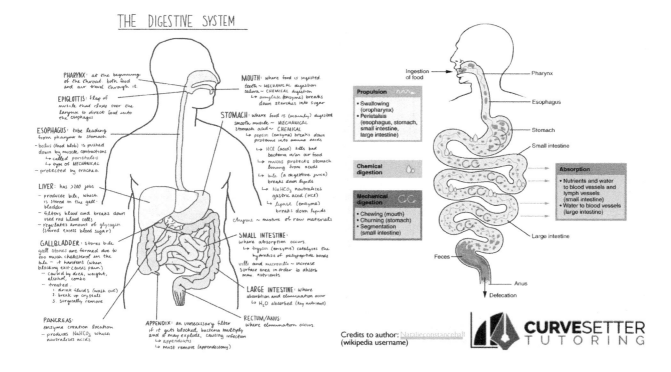

Ingestion

- Food enters the mouth and is chewed (**mastication**), initiating mechanical breakdown
  - Increases surface area of the food facilitates more efficient breakdown by digestive enzymes

- **Saliva** is also mixed into the food, initiating chemical breakdown and lubricating the food
  - Saliva adds water, digestive enzymes, and mucus
  - Digestive enzymes: **amylase** – breaks down polysaccharides into simpler sugars that will be further broken down in the small intestine; also contains **lysozyme** (antimicrobial properties)
  - Cohesive chewed food mass now called a bolus

- The bolus is swallowed and pushed through the **pharynx** and past the **epiglottis,** a small flap that prevents food from entering the windpipe and directs it into the muscular tube called the **esophagus**
  - Esophagus pushes food into the stomach by **peristalsis**
  - **Peristalsis –** involuntary wave-like movements of smooth muscle; enable bolus to even be swallowed while person is upside-down

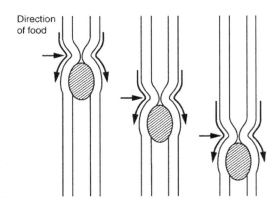

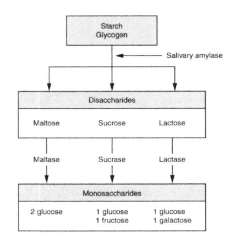

Stomach

Mechanical digestion: the stomach churns and mixes the bolus using peristalsis

Storage: the bolus can be stored in the stomach until ready to be emptied into the small intestine; can stretch to store more

Chemical digestion:
- **Pepsin** – protease that functions optimally in the low pH environment of the stomach; breaks down proteins into small polypeptides
    - Secreted initially in its inactive form, **pepsinogen**, which is activated by HCl into pepsin
- **HCl** – activates pepsinogen into pepsin

Cell types:
- **Mucus/Goblet cells** – secrete mucus lining of the stomach
- **Parietal cells** – secrete HCl, which activates pepsin and destroys pathogens (in response to gastrin)
- **Chief cells** – secrete pepsinogen (which soon become pepsin)
- **G cells** – secrete gastrin, a peptide hormone that triggers parietal cells to secrete HCl
    - Also in the small intestine and pancreas

Structure:

- Expandable bag with inner mucus layer and many layers of smooth muscle
  - **Mucus layer** prevents digestive enzymes and HCl from degrading the stomach lining
- Highly folded (**rugae**) to enable expansion
- Sphincters seal off the top and bottom
  - **Gastroesophageal sphincter** and **pyloric sphincter** – control when bolus can enter and leave the stomach

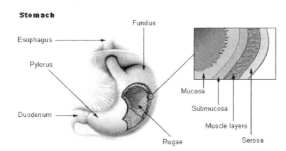

Liver and Bile

Functions:

- Production of **bile,** which facilitates the breakdown of fats
  - Bile transported to the small intestine (duodenum) for use and to the gallbladder for storage
- Filters through blood that has passed through the digestive tract – absorb and process glucose, fatty acids, glycerol, and amino acids; breaks down, stores, or uses these precursors for biosynthesis
  - **Hepatic portal system:** blood travels through capillary beds of the GI tract, which then merge into the hepatic portal vein → hepatic portal vein brings blood to capillary beds of the liver → capillary beds of liver merge into hepatic vein which goes back to the heart
- **Detoxification** and **metabolism/inactivation of drugs**
- Produces **blood clotting factors** (coagulation cascade) and blood proteins such as albumin
- Blood glucose regulation – if BGL rises then the liver stores glucose as glycogen (**glycogenesis**); if BGL too low then liver performs **glycogenolysis** and **gluconeogenesis**

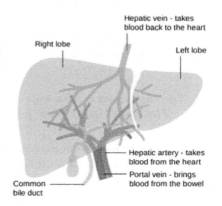

Bile: greenish-brown fluid that facilitates the digestion of fats in the small intestine

- Other functions: enables absorption of fat-soluble vitamins (A, D, E, and K); enables the excretion of bilirubin (by-product of RBC breakdown)

- Produced in the liver, stored in the gall bladder, and released for use in the duodenum of the small intestine during fat digestion

- Fat digestion: bile is an **emulsifying agent,** so it breaks down fats into smaller droplets by surrounding it in a micelle → smaller droplets increase the surface area and make the lipids more accessible to breakdown by **lipase**

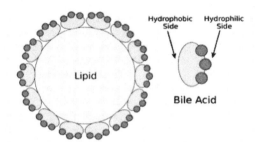

Pancreas

Function: Produces pancreatic juice, which contains the majority of the digestive enzymes as well as bicarbonate (exocrine pancreas); also functions as an endocrine gland as it produces insulin, glucagon, and somatostatin (endocrine pancreas)

- **Islet of Langerhans cells** fulfill the endocrine functions → hormones travel in blood to distant target organs
- **Acinar cells** fulfill the digestive/exocrine functions → pancreatic juice flows through duct into the small intestine

Pancreatic juice components:
- **Pancreatic lipase –** breaks down triglycerides into glycerol + fatty acids
- **Nucleases –** break down nucleic acids
- **Amylase –** breaks down starch into simple sugars
- **Proteases** such as trypsinogen (activated to trypsin) and chymotrypsinogen (activated to chymotrypsin)
- **Bicarbonate (HCO$_3^-$) –** neutralizes the highly acidic bolus coming from the low pH stomach, enabling enzymes to function

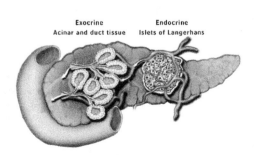

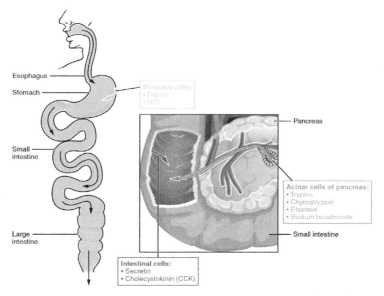

Small Intestine

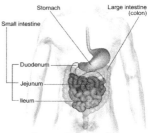

Anatomy of Small Intestine

Structure:

- Composed of three different regions: duodenum → jejenum → ileum
- Duodenum is the short frontal region that receives chyme from stomach, pancreatic juices (enzymes plus bicarbonate), and bile
  - Enzymes enable digestion of nutrient, bicarbonate neutralizes the chyme
- Jejenum and ileum contain villi – maximizes surface area for the absorption of nutrients
  - Villi are finger-like protrusions composed of multiple cells; each cell of the villi has microvilli (tiny cellular appendages)
  - Surface of villi and micorvilli is referred to as a "brush border"
- Crypts contain many different cell types, including: goblet cells (make and secrete mucus), enteroendocrine cells (secrete hormones), and stem cells

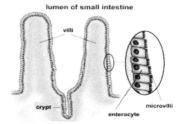

Function:

- Digestion of chyme using enzymes from pancreatic juice (lipase, proteases, and amylase) and some of its own enzymes
  - Carbs, lipids, and proteins degraded into smaller precursors
  - Chyme passes slowly through small intestine via peristalsis

- Absorption of nutrients and minerals from food, some water absorption
  - Products of digestion absorbed into blood vessels of the intestine and eventually go to liver (hepatic portal system)
  - Fatty acids go into lacteals (lymphatic vessels) and are eventually brought back into the blood supply

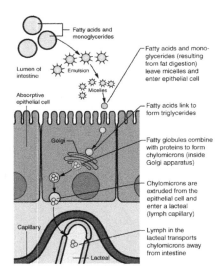

Large Intestine

Structure:
- Large muscular tube with three main segments: ascending, transverse, and descending colon
- Thicker but shorter than small intestine; no villi

Function:
- Converts chyme into feces by the reabsorption of excess water and the actions of a diverse bacterial population
- Water absorption enables the chyme to solidify
  - Solutes such as salts also reabsorbed with the water
- Bacteria digest substances that the human digestive system can't, and release many different types of vitamins (B2, B6, B12, K, etc.)
  - Vitamin K crucial for blood clotting
  - Produce gas byproducts
- Waste stored as feces until ready for excretion

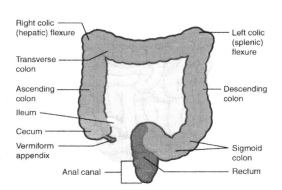

Rectum and Anus

Rectum: begins at the end of the large intestine (colon)

- **Feces** is mainly stored higher up in the colon; when enough feces accumulates that it enters the rectum then an urge to defecate is initiated

Anus: opening at the end of the GI that enables feces to exit

- Usually kept closed by the muscular **anal sphincter** until ready to defecate

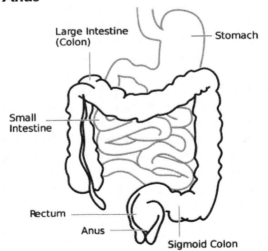

Endocrine control of digestion:

GI Hormones

Hormone	Secreted By	Source & Stimulus	Target Organ	Respone
Gastrin	Stomach mucosa	Stomach in response to food	Stomach, small intestine	•release of HCL •Increase of intestine movement •release of pepsinogen
Secretin	Small Intestine	Duodenum in response to acidic chyme	Pancreas	•secrection of alkaline •digestive pro-enzyme •Inhibits intestine motility
Cholecystokinin (CCK)	Small Intestine	Intestinal cells in response to food	Pancreas, gallbladder	•Secretion of proenzymes and bile
Gastric Inhibitory Peptide (GIP)		Intestinal cells in response to fat	Stomach, Pancreas	•Insulin secretion •Inhibits gastric secretion and motality

The Enteric Nervous System

- The enteric nervous system is the digestive system's own local network of neurons that are embedded in the lining of the GI tract

- Controls autonomous (involuntary) functions of digestion, such as the secretion of digestive enzymes, peristalsis, regulation of blood flow, and sensing/modulating the environment within the GI tract
    - Uses neurotransmitters that are also used by the CNS/PNS, such acetylcholine and dopamine
    - Considered a branch of the autonomic nervous system

- Can operate independently from the CNS but does communicate with the CNS and PNS via the parasympathetic and sympathetic nervous systems

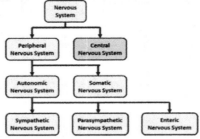

Summary:

Major Digestive Enzymes

Enzyme	Produced In	Site of Release	pH Level
Carbohydrate Digestion:			
Salivary amylase	Salivary Glands	Mouth	Neutral
Pancreatic amylase	Pancreas	Small Intestine	Basic
Maltase	Small intestine	Small intestine	Basic
Protien Digestion:			
Pepsin	Gastric glands	Stomach	Acidic
Trypsin	Pancreas	Small intestine	Basic
Peptidases	Small Intestine	Small intestine	Basic
Nucleic Acid Digestion:			
Nuclease	Pancreas	Small intestine	Basic
Nucleosidases	Pancreas	Small intestine	Basic
Fat Digestion:			
Lipase	Pancreas	Small intestine	Basic

THE EXCRETORY SYSTEM, SKIN, AND THE SKELETAL SYSTEM

Biology Lecture 13

OBJECTIVES

- Function of the excretory system
  - Removal of wastes
  - Blood pressure control, osmoregulation, pH regulation
- Overall kidney structure
- Roles of the ureter, bladder, and urethra
- Nephron function and structure
- Urine formation
  - Filtration, secretion, and reabsorption; concentration gradients
  - Modulating urine concentration
- The structure of the skin system
  - Layers of skin; structural characteristics
- Functions of skin
  - Protection, thermoregulation, osmoregulation, etc.
- The skeletal system
  - Function of the skeleton
  - Structure of the human skeleton
  - Structure and components of bone
  - Cartilage, tendons, ligaments

The Excretory (Urinary) System: Functions

Excretion of waste:
- Elimination of the soluble waste products of metabolism
  - Nitrogenous wastes: the breakdown of proteins produces nitrogenous waste in the form of ammonia; ammonia is toxic to humans and is converted to urea via the **urea cycle**
- Urine = water + urea + salts (Na^+, K^+, bicarbonate, etc.) + sugar

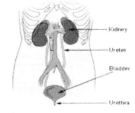

Blood pressure regulation:
- By modulating the rate of filtration and reabsorption in the kidneys, fluid can be increasingly retained or excreted; regulation of blood volume → regulation of blood pressure
- When **BP is too low:**
  - Kidney cells secrete **renin** → renin triggers **angiotensin II** to form → **aldosterone** released from adrenal cortex → increased Na^+ uptake in kidneys → excess water reabsorbed → less fluid excreted; blood volume increases → BP increases
  - ADH released from posterior pituitary increases water reabsorption and also raises BP
- When **BP is too high** the heart releases ANP which counteracts aldosterone

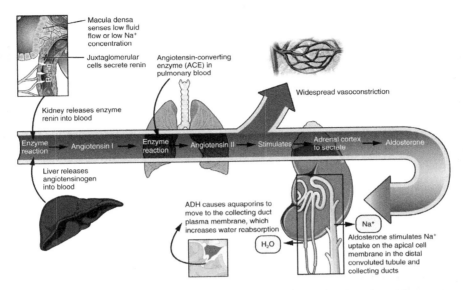

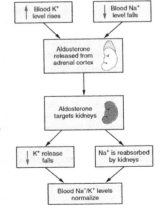

Osmoregulation:

- Through reabsorption and excretion, the kidneys modulate ion concentrations in the blood; specifically, K^+, Na^+, Cl^-, and Ca^+
  - **Aldosterone**: reabsorb Na^+, excrete (less reabsorption of) K^+
  - **Parathyroid hormone**: Ca^{+2} reabsorption
  - **Calcitonin**: decreased Ca^{+2} reabsorption

Acid-base balance:

- In blood, the **bicarbonate buffer system** facilitates acid/base balance; disruption of the buffer occurs is too much or too little bicarbonate is present in the blood
  - By Le Chatelier's Principle – too much bicarbonate leads to an increase in pH; to little bicarbonate leads to a drop in pH
  - In order to counteract a pH shift, the kidneys can excrete or reabsorb more bicarbonate: **acidosis** → bicarbonate reabsorbed by kidneys; **alkalosis** → less bicarbonate is reabsorbed

Figure 1

$$CO_{2(g)} \rightleftharpoons CO_{2(aq)} \rightleftharpoons H_2CO_3 \rightleftharpoons H^+ + HCO_3^-$$

B⁻

HB

Structure of the Kidney

Cortex: inner portion of kidney that contains the uppermost region of nephrons (the glomerulus, Bowman's capsule, convoluted tubules)

Medulla: outer portion of kidney that contains the lower portion of the nephrons (loop of Henle)

Ureter, bladder and urethra

- Fluid (urine) from collecting ducts of the nephrons drains into the **ureter**, which brings urine to the **bladder**

- Urine stored in the bladder until it is ready to be excreted through the **urethra**

- Urination is under control of the parasympathetic nervous system as well as the somatic nervous system
  - External urethral sphincter is controlled voluntarily

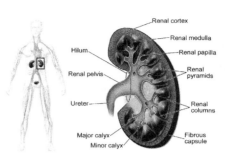

The Structure of a Kidney

The Nephron
- The nephron is the functional unit of the kidney; contains a special tubules through which fluid travels and urine is formed, as well as surrounding blood vessels that exchange solutes and fluid with the tubule
- It performs **filtration** of blood (separating salts and other solutes from plasma), **secretion** (active transport, osmosis, and passive diffusion), and **reabsorption** (removing fluids and other solutes from the filtrate for retention)

Glomerulus – a mass of capillaries through which blood filtration occurs
Bowman's capsule – capsule that surrounds the glomerulus and captures the filtered blood plasma
Proximal convoluted tubule (PCT) – first region of the tubule where reabsorption and secretion occurs
Loop of Henle – reabsorption and secretion of water and salts occurs as tubule passes through concentration gradient of interstitial fluid; interstitial fluid at highest concentration in inner medulla (closer to bottom of the loop)
Distal convoluted tubule (DCT) – region where hormone controlled reabsorption occurs
Collecting duct – tube that DCTs drain into; more hormone-controlled reabsorption; fluid from here eventually drains into the ureter

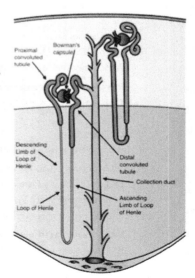

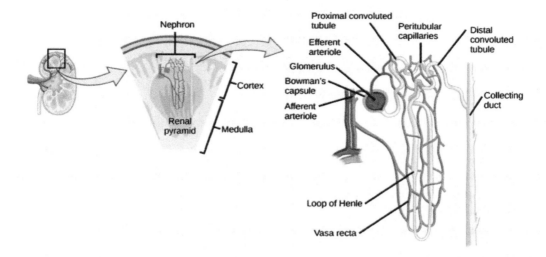

Formation of urine:

Glomerular Filtration –

- Blood at high pressure passes through the glomerulus
- Filtration: hydrostatic pressure pushes fluids and solutes (that are small enough) into the Bowman's capsule
  - Water, ions, glucose, urea pass easily through
  - Large proteins hardly pass though and cells (RBCs and WBCs) never pass through
- Glomerular filtration rate increases as blood pressure increases
- Both good (nutrients and necessary solutes) and bad (wastes) stuff is pushed into the filtrate; some with need to be reabsorbed and some will be excreted

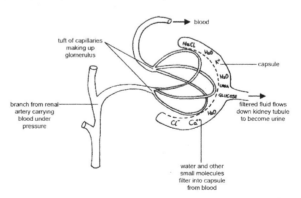

Secretion and reabsorption of solutes; concentration of urine –

- **PCT:** major site of reabsorption and secretion; nutrients and salts reabsorbed, wastes secreted
  - glucose, amino acids, and some other nutrients reabsorbed fully by active transport
  - H_2O, NaCl, and other salts reabsorbed via diffusion as well as active transport
  - Nitrogenous wastes and drugs secreted

- **Loop of Henle:** concentration gradient of interstitial fluid drives the flow of salts and water into or out of the tubule; loop has selective permeability
  - **Descending limb is** permeable to water; as fluid travels down, more water is reabsorbed from the tubule into the interstitial fluid (ends up back in the blood); concentration gradient ensures constant water reabsorption even as filtrate becomes more concentrated deeper into the medulla → forms more concentrated urine
  - **Ascending limb** is permeable to NaCl and K^+; NaCl reabsorbed via passive transport at the bottom of the ascending limb, then reabsorbed by active transport at the top of the limb

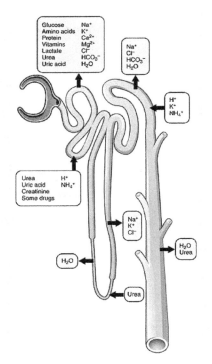

- **DCT:** more reabsorption and secretion; fine tuning based on hormonal cues
  - Salts and water reabsorbed; urea, H^+, and K^+ secreted
  - Reabsorption/secretion of H^+ and/or HCO_3^- enables pH regulation
- **Collecting duct:** some reabsorption of water (as duct descends into concentrated interstitial fluid) and of urea (to maintain high concentration of solutes in interstitial)

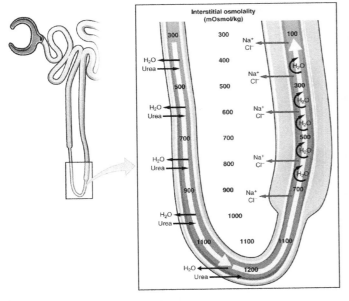

Counter-current multiplier mechanism –

- Countercurrent mechanism system is one that creates a concentration gradient by actively (using energy) transporting solutes across a membrane

- Gradient surround a region in which a fluid flows in opposite directions through a tube (ascending and descending loops of Henle)

The Structure of Skin

Skin is composed of three main layers: **dermis, epidermis, hypodermis**

Epidermis: outermost layer of skin that provides a barrier to the external environment and pathogens, and regulates water loss
- There is no direct blood supply to the epidermis; O_2 can diffuse from the external environment to the cells and the dermis can provide nutrients
- Mainly stratified squamous epithelial tissue
- Greater than 90% of the cells here are **keratinocytes**
  - Produce keratin, a fibrous protein that creates a protective barrier
  - Keratinocytes start as stem cells in basal layer of the epidermis and differentiate as they move upwards
  - Top of epidermis is dead and flattened, keratin-filled cells → shed off and replaced regularly
- Also has **melanocytes** which produce melanin → skin color
  - Melanin protects the body from UV damage
- **Impermeability to water**: cells tightly linked and keratin is water-insoluble

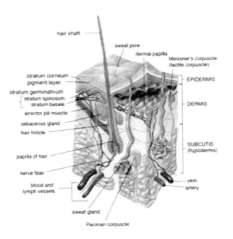

Dermis: thick layer of connective tissue below the dermis that cushions the body

- Connective tissue is full of **collagen** and **elastic fibers** which provide structural support and elasticity
    - Synthesized by **fibroblasts**
- Contains: blood vessels, hair follicles, nerve fibers, sweat glands, mechanoreceptors, thermoreceptors, lymphatic vessels, and muscle fibers that erect hair shafts
    - Capillaries provide nourishment and waste removal for dermis and epidermis
    - Mechanoreceptors are sensory receptors that relay information about stretch, vibration, and pressure
    - Thermoreceptors sense heat
- Macrophages provide immune support

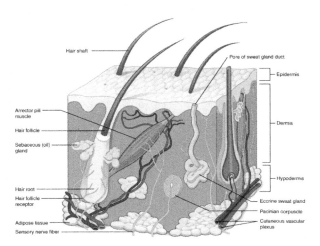

Hypodermis: fatty layer that stores fat and provides the skin with insulation and cushioning

Functions of Skin

Protection: skin protects against stress/strain/abrasion and the external elements (such as chemicals and radiation)
- Skin also provides a barrier to keep out pathogens and unwanted microorganisms
- Nails, calluses, and hair all contain keratin and are addition forms of protection
- Melanin protects against damaging UV rays

Sensory functions: sensory receptors and free nerve endings in the skin sense temperature, pressure, vibration, touch, pain

Homeostasis –
- Protects against water loss = fluid homeostasis
- Thermoregulation = heat homeostasis
- Osmoregulation – sweating enables the excretion of excess fluid, ammonia, urea, and salts

Thermoregulation –
- Blood vessels close to the surface of the skin can dilate (vasodilation) or contract (vasoconstriction) in order to decrease or increase heat loss from capillary beds
- Layer of fat in the hypodermis provides insulation
- Hair on skin surface help insulate the skin; when cold, erector muscles enable hair to stand up → more efficient at trapping heat
- Sweating enables heat loss through evaporative cooling

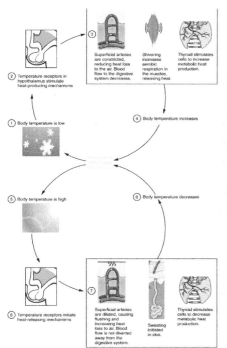

① Body temperature is low

② Temperature receptors in hypothalamus stimulate heat-producing mechanisms

③ Superficial arteries are constricted, reducing heat loss to the air. Blood flow to the digestive system decreases.

Shivering increases aerobic respiration in the muscles, releasing heat.

Thyroid stimulates cells to increase metabolic heat production.

④ Body temperature increases

⑤ Body temperature is high

⑥ Temperature receptors initiate heat-releasing mechanisms

⑦ Superficial arteries are dilated, causing flushing and increasing heat loss to air. Blood flow is not diverted away from the digestive system.

Sweating initiated in skin.

Thyroid stimulates cells to decrease metabolic heat production.

⑧ Body temperature decreases

Thermoregulation:

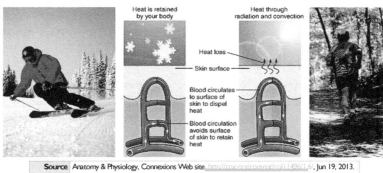

Heat is retained by your body

Heat through radiation and convection

Heat loss

Skin surface

Blood circulates to surface of skin to dispel heat

Blood circulation avoids surface of skin to retain heat

Source Anatomy & Physiology, Connexions Web site. http://cnx.org/content/col11496/1.6/, Jun 19, 2013.

Functions of the Skeletal System

- Forms the framework and shape of the body and provides overall structural support

- Protects delicate internal organs from stress, blunt force, and trauma
  - Ribcage protects the heart and lungs; skull protects the brain

- Bone is a calcium reservoir – it can release calcium when needed by the body or absorb excess calcium

- Production of RBCs and WBCs from hematopoietic stem cells in the bone marrow

- Joints and limbs enable movement and flexibility of our body

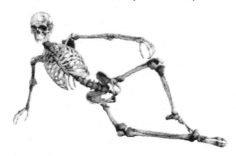

Skeletal Structure

Endoskeleton versus exoskeleton:

- Endoskeleton is inside the body; the skeletons of vertebrates

- Exoskeleton is a rigid external skeleton; found in many invertebrates, such as insects

Bone type by shape:

- Long bones are long and rod-shaped; often acted on by muscles like a lever – humerus

- Short bones are often cuboidal or round (as wide as they are long) – ankle bone

- Flat bones are curved and flat; often protect organs like a shield – ribs, skull

- Irregular bones have unique and irregular shapes – vertebra

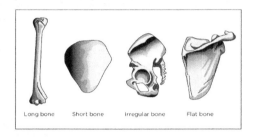

Long bone   Short bone   Irregular bone   Flat bone

Joints

Joint: where 2 or more bones meet; may by mobile (synovial joint) or not mobile

- **Immovable joint** is a connection between bones with fibrous tissue between them providing strength
  - Ex. Multiple skull bones fused at sutures

- **Synovial joints** are freely movable; they contain synovial fluid that lubricates the joint and absorbs shock

- There are classifications of synovial joints based on their movements
  - Main synovial joint types: pivot joint, ball-and-socket joint, plane joint, saddle joint, hinge joint

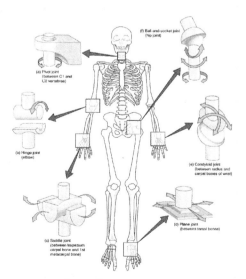

Bone Structure

Gross structure (of a long bone) –

Diaphysis: tubular middle portion and shaft of a bone; mainly compact bone

- Cavity in the middle filled with **yellow bone marrow**

Epiphysis: bulbous end region of bone filled with spongy bone

- Usually capped off with cartilage
- Often contains **red bone marrow**

Metaphysis: between the diaphysis and epiphysis

- Contains the epiphyseal plate - a growth plate composed mainly of cartilage while still growing, then later replace fully with bone

Bone marrow: Yellow and red bone marrow both have high number of blood vessels; both make some RBCs and WBCs (from hematopoietic stem cells), but red marrow makes more; yellow bone marrow has many fat cells

Types of bone –

Spongy bone: lighter and less tough than compact bone; made up of thin threads of bone called **trabeculae**

Compact bone: more compact and tough; made up of **osteons (Haversian systems)**

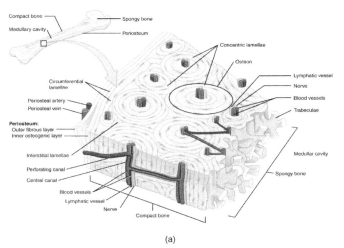

(a)

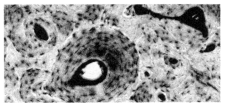

- Bone is made mainly of collagen, calcium phosphate, calcium carbonate, and hydroxyapatite crystals

- Tough yet also has flexibility (collagen, glycoproteins)

- Osteon is a circular unit of bone

- Osteons: concentric bone layers (lamellae) that surround **Haversian canals**, which contain blood and lymphatic vessels, and nerves

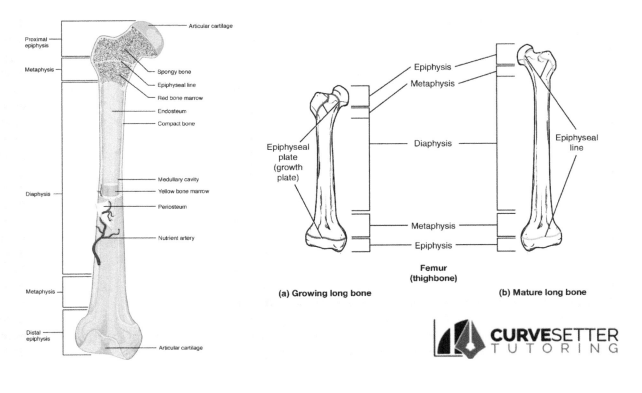

(a) Growing long bone

(b) Mature long bone

Femur
(thighbone)

Bone: Cellular Components

Osteoclast: cells that dissolve/breakdown bone ("resorb" bone), releasing the minerals and releasing Ca^{+2} to the blood
- Found on the surface of bone

Osteoblast: form new bone through Ca^{+2} and mineral deposition and creating collagen

Osteocyte: mature bone cell embedded inside spaces in the bone lacunae)
- Connected to other osteocytes via long cellular extensions, enabling nutrient and waste exchange
- Support and maintain bone; regulate activity of osteoblasts and osteoclasts; sense strain

Osteogenic cell: the only dividing bone cells; differentiate into osteoblats

Bone remodeling: ongoing process of altering the composition of bone due to hormonal cues or stress/strain on the bone

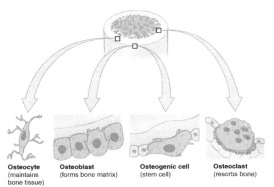

Cartilage, Ligaments, and Tendons

Cartilage – flexible connective tissue involved in supportive framework

- Structural component of many body components such as the nose, ears, and the trachea
- Also found at the end of long bones
- Chondrocytes (cartilage cells) embedded in an extensive ECM made up of collagen, elastin, and other fibers

Ligament – connect bone to bone, stabilizing joints

Tendon – connect muscle to bone, enabling the muscle to move the bone

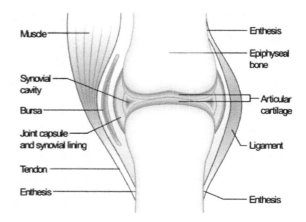

Endocrine Control

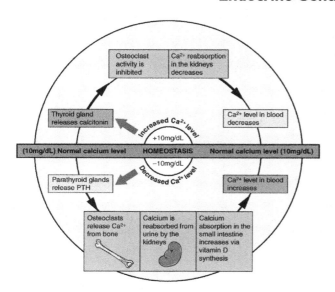

Calcitonin: reduced [Ca^{+2}] by inhibiting osteoclasts

Parathyroid hormone (PTH): increases [Ca^{+2}] by stimulating osteoclasts to break down bone

MUSCLES CELLS AND THE MUSCLE SYSTEM

Biology Lecture 14

OBJECTIVES

- Functions of the muscle system
- Three muscle types and their structures
  - Cardiac, smooth, and skeletal
- The muscle cell
  - Energy sources
  - Actin and myosin filaments; troponin and tropomyosin
  - The sliding filament model of contraction
  - The structure of a sarcomere
  - Role of calcium in muscle contraction
  - T-tubule system and sarcoplasmic reticulum
  - Muscle fiber types and their properties
- Cardiac muscle contraction and regulation
- Oxygen debt
- Nervous system control of muscle
  - Motor neurons and the NMJ
  - Voluntary vs. involuntary muscles
  - Sympathetic and parasympathetic innervation

Functions of the Muscle System

Support and mobility
- Muscles are the only tissue that can contract – enable all body movement
- Maintain our posture and body positions

Circulatory and respiratory assistance
- Cardiac muscle in the heart pumps blood throughout the body
- Smooth muscle in the blood vessels help regulate blood vessel diameter
- Skeletal muscles surrounding the veins help squeeze low pressure blood back to the heart
- Diaphragm and intercostal muscles enable inhalation and exhalation

Thermoregulation
- Muscles enable shivering response to a drop in body temperature

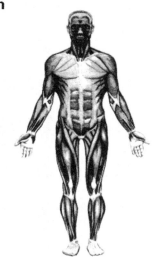

Skeletal, Smooth, and Cardiac Muscle

Skeletal muscle
- Voluntary movements (can be consciously controlled)
- Controlled by the somatic NS
- Striated (contractile units arranged into sarcomeres)
- Long, cylindrical, multinucleated cell; not a syncytium
- Use troponin
- Found throughout the body; often attached to bones

Smooth muscle
- Involuntary movements
- Controlled by the autonomic NS (sympathetic and parasympathetic)
- Non-striated (contractile units scattered throughout the cell)
- Tapered cell; not multinucleated; functional syncytium
- Use calmodulin
- In the digestive tract and blood vessels (walls of visceral organs)

Cardiac muscle
- Involuntary movements
- Controlled by the autonomic NS
- (sympathetic and parasympathetic)
- Striated
- Branched network of cells connected by intercalated disks; generally not multinucleated; functional syncytium
- AP longer that other muscle cells
- Use troponin
- Found in the heart

Smooth muscle cells

Skeletal muscle cells

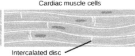

Cardiac muscle cells

Intercalated disc

Skeletal muscle

Smooth muscle

Cardiac muscle

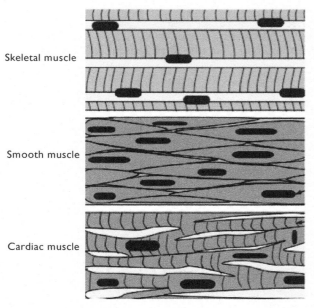

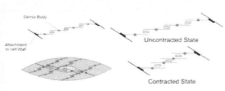

Actin-myosin filaments

The Muscle Cell

Energy Source:

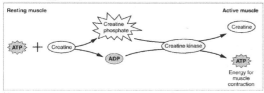

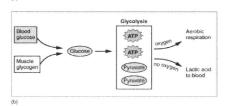

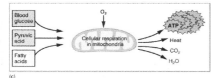

Red muscle fibers
- High endurance muscles but slow contraction
  - Can use for a long duration
- Mainly use aerobic respiration to produce ATP
  - High mitochondria and myoglobin content → red color
  - High capillary density (need high O_2 influx)
- Increased in a marathon runner

White muscle fibers
- Low endurance muscles (fatigue easily) but fast contraction
  - Can only be used for short duration
- Mainly use glycolysis (glycogen as the energy source) and creatine phosphate to make ATP
  - Low mitochondria and myoglobin content
  - Low capillary density
- Increased in a sprinter

Muscle fiber types –
- Muscle fibers can also be classified into: type I, type IIA, and type IIB
- Red fibers are analogous to type I, white fibers are analogous to type IIB, and type IIA fibers are a blend of red and white fibers

Type I (slow twitch oxidative):
- Slow contraction, low force of contraction, high resistance to fatigue
- High myoglobin and mitochondria content
- Mainly use triglycerides as fuel in aerobic respiration

Type IIA (fast twitch oxidative):
- Fast contraction, moderate force of contraction, moderate resistance to fatigue
- Intermediate myoglobin and mitochondria content
- Mainly use creatine phosphate and glycogen as fuel

Type IIB (fast twitch glycolytic):
- Very fast contraction, high force of contraction, low resistance to fatigue
- Low myoglobin and mitochondria content
- Mainly use creatine phosphate and glycogen as fuel

Muscle Contraction: Sliding Filament Model

- **Thin filaments = actin**
    - Linear rope-like protein called **tropomyosin** spirals around the actin filaments and covers the myosin binding site when muscle is not contracting
    - **Troponin** is a protein found on the thin filaments that interacts tropomyosin; moves tropomyosin out of the way (uncovering the myosin binding site) when Ca^{+2} is present during contraction

- **Thick filaments = myosin**
    - Bundles of myosin protein and myosin head groups
    - Myosin head groups bind to actin during contraction and **power stroke** occurs; myosin head groups shift in one direction, pulling the actin filaments towards the center of the sarcomere

Sliding filament theory: muscle contraction occurs when the thin and thick filaments slide past each other due to the interaction between myosin head groups and actin; myosin head groups shift in one direction pulling all the thin filaments in that direction and shortening the sarcomere
- Muscle contraction requires ATP and Ca^{+2} to be present
- Ca^{+2} causes troponin to move tropomyosin away from the myosin binding site → myosin head group interacts with actin forming a cross-bridge → myosin head group cocks back (power stroke), pulling actin filaments towards them → ATP enables myosin to detach from actin and the sarcomere to be reset

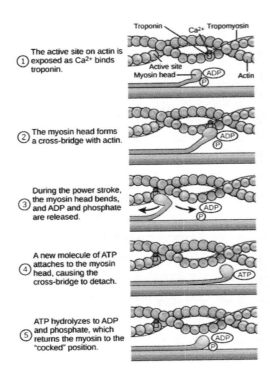

The active site on actin is exposed as Ca²⁺ binds troponin.

(1)

The myosin head forms a cross-bridge with actin.

(2)

During the power stroke, the myosin head bends, and ADP and phosphate are released.

(3)

A new molecule of ATP attaches to the myosin head, causing the cross-bridge to detach.

(4)

ATP hydrolyzes to ADP and phosphate, which returns the myosin to the "cocked" position.

(5)

Sarcomere:

- Actin (thin filaments) and myosin (thick filaments) are organized into sarcomeres in striated muscle (skeletal and cardiac muscle)
- Sarcomeres have certain designated and labelled regions that you need to know
- **M line** is through the **m**iddle of the sarcomere, only ever contains thick filaments
- **H zone** is the region that contains only thick filaments; shrinks during contraction
- **A band** spans the full length of the thick filaments; contains both thin and thick filaments
- **I band** is the region that contains thin filaments only; shrinks during contraction

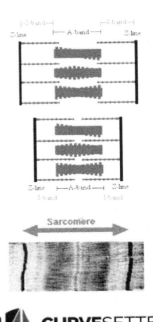

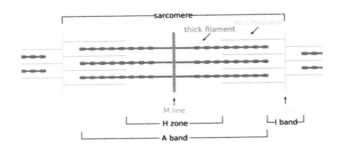

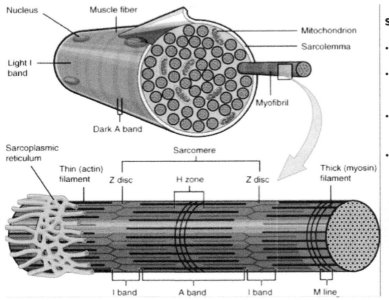

Control of muscle contraction –

- All three muscle types requires Ca^{+2} for contraction

- **T-tubules** (transverse tubules) are channels that surround skeletal and cardiac muscle fibers, enabling an action potential to be rapidly transmitted throughout the cell

- **Sarcoplasmic reticulum** is the smooth ER of muscle cells that stores Ca^{+2} and releases it during contraction

- Nerve fiber stimulates a muscle cell → action potential arrives at the neuromuscular junction (NMJ) → action potential travels through t-tubules → causes sarcoplasmic reticulum to release Ca^{+2} → Ca^{+2} enables myosin head to bind to thin filament and initiate power stroke → contraction occurs

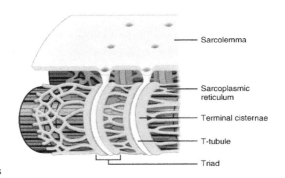

Cardiac Muscle Contraction

- Cardiac muscles must synchronize their contraction and contract as a single unit
  - Muscle cells connected by gap junctions at intercalated disks → enables the spread of action potentials between all connected cells

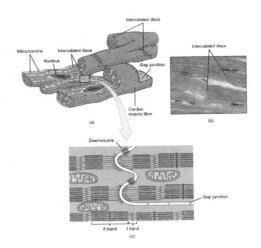

- Cardiac muscle in under control of the autonomic nervous system

- Sympathetic nervous system increases heart rate and contractility (epinephrine and norepinephrine)

- Parasympathetic nervous system decreases the heart rate (acetylcholine)

Oxygen debt –

- Also called post exercise oxygen consumption
- After an intense burst of muscle activity you are still breathing heavily for some time (repaying the oxygen debt)
- This occurs because… during the strenuous activity there was not enough O_2 to keep up with ATP demands with aerobic respiration, so the body uses some anaerobic respiration
- Anaerobic respiration produces lactic acid which must eventually get converted back to CO_2
- After the activity, increased oxygen intake is used to convert lactic acid back to CO_2

Nervous control of skeletal muscle –

- **Motor neuron (efferent nerve)** is a neuron with a cell body in the CNS and an axon that extends to muscle to control movement
  - **Somatic motor neurons** innervate skeletal muscles; often synapse directly onto effector
  - **Visceral motor neurons** innervate smooth and cardiac muscle

- Visceral motor neurons originate in the CNS and synapse onto ganglia in the PNS, specifically the autonomic branch (generally di-synaptic)

Neuromuscular Junction (motor end plate)

- The junction (synapse) between a motor neuron and a muscle fiber
- Motor neurons release neurotransmitter (acetylcholine), causing muscle to contract
- AP reaches axon terminal of motor neuron → voltage-dependent Ca^{+2} channels open and Ca^{+2} rushes into the axon terminal → vesicles containing acetylcholine fuse with the axon terminal and release it into the synaptic cleft → acetylcholine depolarizes the muscle fiber and contraction occurs

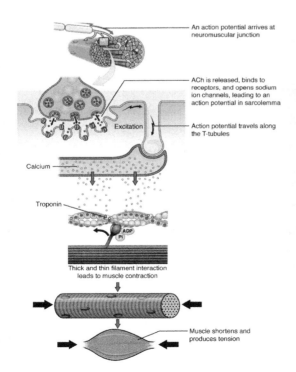

An action potential arrives at neuromuscular junction

ACh is released, binds to receptors, and opens sodium ion channels, leading to an action potential in sarcolemma

Excitation

Action potential travels along the T-tubules

Calcium

Troponin

ADP
Pi

Thick and thin filament interaction leads to muscle contraction

Muscle shortens and produces tension

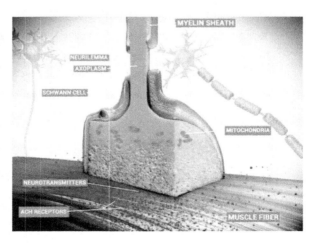

MYELIN SHEATH
NEURILEMMA
AXOPLASM
SCHWANN CELL
MITOCHONDRIA
NEUROTRANSMITTERS
ACH RECEPTORS
MUSCLE FIBER

Sympathetic and parasympathetic innervation –

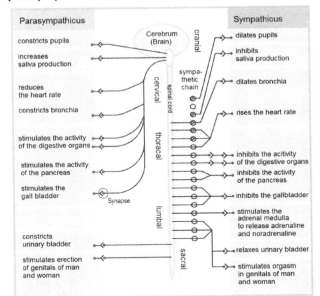

THE REPRODUCTIVE SYSTEM, EMBRYOGENESIS, AND DEVELOPMENT

Biology Lecture 15

The Reproductive System

Gonads – the reproductive organs that produce **gametes** (haploid germ cell; eggs and sperm) and sex hormones

- Gonads are called the "primary reproductive organ"; other organs of the system are called "secondary (or accessory) reproductive organs"
- Gonads are controlled by the hormones FSH and LH, which are released by the anterior pituitary
- Testes and ovaries arise from the same precursor and have homologous functions

Male: testes
- Produce sperm (spermatogenesis) and androgens such as testosterone
- Protected and kept warm by the scrotum
- **Seminiferous tubules** – site of spermatogenesis in the testes

Female: ovaries
- Produce ovum/eggs (oogenesis), as well as estrogen, progesterone, and testosterone

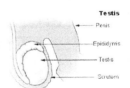

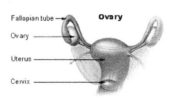

Testes – Sertoli cells and Leydig cells

- Testes have coiled tubes called **seminiferous tubules**
- Inside the seminiferous tubules are **Sertoli cells**, which protect and nourish the developing sperm
  - Sertoli cells also produce **inhibin**, a hormone crucial for negative feedback on the anterior pituitary
- **Leydig cells** are outside the tubules; they produce and release androgens such as **testosterone**
  - Testosterone crucial for negative feedback as well

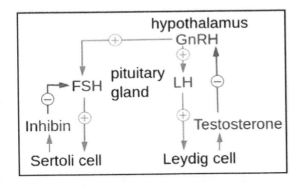

Other reproductive organs–

Male
- Epididymis – seminiferous tubules empty into epididymis; sperm stored here
- Vas (ductus) deferens – sperm travels through here toward the urethra
- Seminal vesicles – produce nearly 70% of semen; containing proteins and nourishment
- Bulbourethral gland – produce a small amount of semen; mucus-like fluid lubricates and neutralizes
- Ejaculatory duct – group of structures that enable ejaculation
- Penis – external muscular structure required for copulation

Male Reproductive System

Pubic bone
Ductus deferens
Penis
Spongy urethra
Bladder
Seminal vesicle
Prostate gland
Epididymis
Testis
Scrotum

Path of sperm during ejaculation:

Seminiferous tubules → Epididymus → Vas deferens → ejaculatory duct → Urethra → Penis

"SEVEn UP" – n is nothing

Female
- Fallopian tubes – tunnel through which ovum is transferred from ovaries to uterus; fertilization occurs here
- Uterus – "the womb"; supports and protects developing fetus
- Endometrium – inner lining of the uterus; where blastocyst is implanted
- Cervix - narrow bottom pertion of the uterus that connects to the vagina
- Vagina – muscular tube connecting to the uterus at the cervix
- Clitoris – enables stimulation/arousal during copulation

- **Arousal** is facilitated by the **parasympathetic NS,** enabling erection, lubrication, etc.
- **Orgasm** and ejaculation are facilitated by the **sympathetic NS**

Differences between male and female reproductive organs:
- Male an female reproductive organs arise from the same undifferentiated structures in early development
- Most structures are homologous, arising from the same precursor but having specialized purposes for male vs. female reproduction
- Males: urethra carries sperm and urine; females: urethra and vagina are distinct

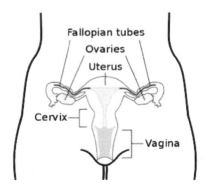

Development of the Reproductive System

- Males and females both start out with the same undifferentiated structures, which begin to differentiate a few weeks after the zygote is formed

- The "default sex" is female – if no other action are taken, the undifferentiated structures will automatically differentiate into female sexual organs

- **Males:** the Y chromosome has the **SRY gene** → SRY proteins causes testes to develop
  - Sertoli cells of testes produce **anti-mullerian hormone (AMH),** which causes regression of the (female precursor) **Mullerian ducts**
  - **Wolffian ducts** become the vas deferens and epididymis
  - Leydig cells produce testosterone which causes other sexual structures to differentiate into the male form

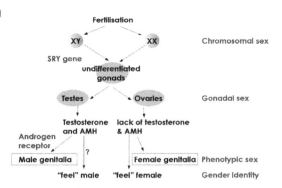

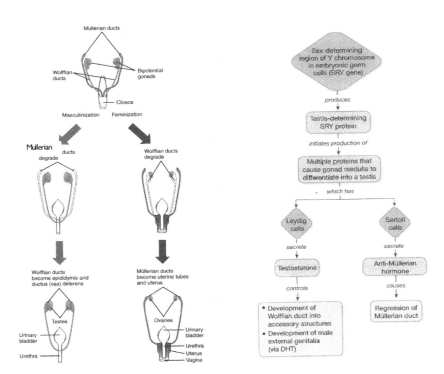

Puberty –

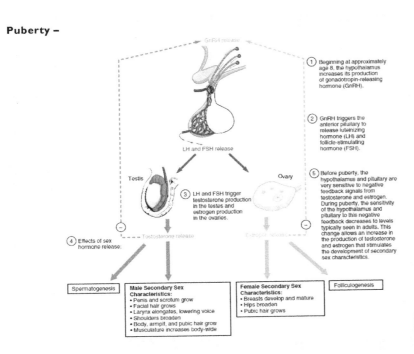

Female Reproductive Cycle

Key terms/concepts:

- LH → ovulation and formation of corpus luteum (ovulation = follicle becomes corpus luteum and egg released)
- FSH and LH trigger the ovary to secrete steroid hormones (estrogen and progesterone)
  - E and P maintain the endometrium and are important in feedback on LH and FSH
- **Corpus luteum-** what the follicle becomes after ovulation; secretes E and P
- **Follicle-** group of associated cells in the ovary; oocyte is housed and matures here
  - One follicle grows/matures and releases a single egg per month
- **Menstruation-** shedding of the endometrium (bleeding); occurs once per month

Follicular Phase

- Begins on first day of menstruation (day 1 of cycle)
- FSH triggers the selection and maturation of one follicle
- Follicle secretes estrogen → E levels begin to increase
- Menstruation is followed by **proliferative phase** in which endometrium begins to thicken; endometrium will continue to thicken for the rest of the cycle, preparing for the implantation of a zygote

Ovulation

- Estrogen produced by follicle trigger a spike in LH (and FSH) levels by positive feedback → egg is released from the follicle into the fallopian tube → egg can now be fertilized by sperm for a brief window of time
  - Released egg is paused in metaphase II of meiosis; completes meiosis II if fertilized
- Follicle becomes the corpus luteum after ovulation
- Occurs around day 14 of cycle

Luteal Phase

- Occurs after ovulation and continues until next menstruation
- Corpus luteum secretes E and P
- E and P cause endometrium to thicken and prevent GnRH, FSH, and LH (via negative feedback) → prevent another follicle from developing as body prepares to accept zygote in the endometrium
- Corpus luteum begins to degenerate if fertilization doesn't occur
- As corpus luteum degenerates at the end of luteal phase, E and P are no longer secreted and levels drop
- Drop in E and P → endometrium no longer maintained and sloughs off (menstruation) → cycle restarts

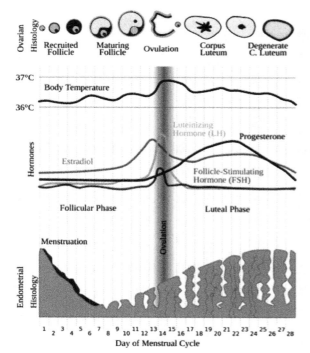

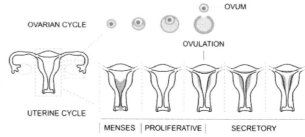

Oogenesis

Before birth –
- **Oogonia** (in primordial follicles) divide by mitosis forming **primary oocytes**

Puberty through menopause –
- Every menstrual cycle, a few primary oocytes complete meiosis I, forming one polar body (not used) and one **secondary oocyte** per primary oocyte
- In maturing follicles during ovulation, secondary oocytes proceed with meiosis II up until metaphase; pause at metaphase

Fertilization –
- When contact with sperm is made, secondary oocyte completes meiosis II, forming a mature **ovum** (and a polar body)
- Then sperm and egg nuclei fuse, forming the zygote

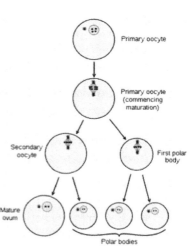

Spermatogenesis

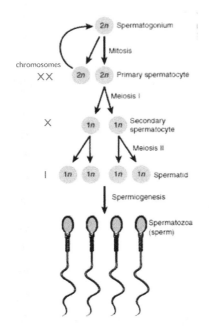

- Begins occurring at puberty and continues for the rest of the male's life
  - Occurs in seminiferous tubules of testes
  - Sertoli cells provide nutrients, protection, and support
- Spermatogonia divide by mitosis, yielding primary spermatocytes
- Primary spermatocytes undergo meiosis I, yielding secondary spermatocytes
- Secondary spermatocytes undergo meiosis II, yielding spermatids
- Spermatids mature into spermatozoa
- Unlike ovum, sperm are motile (flagellum) and much smaller than the egg
- Sperm contributes only its haploid genetic material to the zygote

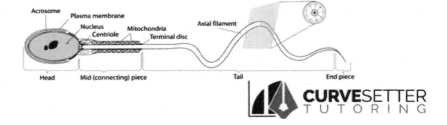

Stages of Reproduction

Fertilization:
- Sperm meets the egg (paused in metaphase II of meiosis) in the fallopian tube
- **Acrosome reaction:** enzymes in tip of sperm are released and degrade through outer layers of egg (zona pellucida and surrounding corona radiata)
  → sperm penetrates egg → sperm and egg plasma membrane fuse and sperm donates its haploid genetic material → form zygote
  - Egg contributes its cytoplasm and all organelles to zygote
- Egg completes meiosis II, producing mature ovum
- **Cortical reaction:** ensures that only a single sperm will fertilize the egg
- After this, many rounds of cell division (mitosis) will occur and cell mass moves through fallopian tubes to eventually reach the uterus

Implantation:
- Blastocyst implants itself into thick, vascularized endometrium around day 9
- Trophoblast cells of the blastocyst penetrate and grow into the endometrium
  → grow into long finger-like projections (chorionic villi) that make contact with maternal blood supply → structure eventually becomes the placenta
- **Ectopic pregnancy:** blastocyst implants in fallopian tubes; not viable

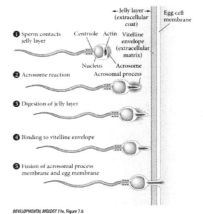

DEVELOPMENTAL BIOLOGY 11e, Figure 7.6
© 2016 Sinauer Associates, Inc.

Pregnancy:
- Lasts approximately 40 weeks; broken into 3 trimesters
- Mother's body nurtures the growing fetus
- High levels of **human chorionic gonadotropin hormone (hCG)** → produced by placenta following implantation
  - Maintains corpus luteum in early pregnancy (no degeneration)
- High estrogen and progesterone (first produced by corpus luteum then placenta takes over); low GnRH, LH, FSH
  - Endometrium is maintained and blastocyst is implanted into it
- **Placenta** = structure that lines uterine wall and supports the fetus → delivers nutrients and oxygen, enables waste elimination and gas exchange (connected to the mother's blood supply), and more
- **Umbilical Cord** = connection between the fetus and the placenta
  - Umbilical arteries and veins enable gas, nutrient, and waste exchange

Birth (parturition):
- Cervix dilates and infant is expelled head-first out of the mother
- Oxytocin thought to play role in triggering labor

Lactation:
- Milk secretion from mammary glands of mother; facilitated by hormones prolactin and oxytocin

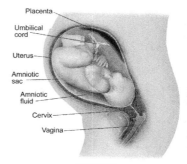

Pregnancy

Embryogenesis: Stages of Development

Fertilization → Cleavage → Blastulation → Implantation → Gastrulation → Neurulation

- **Cleavage:** following fertilization, the zygote undergoes rapid rounds of cell division with minimal growth between the divisions → cells form a compacted mass called the **morula**
  - Morula is the same approximate size as the zygote but has many more cells

- **Blastulation:** morula continues to divide and cells arrange themselves into a **blastula**
  - Blastula is called a **blastocyst** in mammals
  - Blastocyst has an outer ring of cells called the **trophoblast** that surrounds a fluid-filled cavity (**blastocoel**), and has an inner ball of cells called the **inner cell mass**
  - Trophoblast becomes the chorion which contributes to the placenta
  - Inner cell mass becomes the embryo

- **Implantation:** blastocyst implants into endometrium

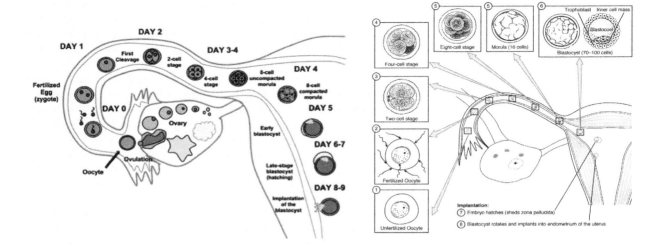

- **Gastrulation:** first cell movements and formation of the three germ layers
  - Cells invaginate at the **primary streak**
  - Embryo sets up its axis
  - Cells begin to differentiate – become one of the three primary germ layers: **endoderm, ectoderm, or mesoderm**
  - Involves extensive **cell migration**

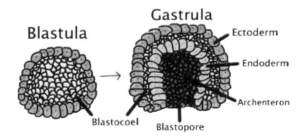

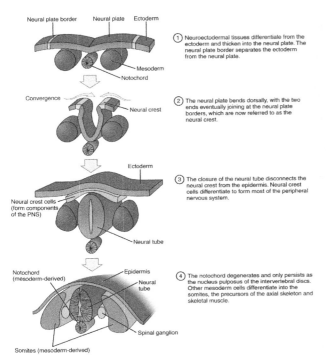

1. Neuroectodermal tissues differentiate from the ectoderm and thicken into the neural plate. The neural plate border separates the ectoderm from the neural plate.

2. The neural plate bends dorsally, with the two ends eventually joining at the neural plate borders, which are now referred to as the neural crest.

3. The closure of the neural tube disconnects the neural crest from the epidermis. Neural crest cells differentiate to form most of the peripheral nervous system.

4. The notochord degenerates and only persists as the nucleus pulposus of the intervertebral discs. Other mesoderm cells differentiate into the somites, the precursors of the axial skeleton and skeletal muscle.

Neurulation: formation of the nervous system from the ectoderm; a type of organogenesis (formation of the organ systems)

- Involves extensive cell migration and differentiation
- **Neural plate** (specialized region of the ectoderm) invaginates, forming the neural folds
- **Notochord** directs cell movement of neurulation; eventually forms part of the vertebra
- Invaginated tissue pinches off, forming the **neural tube**
  - Neural tube will become the brain and spinal cord
- **Neural crest cells** pinch off and migrate to different regions of the developing fetus → form many parts of the PNS, bones and cartilage of the face, the adrenal medulla, nerves of the gut and cranial nerves, melanocytes, glial cells, and more

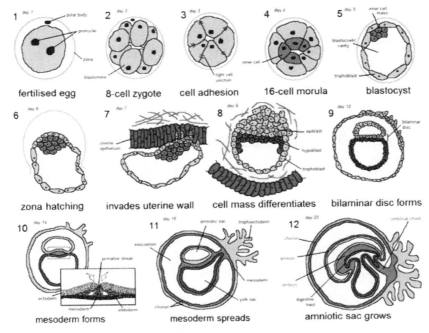

1. fertilised egg
2. 8-cell zygote
3. cell adhesion
4. 16-cell morula
5. blastocyst
6. zona hatching
7. invades uterine wall
8. cell mass differentiates
9. bilaminar disc forms
10. mesoderm forms
11. mesoderm spreads
12. amniotic sac grows

Chorion: outer protective membrane
- Arises from trophoblast
- Contributes to placenta

Amnion: inner protective membrane
- Arises from inner cell mass
- Surrounds embryo and amniotic fluid

Chorion + amnion = amniotic sac

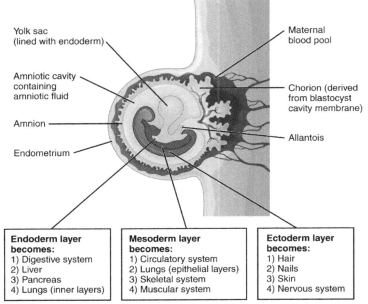

Yolk sac (lined with endoderm)

Amniotic cavity containing amniotic fluid

Amnion

Endometrium

Maternal blood pool

Chorion (derived from blastocyst cavity membrane)

Allantois

Endoderm layer becomes:
1) Digestive system
2) Liver
3) Pancreas
4) Lungs (inner layers)

Mesoderm layer becomes:
1) Circulatory system
2) Lungs (epithelial layers)
3) Skeletal system
4) Muscular system

Ectoderm layer becomes:
1) Hair
2) Nails
3) Skin
4) Nervous system

Primary Germ Layers

Ectoderm:
- Outer-most germ layer

Becomes the…
- Nervous system
- pituitary gland and adrenal medulla
- Eyes, nose, and mouth
- Epidermis, hair, and nails

Mesoderm:
- Middle germ layer

Becomes the…
- Connective tissue - bone, blood, cartilage, adipose tissue, etc.
- Cardiovascular system (heart, blood vessels) and lymph vessels
- Muscles - cardiac, smooth, and skeletal
- Skin dermis
- Most urinary and genital organs - gonads, kidneys, ureter
- Adrenal cortex

Endoderm:
- Inner-most layer

Becomes the…
- Lung inner layers
- GI tract organs - stomach, pancreas, etc.
- Liver, thymus, thyroid and parathyroid glands
- Lining of urethra and bladder
- Majority of all epithelium *inside* the body (i.e. not the epidermis)

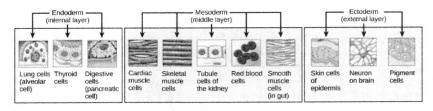

Development: Gene regulation and environment-gene interactions

- Cell differentiation occurs largely by **differential gene expression** – some genes turned on, some turned off
    - Histone and DNA modification (euchromatin versus heterochromatin) – methylation, acetylation, phosphorylation, etc.
    - Transcriptional regulation, alternative RNA splicing, and translation regulation
    - These are all epigenetic changes

- Many different genes and chemicals are involved in **morphogenesis** (development of the shape and body plan of the fetus)
    - **Morphogens** – chemicals that transmit information about pattern formation and cell differentiation based on their concentration gradients
    - **Maternal cytoplasmic determinants** play a key role in early embryogenesis
    - Toxins and environmental cues can alter and disrupt morphogenesis
    - **Hox genes** for organizing body plan; highly conserved across species

- **Teratogen** – chemical that causes birth defects; often does so by disrupting embryogenesis and fetus development
    - Excessive alcohol intake during pregnancy → fetal alcohol syndrome

Determination – cell is committed to become a specific cell type (cell's fate is determined)
- Determined cells may look exactly the same as they haven't started the process of adopting that fate yet

Differentiation – cell is in the process of the becoming that specific cell type; differentiation follows determination

Cell-cell communication –
- **Induction:** one cell signal to another, influencing its developmental fate
- Induction may occur due to the cells being in physical contact, or due to a chemical messenger

Regenerative capacity –
- Regenerative capacity = the ability to restore and renew damaged tissue
    - Generally relies on the presence of adult stem cells
- Differs extensively across species and even across different tissues within an organism
    - Ex. Lizards can regrow a tail if cut off
    - Humans – some tissues and cell types undergo constant regeneration (keratinocytes, erythrocytes) due to the presence of adult stem cell precursors
    - In general, humans are quite limited in their regenerative capacity – we cannot regrow a severed or removed limb or organ

Cell potency:

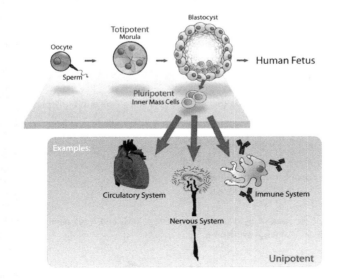

Totipotent –

Pluripotent –

Multipotent –

AMINO ACIDS AND PROTEINS

Biochemistry Lecture 1

OBJECTIVES

- Overview of amino acids
  - Structure
  - Acidic or basic; hydrophilic or hydrophobic
- Isoelectric Point (pI)
- Peptide Linkage (review)
  - Formation and hydrolysis
- Sulfur Linkage
- Protein Structure
  - Primary
  - Secondary
  - Tertiary
  - Quaternary
- Protein folding and denaturing
- Solvation layer and impact on entropy
- Non-enzymatic protein functions

Amino Acids

Amino Acid Backbone:

- Alpha carbon, amine group, carboxyl group, side chain (R group)
- Amino acids are amphoteric
- At low pH both the amine and carboxylic acid are protonated
    - NH_3^+ pKa ≈ 9.5; COOH pKa ≈ 2
- Above pH of 2 but below 9.5: COO^- and NH_3^+ **(zwitterion)**
- Above pH of 9.5: COO^- and NH_2

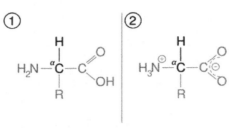

Acidity and Basicity:

- Amino acids are characterized as acidic or basic based on the pKa of their side chain (R group)
    - Acidic if R group contains carboxyl group; basic if R group contains amine
- When the pH of solution = pKa of the side chain, half of the a.a. that R group protonated, and half have it deprotonated; as pH rises, the amount of a.a. with the R group deprotonated increases towards 100%
- pKa's to know: Asp (approx. 4), Glu (approx. 4), His (6.5), Lys (10), Arg (12)

Hydrophilic or Hydrophobic:

- Amino acids are characterized as hydrophilic (polar) or hydrophobic (non-polar) based on their side chains
- Non-polar/hydrophobic: R group is alkyl or aromatic
- Polar/hydrophilic: acidic R groups, basic R groups, and other R groups that contain 1+ very polar bond(s) in R group

Isoelectric Point: pH at which molecule is net neutral

- For basic a.a.: pI = (pKa(R group) + pKa(amine))/2
- For acidic a.a.: pI = (pKa(R group) + pKa(COOH))/2
- For neither acidic nor basic a.a.: pI = (pKa(COOH) + pKa(amine))/2 ≈ (9.5 + 2) / 2 ≈ 5.75
    - Must have NO pKa of side chain (R group cannot be protonated or deprotonated)

Ex. Arg: pI = (12 + 9.5) / 2 = 10.75
- 0 – 2: COOH, NH_3^+, R^+ → NET +2
- 2 – 9.5: COO^-, NH_3^+, R^+ → NET +1
- 9.5 – 12: COO^-, NH_2, R^+ → NET 0
- 12 – 14: COO^-, NH_2, R → NET -1

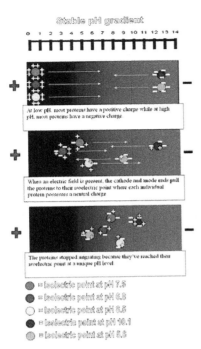

Stable pH gradient

= Isoelectric point at pH 7.6
= Isoelectric point at pH 6.6
= Isoelectric point at pH 8.5
= Isoelectric point at pH 10.1
= Isoelectric point at pH 5.6

Isoelectric Focusing: separate proteins based on their isoelectric point (pI)

- pH gradient set up in gel (low pH is + end, high pH is − end)
- Proteins start at either end and migrates towards the opposite end until they reach the position in the gel's pH gradient that is equal to their pI
- Protein starting at low pH end will be net + and repelled by the positive charge at that end; migrates towards opposite end (- and high pH) until it reaches pI, at which point if it travelled further it would begin to have a net − charge and be repelled

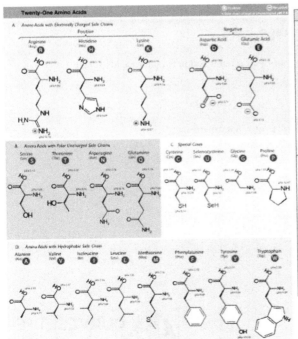

- **Peptide bond:** amide linkage between amino acids in a polypeptide (protein)

- Peptide bond has resonance: increased stability of bond (difficult to hydrolyze)
  - 6 atoms (those of amide bond and those directly adjacent) are planar due to partial pi bond character

- Formation of the peptide bond is a **condensation reaction** (remove H_2O; also called dehydration) and is facilitated by tRNA molecules during translation
  - Addition-elimination reaction between carboxylic acid and primary amine (amine attacks the carbonyl carbon)
  - Reaction is non-spontaneous ($\Delta G > 0$) and requires catalysis and ATP

- Breaking peptide bond is a **hydrolysis reaction**
  - Requires strong base and enzyme catalysis

Sulfur Linkage

- **Disulfide bond/bridge:** covalent bond between the sulfurs of two cysteine residues (amino acids called residues when in a polypeptide)
  - R-SH + R-SH → R-S-S-R (oxidation)
  - "cystine" = 2 linked cysteine residues

- Forms when cysteines are close by each other and in an **oxidizing environment**
  - Cytosol is a reducing environment, so no disulfide bridges there
  - They can form in RER lumen, secreted proteins, proteins on cell membrane exterior

Protein Structure

Primary Structure: the sequence of covalently linked a.a. in a polypeptide chain

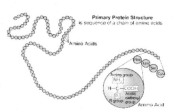

- Held together by peptide bonds

- Only broken by hydrolysis reaction requiring catalysis

- Proteases degrade peptide bonds

- Determined by DNA sequence of gene

Gly   Ser   Gly   Ala   Gly   Ala

Secondary Structure: local regions of folding of the polypeptide chain due to interactions between backbone atoms

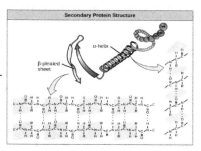

- **Hydrogen-bonding** between backbone atoms: H atom of amino group is the H-bond donor and O of carbonyl group is the H-bond acceptor

- Most common secondary structures: **alpha helix** and **beta pleated sheet**

- Protein may contain one, both, or neither motif

- Amino acids have different propensities for forming alpha helices and beta sheets

Alpha helix:

- Helical structure formed by H-bonds that run parallel to the axis of the helix and form between every 3-4 amino acids

- Right-handed helix with approximately 3.6 residues per turn of the helix

- Forms within one continuous region of a polypeptide chain

- R groups stick outwards from helix (not inwards; not enough space)

- Alpha helix "breakers": proline (cyclic R group sterically hinders helical shape) and glycine (moves very freely because R group is so small)

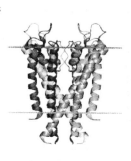

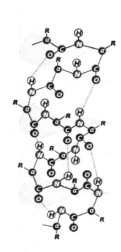

Beta pleated sheet:

- 2 or more different segments of a polypeptide chain align and H-bonds between adjacent strands form perpendicular to the length of the chain
- The aligned sheets are pleated at the alpha C of the backbone
- R groups jut out above and below the sheet
- Large aromatic residues and large alkyl residues favored (tyrosine, tryptophan phenylalanine, isoleucine, etc.)

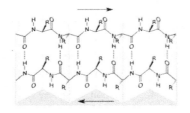

- **Parallel sheet:** N-terminus of one sheet aligns with N-terminus of the other
- **Antiparallel sheet:** N-terminus of one aligns with C-terminus of the other (strands run in opposite directions)

Parallel

Anti-parallel

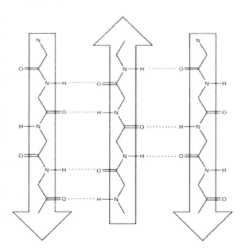

Antiparallel b-sheet

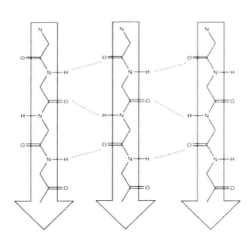

Parallel b-sheet

Tertiary Structure: the overall 3D shape that a polypeptide chain folds into due to interactions between side chains

- Involves mainly non-covalent bonds:

    - **London dispersion forces** between non-polar side chains

    - **Dipole-dipole** between polar side chains

    - **H-bonds** between polar side chains with H-bond donors and acceptors

    - **Ionic bonds** between charged side chains (acidic/basic): **salt bridges**

- **Disulfide bonds** also considered part of tertiary structure
- Tertiary structure is the conformation that is most stable/lowest energy by maximizing IMF

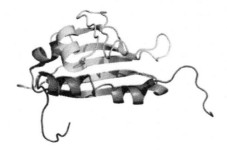

In a polar aqueous environment (physiological conditions): hydrophobic amino acids cluster together on the interior region of the protein while charged and polar residues are exposed on the exterior of the protein

- Enables polar residues to have H-bonding or dipole-dipole interactions with the surrounding water molecules

- **Hydrophobic interactions** (London dispersion forces) are weak individually but present in such high quantity that they contribute immensely to the overall structure and stability of a folded protein

    - This is the main force driving the folding of a protein

    - Favorable because it maximizes the entropy of the folded protein: enables water molecules to engage in a maximum amount of highly dynamic and disordered H-bonds (rather than being trapped in a highly ordered **solvation layer** in which water molecules weakly interact weakly with exposed non-polar side chains)

Isolated Protein   **Protein in aqueous solution**

Quaternary Structure: multiple subunits (folded polypeptide chains) interacting

- Only found in proteins that are composed of more than one polypeptide chain

- Ex. Hemoglobin has 2 alpha subunits and 2 beta subunits

- Held together by same interactions as tertiary structure (disulfide bridges, London dispersion, dipole-dipole, H-bonds, ionic bonds/salt bridges)

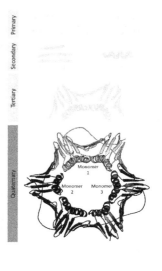

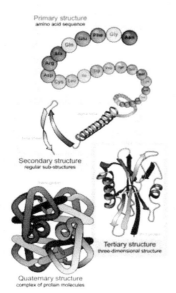

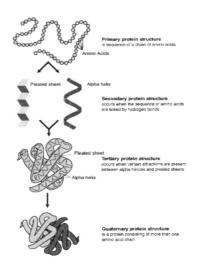

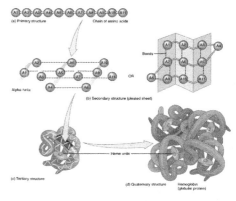

Protein Folding and Denaturing

Protein Folding: the protein's primary structure and the environment it is in (polar versus non-polar) determine what shape the protein will fold into

- Under physiological conditions a protein will fold into its native conformation, which is usually biologically functional
  - Lowest energy state
  - Protein may have more than one native state possible
- Proteins begin folding as they are translated by ribosomes

Denaturation: process by which a protein is unfolded from its native state

- Secondary, tertiary, and quaternary structures are lost (primary isn't)
- Denatured protein can no longer perform its proper function
- Denaturation can occur via changes in: **temperature**, **pH** (adding an acid or base), or chemical environment (adding a **salt** or dramatically changing the polarity of the environment by adding some **organic solvent**)
  - Increases in temperature will generally increase protein activity until the temperature of denaturation is reached, at which point it becomes non-functional
- Usually denaturation is reversible
  - Primary sequence directs protein to refold into the same conformation
  - Chaperones may or may not be required

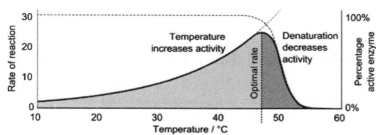

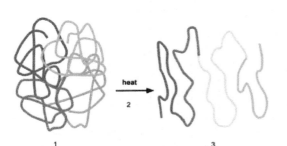

Temperature: molecules move around so rapidly that they break free from ordered structure

pH: salt bridges and H-bonding disrupting by changing residues' protonation state

Salt: disrupts ionic bonds, H-bonds, dipole-dipole

Solvent: disrupts H-bonds and dipole-dipole

Protein Function

Enzymatic proteins:

- Enzymes = protein catalysts → increase the rate of chemical reactions by lowering the reaction's activation energy

- Lowers the activation energy by stabilizing the transition state

- Enzyme may participate in the reaction through transient bonds or IMF, but comes out unchanged

- Substrate = compound the enzyme acts on → enzyme has a specific substrate and only catalyzes a specific reaction (or a few closely related reactions) for that substrate

- Enzyme names usually end in "-ase", and the prefix may indicate what its substrate is

  - Ex. protease, amylase, nuclease

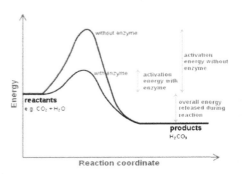

Enzymes are divided into classes, which depict the type of reaction that the enzyme assists in:

- **Oxidoreductase:** catalyze redox reactions (transfers of electrons)

  - Ex. dehydrogenase

- **Transferase:** catalyze reactions in which a group of atoms is transferred from one substrate to another

  - Ex. kinase

- **Lyase:** catalyze reactions in which functional group is added, breaking a double bond (or the reverse)

  - Ex. aldolase

- **Hydrolase:** catalyze hydrolysis reactions (break a molecule with addition of water or form a molecule with removal of water)

  - Ex. lipase

- **Isomerase:** move atoms around on one molecule so that it changes into a new isomer

  - Ex. phosphohexoisomerase

- **Ligase/Synthetase:** catalyze reactions in which two substrates are joined (new C-C, C-O, C-S or C-N bond) and reaction coupled to ATP hydrolysis

  - Ex. DNA ligase

Non-enzymatic proteins have many functions, including transportation, regulation, structural, hormonal, and defense

- **Binding:** proteins have a specific affinity to the molecule that they act on

    - Affinity = how strongly the protein is attracted to/interacts with its target molecule

    - Proteins on the surface of the cell membrane bind to specific substances in the external environment to relay a signal to the inside of the cell or to interact with other cells in the environment

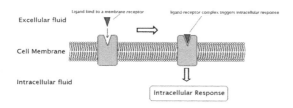

- **Immune system proteins:** antibodies are proteins in the immune system that detect foreign substances (antigens) and mark them for destruction

    - Antigen-antibody specificity is crucial

- **Motor proteins:** enable movement of the entire cell or certain substances with the cell

    - Myosin in muscles enables them to contract

    - Kinesin and dynein use ATP to move along microtubule filament "tracks" and transport substances; dynein also involved in cillia and flagella movement

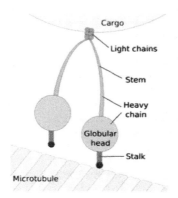

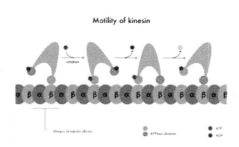

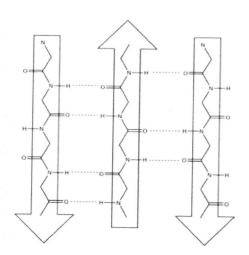

Antiparallel b-sheet

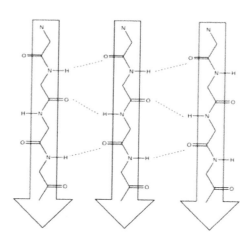

Parallel b-sheet

ENZYMES: ACTIVITY, INHIBITION, AND REGULATION

Biochemistry Lecture 2

OBJECTIVES

- Enzyme-substrate interaction:
  - Active Site Model
  - Induced-fit Model
  - Cooperativity
- Enzyme catalysis mechanisms
  - Helpers: cofactors, coenzymes, vitamins
- Impact of environmental conditions on enzyme activity
- The kinetics of enzyme activity
  - Michaelis-Menten
- Types of enzyme inhibition
  - Competitive
  - Non-competitive
  - Mixed
  - Uncompetitive
- Regulation of enzyme activity
  - Positive and negative feedback
  - Enzymatic forms of regulation

Enzyme-Substrate Interaction

Active Site Model:

- Active site = region of enzyme that substrate binds to (forming the E-S complex) and where catalysis occurs
- 3D shape at that region and chemical interactions from residues to the substrate enable the specificity to that substrate
- Active site model proposes that enzymes and their substrates interact in a "lock and key" fashion → enzyme (lock) has a specific shape that only one substrate (key) will fit into
    - Enzymes are often stereospecific (chiral themselves)

Induced-fit Model:

- This model proposes that the binding of a substrate to its enzyme induces the enzyme to shift its conformation slightly, to one that is even more complementary to the substrate
    - The induced shape change boosts the affinity of the enzyme for the substrate

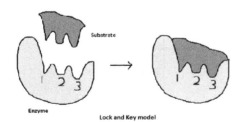

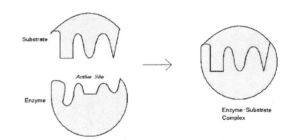

Induced-fit Model - The enzyme active site forms a complementary shape to the substrate after binding

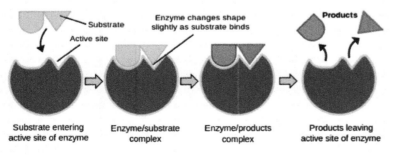

Cooperativity

- Explains how changes in the concentration of the substrate may affect the enzyme's activity
  - Refers to proteins that can bind to more than one of the substrate molecule

- **Positive Cooperativity:** the binding of a substrate to the protein increases the protein's affinity for that substrate, making it easier for more substrates to bind to it
  - Ex. 4 O_2 molecules can bind to 1 hemoglobin protein. After the first O_2 molecule binds to hemoglobin, the 3 other binding sites shift making it easier for the 2nd, 3rd, and 4th O_2 molecules to bind

- **Negative Cooperativity:** once one substrate molecule is bound to the protein, the other binding sites have decreased affinity for subsequent ligands to bind

Enzyme Catalysis: Mechanisms

In general, enzyme lower the energy of the T.S. (make it easier for reactants to reach that state). They do this in a few different ways:

- Enzyme may **preferentially bind to the transition state,** stabilizing it
  - Enzyme interacts more favorably with T.S. than with reactants or products

- **Acid-Base Catalysis:** residues of the enzyme participate in the reaction by donating or accepting hydrogens
  - Enzyme must be regenerated into original form

- **Proximity and Orientation:** enzyme positions the substrates near each other (proximity) and in the correct orientation for them to react

- **Metal Ion Catalysis:** enzyme uses metal ions to assist in catalysis

- **Covalent Catalysis:** residues of the enzyme participate in the reaction by forming temporary covalent bonds with the substrate

Cysteine

Free enzyme   First tetrahedral intermediate   Covalent acyl-enzyme intermediate   Second tetrahedral intermediate   Free enzyme

Serine

Enzyme substrate complex   Tetrahedral intermediate

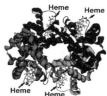

Cofactors: non-protein molecule or ion that helps the enzyme perform its biological function
- Include metals ions, coenzymes, vitamins, prosthetic groups

Metal Ions: required for metal ion catalysis
- Fe^{+2} Fe^{+3} Cu^{+2} Mg^{+2} Mn^{+2} and so on…

Coenzymes: non-protein organic (not metal ions) helper molecules that are loosely associated with the enzyme

Prosthetic groups: non-protein organic helper molecules that are "permanently"/covalently bound to the enzyme
- Ex. Iron of the heme prosthetic group in the center of hemoglobin; required for its function

(Water-soluble) Vitamins: many water soluble vitamins act as cofactors
- May be a precursor to a cofactor or act as a cofactor itself
- Vitamins B (many different types) and C
- Ex. FAD and FMN (electron carriers) made from vitamin B2

Holoenzyme = enzyme complete with its prosthetic groups/cofactors

Enzyme Activity: Environmental Conditions

Temperature:

- Increasing temperature will generally increase enzyme activity until it reaches the temperature at which the protein denatures, at which point the enzyme cannot perform its proper function

pH:

- Enzymes have a specific optimal pH range in which they function best, which depends on their role
- Digestive enzymes, for example, function most optimally at low pH
- Changes in pH will change the protonation state of the protein's residues and disrupt its biological function
- Severe pH changes may denature a protein

Enzyme Kinetics

- Enzymes increase reaction rate by stabilizing the T.S. which lowers the activation energy
  - They impact a kinetic parameter, not a thermodynamic one
  - Enzymes cannot make a non-spontaneous reaction ($\Delta G > 0$) occur, that requires coupling to ATP hydrolysis

Michaelis-Menten:

- $E + S \underset{k_{-1}}{\overset{k_1}{\rightleftharpoons}} ES \overset{k_2}{\rightarrow} E + P$
- k_1 = forward rate constant (formation of ES complex), k_{-1} = reverse rate constant
- Increasing the concentration of the enzyme or substrate will increase the reaction rate because it increases formation of the E-S complex (rate = k[E][S])
- $K_M = (k_2 + k_{-1}) / k_1$

- V_{max} = maximum rate of catalysis when enzyme solution is saturated with substrate
  - $V_{max} = k_2[E]$; k_2 also called k_{cat}
  - Why? Because catalysis (k_2) is the RDS
  - Doesn't depend on [S] because adding more substrate won't increase the maximum rate of the enzymes
  - Depends on [E] because adding more enzymes = more reaction can occur

- V_0 = initial reaction rate

$$V_0 = \frac{vmax[S]}{K_M + [S]}$$

- K_M value equal the substrate concentration required to reach a $v_0 = \frac{1}{2} vmax$
  - When $K_M = [S] \rightarrow v_0 = vmax(1)/(1+1) = \frac{1}{2} vmax$

- K_M is specific for an enzyme and indicates the **binding affinity** of that enzyme for its substrate
  - Higher K_M = lower affinity (more substrate required in order to reach half of its max rate)
  - Lower K_M = higher affinity (less of the substrate is required to reach half $vmax$)

- Efficiency = k_{cat} / K_M = 1/Msec $\rightarrow$ low K_M and high k_{cat} = high efficiency

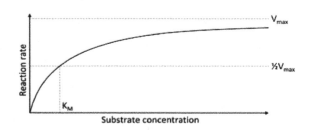

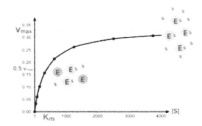

Lineweaver-Burke Plot:

- In order to get a linear plot of rate versus substrate, we can plot the inverse (1/v versus 1/[S])
- Used to determine the impact of inhibitors on enzymes

Slope = $K_m / vmax$

Y-intercept = $1 / vmax$

X-intercept = $-1 / K_M$

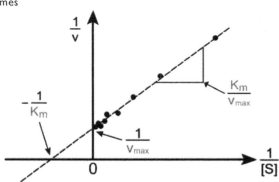

- There are different types of enzyme inhibition
  - Differ in their effect on the binding and/or catalysis mechanisms
  - Differ in how they change (or don't change) $vmax$ and K_M

Competitive Inhibition

- Inhibitor competes with the substrate to bind (reversibly) at the enzyme's active site
  - Inhibitor mimics structure of actual substrate
  - Bind to E, not ES complex
- Competitive inhibition can be overcome by increasing the concentration of the substrate (enabling the substrate to "outcompete" the inhibitor and make its effect negligible)

No change in V$_{max}$
Increase in K$_M$ (because it interferes with the binding of the enzyme to its substrate)

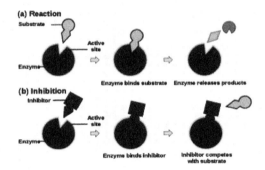

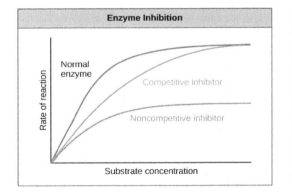

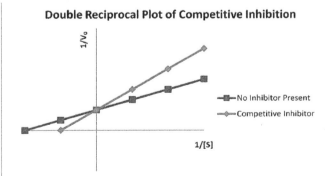

Uncompetitive Inhibition

- Inhibitor binds to the ES complex and reduces the enzyme's catalytic activity
    - Doesn't bind to the active site, so substrate can still bind there
    - Better inhibition when substrate concentration is higher (substrate must be present for it to inhibit)

- ES + I ←→ ESI
    - As the inhibitor binds, forming ESI complexes, Le Chatelier's Principle drives the formation of more ES complexes, resulting in an apparent (and slightly counter-intiutive) decrease in K_M

Decrease in K_M

Decrease in v_{max}

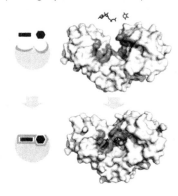

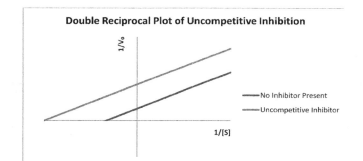

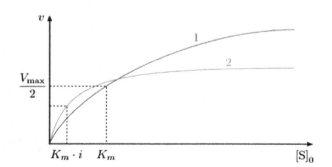

Mixed Inhibitor

- Binds at an allosteric site of the E or ES complex
  - Mix between competitive and uncompetitive inhibition
  - Decreases the maximum reaction rate

- If it acts more like a competitive inhibitor (binds more effectively to E) then it will result in an apparent increase in K_M

- If it acts more like an uncompetitive inhibitor (binds more effectively to ES complex) then it will result in an apparent decrease in K_M

Decrease in v_{max}

Increase OR decrease in K_M

Non-Competitive Inhibition

- Inhibitor binds at a site other than the active site (an allosteric site) and decreases the activity of the enzyme
  - Changes the conformation of the active site, making it less catalytically effective
- Doesn't impact the binding of the substrate to the enzyme
- Can bind to E or ES complex

No change in K_M

Decrease in v_{max}

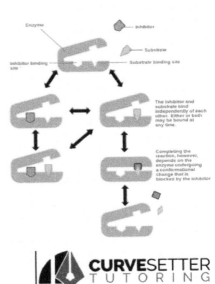

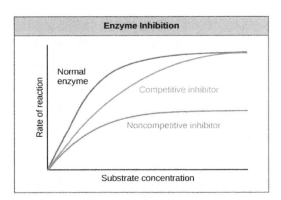

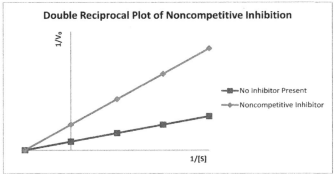

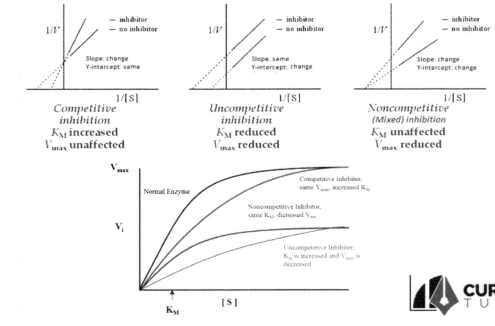

Lineweaver-Burk plots for enzyme inhibition

Feedback Regulation

- A product or later-made compound of a reaction pathway allosterically regulates an earlier enzyme of the pathways
  - feed**back** because regulator goes back to an earlier step of the pathway and increases or decreases the rate of that step (in order to increase or decrease the amount of product that is made)

- **Negative feedback regulation:** A product (or later intermediate) of a metabolic pathway inhibits an earlier step in the pathway
  - When there's already a lot of the product being made and accumulating, the pathway need to slow down in order to conserve energy and resources

- **Positive feedback regulation:** A product (or later intermediate) of a metabolic pathway increases the activity of an earlier enzyme, resulting in even more product being made

Overview of Feedback Inhibition

Feedback inhibition occurs when the biochemical product of a pathway blocks an enzyme in the beginning of the pathway. This occurs when there is a buildup of product/excess of product being produced. Cells use this method to slow down the production, conserve energy and to keep a state of balance (homeostasis) within the cell.

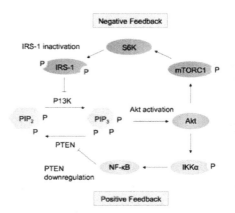

Feedback Inhibition: The final product inhibits enzyme one

Allosteric Enzymes: Enzymes that increase or decrease activity when some compound (allosteric regulator) binds to their allosteric site (a site other than the active site)

- Positive allosteric regulator or negative allosteric regulator
- Binging of the allosteric regulator causes the enzyme to shift its conformation slightly → increases or decreases its affinity for the substrate

Covalently-modified Enzymes: A group of atoms may be covalently added to a protein to change its activity

- Usually another enzyme is required to catalyze this addition/removal
- Phosphorylation/dephosphorylation is the most common type: kinases do the phosphorylation and phosphatases do the dephosphorylation
    - Enables tight control over enzyme activity (like a switch turning them "on" and "off")
- The covalently linked group may increase or decrease the enzyme's activity

Zymogen: the inactive formed of an enzyme which must be modified in some way (usually be cleavage of some region of the zymogen) in order to perform its biological function

- Prevents enzymes from doing damage by performing their function at the wrong time/place
- Digestive enzyme: pepsinogen → pepsin occurs when pepsinogen is exposed to HCl (in a low pH environment)

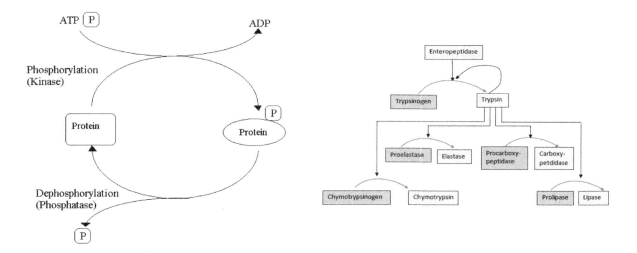

NUCLEIC ACIDS, CARBOHYDRATES, AND LIPIDS

Biochemistry Lecture 3

OBJECTIVES

- Nucleic Acids
  - Structure and function overview
  - Nucleotides and nucleosides
  - Backbone and nitrogenous bases
  - DNA: structure and base pairing
  - RNA structure and function
  - DNA: hybridization, denaturing, annealing
- Carbohydrates
  - Monosaccharides, disaccharides, polysaccharides
  - Stereochemistry (review)
- Lipids
  - Structure and function overview
  - Phospholipids
  - Steroids
  - Terpenes

Nucleic Acids

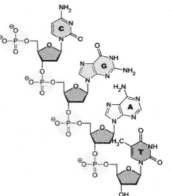

- Nucleic acid = macromolecule (polymer) composed of nucleotide monomers
  - DNA and RNA (mRNA, tRNA, rRNA, snRNA, etc.)

- Roles: DNA carries hereditary genetic information required to build proteins and create and maintain the functioning of an entire organism. RNA also serves as genetic material, as well as having structural, catalytic, and regulatory roles
  - Required by all living organisms as well as viruses

- Structure: linear strand of nucleotides joined by **phosphodiester bonds**
  - May be single stranded or double stranded, with H-bonds linking the two strands

- Nucleic "acid" because of phosphate group (acidic)

Nucleotide = nitrogenous base + sugar + 1-3 phosphates
Nucleoside = nitrogenous base + sugar

- **Nucleic acid backbone =** sugar and phosphate group of each nucleotide linked by phosphodiester bonds (two esters)

- **Glycosidic bond** between sugar and the base

- DNA and RNA differ in the 2' carbon of the sugar: RNA (ribose) has an OH; DNA (deoxyribose) has H

- Base linked to the 1' C of sugar, phosphate linked to 5' C

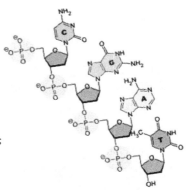

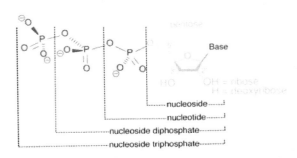

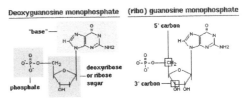

Deoxyguanosine monophosphate   (ribo) guanosine monophosphate

Nitrogenous Bases

Purines: Adenine and Guanine
- Double ring

Pyrimidines: Cytosine, Uracil, Thymine
- Single ring
- Thymine = DNA, Uracil = RNA
- U and T differ in a methyl group
- "Pyramids will CUT you"

* Know these structures *

- Bases allow for the encoding specificity of DNA
    - Sugar-phosphate backbone doesn't change but bases do

adenine

guanine

uracil

thymine

cytosine

"Thymine has a methyl **too**"

Deoxyribonucleic Acid (DNA)

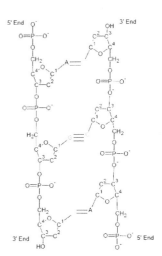

Structure:

- **Double helix** = 2 nucleic acid strands linked by H-bonds between nitrogenous bases (Watson-Crick Model)

- The linked strands are twisted into a **right-handed helix**

- Strands are **"anti-parallel"**: 5' end of one strand is aligned with the 3' end of the other
  - 5' end of strand is where phosphate group (linked to 5' C) is the last group
  - 3' end is where OH (linked to 3' C) marks the end of the strand
  - DNA sequences read/written 5' → 3'

- DNA is built by adding the 5' end of incoming nucleotide to 3' OH of existing strand
  - Pyrophosphate (two phosphates) lost when built from nucleotide triphosphates

Base Pairing:

- Adenine always base pairs with Thymine (with Uracil in RNA → 2 H-bonds

- Cytosine always pairs with Guanine → 3 H-bonds (stronger base pair)

Chargaff's Rule:

- In a DNA double helix, [A] = [T] and [G] = [C]

- So, [A] + [G] = [C] + [T] = 50%

    [purines] = [pyrimidines]

- 1:1 ratio of purines to pyrimidines

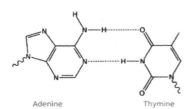

Adenine   Thymine

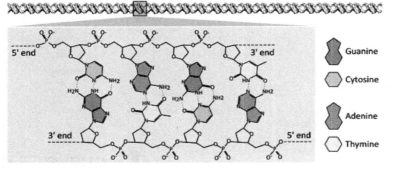

Guanine
Cytosine
Adenine
Thymine

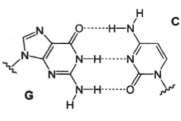

RNA Structure and Function

Structure:

- Usually single stranded
- Single strand may be wound up into a uniquely folded and twisted conformation due to IMF
- Ribose has a 2' OH instead of DNA's 2' H → makes RNA less stable because 2' OH can conduct (intramolecular) nucleophilic attack to the strand and cleave it
    - RNA functions usually more transient than the role of DNA, which requires it to remain stable

Types:

- mRNA = messenger RNA: encode the polypeptide's a.a. sequence, as encoded by the DNA (starts as hnRNA in eukaryotes, then processed to mRNA)
- rRNA = ribosomal RNA: makes up ribosomes
- tRNA = transfer RNA: facilitates the conversion from mRNA → polypeptide chain by carrying and linking a.a.
- snRNA = small nuclear RNA: used in RNA processing
- Ribozyme: any RNA that is capeable of catalysis

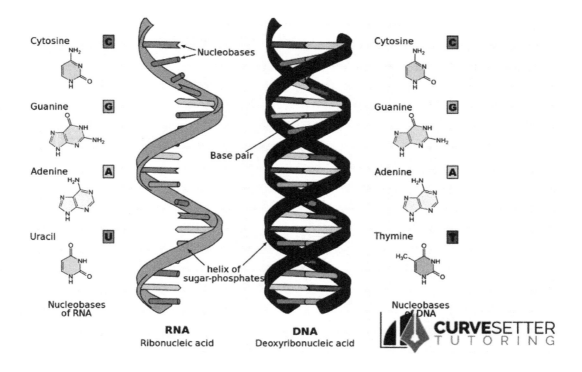

DNA: hybridization, denaturing, annealing

DNA Hybridization/Annealing: Two complementary single strands of DNA (or RNA) come together and bind via H-bonds between the complementary bases

DNA Denaturing: When the H-bonds between bases in DNA are disrupted and the two strands begin to unwind and separate ("melt")
- Usually due to high temperatures
- T_m = melting temperature = temperature at which 50% of the DNA is melted/denatured
- Higher T_m indicated higher CG content

DNA Reannealing: If the conditions that cause denaturation are reversed, DNA strands can join up again

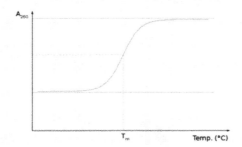
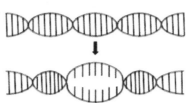

Carbohydrates

Monosaccharides: glucose, fructose, galactose, ribose, deoxyribose

See Organic Chemistry Lecture 4 for more on sugars

Glucose:

Fructose:

Galactose:

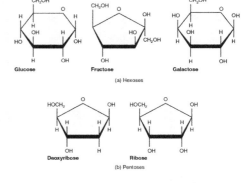

(a) Hexoses

Deoxyribose Ribose

(b) Pentoses

Disaccharides = 2 sugar units

Sucrose = glucose + fructose (beta-1,2)

Lactose = glucose + galactose (beta-1,4)

Maltose = glucose + glucose (alpha-1,4)

Polysaccharide = many sugar units

Cellulose: $\beta(1 \rightarrow 4)$ bonds between glucose units; structural in plants

Starch: $\alpha(1 \rightarrow 4)$ bonds between glucose units energy storage in plants

Glycogen: $\alpha(1 \rightarrow 4)$ bonds between glucose units; energy storage in animals

- Sugars are classified as D/L based on configuration at penultimate carbon (second to last carbon in linear form; last chiral center)

    - D sugars have an R configuration at penultimate carbon
    → Fischer projection of glucose has OH group on the right of penultimate carbon

    - L sugars have an S configuration; L sugars rarely found in nature

    - L and D sugars are enantiomers of each other (every chiral center flips)

- Cyclic sugars are designated as α or β depending on the configuration of the anomeric carbon (Carbon #1; only becomes a stereocenter once molecule is cyclic)

- α sugar: OH of anomeric C and CH2OH groups on OPPOSITE sides of the ring

- β sugar: OH of anomeric C and CH2OH groups on SAME sides of the ring

- α and β sugars are **epimers** (differ at only 1 chiral center); more specifically referred to as **anomers** (epimers that differ at the anomeric C)

α-D-glucopyranose β-D-glucopyranose

Lipids

- Lipids are a broad and diverse category of **non-polar** molecules

- Include: steroids, fat-soluble vitamins (ADEK), waxes, triglycerides, phospholipids

- **Main functions:** energy storage, signaling, and forming cell membranes

Cholesterol

A free fatty acid

A triglyceride

A phospholipid

Phospholipids

- Made up of a polar/hydrophillic "head" (containing phosphate) and two non-polar/hydrophobic "tails" (fatty acids)
  - Amphiphilic = hydrophilic and hydrophobic

- Associate in a spherical bilayer to form cell membrane
  - Hydrophobic tails face the interior of the bilayer (water excluded) while hydrophilic heads face the aqueous cytosol and external environment

- Only small, non-polar molecules (such as O_2 and steroid hormones) can pass directly through the bilayer; larger and polar molecules must be carried by transport proteins
  - Even water requires a protein transporter

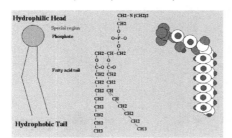
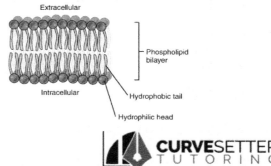

Steroids

- Comprised of 4 connected hydrocarbon rings (6, 6, 6, 5), called the steroid ring system, with different attached functional groups

- Main functions: signaling (steroid hormones) and structural (cholesterol in cell membranes)

- Steroid hormones are derived from cholesterol (more specifically, cholesterol is a sterol- a steroid with an alcohol)

- Cortisol, aldosterone, testosterone, estrogen, progesterone, etc.

Estrogen:

Cholesterol:

Terpenes and Terpenoids

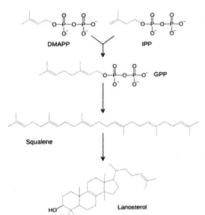

- Terpene: hydrocarbon with the basic formula $(C_5H_8)_n$
  - Terpenes are made up of multiple linked isoprenes (isoprene C_5H_8)
  - Terpenoid = terpene with additional functional groups

- Role: terpenes (specifically squalene) can be used in the synthesis of cholesterol and steroids

isoprene

Squalene:

GLYCOLYSIS, GLUCONEOGENESIS, AND THE PENTOSE PHOSPHATE PATHWAY

Biochemistry Lecture 4

OBJECTIVES

- Bioenergetics Basics
  - ATP hydrolysis and reaction coupling
  - Phosphoryl group transfers
  - Cellular respiration overview
- Glycolysis
  - Substrates, products, and the pathway
  - Pathway regulation
  - Glycogen and starch metabolism
- Anaerobic Conditions
  - Fermentation: alcohol and lactic acid
- Gluconeogenesis
  - Substrates, products, and the pathway
  - Enzymes involved in irreversible steps
  - Glycolysis and gluconeogenesis: reciprocal regulation
- Pentose Phosphate Pathway

Bioenergetics

Adenosine Triphosphate (ATP):
- The "energy currency" of cells
- Nucleotide: composed of a nitrogenous base (adenine), sugar (ribose), and phosphate groups
- The **phosphoanhydride bonds** are very high energy → when broken
  a lot of energy is released (highly spontaneous nature of the hydrolysis)
  - ATP + H2O → ADP + Pi $\Delta G° \approx$ -30 kJ/mol
    - ΔG = -57 kJ/mol under non standard conditions in the cell
  - ATP + H2O → AMP + PPi $\Delta G° \approx$ -46 kJ/mol

Phosphoanhydride bond hydrolysis is so exergonic because...
1. Electrostatic repulsion between the negatively charged phosphate groups makes ATP unstable; ADP and AMP are therefore more stable (lower energy) molecules because they have less of this repulsive strain
2. ADP + Pi have overall more resonance stabilization than ATP does
3. ADP + Pi are higher in entropy than ATP

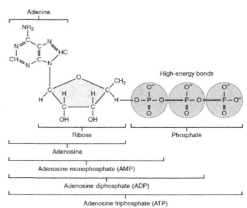

$$P_i = PO_4^{-3}$$

- ATP is considered a coenzyme in the metabolic pathways of cellular respiration
- It is often associated with Mg^{+2}, which stabilizes it
- ATP and AMP are often allosteric regulators of enzymes involved in these pathways
- ATP is also involved in RNA synthesis (it is a nucleotide after all!)
- Phosphorylation of enzymes (done by kinases) can be used to regulate enzymes; like an "on" and "off" switch

Reaction coupling:

- Hydrolysis of ATP releases energy in the form of heat; this energy can be harnessed through reaction coupling
- Reaction coupling occurs when two reactions, one spontaneous and one non-spontaneous, are "added together" to yield a net reaction that is spontaneous (overall negative ΔG)
    - $\Delta G_1 = 20$ kJ/mol, $\Delta G_2 = -57$ kJ/mol $\rightarrow$ $\Delta G_{net} = -37$ kJ/mol
- Usually a phosphate group from ATP is transferred to one of the substrate molecules (phosphoryl group transfer), yielding a phosphorylated intermediate whose hydrolysis is spontaneous (releasing P_i)

Phosphoryl group transfers: one of the phosphate groups of ATP can be transferred to another substrate to make an unfavorable reaction favorable

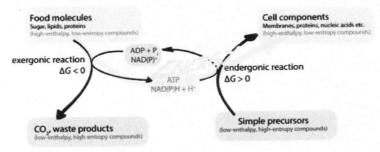

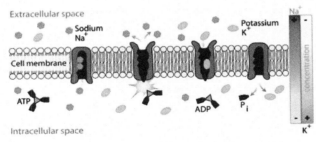

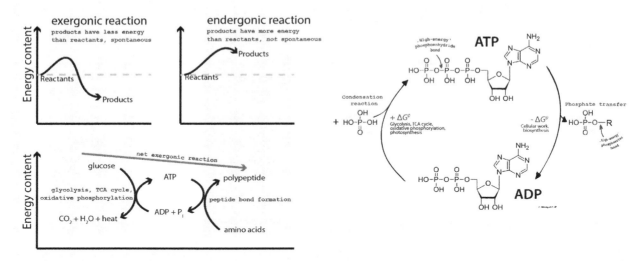

Cellular Respiration Overview

- Cellular respiration = the metabolic pathways that convert energy from food nutrients (carbohydrates, fats, proteins) into energy stored in ATP
- Aerobic respiration = Glycolysis + PDH complex + Citric Acid (TCA) Cycle + Oxidative Phosphorylation
- Overall: $C_6H_{12}O_6 + 6O_2 \rightarrow 6CO_2 + 6H_2O$

    oxidized   reduced

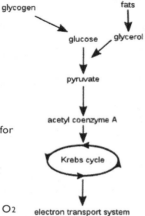

- Glycolysis: occurs in cytoplasm, doesn't require O_2
- PDH Complex/PDC (pyruvate dehydrogenase complex): occurs in mitochondrial matrix for eukaryotes, cytosol for prokaryotes; indirectly requires O_2
- Citric Acid/Kreb's/TCA Cycle: occurs in mitochondrial matrix for eukaryotes, cytosol for prokaryotes; indirectly requires O_2
- Oxidative Phosphorylation: occurs in mitochondrial IMS for eukaryotes; directly requires O_2

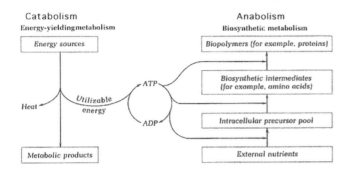

Catabolism
Energy-yielding metabolism

Anabolism
Biosynthetic metabolism

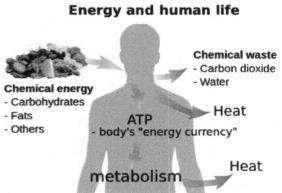

Energy and human life

Chemical energy
- Carbohydrates
- Fats
- Others

Chemical waste
- Carbon dioxide
- Water

ATP
- body's "energy currency"

Heat

metabolism

Heat

Catabolism: breaking larger molecules (polymers) into smaller ones (monomers), releasing energy

Anabolism: Building larger molecules from smaller precursors, requiring energy

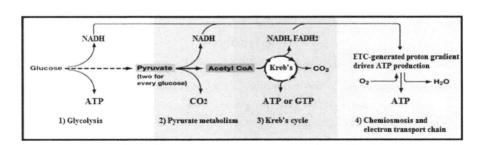

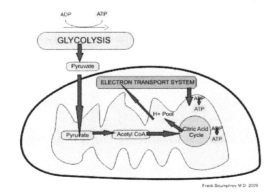

Frank Boumphrey M.D. 2009

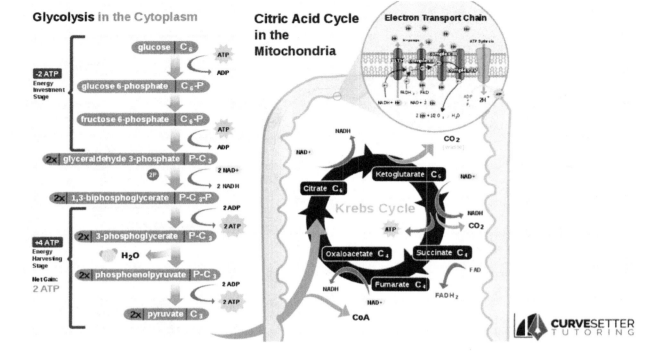

Glycolysis

- Glucose + 2ADP + 2P$_i$ + 2NAD$^+$ → 2pyruvate + 2ATP + 2NADH + 2H$_2$O + 2H$^+$

- All living things utilize glycolysis for energy production (no oxygen required)

- 2 phases: energy investment phase uses up 2 ATP per glucose; energy output phase makes 4 ATP and 2 NADH per glucose → NET 2 ATP and 2 NADH made

    - NADH is the reduced form of NAD$^+$ and is an electron carrier molecule (like FADH$_2$) that drops e- into the electron transport chain during oxidative phosphorylation

- Anaerobic conditions: PDC, Kreb's cycle, and oxidative phosphorylation stop → glycolysis speeds up to compensate

- Overall, glucose (6-C sugar) is broken into 2 3-C sugars called pyruvate

    - Energy input phase breaks glucose into 2 3-C sugars (DHAP and G3-P) and requires 2 ATP per glucose for the phosphorylation steps

    - DHAP & G3-P → 2 x G3-P (G3-P is more stable than DHAP)

    - G3-P → pyruvate (energy output phase) releases 1 NADH and 2 ATP per G3-P and occurs twice per glucose

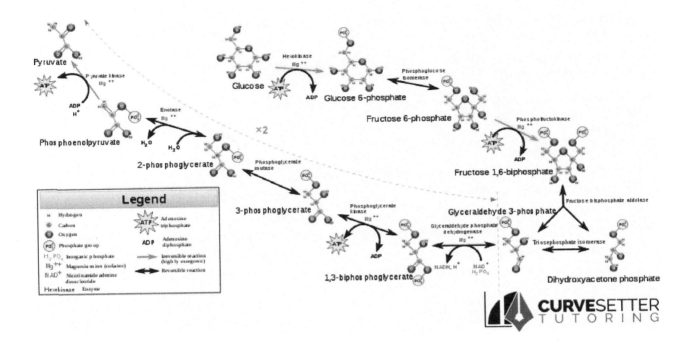

Legend

H	Hydrogen	ATP	Adenosine triphosphate
C	Carbon	ADP	Adenosine diphosphate
O	Oxygen		
PO₄	Phosphate group		Irreversible reaction (highly exergonic)
H₂PO₄	Inorganic phosphate		Reversible reaction
Mg⁺⁺	Magnesium ion (cofactor)		
NAD⁺	Nicotinamide adenine dinucleotide		
Hexokinase	Enzyme		

- Glucose $\xrightarrow{Hexokinase}$ G 6-P occurs in order to jumpstart glycolysis by trapping G 6-P in the cell
  - Phosphoryl group transfer; spontaneous because coupled to ATP hydrolysis

- G 6-P → F 6-P occurs via phosphoglucose **isomerase**

- F 6-P $\xrightarrow{Phosphofructo\ kinase}$ Fructose-1,6-Bisphosphate is another phosphoryl group transfer, coupled to ATP hydrolysis
  - Rate determining step of glycolysis; also referred to as the "committed step"

- Fructose-1,6-Bisphosphate is then split into 2 3-C sugars, dihydroxyacetone phosphate (DHAP) and glyceraldehyde-3-phosphate (G3P); only G3P can be used in the next step so DHAP must be converted into G3P via an isomerase

- G3P is then oxidized (aldehyde oxidized to a carboxyl group) to 1,3-Bisphophoglycerate, and the e- it loses are used to reduce NAD⁺ to **NADH**
  - Energy released by the redox reaction is used to incorporate an P_i to the molecule at carbon 1

- Phosphoglycerate **kinase** transfers a phosphate group from 1,3-Bisphosphoglyerate to ADP, forming ATP (substrate-level phosphorylation)

- 3-Phosphoglycerate → 2-Phosphoglycerate (isomers)

- 2-Phosphoglycerate is converted into phospho**enol**pyruvate (PEP) by **enol**ase, through the removal of a water molecule

- Pyruvate kinase transfers a phosphate group from PEP to ADP, forming another ATP molecule via substrate-level phosphorylation, and the end molecule pyruvate

- "**Irreversible steps**" of glycolysis are those that have large negative ΔG values and cannot be easily reversed
  - Steps 1, 3, and 10 are irreversible

Glycolysis Regulation

- Hexokinase is inhibited by its product, G6-P (feedback inhibition)
- Phosphofructokinase is inhibited by ATP (if cell already has a lot of ATP, glycolysis should slow down) and by citrate (an intermediate of TCA cycle)
- Phosphofructokinase is activated by ADP/AMP (if ADP/AMP are abundant, ATP is scarce and glycolysis needs to run) and by fructose 2,6-bisphosphate
- Pyruvate kinase is activated when fructose 1,6-bisphosphate builds up (if first half of glycolysis is running quickly, then the second half needs to keep up)

Glycogen Metabolism:

* Glycogen is a highly branched polymer of glucose that is readily broken down into glucose monomers, which then enter glycolysis

    * Glycogen stored in liver and skeletal muscle
    * Muscle glycogen primarily used as a source of glucose during bursts of activity (the glucose mobilized is used by the muscle themselves)
    * Liver glycogen used to mobilize glucose during a fasted state in order to maintain the blood glucose level

* **Glycogenolysis** = metabolizing glycogen into glucose monomers

$$glycogen \xrightarrow{glycogen\ phosphorylase} G\text{-}1\text{-}P \rightarrow G\text{-}6\text{-}P \xrightarrow{glucose-6-phosphatase} glucose$$

    * Occurs when blood glucose level low; glucagon and epinephrine trigger
    * G-6-P → glucose (released into bloodstream) only occurs in liver

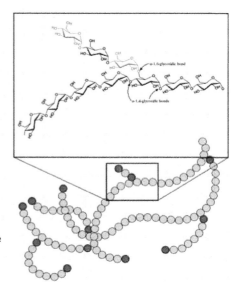

* **Glycogenesis** = forming glycogen from glucose

    * $glucose \xrightarrow{hexokinase} G\text{-}6\text{-}P \rightarrow G\text{-}1\text{-}P + UTP \rightarrow$ **UDP-glucose** $\xrightarrow{glycogen\ synthase} glycogen$

* Occurs when blood glucose level is high → insulin released by pancreas triggers glycogenesis

* Glucose monomers added one to one onto the growing chain

* UTP = source of energy and "activates" the incoming glucose monomer, which can only be added to the chain as UDP-glucose

Glucose metabolism

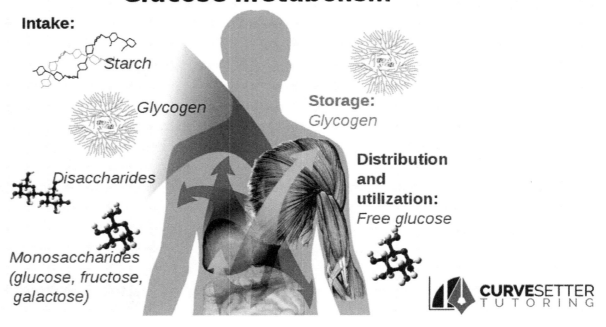

Intake:
Starch
Glycogen
Disaccharides
Monosaccharides
(glucose, fructose, galactose)

Storage:
Glycogen

Distribution and utilization:
Free glucose

Starch Metabolism:

- Starch is the main carbohydrate in humans' diet (rice, corn, potatoes, wheat, etc.)
- Amylase (enzyme in saliva) breaks down starch into maltose (glucose-glucose disaccharide), which can then be broken down into glucose monomers
- Starch is composed of amylose and amylopectin
    - Amylose is unbranched; $\alpha(1 \rightarrow 4)$ glycosidic bonds between glucose monomers
    - Amylopectin is branched; $\alpha(1 \rightarrow 6)$ glycosidic bonds at branch points

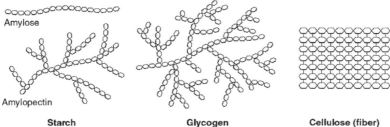

Amylose

Amylopectin

Starch   Glycogen   Cellulose (fiber)

Anaerobic Conditions

- Anaerobic conditions = limited/no oxygen available; cell cannot do PDH complex reactions, Kreb's cycle, or oxidative phosphorylation → glycolysis is the only method to make ATP

- In order for glycolysis to continue running, NAD^+ must be regenerated (it is reduced to NADH in glycolysis) because it is a substrate of the GAPDH enzyme

- Pyruvate accepts e- from NADH, becoming reduced to lactate or ethanol, while NADH is oxidized to NAD^+

- NADH + pyruvate → NAD^+ + lactate/ethanol

  e-   glycolysis

- Lactic acid fermentation occurs in humans

- Alcoholic fermentation occurs in yeast

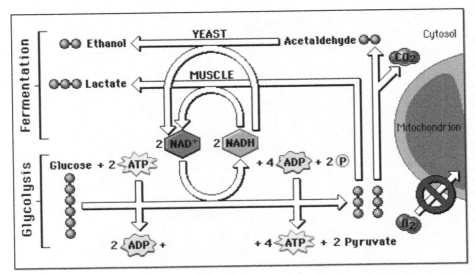

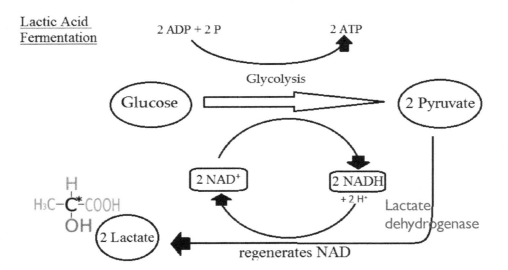

Lactic Acid Fermentation

2 ADP + 2 P → 2 ATP

Glycolysis

Glucose → 2 Pyruvate

2 NAD⁺   2 NADH + 2 H⁺

Lactate dehydrogenase

$H_3C-\overset{H}{\underset{OH}{C^*}}-COOH$

2 Lactate   regenerates NAD

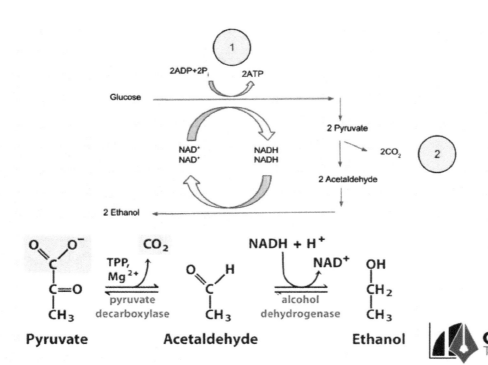

2ADP+2Pᵢ   2ATP

1

Glucose

NAD⁺   NADH
NAD⁺   NADH

2 Pyruvate

2CO₂   2

2 Acetaldehyde

2 Ethanol

Pyruvate — TPP, Mg²⁺, pyruvate decarboxylase → CO₂ → Acetaldehyde — NADH + H⁺, NAD⁺, alcohol dehydrogenase → Ethanol

Pyruvate   Acetaldehyde   Ethanol

Gluconeogenesis

- Making new glucose from other substrates such as amino acids, lactate, Kreb's cycle intermediates, etc.
  - Anabolic pathway → requires ATP

- Cycle is the reverse as glycolysis
  - Enzymes used in the reversible steps of glycolysis and are also used in gluconeogenesis; enzymes used in the irreversible steps of glycolysis require a different enzyme for gluconeogenesis

- Operates in the liver and kidneys

- Blood glucose level must stay within a very constant range: **homeostasis**
  - In **fed state**: glucose consumed in food goes into glycolysis to make ATP; excess glucose stored as glycogen (glycogenesis)
  - In an **initially fasted state**: glycogenolysis runs in order to degrade stored glycogen and release glucose monomers in the blood
  - In a **long-term fasted state**: stored glycogen runs out in less than 24 hours; gluconeogenesis must run in order to create new glucose

- Requires 4 ATP, 2 GTP, 2 NADH per glucose made (2 ATP, 1 GTP, 1 NADH per pyruvate used)

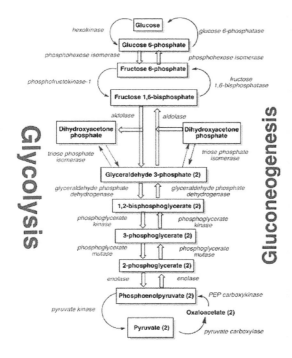

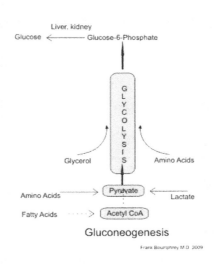

Gluconeogenesis

Enzymes of irreversible steps:

Glycolysis	Gluconeogenesis
Hexokinase	Glucose-6-phosphatase
Phosphofructokinase	Fructose-1,6-bisphosphatase
Pyruvate kinase	Pyruvate carboxylase and PEP carboxykinase

- Only glucose (uncharged) can cross the cell membrane and enter the bloodstream (not glucose-6-phosphate)

- Glucose-6-phosphatase is required in order to remove the phosphate from G-6-P

- Only found (in discernable quantities) in the liver therefore the liver releases majority of glucose into the bloodstream
  - Without this enzyme → hypoglycemic

- Precursors to gluconeogenesis:
  - "glucogenic" amino acids: all except leucine and lysine
  - Lactate
  - Oxaloacetate
  - Glycerol (from triglycerides)

Reciprocal Regulation

- Glycolysis and gluconeogenesis are reciprocally regulated → the same substrate regulates opposing enzymes oppositely
  - One substrate will inhibit an enzyme of glycolysis while activating an enzyme of gluconeogenesis (or vice versa)
  - Overall impact is that when one of the pathways is being strongly activated, the other is inhibited

- Occurs at the later 2 irreversible steps of the cycles: F-6-P ↔ F-1,6-BP and PEP ↔ Pyruvate

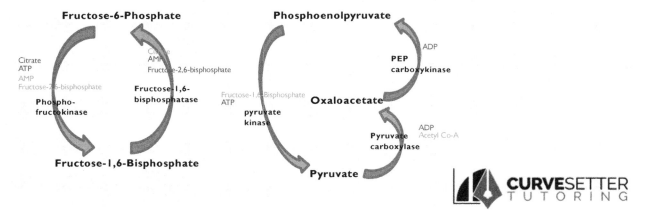

Pentose Phosphate Pathway (PPP)

- Pathway that uses G-6-P (diverted away from glycolysis) as a substrate to make NADPH, ribose-5-phosphate, and other pentoses

- **Ribose-5-phosphate** required in order to make nucleotides for DNA/RNA

- **NADPH** (don't mix up with NADH) has a role of being an e- donor in the cell (gets oxidized; is a reducing agent)
  - Required for many anabolic reactions, such as **fatty acid synthesis**
  - Used to **reduce antioxidants**, thereby regenerating them
  - Very important in red blood cells

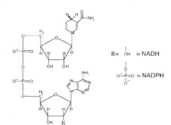

- Occurs in the cytosol of cells (linked to glycolysis)

- Doesn't use or require any ATP

- Flexible pathway; depends entirely on the immediate needs of the cell

Two phases of the pathway
- **Oxidative Phase:** Forms NADPH and ribulose-5-P; irreversible reactions

- **Non-oxidative Phase:** Forms ribose-5-phosphate and other glycolytic intermediates; reversible reactions

  - The glycolytic intermediates that are involved (F-6-P and G-3-P) may leave the PPP and enter glycolysis, depending on the needs of the cells)

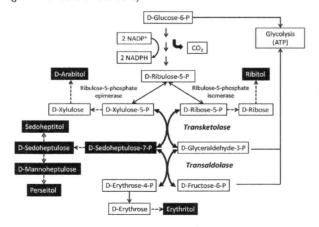

THE CITRIC ACID CYCLE AND OXIDATIVE PHOSPHORYLATION

Biochemistry Lecture 5

OBJECTIVES

- The Pyruvate Dehydrogenase Complex
  - The enzyme complex and its cofactors
  - Reaction of the PDC and regulation
- The Citric Acid Cycle
  - Reactions, intermediates, and enzymes of the pathway
  - Regulation of the cycle
  - Net energetic results
- Oxidative Phosphorylation
  - Review of biological redox
  - Substrates, products, and enzymes of the ETC
  - Proton gradient/proton motive force
  - ATP synthase protein and chemiosmosis
  - Regulation of Oxidative Phosphorylation
- Apoptosis and oxidative stress

The Pyruvate Dehydrogenase Complex

- The PDH Complex/PDC is a complex of three enzymes that facilitates the pyruvate decarboxylation reactions, turning pyruvate (product of glycolysis) into acetyl CoA (substrate of Krebs Cycle)

- Pyruvate + CoA-SH (Coenzyme A) + NAD$^+$ → Acetyl CoA + CO_2 + NADH + H$^+$

- Pyruvate is oxidized and NAD$^+$ is reduced; decarboxylation occurs (oxidative decarboxylation)

- Acetyl CoA is an acetyl group attached to Coenzyme A, which functions to deliver the acetyl to the Krebs Cycle

- NADH will be used to make ATP

- PDC consists of three complexes (abbreviated E1, E2, and E3), each of which carries out a different reaction

- Cofactors: NAD$^+$; prosthetic groups (bound to the enzyme): TPP (vitamin B1) , FAD, lipoic acid

Regulation of the PDC:

- Low energy charge (high AMP or ADP)
- High levels of pyruvate
- PDH Phosphatase is an enzyme that turns the PDC "on"

Inhibited by:
- High ratio of ATP/ADP (high energy charge)
- High ratio of NADH/NAD$^+$
- Acetyl CoA (feedback inhibition)
- PDH Kinase turns the complex "off"

Location:
- In eukaryotes, pyruvate is produced in the cytoplasm and is then transported to the mitochondrial matrix, where the PDC resides
- In prokaryotes, the PDC complex exists in the cytoplasm

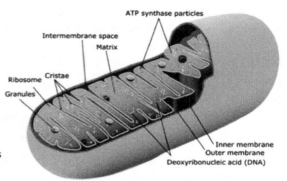

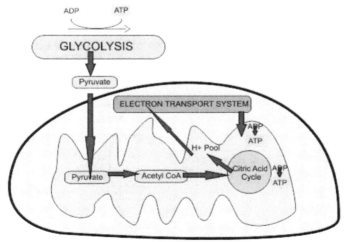

Frank Boumphrey M.D. 2009

The Citric Acid Cycle

- TCA Cycle/Kreb's Cycle/Citric Acid Cycle is a series of reactions used in aerobic respiration to produce energy precursor molecules (which will then be used in oxidative phosphorylation to produce ATP)

- Acetyl CoA is the initial substrate and oxaloacetate (OAA) is the final "product" of the cycle; OAA can feed back into the cycle and combine with the acetyl group of acetyl CoA to form citrate, the first intermediate

- Net production (per glucose molecule/per 2 pyruvates): **6 NADH, 2 FADH₂, 2 GTP, 4 CO₂**
  - In one turn of the cycle you form half of the above quantities, but the cycle occurs twice per glucose because 1 glucose forms 2 pyruvates in glycolysis

- Energy equivalency: 1 NADH ≈ 2.5 ATP
  1 FADH₂ ≈ 1.5 ATP } Conversion occurs in oxidative phosphorylation; equivalency depends on how many H⁺ are pumped as a result of NADH and FADH₂ entering the ETC
  1 GTP ≈ 1 ATP → conversion occurs via substrate level phosphorylation

- Glucose (6C) → 2 x pyruvate (3C) → 2 CO₂ + 2 Acetyl CoA (2C)
- 1 Acetyl CoA (2C) + 1 OAA (4C) → 1 citrate (6C) → → → → 2 CO₂ + 1 OAA (4C)

- TCA cycle occurs in the mitochondrial matrix of eukaryotes and the cytoplasm of prokaryotes

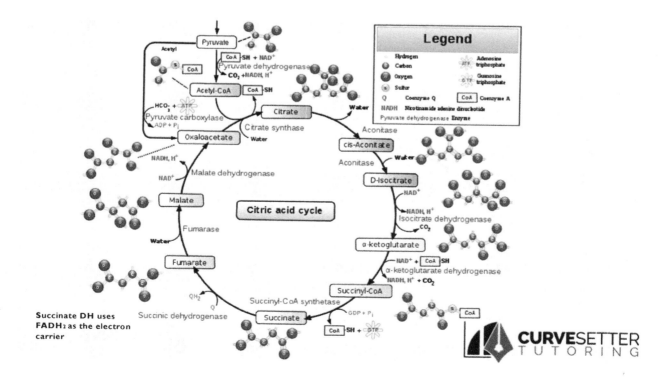

Succinate DH uses FADH₂ as the electron carrier

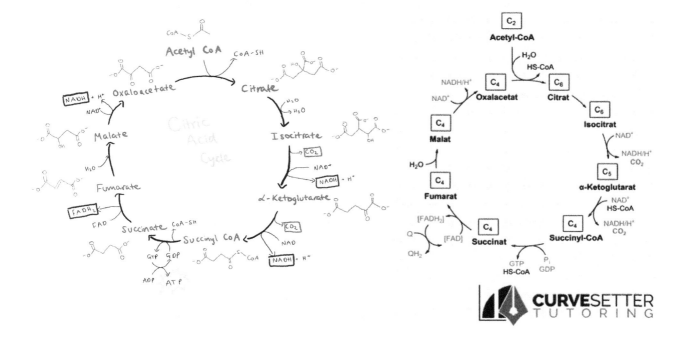

- It is important to be able to track the carbons as they cycle through glycolysis, PDC, and TCA cycle → carbon tracing will require this understanding

- Citrate is not chiral but is asymmetrically converted to isocitrate (only one of the isomers) due to the specificity of aconitase
  - Hydroxyl group added to CH_2 from OAA not from acetyl CoA

- Decarboxylation occurs with isocitrate DH and α-ketoglutarate DH; the carbons removed are those that were from the OAA, not the acetyl CoA
  - Oxidative decarboxylation because NAD^+ reduced to NADH and carbon oxidized

- In succinate, 2 or the carbons are from the original OAA and 2 are from the acetyl CoA

- Starting with OAA, after 1 turn of the TCA cycle, 50% of its carbons remain and 50% have been lost as CO_2; after 2 turns of the cycle 25% of the original carbons remain
  - Using radioactively tagged OAA you could track and quantify the fluorescence

- Intermediates may be diverted away from the TCA cycle for other uses (gluconeogenesis, for example); to keep the cycle running, OAA must be replaced

- Pyruvate carboxylase is an enzyme that converts pyruvate (from glycolysis) into OAA
  - Requires 1 ATP and 1 CO_2 per pyruvate used/OAA produced

- Pyruvate + ATP + CO_2 → OAA

Pyruvate   Pyruvate carboxylase   Oxaloacetate

Regulation of TCA Cycle:

- A key point of regulation is control over how much Acetyl CoA is present → PDC regulated (see earlier slide)
- In general, the TCA cycle slows when energy charge is high (a lot of ATP), when the NADH:NAD$^+$ ratio is high, and due to feedback inhibition

  - Succinyl-CoA inhibits $\propto$-ketoglutarate DH and citrate synthase
  - Citrate inhibits citrate synthase

Net energetic results, per glucose:

- Glycolysis- 2 ATP, 2 NADH ($\approx$ 7 ATP)
- PDC- 2 NADH ($\approx$ 5 ATP)
- TCA Cycle- 6 NADH, 2 GTP, 2 $FADH_2$ ($\approx$ 20 ATP)
- Total $\approx$ 32 ATP / glucose

- In eukaryotes the 2 NADH of glycolysis must be transported into the mitochondrial matrix in order to be useful for the ETC. The glycerol phosphate shuttle achieves this but at the expense of losing $\approx$ 2 ATP

  - e- of NADH → $FADH_2$; $FADH_2$ are "worth" less ATP than NADH because the electrons of $FADH_2$ enter the ETC at a later point and therefore contribute less to the proton motive force

- Therefore, net energetic result: Prokaryotes $\approx$ 32 ATP   Eukaryotes $\approx$ 30 ATP

Biological Redox

Electron carriers:

- The ETC consists of multiple of electron carriers, which are molecules (some protein, some not) that can accept and then donate e- in a series of redox reactions
- The electron carriers may be characterized as water soluble or lipid soluble
    - Lipid-soluble carriers are embedded in the mitochondrial inner-membrane
    - Quinones (aromatic molecules) are lipid soluble and mobile electron carriers. Specifically, **ubiquinone/Coenzyme Q** is in the ETC.
    - Cytochromes are pigment molecules that contain iron and are also commonly e- carriers. In the ETC, **cytochrome c** is a water soluble and mobile e- carrier that shuttles e- between other embedded proteins. There are also immobile cytochromes embedded in protein complexes 3 and 4 of the ETC.

Flavoproteins: proteins that contain flavin molecules such as FAD and FMN, which often serve as redox prosthetic groups
- Complex II of the ETC (succinate dehydrogenase) has an FAD prosthetic group that gets reduced to FADH2 during the TCA Cycle (when succinate is oxidized to fumarate)

Reduction potential ($\varepsilon°$): measures the tendency of a molecule to be reduced

Oxidative Phosphorylation

- The series of reactions through which electron carriers (NADH, FADH2) are **oxidized** in order to create energy in the form of a proton gradient that can be harnessed by to make ATP via substrate level **phosphorylation**

    - "ETC" refers to the electron transport chain in which e- are passed between carrier molecules and/or proteins

    - Chemiosmosis refers to the process used by ATP synthase to harness the energy in an ion gradient

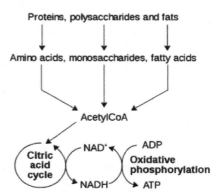

ETC and the Proton Gradient

- Electrons are passed to electron carriers in the order of increasing reduction potential
  - positive $\varepsilon°$ of the redox reaction = $-\Delta G$ → spontaneous
    - The final electron carrier is O_2 which gets reduced to H_2O

- The highly spontaneous/exergonic electron transport reactions are couple to the (non-spontaneous) pumping of H^+ from an area of low concentration (mitochondrial matrix) to are area of high concentration (inner-membrane space)
  - This proton gradient is a source of stored chemical energy, which can be harnessed when the H^+ are allowed to flow back down the gradient (from the IMS back into the matrix)
  - The mitochondrial inner-membrane is not permeable to H^+, so the gradient is sustained

- Protons are allowed to flow only through ATP synthase; the energy released by diffusing this gradient is converted to mechanical energy of ATP synthase and enables substrate-level phosphorylation to occur

Components of the ETC:

Complex I: Receives e- from NADH and passes them to ubiquinone

Coenzyme Q/Ubiquinone: Receives e- from complexes I and II and passes them on to complex III
- Mobile and lipid soluble (embedded in mitochondrial IM)

Complex II/Succinate DH: Receives e- from succinate of the TCA cycle

Complex III: Receives e- from ubiquinone and passes them to cytochrome c

Cytochrome c: Receives e- from complex III and passes them to complex IV
- Mobile and water soluble

Complex IV: Receives e- from cytochrome c and passes them to O_2, reducing it to form H_2O

Uncouplers:
- Uncouplers are substances that allow H^+ ions through the mitochondrial inner-membrane, thereby diffusing the proton gradient but not harnessing the energy to make ATP

- What are the affects of adding an uncoupler protein?

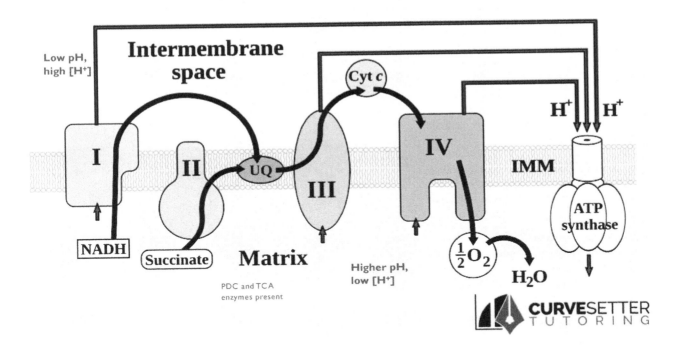

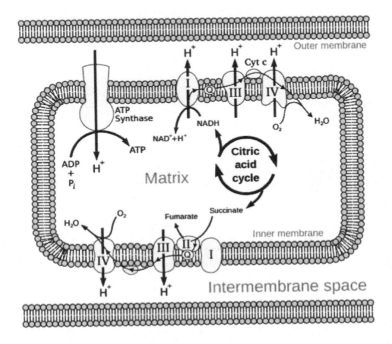

ATP Synthase

- Located in the inner-mitochondrial membrane

- Harnesses the stored energy in the proton gradient (electrochemical gradient) to make ATP through substrate level phosphorylation

- As H⁺ ion flow through the ATP synthase channel, the protein rotates like a molecular motor and joins together ADP + Pi

- All proteins of the ETC as well as ATP synthase are located in the cell membrane of prokaryotes (lack mitochondria)

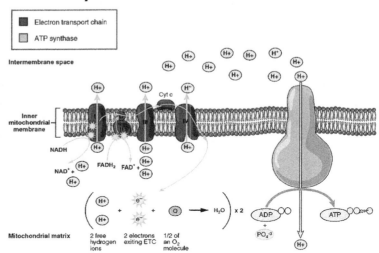

Regulation of Oxidative Phosphorylation:
- The ratio of ATP/ADP within the mitochondrial IMS functions as a method to control the activity of ATP synthase
  → high levels of ATP result in allosteric inhibition of ATP synthase
- It is also regulated by the availability of substrates of the ETC/ATP synthase (NADH, FADH2, ADP, O2)

Oxidative Stress: Occurs when there are many reactive oxygen species (ROS) and not enough antioxidant species to defend against them
- ROS = O_2^-, OH (hydroxyl radical), and H2O2 → natural byproducts as a result of metabolic processes involving oxygen, such as oxidative phosphorylation
- ROS cause damage to proteins, lips, and the bases of DNA/RNA (take e- away from other molecules, cause DNA strand breaks, etc.)
- Oxidative stress is involved in numerous diseases such as cancer, Alzheimer's, ADHD, autism, and more
- Oxidative stress can trigger **apoptosis** (programmed cell death)

FATTY ACID AND PROTEIN METABOLISM

Biochemistry Lecture 6

OBJECTIVES

- Fatty Acids
  - Description
  - Mobilization and use of fats in the body
- Fatty Acid Oxidation
  - Enzymes, reactions, and energetic results
- Fatty Acid Synthesis
  - Enzymes, substrates, and reactions
- Ketogenesis
  - Ketone bodies and their usage
  - Keto acidosis
- Protein metabolism
  - Peptide bond hydrolysis (polypeptide → amino acids)
  - Amino acid catabolism
  - Products of amino acid catabolism and their uses

Fatty Acids

- **Fatty acid** = carboxylic acid with a long hydrocarbon tail (commonly around 8-26 carbons)

- **Saturated** fatty acid: contain no double bonds (saturated with hydrogens)
  - Usually solid at room temperature

- **Unsaturated** fatty acid: contain one or more double bonds
  - Results in hydrocarbon chain being bent/kinked → less London dispersion forces than saturated fats → usually liquid at room temperature
  - **Cis/trans:** designates the conformation of the double bond; H atoms of the unsaturated carbons on the same side of the double bond = cis

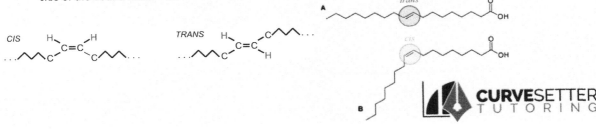

- Fatty acids are important sources of fuel, and also serve as precursor molecules to phospholipids, prostaglandins (regulate inflammation in the body), etc.
  - As a source of fuel they are broken down via **fatty acid/beta oxidation**
  - Compared to glycogen, fats have higher energy density (9 kcal/g versus 4 kcal/g)

- Fatty acids can be mobilized by the break down of stored triglycerides, and can be synthesized via fatty acid synthesis

- Most fatty acids our body can synthesize; essential fatty acids cannot be made from other substrates and must be acquired from our diet (omega 3 and 6)

- Fat is humans' main source of stored fuel; glycogen stores are depleted within a day, and after this point we rely on fats to provide energy to all our cells
  - In animals there isn't a mechanism to convert fats into glucose

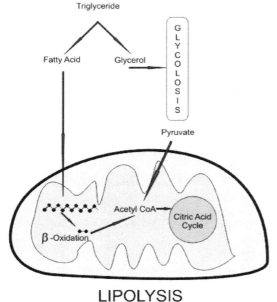

LIPOLYSIS

Frank Boumphrey M.D. 2009

Fat digestion:

- **Lipases** cleave triglycerides (usually in adipocytes) into fatty acids and glycerol

- Free fatty acids travel in the bloodstream attached to the protein albumin

- Fatty acids can be used for fuel by all cells except RBCs (no mitochondria) and cells of the central nervous system (long chain fatty acids are unable to cross the blood brain barrier that encases the CNS)

Fatty Acid (β) Oxidation

- Overall, fatty acids undergo a repeated series of 4 reactions (one cycle), to liberate **1 acetyl CoA, 1 FADH2, and 1 NADH** per "turn" of the cycle
    - Each turn of the cycle cleaves 2 carbons (which become acetyl CoA) from the activated fatty acid chain, then the rest of the chain re-enters the cycle
    - Acetyl CoA then enters the TCA cycle

- Fatty acid must first be **activated** before it can enter beta oxidation, which occurs in the mitochondrial matrix
    - Activation occurs in the endoplasmic reticulum, cytosol, or outer mitochondrial membrane
    - Product of activation is a "fatty acyl CoA" molecule
    - Activation requires 2 ATP and 1 CoA

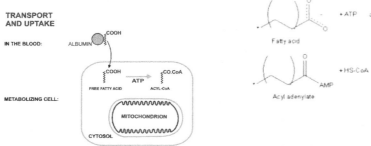

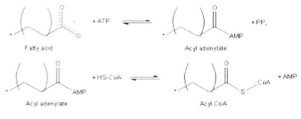

- Activated fatty acid is first transported into to mitochondria

- Then it is oxidized, producing a double bond in the chain and producing FADH2

- Hydration step occurs with the addition of H2O, adding a hydroxyl to the β carbon of the chain

- Hydroxyl in oxidized to a carbonyl, producing NADH

- Molecule is cleaved between the alpha and beta carbons; the 2 carbons cleaved from the chain are added to CoA-SH, forming acetyl CoA

- For a fatty acid with n carbons…
  - # acetyl CoA produced = n/2
  - # cycles of β-oxidation = # NADH = # FADH2 $= \dfrac{n}{2} - 1$
    - "- 1" because the last round produced 1 acetyl CoAs

β-OXIDATION OF FATTY ACIDS

β-oxidation of unsaturated fatty acids:

- Two additional enzymes required (isomerase and reductase)

- Unsaturated fatty acids are more oxidized due to the double bond, and the first step of β-oxidation (which produces a double bond) must be skipped

- ATP yield is less as a result (approximately 2 less ATP per double bond)

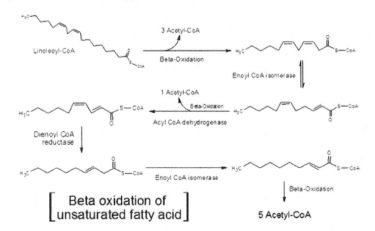

[Beta oxidation of unsaturated fatty acid]

A 12 carbon fatty acid would produce how many NADH, FADH2, and GTP in total (i.e. after the acetyl CoAs have gone through the TCA cycle)?

For a 12 carbon fatty acid there will be 5 rounds of β-oxidation, producing 5 NADH and 5 FADH2. There will also be 6 acetyl CoA molecules produced, and in the TCA cycle each of these will produce 3 NADH, 1 FADH2 and 1 GTP (18 NADH, 6 FADH2, 6 GTP).

So, in total: 23 NADH, 11 FADH2, and 6 GTP produced

Which equates to approximately 80 ATP − 2 ATP (activation) = 78 ATP

Fatty Acid Synthesis

- Fatty acid synthesis produces 16 carbon fatty acids using acetyl CoA and NADPH as the substrates, and fatty acid synthase as the enzyme
  - Acetyl CoA usually acquired from carbohydrates that went through glycolysis followed by PDC
  - Fatty acid product can be further modified by other enzymes

- **NADPH** serves as the reducing agent; **ATP** provides energy
  - Per cycle, 2 NADPH required and 1 ATP required

- **Fatty acid synthase** is a large complex of many enzymes

- Occurs in the cytoplasm of cells, when excess fuel present (insulin triggers it)

- Process may occur to store excess fuel in the form of fat (lipogenesis) or to make other lipid molecules such as phospholipids

- 2 acetyl CoA molecules (2 carbon) are required, and one of them must first by converted to malonyl CoA (3 carbons) through the addition of ATP and CO_2

- ACP (acyl carrier protein) replaces CoA and is used to transfer the acyl and malonyl groups

- Malonyl is added to acetyl-ACP and an ACP as well as a CO_2 molecule are lost

- A ketone is reduced to an alcohol and NADPH is oxidized

- Water removed, then another reduction of the carbon chain occurs (oxidizing another NADPH)

Ketogenesis

- Ketogenesis is the formation of ketone bodies from acetyl CoA (usually derived from fatty acids) and from ketogenic amino acids
    - Ketone bodies and can be used by other tissues of the body as fuel by converting the ketone body is back into acetyl CoA and putting it through the TCA cycle
    - Ketone bodies: acetoacetate, acetone, β-hydroxybutyrate

- Process occurs in the mitochondrial matrix of cells in the liver

- Ketogenesis occurs in a **fasted state** when blood **glucose levels are low** (no intake of carbohydrates and glycogen has been mainly used up)

- In fasted state: fatty acid oxidation occurs in order to make acetyl CoA as an energy source. Excess acetyl CoA molecules in the liver (that aren't immediately put into the TCA cycle) are combined to form ketone bodies. Ketone bodies can then be sent to other tissues as a source of fuel during the glucose-deprived state.

- Long chain fatty acids can't cross the blood brain barrier, so the brain relies heavily on ketone bodies for fuel when glucose levels are low

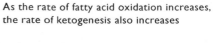

Acetyl CoA's produced mainly by fatty acid oxidation.

As the rate of fatty acid oxidation increases, the rate of ketogenesis also increases

Ketoacidosis

- Ketone bodies are acidic and can therefore lower the pH of the blood when they are released into the bloodstream

- Excessive and uncontrolled ketogenesis results in **ketoacidosis**

- Main symptoms: blood pH drops; heavy breathing (to alter the blood pH via the bicarbonate blood buffer system); fruity breath smell (due to acetone)
  - Extreme cases can result in death if untreated
  - Diabetic ketoacidosis would show high blood glucose levels (unlike non-diabetic ketoacidosis)

- Ketoacidosis is common to individuals with type I diabetes mellitus: shortage of insulin → blood glucose levels are high but glucose cannot be taken into the cells and used for fuel → cells switch to fatty acid oxidation → excessive fatty acid oxidation also results in build up of acetyl CoA and excessive ketogenesis

Protein and Amino Acid Metabolism

- **Proteolysis:** breaking a protein down into smaller chains and/or into its constituent amino acids
  - The peptide bonds are hydrolyzed by proteases and by low pH
  - May occur during metabolism of proteins, zymogen activation, or apoptosis

- Amino acid catabolism first involves deamination (removing the amine group), turning an amino acid into a keto acid
  - The removed amine group may be incorporated into nitrogen containing compounds, or turned into urea by the area cycle and excreted

- The remaining part of amino acids may be metabolized into other products that serve as fuel sources
  - **Glucogenic amino acids** can be metabolized into molecules (TCA intermediates) that can enter gluconeogenesis after being converted to oxaloacetate
    - Ex. Methionine → succinyl-CoA → → → oxaloacetate → → → glucose
  - **Ketogenic amino acids** can be metabolized into molecules that enter ketogenesis (acetyl CoA)
  - Both types can also produce fuel by contributing to the flux of the TCA cycle

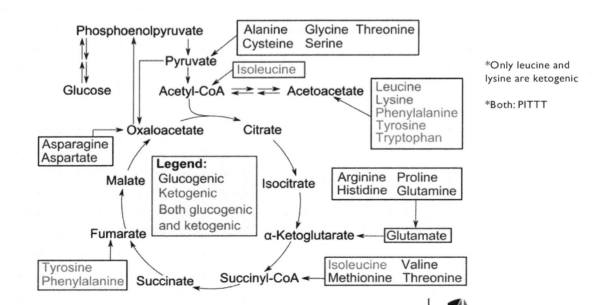

*Only leucine and lysine are ketogenic

*Both: PITTT

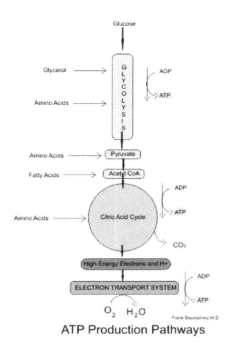

ATP Production Pathways

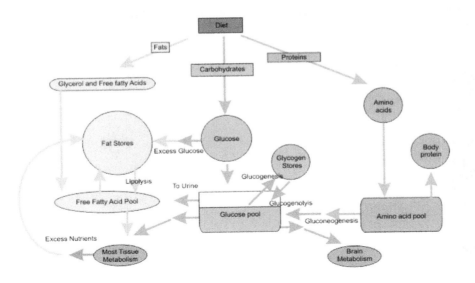

Metabolism Summary

METABOLIC REGULATION AND HORMONAL CONTROL

Biochemistry Lecture 7

OBJECTIVES

- Homeostasis, Steady State, and Equilibrium
  - Maintenance of steady state in the body
  - Different methods of maintaining homeostasis
  - Glycolysis and gluconeogenesis
- Regulation of Glucose Levels and Fuel Sources
  - Hormonal control: Insulin and glucagon
  - Fatty acid oxidation and synthesis
  - Well-fed state
  - Short-term starvation
  - Prolonged starvation
- Tissue-specific metabolism
- Body mass regulation

Homeostasis: the maintenance of a relatively constant internal environmental (temperature, blood glucose level, etc.)
- Usually referring to the entire organism or system

(Chemical) Equilibrium: the forward and reverse reactions are occurring at equal rates so there's no net change in the concentration of products or reactants

- Ion concentrations across a cellular membrane are often not in equilibrium, because the ion has a higher concentration on one side than the other (ex. Na^+, Ca^{+2}, K^+)
- No energy entering or leaving the system

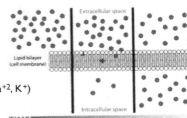

Steady-state: maintaining relatively constant conditions of a certain parameter or reaction; maintenance of steady-state in an organism is, as a whole, homeostasis

- Requires constant work/energy input in order to maintain that condition
- Ex. Concentrations of Na^+ and K^+; requires Na/K ATPase pump
- Sometimes referred to as "dynamic equilibrium", but not the same as chemical equilibrium

Maintenance of steady-state in the body:

Control of the flux through metabolic pathways is achieved by a number of methods operating on different time scales. We will explore this using the regulation of glycolysis and gluconeogenesis as an example:

fast

- Le Chatelier's Principle maintains chemical equilibrium in reactions; higher concentration of reactants than products induces the reaction to flow in the forward direction
  - Sudden influx of glucose into the cell stimulates glycolysis to run
  - Low blood sugar levels and the subsequent breakdown of glucogenic a.a. to pyruvate or oxaloacetate stimulates gluconeogenesis

- Allosteric regulation: results in enzyme inhibition when certain products of the pathways buildup or enzyme stimulation when reactants buildup. This is caused by **specific** substrates that act as allosteric regulators.
  - Hexokinase of glycolysis is inhibited by its product glucose 6-phosphate
  - Phosphofructokinase of glycolysis is stimulated by high levels of AMP, whereas enzymes of gluconeogenesis would be inhibited by high levels of AMP

- Hormonal regulation: insulin and glucagon are released into the bloodstream and control blood sugar levels through the regulation of specific enzymes of glycolysis and gluconeogenesis. Most commonly these enzymes trigger an intracellular signal that results in the phosphorylation or dephosphorylation of enzymes.

- Transcriptional regulation: Certain substances may upregulate or downregulate transcription of enzymes involved in metabolic pathways. Often times, hormones trigger a signal cascade that results in transcriptional activation/inhibition

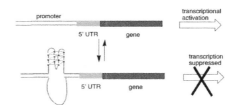

Pancreatic Hormones

- The islets of Langerhans region of the pancreas has different cell types, each of which releases a different hormone. Beta cells make and release insulin, alpha cells release glucagon, and delta cells release somatostatin. Insulin and glucagon control blood glucose levels within a tight range.

Insulin: Lowers blood glucose levels (BGL) by triggering liver, muscle, and adipose cells to take up glucose. Released after a meal when BGL spikes. In general, insulin...

- Stimulates glycolysis, glycogenesis, fatty acid synthesis, and protein synthesis (because the substrates for these processes is present at high BGL)
- Inhibits fatty acid oxidation, gluconeogenesis, glycogenolysis, and protein catabolism

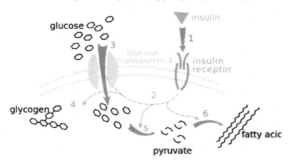

Glucagon: Increases BGL by inhibiting cellular uptake and usage of glucose. Released when BGL low ("glucose-gone"). In general, glucagon...

- Stimulates gluconeogenesis, glycogenolysis, lipolysis/fatty acid oxidation
- Inhibits fatty acid synthesis, glycolysis, glycogenesis

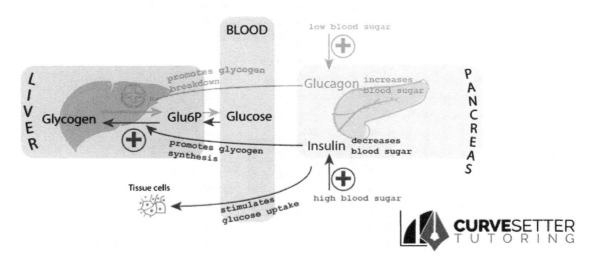

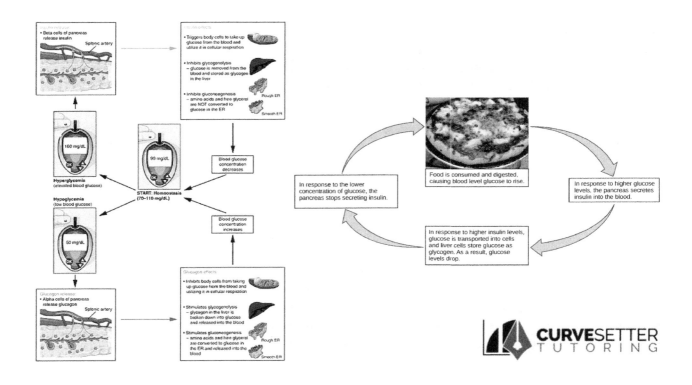

Tissue Specific Metabolism

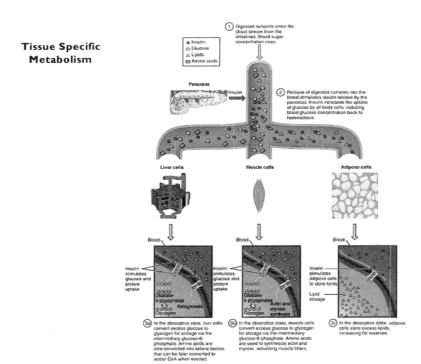

Fructose 2,6-Bisphosphate: allosteric regulator of phosphofructokinase (of glycolysis) and fructose 1,6-bisphosphatase (of gluconeogenesis) → reciprocal regulation

- Stimulates PFK to increase flux through glycolysis
- Inhibits F1,6-BPase to decrease flux through gluconeogenesis
- Abundance of fructose 2,6-bisphosphate is under hormonal control

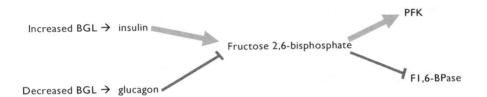

Glycogenesis: glucose $\xrightarrow{hexokinase}$ G-6-P → G-1-P → UDP-glucose $\xrightarrow{glycogen\ synthase}$ glycogen

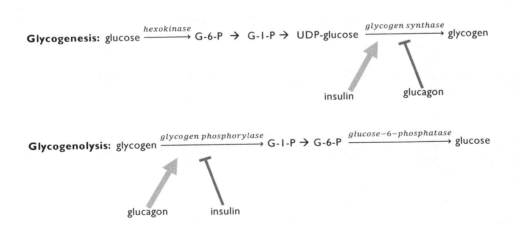

Glycogenolysis: glycogen $\xrightarrow{glycogen\ phosphorylase}$ G-1-P → G-6-P $\xrightarrow{glucose-6-phosphatase}$ glucose

Fatty Acid Oxidation and Synthesis:

- Fatty acid oxidation occurs during a "starvation" state when blood glucose levels are low. This may occur due to lack of nutrient intake, or inability to take glucose into cells (diabetics).
  - Stimulated by ADP and inhibited by high levels of ATP; occurs when insulin is low and glucagon high

- When acetyl Co-A levels rise (due in part to increased fatty acid oxidation), some of it goes into the TCA cycle to produce ATP and some goes into ketogenesis, forming ketone bodies that are taken up by various organs

- If levels of ATP and NADPH are high, acetyl Co-A molecules go into fatty acid synthesis
  - Stimulated by insulin

Integration of Metabolic Regulation

Well-fed state → high BGL → Cells uptake glucose to use it as fuel; glycolysis, TCA cycle and oxidative phosphorylation stimulated to make ATP; glycogenesis occurs in the liver and muscle cells, storing excess glucose as glycogen; high ATP and NADPH enables fatty acid synthesis to occur, storing excess fuel as fat; anabolic processes such as protein synthesis also likely

Starvation state → low BGL → liver performs glycogenolysis, liberating glucose into the bloodstream to raise BGL and send glucose to other organs; some gluconeogenesis also occurs in order to produce glucose and raise the BGL

Prolonged starvation state → low BGL and glycogen depleted → lipolysis occurs releasing fats into the bloodstream which are taken up by cells; fatty acid oxidation occurs to provide fuel for the cell; some acetyl CoA goes into ketogenesis to make ketone bodies so that other organs (brain) can get fuel; protein catabolism occurs so that glucogenic amino acids can be turned into glucose and ketogenic amino acids into ketone bodies

very simplified summary; reality isn't quite so clear cut

Body Mass

- **BMI** = mass/height^2 = kg/m^2
  - Normal = 18.5 – 25
  - Overweight = 25 – 30
  - Obese = 30+

- Excess weight occurs when the amount of calories taken into the body are more than the amount of calories burned → excess fuel is stored as fat in adipose tissue → adipose cells grow in size

- **Leptin:** released by adipose cells when excess fuel is present → decreases hunger
  - Leptin resistance in obesity

- **Ghrelin:** released when hungry (stomach empty) → increases hunger and prepares GI tract for food

- Leptin and ghrelin act on the hypothalamus to control appetite; their opposing effects maintain homeostasis

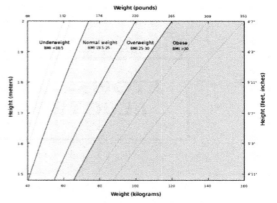

ATOMS- NOTATION, STRUCTURE, ELECTRON CONFIGURATIONS

General Chemistry Lecture 1

OBJECTIVES

- Overview of atoms
  - Composition of an atomic nucleus
  - General atomic structure
  - Notation
  - Isotopes and Ions
  - Binding energy
- Atomic structure and behavior
  - Emission spectrum
  - Bohr model of an atom
  - Electron configurations and orbital structure
  - Diamagnetic vs paramagnetic
  - Reactivity
  - Excited vs ground state
  - Photoelectric Effect

- The nucleus of an atom consists of **protons** (mass = 1 amu, charge = +1) and **neutrons** (mass = 1 amu, charge = 0). Electrons circulate in a cloud around the nucleus (mass = 0 amu, charge = -1)
  - The subatomic particles ("nucleons") within the nucleus are held together by the **strong nuclear force** (this is the strongest of nature's 4 basic forces: strong nuclear force, weak nuclear force, gravity, electromagnetic force)
  - The **electromagnetic force** (attraction between + and – or repulsion between like charges) also acts within the nucleus as repulsion between positively charged protons. The strong nuclear force overcomes this repulsion.

- **Atomic number** (Z): # protons
  - fingerprint of an atom, never changes for that element
- **Mass number** (A): # protons + # neutrons

$$^A_Z X$$

  - # neutrons = A – Z
  - # electrons = # protons IF atoms is neutral. If atom is +2 charge, it has 2 less e- than the number of protons (Ni^{+2} has 26 e-). If atom is -2 change, it has 2 more e- than the number of protons (O^{-2} has 10 e-)
  - The actual weight of any one atom is approximately equal to its mass number in amu or Daltons (1 amu = 1 Da = 1.66×10^{-27} kg)
  - The weight of 1 mole of any element is equal to its mass number in grams

Ex. Carbon-12: mass #=12, atomic #=6; 6 protons and 6 neutrons.
Neutral atom therefore has 6 e-.
Mass of one C-12 atom = 12 amu (12 Daltons)
Mass of one mole of C-12 = 12 g

$$^{12}_6 C.$$

- **Isotope**: same # of protons, different # neutrons (isotopes of an element differ only in the # neutrons; i.e. C-12 and C-13 → C-12 has 6 neutrons while C-13 has 7)
  - The mass number noted below each element on the periodic table is a weighted average (by relative abundance) of all the naturally occurring isotopes of that element
  - ex. Hydrogen has 3 naturally occurring isotopes; their names occasionally come up

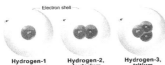

Isotopes generally have similar chemical properties but differing stabilities (some may be so unstable that they undergo a form of radioactive decay)

- **Ion**: Atom with a net non-zero charge because it has gained or lost e- from its neutral state
  - Cation: + → has lost e-   (*The 't' in cation looks like a '+')
  - Anion: - → has gained e-

- **(Nuclear) Binding energy**: the energy required to break the nucleus down into its constituent parts
  - This amount of energy was released when the nucleus formed from individual nucleons

- **Mass defect:** the mass of an intact nucleus is less than the sum of the masses of the nucleons that make it up. This difference is the mass defect.

    - This amount of mass was converted to energy and released when the nucleus formed (nuclear binding energy) and these quantities are related by $E=mc^2$

- **Excited state vs. ground state of an e-:** Electrons are usually at their "ground state" energy level but can absorb energy and be promoted to an "excited state" of higher energy. When an e- falls from the excited state back to the ground state, it releases energy (same amount of energy as was required to excite it)

Absorption spectrum:
- Shine light through a substance and it will absorb certain specific frequencies (or colors) of that light. It is visualized as dark bands on a rainbow spectrum. The dark bands show which frequencies of light were absorbed.

Emission spectrum:
- Pass light through a substance and certain frequencies of light are emitted. It is visualized as bright bands (the colors of the bands represent which frequencies of light were emitted) on a dark surface.
- Light is emitted from the substance when an atom transitions from a high energy state (due an to excited electron) to a low energy/ground state. The difference in energy between these two states is exactly equivalent to the energy of the photon released.
- Since there are many different electron transitions possible for each atom, there are multiple different energies of photons (colors) released
- Seen as the "fingerprint" of an atom
- $E_{photon} = h\nu = h(c/\lambda)$; $h = 6.63 \times 10^{-34}$ Js

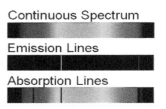

Continuous Spectrum

Emission Lines

Absorption Lines

Bohr Atom:

- Simplified model of an atom in which electrons orbit the nucleus in a circular path
- The distance of the e- from the nucleus is related to the energy of the e- (further away = higher energy e-; because negative e- want to be close to +ly charged nucleus)
  - E- can only possess discrete energy quantities (quantized energy states) and can "jump" between these discrete energy levels
- Transitions between energy levels are accompanied by an input of energy (if e- goes to higher energy level) or a release of energy (if e- goes to lower energy level)

$$E(n) = -\frac{1}{n^2}(13.6\ eV)$$

$$E(1) = -13.6\ eV$$

$$\Delta E = E_{nf} - E_{ni}$$

- First equation is used to calculate the energy of an e- at the nth energy level. The value will be negative because it's relative to a free electron (0 eV because n = ∞), and bound e- are more stable than free e-. Larger -# = more stable

- Third equation shows how to calculate the energy absorbed or emitted when an e- transitions between energy levels.
  - Using this equation you could set $\Delta E = hv = h(c/\lambda)$ to determine the frequency or wavelength of the light emitted/absorbed

Ex. n = 1 → E₁ = -13.6 eV

n = 2 → E₂ = -3.4 eV (smaller -# because higher energy e-)

If the e- transitions from n = 1 to n = 2, you must provide it with 10.2 eV

Why? ($\Delta E = E_2 - E_1 = -3.4 - (-13.6) = 10.2$ eV

+# therefore energy must be provided because the transition indicates that the e- will increase in energy

Ex. To ionize (fully remove) an e- from the n = 1 energy level, how much energy must be provided?

Reality:

- The Bohr model only works for an atom with one electron (H, He⁺¹, Li⁺²) because the presence of more e- results in repulsion and the model no longer depicts reality
- The idea that e- occupy certain "shells" or "levels" of fixed energy levels is still used. But the idea that these electrons have a fixed circular orbit was rejected.

- **Heisenberg's Uncertainty Principle:** The exact position or speed of an e- cannot be calculated, only the probability of it being in a certain region can be calculated
  - Modern quantum mechanical model

Electron Orbitals and Configurations:
- We can estimate the general "location" of an electron by noting its principle quantum number (the energy shell) and the orbital type (the energy subshell)

- The **principle quantum number (n)** tells you the energy shell of the electron and ranges from 1 onwards (whole numbers only)
  - n = 1, 2, 3, …
  - Higher n values = further from the nucleus = higher in energy
  - The *value* of n also tells you *how many* different subshells there are in that energy level (n = 1 has 1 subshell: s; n = 2 has 2 subshells: s and p; n = 3 has 3 subshells: s, p, d)

- The **sub-shell** describes the shape of the region of space in which an electron may exist. The possible subshells are s, p ,d, and f. Each subshell type has a set number of individual orbitals.
  - s<p<d<f in terms of energy and complexity
  - "s" has 1 orbital, "p" has 3 (px, py, pz), "d" has 5, "f" has 7
  - Each individual orbital can have a maximum of 2 e-. Therefore the s subshell can have 2 e- in it, the p subshell can have 6 e- in it (2e- x 3 p-orbitals), etc.

- Putting it all together:
  - n = 1: $1s^2$
  - n = 2: $2s^2\ 2p^6$
  - n = 3: $3s^2\ 3p^6\ 3d^{10}$
  - n = 4: $4s^2\ 4p^6\ 4d^{10}\ 4f^{14}$

subshell	# orbitals	Total # e- possible per orbital
s	1	2 e-
p	3	6 e-
d	5	10 e-
f	7	14 e-

- The actual order of these orbitals in terms of increasing energy (order of e- filling) doesn't exactly follow what you would expect.
  - 1s 2s 2p 3s 3p 4s 3d 4p 5s 4d 5p 6s (see "diagonal rule" below)

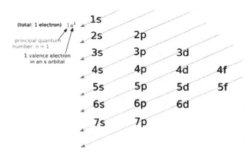

- Finally, each e- has a spin number which describes whether its spin is up or down. In each orbital, one e- has an up spin and one e- has a down spin.

Writing Electron Configurations:
- Electrons occupy the lowest energy level orbital first (1s), then fill in order of increasing energy (Aufbau's Principle)
- The order of filling and also order of notation can be found by tracing across the rows (also called "periods") of the periodic table.
- Note that the "n" value is the same as the period number for every block except the d-block, where it's the row # – 1, and the f-block (row # - 2)
- By tracing across the periodic table, you can see that the order of filling is: 1s, 2s, 2p, 3s, 3p, 4s, 3d, 4p, 5s, 4d... etc.

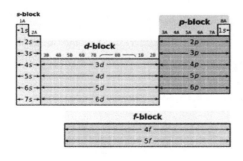

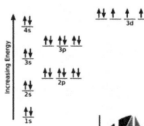

- **Pauli Exclusion Principle:** There can be no more than 2e- per orbital, one with up spin and one with down spin (see arrows as notation for spin in diagram below)
- **Hund's Rule:** Electrons in the same subshell (s, p, d, or f) occupy available orbitals singly first before pairing up

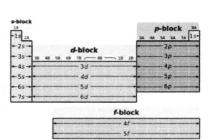

- When writing the e- configuration, find the element on the periodic table, and then trace across the rows noting down each new orbital type as you cross it
- Count the number of elements (represents the number of e-) in that orbital type and note it as a subscript on the label ($1s^2$, $3d^{10}$)
  - If the element has a charge, add (if -) or subtract (if +) accordingly from this e- count for the last orbital type that you note down for that element

He: $1s^2$,   Be: $1s^2 2s^2$,   Ne: $1s^2 2s^2 2p^6$,   Na$^+$: $1s^2 2s^2 2p^6$

- Noble gas short-cut: In e- configuration, note in brackets the noble gas element (last row of periodic table) that is in the row above the row of the element you are dealing with. Now you can just write the notation that follows from that noble gas, without having to rehash the orbitals that constitute that noble gas.

  Mg: $1s^2 2s^2 2p^6 3s^2$ →   Mg: $[Ne]3s^2$

- **Valence shell:** highest energy (least stable) shell of that element
  - Except for transition metals, can count # valence e- by counting column # of that element (from 1 – 8, skipping over d-block)

- Noble gases are inert (unreactive) and very stable because they have a full valence shell ("full octet")

- **Isoelectronic** elements are elements that have the same electron configuration
  - Ex. S^{-2} and Ar: $[Ne]3s^2 3p^6$

- Many elements will lose or gain electrons to achieve a full valence shell (therefore become isoelectronic to the closest noble gas)→   Ex. Na$^+$, Ca^{+2}, S^{-2}

- Almost all elements will lose e- in the reverse order as they filled
  - Exception: Transition metals will lose e- from the s-subshell before d-subshell

  Ex. Zr: $[Kr]5s^2 4d^2$,   Zr^{+2}: $[Kr]4d^2$

Another exception...

- Some transition metals can achieve higher stability by promoting an e- in order to achieve a half filled (5e-) or fully filled (10e-) d-subshell
    - Cu, Cr, Ag, Au
    - Cu: [Ar] $4s^1 3d^{10}$
    - Cr: [Ar] $4s^1 3d^5$
    - Pd: [Kr] $4d^{10}$ → NO s-subshell

Diamagnetic vs. Paramagnetic

- Diamagnetic: All e- are spin paired (each orbital has 2e-)
    - Ex. Ne, He, Be
    - Diamagnetic elements have no internal magnetic field but are repelled by the presence of an external magnetic field
- Paramagnetic: Not all e- are spin paired
    - E, N, O, F
    - Attracted to an external magnetic field

paramagnetic

diamagnetic

N $1s^2 2s^2 2p^3$

O $1s^2 2s^2 2p^4$

F $1s^2 2s^2 2p^5$

Ne $1s^2 2s^2 2p^6$

Excited vs. Ground State:

- An atom may achieve an excited state by promoting an e- to a higher orbital than it usually occupies in the ground state
- Ex. Ground state→ O: $1s^2 2s^2 2p^4$

    Excited state→ O*: $1s^2 2s^2 2p^3 3s^1$

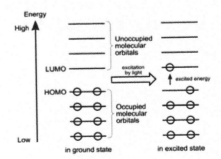

The Photoelectric Effect

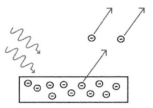

- If a light shines on certain metals, e- can be ejected from the metal (now called photoelectrons
- The incident light has a certain amount of energy (E_{photon}), which is used to overcome the work function of the metal (Φ) and to give the e- some kinetic energy (KE_{e-}) once it is ejected
- Energy is conserved, so: $E_{photon} = \Phi + KE_{e-}$

$$h\nu = \Phi + KE_{e-}$$

- As long as $E_{photon} > \Phi$, then the KE of the photoelectrons will increase as the frequency of incident light increases

- Increasing the amplitude of the incident light (more photons) results in increased outgoing current (more e- ejected) but no change in KE_{e-}

THE PERIODIC TABLE- GROUPS, PROPERTIES AND TRENDS

General Chemistry Lecture 2

OBJECTIVES

- Review key groups of the periodic table
  - Alkali metals
  - Alkaline earth metals
  - Halogens
  - Noble gases
  - Transition metals
  - Metals vs. Non-metals
- Periodic Trends and Properties
  - Shielding
  - Atomic radius
  - Ionization energy
  - Electron affinity
  - Electronegativity

Alkali metals

- Group 1
- 1 valence e- → VERY reactive because they want to lose this 1 e- to achieve full octet
  - For example, some react violently with water → form OH⁻ releasing H⁺

    $(2K_{(s)} + 2H_2O_{(l)} \rightarrow H_{2(g)} + 2K^+_{(aq)} + 2OH^-_{(aq)})$
- Usually found in +1 oxidation state (see above)

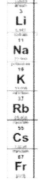

Alkaline Earth Metals

- Group 2
- 2 valence e- → very reactive
- Often found in +2 oxidation state
- React with water to produce OH- and H+
  - Usually produce $X(OH)_2$ with water
- Not found freely in nature but distributed in Earth's crust
- React vigorously with H_2O

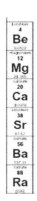

Halogens

- Group 17 (second to last column)
- 7 valence e- → very reactive because want to gain 1 e- to achieve full octet
- Usually found in -1 oxidation state
- Form acidic compounds (such as HCl, HF, HBr)
- React with metals forming salts
- Found naturally in all 3 states (s, l, g)

Noble Gases

- Group 18
- Full octet (ns^2np^6) → unreactive (inert) therefore rarely participate in chemical reactions
- Found in oxidation state of 0

Transition Metals

- "d-block" elements
- Partially filled d orbital e-
    - Can form many different oxidation states (almost always +)
    - Often colored due to e- jumping between different d-orbitals
- Metals --> conduct electricity
    - Loosely bound d-orbital e-

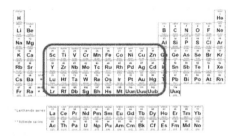

Metals vs. Non-metals

Metals

- Malleable; shiny; solid @ room temp (except Hg)
- Good conductor of heat and electricity
- Easily lose valence e- (often + ox state)
- Good reducing agent
- Lower EN

Non-metals

- Non-malleable; dull; s, l, or g
- Poor conductor of heat and electricity
- Gain or share valence e- (often − ox state)
- Good oxidizing agent
- Higher EN

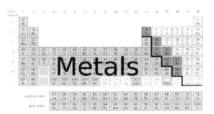

Shielding: Filled shells between the nucleus and the valence e- "protects" or shields the valence e- from the pull of the positively charged nucleus

Effective nuclear charge (Z_{Eff}): Represents the "charge" or amount of pull that an e- experiences due to the + nucleus

- $Z_{eff} = Z - S$, where Z is the atomic # of the atom and S is the effect of the "sheilding" electrons
- $Z_{eff} < Z \rightarrow$ In other words, the shielding e- decrease the positive pull of the nucleus

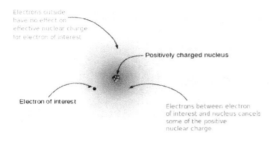

Periodic Trends

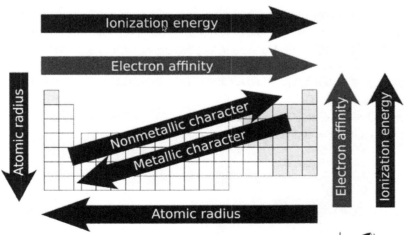

Atomic Radius: size of the atom; depends on number of electron shells as well as how much the + nucleus pulls on those e- (increased pull on e- → decreased radius)

Across row/period: radius decreases
- Within one row, all elements have the same number of e- shells. When moving across row, Z increases (increased # protons) → Increased pull on the electron cloud → Decreased radius

Down column/group: radius increases
- As you move down a column, more e- shells are added → More shielding (Z_{eff} decreases) → Less pull on e- cloud → Increased radius

Ions of one element:
- cation < neutral < anion

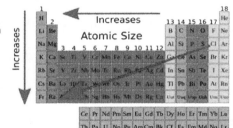

Ionization Energy (IE): Energy needed to remove an electron (+ nucleus attracts e- therefore energy is needed to remove them)
- First IE = Energy needed to remove the first valence e-
- Second IE = Energy needed to remove a second e-
  - Second IE > First IE → Once one e- is removed, there is a higher proton:electron ratio, therefore increased pull on that second e- from the nucleus and it's harder to remove
- Across row/period: IE increases
  - Increased Z → more pull on e- cloud so harder to remove e-
- Up column: IE increases
  - Less e- shells → less shielding → more pull on e- and harder to remove
- IE highest for noble gases and very low for alkali metals → why?

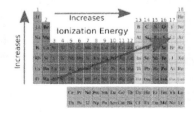

Electron Affinity (EA): Amount of energy released with the addition on an e- (to neutral atom)

- -EA value implies a favorable (exothermic) process because energy is released
- By "high EA" we mean a large negative EA value (-50J EA > -30J EA) because more energy is released with the addition of that e-
- Can be thought of as the willingness of a neutral atom to gain an e-

Across row: EA increases

- Atoms are more willing to accept an e- in their valence shell if they are closer to achieving a full octet (think of Halogens versus alkali metals!)

Up column: EA (generally) increases

- Less e- shells → added e- is closer to + nucleus
- Only really applies to group I

Electronegativity (EN): How much an atom pulls e- towards itself.

- Comparing the EN of bonded atoms indicates whether the bond is covalent (lower EN difference so more of a "sharing" of e-) or ionic (larger EN difference so one atom in effect "donates" e- to the other, more EN, atom)

- In covalent bond, the more EN atom pulls the bonded e- pair closer to its own nucleus ("hoards") → acquires a partial negative charge (δ-). The other atom in the bond has a partial positive charge (δ+)

$$EN\ O = 3.44$$
$$EH\ H = 2.2$$

$$\overset{\delta^-}{O} \quad \delta^+_H \diagdown \overset{}{} \diagup \delta^+_H$$

- Elements are given a numerical value for EN that ranges from 0 → 4

Across row: EN increases
- Increased Z (# protons) across row → nucleus pulls more strongly on e-

Up column: EN increases
- Less e- shells (less shielding) → e- are closer to nucleus and held more tightly

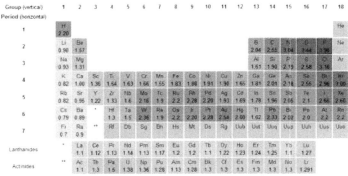

Periodic table of electronegativity using the Pauling scale

- Fluorine = most EN atom

- **Know** this trend for the commonly encountered elements:

FONCIBRISCH   ("fonkle brish")

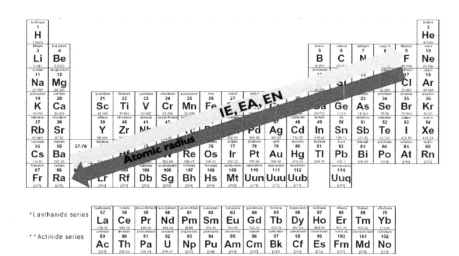

RADIOACTIVITY AND ELECTROCHEMISTRY

General Chemistry Lecture 3

OBJECTIVES

- Radioactivity
  - Types of radioactive decay and their products
  - Half-life
  - Exponential decay
  - Plots of decay

- Electrochemistry
  - "Redox" overview
  - Electrolytic cells
  - Voltaic cells
  - Concentration cells

Radioactive Decay

- Spontaneous process by which an unstable nucleus emits particles and/or energy from the nucleus

- Unstable parent atom/isotope → daughter atom/isotope
  - Net mass and charge of reactants must equal that of products

- Three main types: alpha (α), beta (β), gamma (γ)
  - Beta has three subtypes: β-, β+ (positron), e--capture

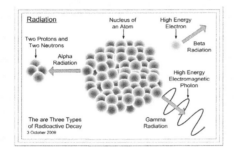

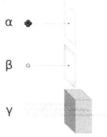

Alpha Decay

$$^A_Z X \rightarrow {}^4_2 He + {}^{A-4}_{Z-2} Y$$
$$\alpha = {}^4_2 He$$

- Nucleus releases α particle, which is a Helium nucleus (2 protons + 2 neutrons)
  - Daughter molecule has 2 less protons and 2 less neutrons (mass decreased by 4, atomic # decreased by 2)

- α particle: Low energy; ejected at low velocity; dangerous if inside the body
  - Easily blocked by material because large and slow

Ex. U → Th + α $\qquad$ $^{238}_{92} U \rightarrow {}^{234}_{90} Th + {}^4_2 He$

Beta (minus) Decay

$$_Z^A X \rightarrow \ _{-1}^{0} e + \ _{z+1}^{A} Y$$

$$_{-1}^{0}\beta = \ \beta = \ _{-1}^{0}e = e^-$$

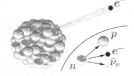

- Nucleus releases a β- particle, which is an electron (mass = 0, charge = -1)
  - Daughter nucleus has same total mass but one more proton (and one less neutron)

- In reality, a neutron of the parent nucleus decays into a proton (stays in nucleus), an electron (gets released), and an anti-neutrino (v_e)
  - $n \rightarrow p^+ + e^- + v_e$
  - Happens as a consequence of the "weak force"

- Beta particles are harder to stop and more energy than an alpha particle

- Ex. $_6^{14}C \rightarrow \ _7^{14}N + \ _{-1}^{0}e$

Positron Emission/β⁺ Decay

$$_Z^A X \rightarrow \ _{+1}^{0}\beta + \ _{z-1}^{A} Y$$

$$_{+1}^{0}\beta = e^+$$

- Nucleus releases a β⁺ particle, which is like the opposite of an electron (mass = 0, charge = +1)
  - Daughter nucleus has one less proton (atomic # decreases by 1) but one more neutron, so same total mass

- In reality, a proton of parent nucleus decays into a neutron (stays in nucleus), a positron (gets released), and a neutrino (v_e)
  - $p^+ \rightarrow n + e^+ + v_0$
  - Also relies on the "weak force"

- Ex. $_6^{11}C \rightarrow \ _5^{11}B + \ _{+1}^{0}e$

Electron Capture

$$^{A}_{Z}X + ^{0}_{-1}e \rightarrow ^{A}_{z-1}Y$$

- Nucleus captures an electron from its own electron cloud and uses it to convert a proton into a neutron
  - Daughter nucleus has one less proton (atomic # decreases by 1) but one more neutron, so same total mass (same as positron emission)
  - Does net charge on atom change?

- $e^- + p^+ \rightarrow n + v_0$

- Ex. $$^{11}_{6}C + ^{0}_{-1}e \rightarrow ^{11}_{5}B$$

Gamma Radiation

$$^{A}_{Z}X \rightarrow ^{0}_{0}\gamma + ^{A}_{Z}X$$
$$\gamma = gamma\ ray$$

- Nucleus in an excited state (may be noted as X^*) releases gamma rays and falls back to ground state

- Gamma rays are a form of EM radiation $\rightarrow$ no change in mass or charge of the parent nucleus, just change in energy state)

- Gamma rays are photons of high frequency (high energy) and very difficult to stop

Half-life ($T_{1/2}$)

- The time it takes for half of a sample of radioactive material to undergo decay (time for half of the original sample of parent nuclei to become daughter nuclei)

- If $T_{1/2}$ = 1 hour, after 1 hour 50% of the original nuclei remain, after 2 hours 25% remain, after 3 hours 12.5% remain, etc.

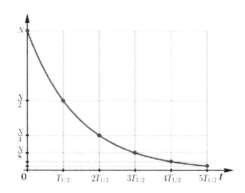

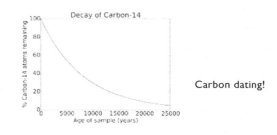

Carbon dating!

$$N = N_0 \left(\frac{1}{2}\right)^{\frac{T}{t_{\frac{1}{2}}}}$$

$$N = N_0 e^{-kt}$$

$$where\ k = \frac{ln2}{t_{1/2}}$$

- N = amount of original material left
- N_0 = original amount
- T = time passed, $T/t_{1/2}$ = # of half-lives passed
- k = decay constant
  - Larger k = lower $t_{1/2}$ = faster decay

- Exponential decay: Substance is undergoing exponential decay if the rate at which it decays is directly proportional to the amount present at that time
  - $N = N_0\ e^{-\lambda t}$ → λ is the decay constant for that material (related to k but not calculated using ln 2; usually given)
  - Radioactive materials undergo exponential decay

    Graph of amount vs. time:

- Semi-log plot = Graph of log(amount) vs. time is linear and the slope corresponds to the decay constant for that substance
  - Y- axis values are labeled in terms of amount but spacing is in terms of log (amt)

"Redox" overview for electrochemistry

- "Redox" = "reduction and oxidation" = reactions in which there's a transfer of e-

- Oxidation #/state indicates how much an atom is donating or receiving electrons in a bond (can be -, +, or 0)
  - Oxidation states of all atoms add up to the net charge of the molecule
  - Ex. Fe Cl_3 → Cl is -1, Fe is +3
  - Atoms alone have an oxidation # of 0
  - Many elements have predictable oxidation #s: group 1 = +1; group 2 = +2; O and S often = -2; Halogens often = -1; H = +1 or -1

- Reduction is the gaining of e-
  - Species that is reduced = the oxidizing agent
  - Oxidation state will decrease

- Oxidation is the loss of e-
  - Species that is oxidized = the reducing agent
  - Oxidation state will increase
        "LEO GER"

Voltaic/Galvanic Cells

- A spontaneous redox reaction occurs and generates a flow of e- (a current)
  - Chemical reaction (redox) used to create electrical energy

- Parts:
  - Two electrodes (metal rods): anode = electrode that is oxidized, cathode = electrode that is reduced (an-ox, red-cat)

  - Half-cells: the two halves of the cell are separated, one has anode and one has a cathode, both electrodes sitting in a solution

  - E- flow along wire from the anode → cathode
    - Can harness current by connecting a device (light-bulb) to the wire or measure current with a voltmeter

  - Salt bridge or porous membrane allows for ion flow between the half-cells

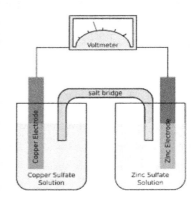

- Two half reactions: one describes the species (electrode) that is oxidized and the other describes the species that is reduced
  - Oxidation half rxtn: $Zn \rightarrow Zn^{+2} + 2e^-$
  - Reduction half rxtn: $Cu^{+2} + 2e^- \rightarrow Cu$

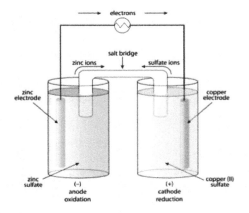

- **Reduction potential** (ε): the tendency of a species to be reduced (how much it "wants to" acquire e-)
  - Measured in Volts
  - $\varepsilon > 0 \rightarrow$ reduction of species is spontaneous
  - More + $\varepsilon \rightarrow$ better oxidizing agent (will be cathode)
  - Q: For species with a high EA, smaller or larger ε?

- Standard Reduction Potential ($\varepsilon°$) is this property measured at standard conditions
  - For MCAT you will use a table of $\varepsilon°$ and for voltaic cells you can almost always assume standard conditions

Cell potential: $\varepsilon_{cell} = \varepsilon_{e\text{- acceptor}} - \varepsilon_{e\text{- donor}} = \varepsilon_{cathode} - \varepsilon_{anode}$

Also, $\varepsilon_{cell} = $ (reduction potential) + (oxidation potential)

- Oxidation potential = - (reduction potential) = - (ε)

- Measured in Volts

- Voltaic cells are spontaneous and create a net current, so cell potential > 0

Q: ε of the cathode species should be larger or smaller?

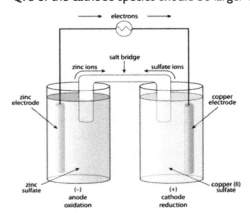

$Zn^{+2} + 2e^- \rightarrow Zn \qquad \varepsilon° = -0.76\,V$

$Cu^{+2} + 2e^- \rightarrow Cu \qquad \varepsilon° = 0.34\,V$

$\varepsilon°_{cell} = 0.34 - (-0.76) = 1.10\,V$

- For redox reactions, spontaneity of the reaction and the cell potential are related:
  $\Delta G° = -n\,F\,\varepsilon_{cell}°$
  n = moles electrons; F = Faraday's constant = 96,485 Coul/mol e-

  - Voltaic cells: **$\Delta G° < 0$ because $\varepsilon_{cell}° > 0$**

- If the species are not at standard state (because species not at 1M)…

  $\Delta G = \Delta G° + RT(\ln Q)$
  R = gas constant = 8.314 J/molK , T = temperature (K), Q = reaction quotient

  $\varepsilon = \varepsilon° - (RT/nF)\,\ln Q$

Concentration Cell

- A form of a voltaic/galvanic cell in which the half cells have equivalent species but differ in concentration (or occasionally temperature)
  - Same metal at the anode and cathode; same solution but differing concentration
  - Electrons flow and voltage is created as the solutions equilibrate to the same concentration

- To calculate ε_{cell}, you must use: **$\varepsilon = \varepsilon° - (RT/nF)\,\ln Q$**

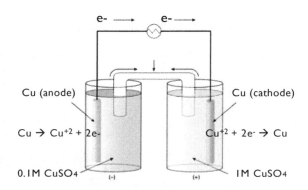

$Cu^{+2} + 2e^- \rightarrow Cu \quad \varepsilon° = 0.34V$

ε_{cell} depends on the difference between the two concentrations; once they are equal $\varepsilon_{cell} = 0$

Electrolytic Cell

- An external current source (battery) provides a flow of e-, forcing a non-spontaneous redox reaction to occur
    - Opposite process as galvanic cell
    - $\Delta G > 0$ and $\varepsilon°_{cell} < 0$ but process occurs because of external voltage source
    - Electrolysis (breaking a molecule into its constituent atoms) may also occur of the molecules in solution

- Parts:
    - 2 electrodes: anode = oxidation occurs, positively charged; cathode = reduction occurs, negatively charged
    - Electrolyte = solution in which ions are dissolved
    - Ions of electrolyte are attracted to the electrode with an opposite charge to their own
    - End result: Either a metal electrode is plated OR gas is liberated

- Uses: plating a metal, electrolysis of a molecule

Faraday's Law:

- Can use to solve for the # moles of e- that power the electrolytic cell

- With stoichiometry and half-equations, we can use the moles e- to find how much of the element is deposited on the electrode or how much gas is liberated
    - After all, that is the end result and purpose of this type of cell

$I = q/t \rightarrow q = It;$ $F = Coul/mol\ e- = q/n \rightarrow q = nF$

$It = nF$

$n = It/F$ where n = mole e-, I = current (Coul/s), t = time (s)

Common Oxidizing Agents

- O_2 and O_3

- Ag^+, Cu^{+2}

- F_2, Cl_2 (high EN)

- MnO_4^- (Mn reduced)

- H_2O_2

- H_2SO_4/SO_4^{-2}

- HNO_3/NO_3^-

- CrO_4/Cr_2O_7 (Cr reduced)

- In general, Lewis acids

Common Reducing Agents

- K, Na, Mg → Why?

- Al, Zn, Fe, Pb

- H_2

- $NaBH_4$ (sodium borohydride)

- $LiAlH_4$

- Lewis bases

STOICHIOMETRY & CHEMICAL EQUATIONS

General Chemistry Lecture 4

OBJECTIVES

- Metric units commonly used
- Moles, Avogadro's #
- Empirical formula and molecular formula
- Molecular weight
- Composition by % mass (% composition)
- Chemical equations
  - Writing and balancing general equations
  - Balancing redox equations
- Limiting Reactants
  - Yield (theoretical vs. actual)

Metric Units

- S.I. units = base units most commonly used = "mks" system
  - Meter, kilogram, second   (and Kelvin)

- Helpful to know:
$1L = 1\ dm^3 = 1000cm^3$; $1\ m^3 = 1000L$; $1\ mL = 1\ cm^3$
$1\ m^3 \times (10\ dm/1\ m)^3 \times (1\ L/1\ dm)^3 = 10^3\ L$

- Density = ρ = mass/volume
  - $\rho = kg/m^3$ (SI units)
  - $\rho = g/cm^3$ (often used) × 1000
  - $\rho_{water} = 1\ g/cm^3 = 1000\ kg/m^3$

PREFIX	tera	giga	mega	kilo	**g** (gram) **m** (meter)	deci	centi	milli	micro	nano	pico
SYMBOL	T	G	M	k		d	c	m	μ	n	p
NUMBER	10^{12}	10^9	10^6	10^3	10^0	10^{-1}	10^{-2}	10^{-3}	10^{-6}	10^{-9}	10^{-12}

$3 - (-1) = 4$

How many dg are in 2.6 kg? ➡ $2.6\ \text{kg} \times \dfrac{\boxed{}\ \text{dg}}{1\ \text{kg}}$

1. Write amount & unit given
2. Mulitply by a fraction with
   A. Given unit on bottom, wanted unit on top
   B. Fill in numerical relationship between units:
      Larger unit: gets 1; **Smaller unit:** subtract exponents, result is exponent for the smaller unit. ✓

Moles and Avogadro's Number

- A mole is a unit used to discuss the quantity of a substance that's made up of many individual repeating particles
    - Particles = individual atoms or molecules
    - Like a baker's dozen (1 dozen = 12 pastry units)

- 1 mole = 6.022×10^{23} particles (called Avogadro's number, abbreviated N_A)
    - 1 mol Cu = 6.022×10^{23} atoms Cu

    - 1 mol H_2O = 6.022×10^{23} molecules H_2O
        - 2 mol H; 12.044×10^{23} atoms H (2 atoms H / 1 molecule H_2O)
        - 1 mol O; 6.022×10^{23} atoms O (1 atom O / molecule H_2O)

- Can convert between particles X, mass X, and moles X

Molecular weight; empirical and molecular formulae

- Molecular weight = amu (atom mass unit) → the weight of one molecule/atom of that substance, given that 1 neutron and 1 proton each weigh approximately 1 amu
    - For each element, the avg MW (of all isotopes) is found on the periodic table. For a molecule, add up the MWs of all constituent atoms

- MW (amu) is numerically equivalent to the molar mass (MM = g/mol)
    - # g X/MM X = # mol X

- Molecular formula: describes the atomic constituents of a molecule with a subscript denoting how many of each atom
    - C_6H_{14}; $C_6H_{12}O_6$

- Empirical formula: essentially a ratio of the elements in a compound to each other. Find by reducing subscripts of molecular formula by a common denominator (whole #s only).
    - C_3H_7; CH_2O

Percent Composition by Mass

- The % (by mass) of each element in a certain compound

Finding the % composition of X by mass when given the molecular or empirical formula:
   Ex. H in $C_6H_{12}O_6$

- Reduce the molecular formula to the empirical formula
   - CH_2O

- Using the periodic table MWs, calculate the: (mass of all X atoms) / (total mass); multiply the calculated decimal by 100 to get %
   - $(1.01 \times 2) / [12.01 + (2 \times 1.01) + 16.00] = 2.02/30.03 = 0.067 \rightarrow 6.7\%$

Finding empirical formula when given the % composition of each element:
Ex. 40% C, 6.7% H, 53.3% O

- Assume there's 100g of the compound, and note mass of each atom present
   40g C, 6.7g H, 53.3g O

- Determine moles of each atom using the above assumption and their molar masses (MWs)
   C: 40g /12.01 gmol^{-1} = 3.33
   H: 6.7g/1.01 gmol^{-1} = 6.63
   O: 53.3g/16 gmol^{-1} = 3.33

- Now you have the molar ratio of elements. Find empirical formula by dividing those numbers by a common denominator (here; ≈3.33)
   C = 1, H = 2, O = 1 $\rightarrow$ CH_2O

Chemical Equations

- Describes a chemical reaction: Products → Reactants
- Phase of each substance usually noted as subscript (s, l, or aq)
    - H_2O = liquid, almost all other liquids are aq (aqueous means a solution of compound dissolved in H_2O)
- Charge of substance noted as superscript
- Coefficient denotes the ratio of substances to each other in a balanced reaction
    - "balanced reaction" = Products and reactants have the same total # of atoms of each element
- Above the arrow: catalyst may be written; "Δ" implies that reaction is heated

$$2H_{2(g)} + O_{2(g)} \rightarrow H_2O_{(g)}$$

$$2Na_{(s)} + 2H_2O_{(l)} \rightarrow 2NaOH_{(aq)} + H_{2(g)}$$

Balancing chemical equations

- Always check if an equation is balanced or not on the MCAT before calculations!!

- To check if balanced, add up the total # of each element on both sides of the equation and see if equal (remember to account for subscripts and coefficients)
    - Ex. $2Na_{(s)} + 2H_2O_{(l)} \rightarrow 2NaOH_{(aq)} + H_{2(g)}$
    - R: 2 Na, 2x2= 4 H, 2 O   P: 2 Na, 2 O, 2+2=4 H

- Balancing is trial and error. Try adding coefficients that make one element equal on both sides, and keep checking all elements and adjusting till it works!

Try it...

$P_4O_{10} + H_2O \rightarrow H_3PO_4$

$BaCl_2 + Al_2(SO_4)_3 \rightarrow BaSO_4 + AlCl_3$ (treat the entire polyatomic ion (SO_4) as one atom/unit)

Balancing redox equations

- Mass and e- transfer must be balanced
- How do you know if it's a redox equation?

$$2Na^0 + Cl_2 \rightarrow 2NaCl$$
$$2(Na^0 - e^- \rightarrow Na^+)$$
$$Cl_2 + 2e^- \rightarrow 2Cl^-$$

1. Assign oxidation #s to each species and determine which species was oxidized versus which was reduced → write the half-reactions (ignore species that don't change ox. #, often called "spectator ions")
   $Cu + HNO_3 \rightarrow Cu(NO_3)_2 + NO + H_2O$
   Cu: 0 → 2,   H: 1 → 1,   N: 5 → 2 (in NO),   O: -2 → -2
   Oxidation: Cu → Cu^{+2} ;   Reduction: NO$_3^-$ → NO

2. Balance all atoms in the half reactions except O and H

3. Balance O by adding H$_2$O as needed
   NO$_3^-$ → NO + **2H$_2$O**

4. Balance H by adding H$^+$ as needed
   - Basic Solutions: now you must "neutralize" the H$^+$ by adding as many OH$^-$ as there are H$^+$ on both sides of the equation (H$^+$ and OH$^-$ will become H$_2$O)
   Acidic: **4H$^+$** + NO$_3^-$ → NO + 2H$_2$O   Basic: **4H$_2$O** + NO$_3^-$ → NO + 2H$_2$O + **4OH$^-$**

5. For each half reaction, add as many e- as necessary to balance out the total ionic charge on the products and reactant sides
   Cu → Cu^{+2} + **2e$^-$**
   3e$^-$ + 4H$^+$ + NO$_3^-$ → NO + 2H$_2$O

6. Now make sure both half reactions transfer the same number of e-, and if they don't, multiple the entire half reaction by a coefficient so that they do
   3(Cu → Cu^{+2} + 2e$^-$)
   2(3e$^-$ + 4H$^+$ + NO$_3^-$ → NO + 2H$_2$O)

7. Add the half reactions together. Cancel anything that both side have (including e-), and combine any like terms. You may or may not have to add the spectator ion back in.
   3Cu + 8H$^+$ + 2NO$_3^-$ → 3Cu^{+2} + 2NO + 4H$_2$O

Limiting Reactant

- If you had 20 wheels and 12 frames,
  you could only make a maximum of 10 bikes.
  So the wheels are the limiting factor.

- Similarly, in chemical reactions, one species will be in a quantity that limits how much of each product species can be made. Once that limiting reactant is all used up, the reaction will cease. The other reactants may be leftover ("in excess")

- Given a certain amount of each reactant, in order to find out how much total product is made you must determine which reactant is limiting.
  - Use the starting amount of each reactant and the stoichiometric coefficients to determine how much product each reactant could yield (assuming an excess of the other reactants). The one that yields the least is limiting.
  - If given masses of the reactant species, convert them to moles

Ex. $Cu + 2AgNO_3 \rightarrow Cu(NO_3)_2 + 2Ag$;   60 g Ag and 140 g 2AgNO₃

- Find mol of each reactant:

60 g Cu/63.55 gmol⁻¹ = 0.94 mol

140 g AgNO₃/(107.9 + 14.01 + 3(16)) gmol⁻¹ = 0.82 mol

- Find out how many mol product that each reactant quantity can produce:

.94 mol Cu x (1 mol Cu(NO₃)₂ / 1 mol Cu) = 0.94 mol Cu(NO₃)₂

0.82 mol AgNO₃ x (1 mol Cu(NO₃)₂/**2** mol AgNO₃) = 0.41 mol Cu(NO₃)₂

AgNO₃ is the limiting reactant!

Theoretical yield: How much product can theoretically be produced given the starting amount (see previous slides on how to determine)

Actual/Experimental yield: How much product is actually made in the procedure

% yield = (actual yield)/(theoretical yield) x 100
- Want to get 100% yield in practice

Can calculate using moles or grams product

GASES: PROPERTIES, BEHAVIOR AND IDEAL VERSUS REAL

General Chemistry Lecture 5

OBJECTIVES

- Temperature, Pressure, and Volume basics

- Gas Laws
  - Ideal Gas Law
  - Boyle's Law
  - Charles' Law
  - Avogadro's Law

- Kinetic Molecular Theory

- Deviation of real gases from the "ideal gases"

- Partial pressure

- Effusion

Temperature

- Temperature: a measure of the average KE of the molecules of a substance

- Scales: Kelvin, Celsius, Fahrenheit
    - Kelvin = S.I. Unit

- $°K = °C + 273.15$

- $°F = \frac{9}{5}°C + 32$

- "Absolute zero" = 0 °K = -273.15 °C
    - Theoretically 0 entropy

- Freezing point of H_2O = 273.15 °K = 0 °C

- Boiling point of H_2O = 373.15 °K = 100 °C

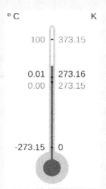

Volume and Pressure

- **Volume:** The amount of 3D space that a substance occupies
    - S.I. unit = m^3
    - $1 cm^3 = 1 cc = 1 mL$
    - $1 dm^3 = 1 L$
    - $1 m^3 = 1000 L$

- **Pressure** = Force/Area = Energy/Volume
    - S.I. unit = Pascal (Pa)
    - $1 Pa = 1 N/m^2$
- **101,325 Pa = 1 atm = 760 Torr**
    - 1 Torr = 1 mmHg → BP measured in mmHg

- **Mercury barometer:** used to measure atmospheric pressure
    - Reservoir of mercury at base, open to pressure from atmosphere. Pressure of atmosphere pushes down on mercury, which rises into a column (with vacuum at top of column). How high the mercury rises indicates the amount of atmospheric pressure. Calibrated so that 1 atm of pressure pushes mercury up to 760 mm in tube

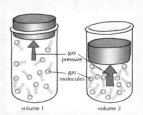

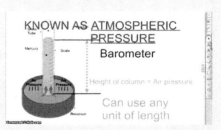

Standard Temperature and Pressure (STP) and Ideal Gases

- "STP" refers to specific conditions: $0°C$ $(273.15 °K, 32 °F)$ *and* 1 atm

- When any **ideal gas** (identity of the gas doesn't matter) is at STP, one mole of it occupies a volume of 22.4 L
  → **STP gas = 22.4 L/mol**
    - If you know gas is at STP and you're given the # mol you can determine the volume, and vice versa

"Ideal gas":
- Volume of molecule is negligible (insignificant as compared to volume of container)
- All collisions are elastic (KE conserved)
- No intermolecular forces (no attraction or repulsion between molecules)

- No gases are exactly ideal but we can approximate these conditions (for example at STP)

Ideal Gas Law

Ideal Gas Law: **PV = nRT**

- P = pressure, V = vol, n = # mol, T = temp, R = gas constant = 8.314 J/molK = 0.0821 Latm/molK

Combined gas Law: $\frac{P_1 V_1}{T_1 n_1} = \frac{P_2 V_2}{T_2 n_2}$ → as condition change, solve for missing parameter

You can derive Avogadro's Law, Charles' Law and Boyle's Law all from the ideal gas law

Avogadro's Law: $\frac{V_1}{n_1} = \frac{V_2}{n_2}$ & V/n = RT/P & V/n = constant @ constant temp and pressure
   At STP, V/n = 22.4 L/mol

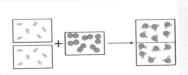

Equal volumes of gas contain the same
moles and same # molecules

3 L / 3 mol   =   2 L / 2 mol

Boyle's Law: @ constant temperature, $P_1 V_1 = P_2 V_2$

Inverse relationship btwn P and V

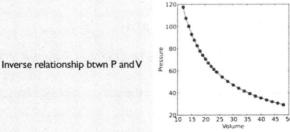

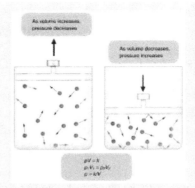

Charles' Law: @ constant pressure, $\dfrac{V_1}{T_1} = \dfrac{V_2}{T_2}$

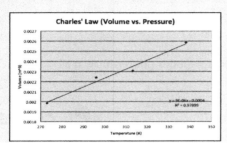

Kinetic Molecular Theory (KMT) of Gases

- Model that is used to describe how (ideal) gases behave
  - Rests on assumptions of ideal gas law (no IMF, volume of gas molecules negligent, KE conserved)

- Pressure of gas = average Force/Area of all collisions (of gas molecules on the surfaces of container)

KMT and Temperature:
- Average KE of all gas particles is proportional to the temperature of the gas
- Average KE is the same for ALL gases at a given temperature (independent of the identity of the gas)
- KE $= \frac{3}{2} k_b T$
  - k_B = Boltzmann's constant = 1.381×10^{-23} m²kg/s² K (or J/K)   and   T = temp in Kelvin

KMT and heat capacity:
- Gases have a certain hear capacity at constant V (C_V), and a different one at constant P (C_p)
- Numerical values: C_V = 3/2 R, C_p = 5/2 R
- Heat capacity = Energy/Temperature → $\Delta Q = n\, C\, \Delta T$

Deviation of Real Gases from Ideal Gases

- Gases are MORE ideal at HIGH temperature and LOW pressure (plus weaker IMF)
  - WHY? molecules far apart at high T and low P → molecular V more negligible and IMF weaker

- LOW temperature and HIGH pressure → larger deviations from an ideal gas
  - WHY? IMF (at low T) and molecular size/volume (at high P) become more significant

Quantitative Deviations

- Van der Waals' Equation: $P = \dfrac{nRT}{V - nb} - \dfrac{n^2 a}{V^2}$

  - "nb" term accounts for repulsive forces → larger b = more repulsion forces = larger P than expected
  - "n²a" term accounts for attractive forces → larger a = more attractive forces = lower P than expected

Partial Pressure and Mole Fraction

- **Partial pressure** = the pressure that is exerted by one gas species in a mixture of gases

- Ideal gases: Total pressure of a mixture of gases is equal to the sum of all partial pressures

- **Mole fraction** = the fraction of a mixture of gases that is one specific species
  - **Mole fraction A** $= \dfrac{\# \, mol \, A}{Total \, \# \, mol} = \dfrac{n_a}{(n_a + n_b + n_c + \ldots)}$
  - Sum of all mole fractions in a mixture = 1

- **Dalton's Law:** relates mole fractions and partial pressures to total pressure

  - $P_{total} = P_a + P_b + P_c + \ldots$

  - $P_a = X_a(P_{total})$, where X_a = mole fraction A

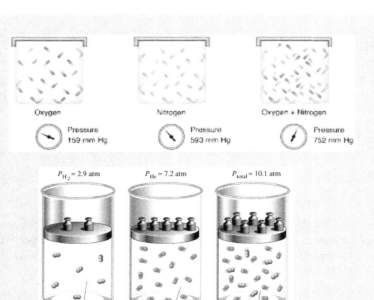

Effusion and Graham's Law

- **Effusion** = gas escaping through a small hole

- If you have a container of 2 gases, both at the same temperature…
  - Both gases have the same KE (because same temp) therefore the larger gas molecules move slower (KE = ½ mv²)
  - Larger gas molecules move more slowly therefore effuse more slowly

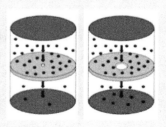

- $$\frac{\text{rate effusion } a}{\text{rate effusion } b} = \sqrt{\frac{molar\ mass\ b}{molar\ mass\ a}}$$

LEWIS DOT DIAGRAMS, CHEMICAL BONDS, AND INTERMOLECULAR FORCES

General Chemistry Lecture 6

OBJECTIVES

- Lewis Dot Diagrams
  - Resonance structures, formal charge
  - Lewis acids and bases
- Bond types
  - EN and bonding
  - Non-polar covalent, polar covalent, ionic, metallic, coordinate covalent
  - Dipole moment
- Multiple bonds → length and energy characteristics
- Intermolecular forces
  - Types and strengths: London Dispersion forces, dipoles, hydrogen-bonds
  - Effect of IMF strength on various properties

Lewis Dot Diagrams

- Pictorially represents the electrons present in bonds and lone pairs
- For monoatomic species: # dots around chemical symbol of element = # valence e-
  - To determine how many valence e- an element has, count which column of the the periodic table it is in (skipping over transition metals)

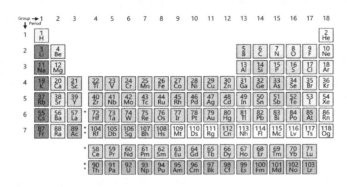

To make the Lewis dot structure of a molecule, often you can use the following shortcut

- Central atom = usually least EN atom (but never H)
- # bonds to central atom: (want − have) ÷ 2
  - Want = # e- it theoretically wants to have in its valence shell (almost always 8 but 2 for H)
  - Have = # e- it has (count column in periodic table, add or subtract e- if molecule has a net charge)
- "sticks" represent covalent bond (2 e- being shared between the connected atoms) while each "dot" represents a lone e- (lone pairs may be shown with sticks as well)

Nitrite: NO_2^{-1}

- Sometimes the shortcut isn't useful (no single central atom)
- Try to satisfy an octet for all atoms (except H) and make sure the diagram doesn't depict anymore e- than are present (sum of valence e- for each atom and then add/subtract e- depending on molecule's net charge)
- Notable exceptions: PO_4^{-3} (P has 10 e- in valence shell because 5 bonds to it), SO_4^{-2} (S has 12 e-), Boron usually best with 6 (wants 6, not 8) e-
- Practice, practice, practice...

Want = 8 + 2 + 2 = 12
Have = 6 + 1 + 1 = 8
(Want − have) / 2 = 2 bonds to O

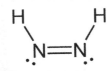

Formal Charge: charge of each atom in a molecule (sum should add to net charge of molecule)

- $FC = V - \left(\frac{1}{2}B\right) - L$
- V = valence e-, B = # e- in a bond (so ½ B = # bonds/"sticks" to that atom), L = # lone e- ("dots")
- So, FC = (valence e-) − (dots + sticks)
- Label FC next to each atom
- FC can help you determine which Lewis dot diagram best represents the molecule → diagram with all atoms with FCs closest to 0 is best

Ex. CO_3^{-2}:   want = 4(8) = 32, have = 18 + 4 + 2 = 22
- (32 − 22)/2 = 5 bonds to C
- FCs: C = 4 − 4 = 0; O_{top}= 6 - 6 = 0; O_{bottom}= 6 − 7 = -1

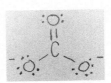

Resonance Structures: account for true distribution of e-

- E- in pi bonds (second, third, etc.) are delocalized and not fixed to one bond but instead move around

- Electron delocalization lowers the energy of the structure (more stable)

- "True" structure is a blend (hybrid) of all contributing resonance structures (may have partial bonds noted)

Some resonance rules:

- NEVER move atoms from one resonance structure to another (don't move a H atom- common pitfall)

- Net charge of molecule must be the same across all contributors

- Some, more stable resonance contributors will contribute more to the true structure of the molecule:

  - Full octets on all atoms (most important stipulation)

  - Least amount of formal charges

  - Negative FC on more EN atoms and vice versa

Lewis acid: e- acceptor (such as H⁺, which can accept an e- pair)

Lewis base: e- donor (usually have lone pairs on the central atom which get shared with Lewis acid)

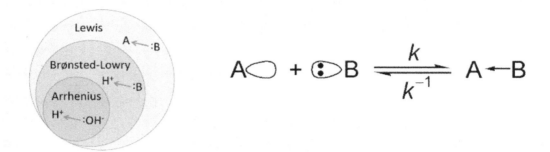

Main bond types (<u>intra</u>molecular forces):

- **Covalent bond:** e- shared between atoms in the bond (two non-metals)
  - Can be **polar** covalent or **non-polar** covalent, depending on ΔEN
  - Polar covalent = e- unequally shared; non-polar covalent = e- equally shared
  - **Network covalent solid:** All atoms are connected by covalent bonds in a continuous network/lattice structure; stronger than normal covalent bond (ex. SiO_2, $C_{graphite}$, $C_{diamond}$)
- **Coordinate Covalent bond:** Atom with a lone pair donates them
    to an e- deficient species (both e- are from the Lewis base)
- **Ionic bond:** Bond between a metal and a non-metal; one atom donates e- (becomes +, cation) , one atom receives e- (becomes -, anion)
- **Metallic bond:** bond between metals; delocalized valence e-
    of metals shared amongst the molecules

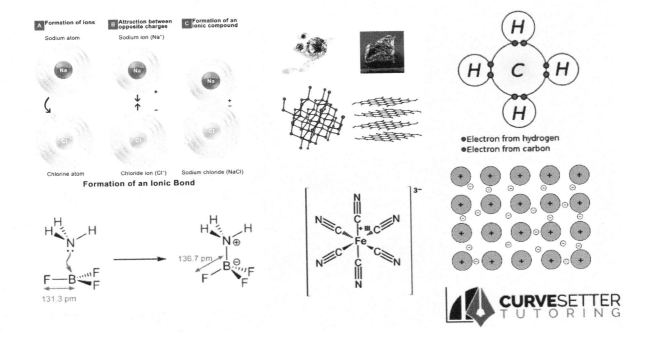

The role of EN:

- To characterize the bond between two atoms you should know the difference between their electronegativities (ΔEN)

- Largest ΔEN = ionic bond (approximately > 2)
  - Larger ΔEN = stronger ionic bond

- No ΔEN = non-polar covalent

- Some ΔEN = polar covalent (partial ionic character)
  - Results in partial charges (more EN atom is $\partial -$ and less EN atom is $\partial +$)

$$\overset{\delta+}{C}\text{—}\overset{\delta-}{F}$$

- **Dipole moment** results from asymmetrical charge distribution. Larger ΔEN = larger dipole moment.
  - Symmetrical molecules (CCl_4, BF_3, PF_5, SF_6) have NO net dipole moment and are overall non-polar because the individual dipole moments cancel out

    The polarity of individual bonds versus the overall molecule are described separately and may be different!

	Bond type		Molecular shape		Molecular type
Water	δ− O H δ+ Polar covalent		δ+ H H δ+ O δ− Bent		Polar
Methane	C H Nonpolar covalent		H C H H H Tetrahedral		Nonpolar
Carbon dioxide	δ− O = C δ+ Polar covalent		O = C = O Linear		Nonpolar

acetone

net dipole

H₃C—C—CH₃

H₃C—C—CH₃

Multiple bonds:

- Bond length= the distance between the nuclei of two atoms in a bond

- Bond Dissociation Energy (BDE)= the energy required to break a bond (homolytic cleavage- each atom receives same # e- from the bond)
  - Also a measure of the strength of that bond
  - + # because energy required to break a bond (bonded atoms are more stable)
  - Larger BDE = more stable bond

Effect of multiple bonds on length and BDE:
- Multiple bonds = Shorter bond length, larger BDE (bc stronger bond)

Effect on rigidity:
- More bonds = more rigid (atoms less able to rotate about the bond)
- Atoms in single bond are free to rotate about the bond
- Partial double bond (due to resonance and delocalized e-) restricts movement
- Atoms involved in double-triple bond fixed

"Bond Order" = # bonds between two atoms

Intermolecular Forces

Ion-dipole: Polar molecule (permanent partial charges) attracted to ion (permanent full charges)

Hydrogen bond: Molecule with a ∂ + H atom (bonded to highly EN atom), which interacts with the lone pair on a highly EN atom (usually N, O, F).
∂ + H is the H-bond donor, EN atom with lone pair is the H-bond acceptor. More ∂ + H = stronger H-bond

Dipole-dipole: Attraction between two polar molecules (both with permanent dipoles). Attraction is between the ∂ − of one and the ∂ + of the other

Dipole-induced dipole: One molecule with a permanent dipole attracted to another (NP) molecule

London dispersion forces (induced-induced): Due to nearby e- clouds inducing temporary dipoles in each other. Exist in all molecules; very weak and transient (momentary and constantly changing); as size of molecules and # e- increases, this force increases

Van der Waals forces: involve only partial charges (dipole-dipole, dipole-indiced dipole, London dispersion)

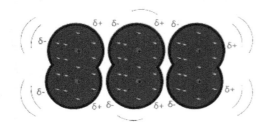

Adenine   Thymine

Which interactions are present in a solution of each of the following species? Based on that, which has the lowest melting point?

SiO_2 Pb   NaI H_2Se

What is the strongest IMF acting between…

a. H_2O and NaCl?

b. O_2 and N_2?

c. HCl and $CHCl_3$

d. NaCl and NH_3?

e. H_2O and C_8H_{18}?

Effects on various properties:

- ⬆ IMF = ⬆ melting point, ⬆ boiling point, ⬇ vapor pressure and ⬇ volatile (evaporates less easily), ⬆ viscosity

IMF of hydrocarbons (in general)...
Decreased branching, increased length, increased #C, decreased # double bonds, and increased MW → HIGHER IMF

a)   b)

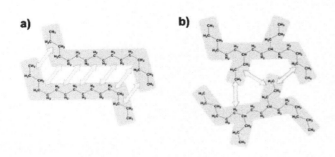

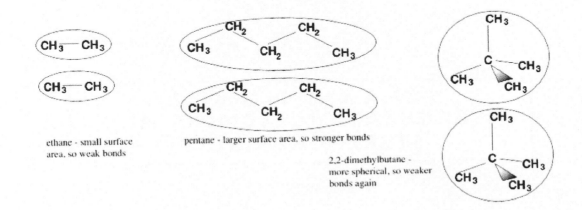

ethane - small surface area, so weak bonds

pentane - larger surface area, so stronger bonds

2,2-dimethylbutane - more spherical, so weaker bonds again

CURVESETTER
TUTORING

SIGMA AND PI BONDS, HYBRIDIZATION, ISOMERS, AND STEREOCHEMISTRY

General Chemistry Lecture 7

OBJECTIVES

- Sigma and Pi bonds
  - Hybridization of orbitals
  - Orbital/molecular geometry and bond angles
  - Delocalized electrons and resonance
- Stereochemistry
  - Structural isomers versus stereoisomers versus conformational isomers
  - Stereoisomer types
  - Absolute and relative configurations
  - Light polarization

Sigma (σ) bond = single covalent bond

- End-to-end overlap of electron orbitals

Pi (π) bond = any subsequent covalent bond (2nd, 3rd, 4th)

- Side-to-side (parallel) overlap

- Single bond = 1 σ, double bond = 1 σ, 1 π, triple bond = 1 σ, 2 π
- Individually, sigma bonds are stronger than pi bonds. Still, a double bond (1 sigma and 1 pi) is stronger than a single (sigma) bond.

Hybridization: We discussed that e- exist in regions of space called orbitals (s, p, d, etc.). When atoms are involved in covalent bonds, an atom's distinct orbital types may fuse, becoming new "hybrid" orbitals (sp hybrid orbital has 50% s character and 50% p character). This enables the atom to make multiple bonds. Single (sigma) bonds usually form from the overlap of these hybrid orbitals. Lone pairs also usually occupy them.

1 s orbital and 1 p orbital hybridize → 2 **sp** hybrid orbitals (the # of orbitals is conserved)
1 s orbital and 2 p orbitals hybridize → 3 **sp²** hybrid orbitals
1 s orbital and 3 p orbitals hybridize → 4 **sp³** hybrid orbitals

Remember, there is one s orbital in an atom but 3 p orbitals (p_x, p_y, and p_z). If an atom is sp hybridized, there's still 2 leftover p orbitals (only 1 p orbital hybridized with s). Similarly, in an sp² hybridized atom there is 1 leftover p orbital. In an sp³ hybridized atom, there are no leftover p orbitals. These leftover p orbitals are the orbitals involved in pi bonds. A pi bond forms from the overlap of two un-hybridized p orbitals.

What to know…
- The hybridization of each atom in a given molecule
- Which bonds are formed from which orbitals (hybridized or un-hybridized)
- The resultant (molecular) geometry of a molecule
- Name of the geometry and bond angles

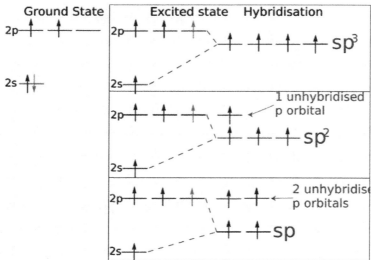

Figure 11.5 continued   **The *sp³* hybrid orbitals in H₂O.**

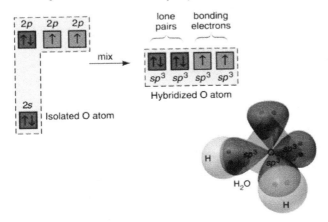

To determine the hybridization of an atom in a certain molecule, first draw the Lewis dot diagram of the molecule. Count the # of "electron groups".

An electron groups refers to attached atoms and/or lone pairs. An attached atom only counts as 1 e-group, whether the bond is single double or triple.

S: 3 electron groups   C: 2 e- groups   C: 3 e- groups   C: 4 e- groups

2 e- groups: sp hybridized (2 sp hybrid orbitals, 2 un-hybridized p orbitals)
3 e- groups: sp² hybridized
4 e- groups: sp³ hybridized

What is the hybridization of each atom in H₂SO₄?

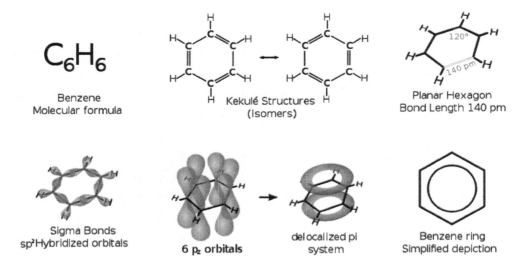

C_6H_6

Benzene
Molecular formula

Kekulé Structures
(Isomers)

Planar Hexagon
Bond Length 140 pm

Sigma Bonds
sp²Hybridized orbitals

6 p_z orbitals

delocalized pi
system

Benzene ring
Simplified depiction

The # of attached "e- groups" (also called an atom's steric number) on the central atom determine the shape of that molecule. Whether the e- groups are lone pairs or actual attached atoms also determines the shape. Know the names of each type of molecular geometry and the bond angles (angle between two atoms attached to the central atom of a molecule).

Orbital vs. molecular geometry (you will be asked about molecular)
- Orbital geometry: only care about the steric number (and don't distinguish between attached atoms versus lone pairs). An sp³ atom is tetrahedral, sp² atom is trigonal planar, sp is linear
- Molecular geometry: distinguish between attached atoms and lone pairs. Theoretically describes the shape you would actually see if looking at a 3D representation of the molecule (because lone pairs wouldn't be visible but atoms would be).

- Try to look over the chart and visualize the shapes; then most will become intuitive (less memorizing)

VSEPR Geometries

Steric No.	Basic Geometry 0 lone pair	1 lone pair	2 lone pairs	3 lone pairs	4 lone pairs
2	CO_2 X—E—X 180° Linear				
3	X—E(—X)—X 120° Trigonal Planar	X—E—X <120° Bent or Angular			
4	X—E 109° Tetrahedral	NH_3 <109° Trigonal Pyramid	H_2O <<109° Bent or Angular		
5	120° / 90° Trigonal Bipyramid	<90° / <120° Sawhorse or Seesaw	<90° T-shape	180° Linear	
6	90° Octahedral	<90° / <90° Square Pyramid	90° Square Planar	<90° T-shape	180° Linear

Lone pairs are repulsive and push more strongly than an attached atom, so squish the atoms closer and decrease the bond angle below what's expected (<120, etc.)

101.7 pm

N
H   H
H   107.8°

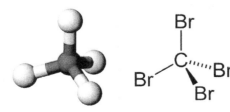

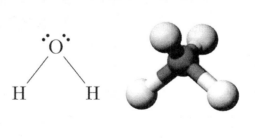

O
H   H

Br
|
Br—C''''Br
|
Br

"Structural formulas for molecules involving H, C, N, O, F, S, P, Si, Cl" (from the AAMC Content List)

- H has 1 valence e- and usually makes a single bond. Has 1 s orbital (never hybridized)
- C almost always makes 4 bonds
- N usually makes 3 bonds and then has a lone pair (NH_3). This enables it to have a FC of 0. If it makes 4 bonds then it has no lone pair and a +1 FC
- O usually makes 2 bonds and has 2 lone pairs
- F and Cl usually make a single bond and have 3 lone pairs
- S usually makes 2 bonds and has 2 lone pairs (like O)
- P usually makes 3 bonds and has a lone pair or it makes 5 bonds (both enable 0 FC)
- Si usually makes 4 bonds (2 double bonds in SiO_2)

Delocalized electrons and resonance:

- If a molecule has resonance, one or more pairs of electrons is not fixed to a specific bond or atom and instead shifts around (as seen when drawing the different resonance structures)
- The atoms with partial double bond character are sp^2 hybridized (not sp^3)

- These e- are said to be "delocalized"

- When ions have resonance, the charge is distributed across multiple different atoms (good for stability)

Delocalized electrons and resonance:

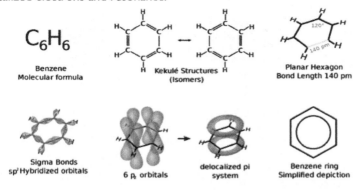

C_6H_6

Benzene
Molecular formula

Kekulé Structures
(Isomers)

Planar Hexagon
Bond Length 140 pm

Sigma Bonds
sp² Hybridized orbitals

6 p_z orbitals

delocalized pi
system

Benzene ring
Simplified depiction

Chiral carbon = stereocenter = Carbon atom that is sp³ hybridized and has **4 different** atoms/groups attached to it

The anti-cancer drug TAXOL

Thalidomide

In a molecule with n different chiral centers, there will be 2^n stereoisomers.

Each chiral center has an "absolute configuration" which is either R or S.
To determine the configuration at each chiral center…

- Assign priority to all groups around the chiral carbon (from 1 → 4)
  - Assign priority using atomic number (but $C^{13} > C^{12}$)
  - If two larger attached groups/chains have the same first atom, follow them until they differ. Treat double bonds as if two attachments of that atom (C=O > C-OH)
- When lowest priority group is on a dashed wedge (facing backwards):
  - If groups numerically (1 → 4) increase in the clockwise direction: R; if counterclockwise: S
- When lowest priority group is on solid wedge:
  - Reverse as above (CW: S, CCW: R)
- When lowest priority group is planar (solid line)
  - Redraw, switching group of dashed wedge with the lowest priority group. Now, CW: S, CCW: R

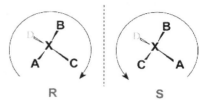

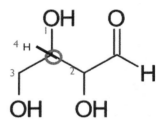

1a

1b

2a

2b

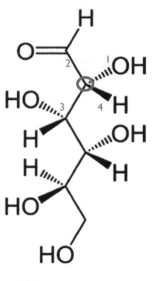

(R)-(–) (S)-(+)

(S)
(R)

(R)
(S)

(R)-Enantiomer **(S)-Enantiomer**

- "R" and "S" label the absolute configuration at each chiral center. They may be included in the chemical formula.
  - (2S,3S)2-bromo-3-iodobutane

Enantiomers: Opposite configuration at every chiral center. Ex. C1 R, C2 S, C3 S and C1 S, C2 R, C3 R
- A pair of enantiomers are optically active (light passed through it will be rotated either to the left or right). They will rotate light in opposite directions.
  - Rotate light to the left = levorotatory, denoted "l" or "-"
  - Rotate light to the right = dextrorotatory, denoted "d" or "+"
  - In a pair of enantiomers, you cannot tell which enantiomer will be d and which will be l. Therefore R/S do not correspond to d/l. You can only determine whether d or l in the lab!
- **Racemic mixture:** a 50:50 mixture of two enantiomers. Optically inactive because cancel each other out.

Meso compound: One stereoisomer in of a set of them for a molecule with at least 2 chiral centers and an internal plane of symmetry (can draw a line somewhere in the middle of it and the two halves will be mirror images). Optically inactive

meso compounds

Isomers

Constitutional/structural isomers: same molecular formula, different bond connectivity

Enantiomers: molecule must have chiral centers; the isomers have opposite orientations at every chiral center. Isomers are "non-superimposable mirror images" (like our hands).
- have the same physical and chemical properties

Diastereomers: Any stereoisomer that isn't an enantiomer. May be optically active (have chiral centers) or not (no chiral center; i.e. conformational and geometric isomers). Optically active diastereomers have different orientations at some (but not all) chiral centers;
- have different physical and chemical properties

Conformational isomers: different momentary rotation about a sigma bond

Geometric isomers: different orientation of groups across a double bond or ring (cis/trans; E/Z)

Stereoisomers

no chiral center

Enantiomers:

(R)-Enantiomer   **(S)-Enantiomer**

(Chirally active) diastereomers:

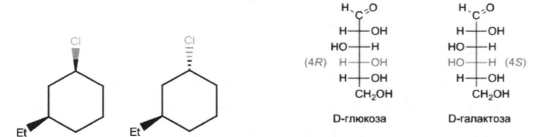

D-глюкоза   D-галактоза

Diastereomers

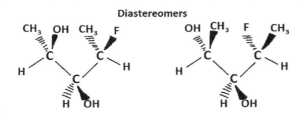

Specific types of diatereomers:

- **Anomers:** the stereocenter that differs is the anomeric Carbon (in a sugar, the C attached to an OH group and to the O in the ring)

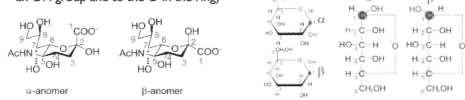

α-anomer   β-anomer

- **Epimers:** isomers that differ at only **one** stereocenter

Epimers

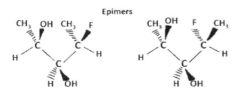

Conformational isomers:

Anti (most stable)

Eclipsed (least stable/ highest energy)

Gauche

Gauche (g-)

Anti

Gauche (g+)

ΔG

Dihedral angle θ

0   60   120   180   240   300   360

Geometric isomers:

Cis/trans: use when there is one atom/group that appears on both sides of the double bond.
  cis: same sides of the double bond
  trans: opposite sides

E/Z: Based on the arrangement of the highest priority groups on either side of a double bond.
  E: highest priority groups on opposite sides of the double bond
  Z: highest priority groups on the same side

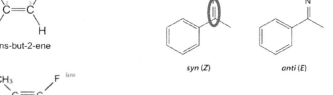

cis-but-2-ene   trans-but-2-ene

syn (Z)   anti (E)

Z-1-bromo-1-fluoropropene   E-1-bromo-1-fluoropropene

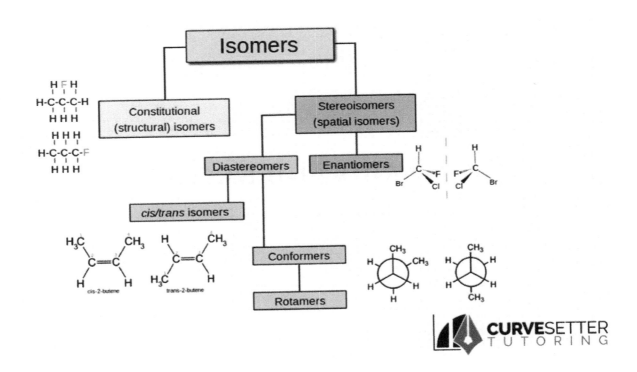

Trans

Cis

(–)-cis

(–)-trans

trans-Azobenzol

cis-Azobenzol

cis

trans

CH₃ CH₃

CH₃

CH₃

CURVESETTER
TUTORING

Isomers

Constitutional
(structural) isomers

Stereoisomers
(spatial isomers)

Diastereomers

Enantiomers

cis/trans isomers

Conformers

Rotamers

cis-2-butene

trans-2-butene

CURVESETTER
TUTORING

ACIDS AND BASES

General Chemistry Lecture 8

OBJECTIVES

Various definitions of acids and bases

pH scale

Ionization of water

K_a and K_b equilibrium constants; K_w

Conjugates

Strong versus weak acids and bases

   Definition and examples

Calculating the pH of acids and bases

Salts

   Calculating the pH of salts

Buffers

   Definition, uses, and application to medicine

Definitions of Acids and Bases

Lewis: Acid = electron acceptor; Base = electron donor

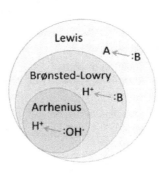

Bronsted-Lowry: Acid = proton (H^+) donor; Base = proton (H^+) acceptor

Arrhenius: Acid = releases H^+, Base = releases OH^- (both in aqueous solution)

- pH: scale (from 0 → 14) used to measure acidity/basicity of an aqueous solution
  - < 7 = acidic; > 7 = basic
  - Lower pH = more acidic; higher pH = more basic
  - Depends on the identity of the solution and its concentration

$$pH = -\log_{10}[H^+] \quad \rightarrow \quad [H^+] = [H_3O^+] = 10^{-pH}$$

$$pH + pOH = 14$$

$$pOH = -\log_{10}[OH^-]$$

Reminder: [X] means concentration of an aqueous solution of X

Molarity (M) = moles solute / L solvent

If $[H^+] = A \times 10^{-n}$, then pH is between n-1 and n

- Pure water has a pH of 7 (neutral); therefore $[H^+] = [OH^-] = 1 \times 10^{-7}$ M (at 25°C and 1 atm)

- Ionization/auto-dissociation of water: pure water ionizes slightly; a fraction of the H_2O molecules dissociate into H^+ and OH^-, and the H^+ immediately combines with another free H_2O molecule forming H_3O^+

- Amphoteric = solution that can act as an acid or a base (ex. H_2O: $H_2O + H_2O \rightarrow H_3O^+ + OH^-$)
  - Bicarbonate: HCO_3^-

- Polyprotic acid = acid that can donate more than one H^+ (ex. H_2CO_3)

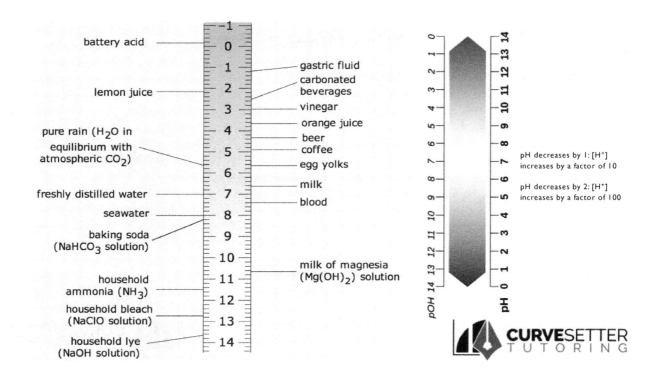

- Equilibrium constant for the auto-ionization/dissociation of water = K_w
  $$K_w = [H_3O^+][OH^-] = 1 \times 10^{-14} \quad \text{(at 25°C and 1 atm)}$$

- Equilibrium constant for acids and bases = K_a and K_b (constants; do not depend on concentration)

- Acid dissociation constant: $K_a = \dfrac{[A^-][H_3O^+]}{[HA]}$
  - Measures the strength of the acid (stronger acid dissociates more/more readily donates that proton)
  - Stronger acid = larger K_a
  - Polyprotic acid K_a's: $H_2A > HA^- > A^{-2}$ (aka $K_{a1} > K_{a2}$) → why?

- $pK_a = -\log_{10}(K_a)$
  - Lower pK_a = stronger acid
  - $pK_a < -2$ → strong acid

$$HA + H_2O \rightarrow A^- + H_3O^+$$

$$B + H_2O \rightarrow OH^- + BH^+$$

- Base dissociation constant: $K_b = \dfrac{[BH^+][OH^-]}{[B]}$
  - Measures the strength of the base (how willing is it to accept a proton)
  - Stronger base = larger K_b

- $pK_b = -\log_{10}(K_b)$
  - Lower pK_b = stronger base

Conjugates

- Conjugate acid base pair: One species before (conjugate acid) and after (conjugate base) having donated a proton
  - $HA + H_2O \leftrightarrow A^- + H_3O^+$
  - $H_2A + H_2O \leftrightarrow HA^- + H_3O^+$
  - $B + H_2O \leftrightarrow BH^+ + OH^-$

- For all conjugate pairs: $K_a \times K_b = K_w = 10^{-14}$ and $pK_a + pK_b = 14$ (at 25°C and 1 atm)
  - Use to convert between K_a and K_b of conjugate pairs

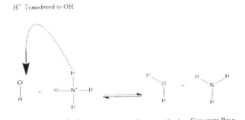

- Strong acid's conjugate has no basic properties
- Strong base's conjugate has no acidic properties
- Acidic substance: $K_a > 10^{-7}$, $K_b < 10^{-7}$
- Conjugate of a weak acid is weakly basic, and v.v.

Strong Acids

- Strong acids dissociate almost completely in water (nearly 100% of the molecules of HA donate a proton to water, to form A⁻ and H₃O⁺)
  - Add a strong acid to water, [H₃O⁺] will increase almost instantly, forming an aqueous solution with low pH

- Because strong acids have weak conjugate bases, the conjugate base that forms following the dissociation (A⁻) will hardly react with H₂O molecules (why? Because it is very stable)

- High K_a values because the molecule readily donates a proton; ex. K_a of HCl = 1×10^6

- Strong acids: **HClO₄, HI, HBr, HCl, H₂SO₄, HNO₃**

Calculating the pH of a strong acid:

Which is a stronger acid, HCl or H₃O⁺?

- We assume that 100% of the acid dissociated, so if we have 10 molecules of HCl and add them to water, then 10 molecules of H₃O⁺ will theoretically form.

- Therefore, a solution of strong acid at 6 M concentration creates 6 M of H₃O⁺ ions

- **[HA] = [H₃O⁺], so pH = -log₁₀[HA]**

  Can the pH be negative?

  - 1 M HCl has a pH of 0; .01 M HCl has a pH of 2

Weak Acids

- Don't fully dissociate in water; less capable of releasing protons than strong acid because conjugate base is less stable than that of strong acid (stable = favorable to form and unlikely to react)

- Common weak acids: HCOOH (formic acid), CH₃COOH (acetic acid), HF, HCN (hydrocyanic acid), H₂S, C₇H₆O₂ (benzoic acid)

Calculating the pH of a weak acid (ICE table!)
   Ex. 0.2 M HA; $K_a = 1 \times 10^{-6}$

	HA ← →	H⁺ +	A⁻
Initial	0.2 M	0	0
Change	- x	+ x	+ x
Equilibrium	0.2 - x	x	x

*Assumption: you can get rid of the "- x" term in denominator, as long as K_a is small enough (approximately less than 10^{-5})

$K_a = x^2 / (.2 - x)$
$1 \times 10^{-6} \approx x^2 / .2$ *
$x = [H^+] \approx (.2 \times 10^{-6})^{.5}$
Use x to find pH → pH = -log₁₀[H⁺];   pOH = 14 – pH
IF K_b is given, use $K_a = 10^{-14} / K_b$

Strong Bases

- Strong bases completely dissociate in water, forming nearly 100% BH$^+$ and OH$^-$
  - B + H$_2$O → BH$^+$ + OH$^-$

- The conjugate acid formed (BH$^+$) is very stable and hardly reacts with water

- Strong bases: **LiOH, NaOH, KOH, Sr(OH)$_2$, Ba(OH)$_2$, Ca(OH)$_2$**   "Linack Sir Baca"

  - Hydroxides of alkali metals and alkaline earth metals

Calculating the pH or pOH of a strong base:

- Very similar to the process for strong acids; assume 100% dissociation of the strong base

- [B] = [OH$^-$], so   pOH = -log$_{10}$[B]   and pH = 14 - pOH

Weak Bases

- Don't fully dissociate in water; less capable of accepting protons than strong base because conjugate acid is less stable than that of strong base

- Common weak bases: NH$_3$ (ammonia), NR$_3$ (tertiary amine), C$_5$H$_5$N (pyridine), HS$^-$, CO$_3^{-2}$ (carbonate ion)
  - Often N with lone pair accepts H$^+$ (forms a bond with it)
  - How can you tell if weak base? → Anything that isn't a strong base is a weak base (to some extent)

Calculating the pOH or pH of a weak base: similar process to that of weak acids (ICE chart); Ex. [B] = 0.2 M

	B ← →	BH$^+$ +	OH$^-$
Initial	0.2 M	0	0
Change	- x	+ x	+ x
Equilibrium	0.2 - x	x	x

Use assumption if K$_b$ is small enough (approximately less than 10^{-5})

K$_b$ = x^2 / (.2 - x)
K$_b$ ≈ x^2 / .2 *
x = [OH$^-$] ≈ (.2 x K$_b$)$^{.5}$
Use x to find pOH → pOH = -log$_{10}$[OH$^-$];   pH = 14 – pOH
IF K$_a$ is given, use K$_b$ = 10^{-14}/ K$_a$

Table 5-4

Dissociation Constants of Some Weak Bases* at 25°C

Base	B	BH+	K_b	pK_b
Aniline	 (—NH₂)	(—NH₃⁺)	4.3×10^{-10}	9.37
Pyridine	(N)	(N⁺—H)	1.8×10^{-9}	8.75
Imidazol	(N, H—N)	(H—N, N—H)	9.1×10^{-8}	7.05
Hydrazine	N_2H_4	$N_2H_5^+$	9.8×10^{-7}	6.01
Ammonia	NH_3	NH_4^+	1.79×10^{-5}	4.75
Trimethylamine	$(CH_3)_3N$	$(CH_3)_3NH^+$	6.4×10^{-5}	4.19
Methylamine	$CH_3—NH_2$	$CH_3—NH_3^+$	3.7×10^{-4}	3.34
Dimethylamine	$(CH_3)_2NH$	$(CH_3)_2NH_2^+$	5.4×10^{-4}	3.27

*If B represents the base, the equilibrium equation is $B + H_2O \rightleftarrows BH^+ + OH^-$, in which BH^+ is the conjugate acid. Base strengths increase down the table, and conjugate acid strengths decrease. The equilibrium-constant expression is

$$K_b = \frac{[BH^+][OH^-]}{[B]} \qquad pK_b = -\log_{10} K_b$$

Salts

- Acid + Base → Salt + H2O; HA + BOH → AB + H2O
    - The H⁺ released by the acid and the OH⁻ released/formed by the base combine to from H2O, the remaining ions of the acid and base combine to from the salt
    - Ex. HCl + NaOH → NaCl + H2O *

- The ions of the salt normally exist in the solution and form an ionic solid (think of NaCl; table salt) when the water is removed

- Salts may be acidic, basic, or neutral. You will have to know which!

- **Neutralization reaction:** strong acid and a strong base react to form a neutral salt plus water (see ex. above*)
    - MaVa = MbVb → equal moles of acid and base must be added for end pH to be 7

- **strong acid + strong base = neutral salt**
    - Neutral salt contains the (very weak) conjugate base of a strong acid and the (very weak) conjugate acid of a strong base → these ions of the salt hardly react with H2O
    - Ex. NaCl, CaCl2, KBr, etc.

- **Strong acid + weak base = acidic salt**
  - $HCl + NH_3 \rightarrow ClNH_4 + H_2O$
  - Cl^- is a very weak base (conjugate of a strong acid; $K_b = 10^{-18}$) so essentially does not react with water
  - NH_4^+ is a weak acid (conjugate of a weak base) but still has some acidic tendencies ($K_a = 10^{-10}$); reacts slightly with water to protonate it

- **Strong base + weak acid = basic salt**
  - $NaOH + HCN \rightarrow NaCN + H_2O$
  - Na^+ hardly reacts with water
  - CN^- is weakly basic ($K_b = 10^{-5}$)

- **Weak base + weak acid = ?** → must compare the dissociation constants to determine if acidic or basic
  - $HA + BOH \rightarrow AB + H_2O$; if A^- is a stronger base than B^+ is an acid (K_b of A^- > K_a of B^+) → basic salt
  - $HClO + NH_3 \rightarrow NH_4ClO + H_2O$
  - NH_4^+ $K_a = 10^{-10}$ and ClO^- $K_b = 10^{-7}$ → slightly basic salt

Calculating the pH of Salts

pH of the salt of a weak acid:
- Ex. CH_3COOK (formed from weak acid CH_3COOH + strong base KOH)
- Salt is weakly basic because CH_3COO^- is slightly basic and a small fraction of them remove an H^+ from H_2O

	CH₃COO⁻ ← →	CH₃COOH +	OH⁻
Initial	M	0	0
Change	- x	+ x	+ x
Equilibrium	M - x	x	x

$K_b = x^2 / (M - x)$ → solve for x; $x = [OH^-]$
$-\log_{10}(x) = pOH$ → $pH = 14 - pOH$

K_a of CH_3COOH > K_b CH_3COO^-, but still not small enough that we can ignore the effect of the conjugate base on water (as we can for Cl^-)

AAMC content guide:"dissociation of weak acids and bases with or without added salt"

- Dissociation of CH_3COOH (weak acid) is reduced if it is placed in solution with a salt of the weak acid, CH_3COOK
  - The salt exists in solution as CH_3COO^- and K^+
  - Weak acid only dissociates until $[A^-][H_3O^+]/[HA]$ is equal to the K_a value
  - Since there is already some of the A^- in the solution (due to the salt), less of the weak acid will dissociate than expected in a solution without the salt
  - Also think about it in terms of LeChatelier's Principle

- Same goes for the dissociation of a weak base in a salt

Buffers

- Buffer = weak acid and base conjugates together in solution
  - Ex. CH_3COOH and CH_3COO^-

- Buffers resist changes in pH
  - If there is an addition of H^+, the A^- (weak base) in the buffer can accept protons to resist a pH drop
  - If there is an addition of OH^-, the HA (weak acid) can donate protons to resist a pH spike

- Best buffer system has a 1:1 ratio of $HA:A^-$
  - At this ratio, the buffer is best at being BOTH a proton source and a proton sink
  - This is true when pH of the buffer = pK_a of the acid species in the buffer

- Buffer's pH = $pK_a + \log([A^-]/[HA])$

- How to make a buffer:
  - Create buffer solution by adding some of each conjugate species (preferably equal amounts)
  - Add some strong base to a weak acid → the strong base will remove a proton from some of the weak acid, creating its conjugate base (preferably add half as many moles of strong base as there are weak acid)
  - Add some strong acid to a weak base

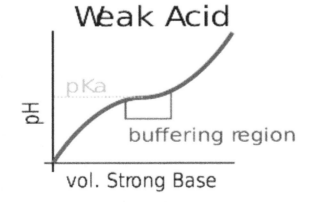

If $pK_a = 7$

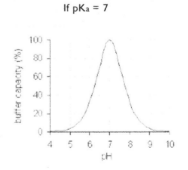

Buffers are crucial to homeostasis in our bodies

Blood buffer system: H_2CO_3 and HCO_3^- in our blood
- Resist changes in the pH of our blood which must be kept within a narrow range (7.35 → 7.45)

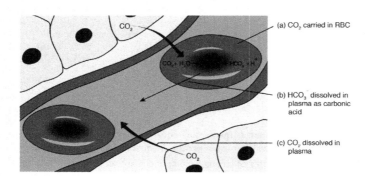

(a) CO_2 carried in RBC

(b) HCO_3^- dissolved in plasma as carbonic acid

(c) CO_2 dissolved in plasma

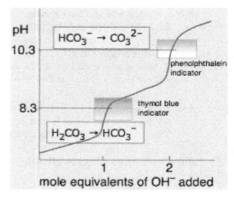

$HCO_3^- \rightarrow CO_3^{2-}$

phenolphthalein indicator

thymol blue indicator

$H_2CO_3 \rightarrow HCO_3^-$

mole equivalents of OH^- added

IONS, SOLUBILITY, AND TITRATIONS

General Chemistry Lecture 9

OBJECTIVES

- Common polyatomic ion names and formulas
  Hydration of ions
  Concentration
  - Molarity, molality, normality
  Solubility product constant
  The common ion effect and its application
  Complex ions
  Solubility of acids and bases
  Titration
  - Half-equivalence point and equivalence point
  - Calculations and titration curves
- Indicators
- Redox titrations

Common ions to know (names and formulas)

OH^- = hydroxide
H_3O^+ = hydronium
NH_4^+ = ammonium
ClO^- = hypochlorite
ClO_3^- = chlorate
ClO_4^- = perchlorate
CO_3^{-2} = carbonate
HCO_3^- = bicarbonate
SO_4^{-2} = sulfate
NO_3^- = nitrate
PO_4^{-3} = phosphate
CH_3COO^- = acetate
CN^- = cyanide
CrO_4^{-2} = chromate
$Cr_2O_7^{-2}$ = dichromate
MnO_4^- = permanganate

Hydration / solvation: describe the interaction between ions and water molecules

- Ions in solution interact with water molecules through the ion-dipole force
- The $\partial-$ of the O in water is attracted to cations, while the $\partial+$ of the H atoms in water is attracted to anions
- In water, individual ions become surrounded by water molecules; anions have the H atoms of water facing directly towards them and cations have the O atom of water facing towards them
- This favorable interaction decreases the potential energy of the involved molecules, resulting in a release of energy

So if ionic solids are so strong why can we easily dissolve them in water? (think of dissolving table salt, NaCl, in water)

- Although it requires quite a bit of energy to break apart the crystalline lattice structure of an ionic solid, all of this energy is provided by the energy that is released when the individuals ions become surrounded by water molecules. Therefore the overall process is favorable/spontaneous.

Hydrated Na+ Ion

Hydrated Cl- Ion

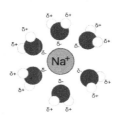

"electrolytes" = ions dissolved in solution

Van't hoff factor = i = how many ions one unit of a substance will dissolve into

Concentration Units

Molarity $= \dfrac{moles\ solute}{L\ solvent}$ **(M)**

- If 2 moles of $CaCl_2$ are added to 1 L water: $[CaCl_2]$ = 2 M; $[Cl^-]$ = 4 M

Molality $= \dfrac{moles\ solute}{kg\ solvent}$ **(m)**

- If water is the solvent, molarity ≈ molality   (because water weighs 1 kg per 1 L)

Normality: the number of moles of equivalents (of H^+ or OH^-) per L of solution
- Used for acids and bases
- Multiple the molarity of the acid or base by how many units of H^+ or OH^- it releases per unit
    - 1 M HCl = 1 N
    - 1 M H_2CO_3 = 2 N
    - 1 M $Ca(OH)_2$ = 2 N
    - 1 M H_3PO_4 = 3 N

Solubility

- Solution = **solute** dissolved into a **solvent**

    - If water is the solvent, it is an aqueous solution

    - In general, it's favorable for a solute to dissolve if the IMF formed between solute and solvent particles are

        overall stronger than those being broken (between the solute molecules)

    - **Saturated solution** = no more solute can be dissolved in the solvent

The Solubility Product Constant (K_{sp}): the equilibrium constant for a solid dissolving in an aqueous solution

     $aA_{(s)} \rightarrow bB_{(aq)} + cC_{(aq)}$ $\rightarrow$ $K_{sp} = [B]^b\,[C]^c$ *solids and liquids not included in equilibrium constants*

- Indicates how soluble a certain substance is: higher K_{sp} = more soluble

- Like all equilibrium constants, K_{sp} tells us how for the reaction will proceed

    - At this point, rate of fwd reaction = rate of reverse reaction (fwd = dissolution, backward = precipitation)

K_{sp} depends on the temperature (and pressure):

- Solubility of solids in liquids increases with increasing temp
    - Putting sugar crystals in hot versus cold coffee
- Solubility of gases in liquids increases with decreasing temp and increasing pressure
    - Soda is most carbonated when it's cold and pressurized

Solubility example:

$PbCl_2$: $K_{sp} = 1.6 \times 10^{-5}$; At what concentration of Pb^{+2} and Cl^- will a solution be fully saturated?

$PbCl_{2(s)} \leftarrow \rightarrow Pb^{+2}_{(aq)} + 2Cl^-_{(aq)}$

$\quad\quad x \quad \leftarrow \rightarrow \quad x \quad + \quad 2x$

$K_{sp} = [Pb^{+2}][Cl^-]^2 = (x)(2x)^2 = 4x^3$

$1.6 \times 10^{-5} = 4x^3$

$x^3 = 4 \times 10^{-6} \rightarrow x = 1.6 \times 10^{-2}$

Solution fully saturated when $[Pb^{+2}] = .016$ M and $[Cl^-] = .032$ M

When the reaction is not at equilibrium, we use **the reaction quotient, Q_{sp}**

- Calculated in the same way as K_{sp}
- Compare Q with K to determine which direction the reaction will procede
    - If $Q_{sp} < K_{sp} \rightarrow$ more salt/solute can be dissolved in the solution; the forward reaction will dominate
    - If $Q_{sp} = K_{sp} \rightarrow$ the reaction is at equilibrium (fully saturated)
    - If $Q_{sp} > K_{sp} \rightarrow$ excess solute is dissolved; the reverse reaction (precipitation) will dominate

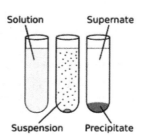

Solution   Supernate

Suspension   Precipitate

Common Ion Effect

- The solubility of a partially soluble salt will decrease if there is a "common ion" (an ion that that salt will dissolve into) present in the solution
    - More AgCl will dissolve in pure water than in a solution which has some Ag^+ and/or Cl^- ions present
    - LeChatelier's Principle in action!
        - $AgCl \leftarrow \rightarrow Ag^+ + Cl^-$
    - If some HCl is added to a fully saturated solution of AgCl, then the reverse reaction will begin to occur and some of the AgCl will precipitate out of the solution
- The common ion effect does NOT suggest that K_{sp} changes

- Application in the lab: the phenomenon can be used in order to force a certain compound to precipitate out of the solution (remove one species from a solution)

Complex Ion

- Complex ion = metal ion surrounded by many ligands (lewis bases: electron donors)
    - M^{+n} + Lewis base: $\rightarrow$ Complex ion
    - Coordinate covalent bond
    - Examples: $[Fe(C_2O_4)_3]^{3-}$, $[Ni(CN)_4]^{2-}$, $[Cr(OH)_4]^-$, $[AlF_6]^3$, $[Cu(NH_3)_4]^{2+}$
- Equilibrium constant = K_f ("formation constant")
- Lewis bases = "ligands" = e^- donating molecules (have lone pair)
- Central metal ion = Lewis acid
    - Cu^{+2}, Ru^{+3}, Ag^+, Fe^{+3}, Cr^{+3} etc.

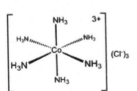

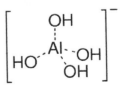

- Effect on solubility: If you add the Lewis base ion to aqueous solution of a partially soluble salt, the solubility of that salt will increase
    - Lewis base ions surround metal cation of the salt (almost as if 'removing it' from the solution) $\rightarrow$ by Le Chatelier's Principle this will drive the forward reaction (dissolution of salt)
    - Ex. Add NH_3 to $Co(OH)_2$ ($Co(OH)_2 \rightarrow Co^{+2} + OH^-$)

Titrations

- One solution (titrant) added dropwise to another (of unknown identity or concentration) solution until neutralization occurs
    - Neutralization has occurred at equivalence point: indicated by color change of indicator compound
- Use to determine concentration or identity (by finding K_a/K_b) of acid/base solution
- Strong added to strong; strong base added to strong acid; strong base added to weak acid
- Goal: determine how much titrant must be added to reach the equivalence point

Equivalence point:
- Point at which the neutralization reaction has fully occurred (acid + base $\rightarrow$ salt + H_2O)
- Only salt and water exist in the solution at this point
- The titrant has converted ALL of the unknown compound into its conjugate
- To reach this point, must have equal moles of acid and base in solution
- mol acid = mol base $\rightarrow$ $M_aV_a = M_bV_b$
    - Knowing the concentration of the titrant and the volume of it added to reach that point, as well as the volume of the unknown solution that you started with, you can determine molarity of the unknown

Salt that has formed at the equivalence point may be acidic, basic, or neutral
- Strong acid/base titrated with strong acid/base: pH = 7
- Weak acid titrated with strong base: pH > 7 (basic salt)
- Weak base titrated with strong acid: pH < 7 (acidic salt)

- To calculate pH of equivalence point (if not told which indicator is used), you must know what the species is at this point and its concentration, then calculate pH normally with ICE chart
    - Ex. CH_3COOH titrated with NaOH; at equivalence point you have $NaCH_3COO$
        Only the CH_3COO^- impacts pH; to calculate its concentration, determine total volume (original plus added volume) and moles of it (= moles titrant added, because mol acid = mol base at equivalence pt.)

pH at any point during titration: $pH = pK_a + \log [A^-]/[HA]$
- $pH - pK_a = \log [A^-]/[HA]$
- $10^{pH - pK_a} = [A^-]/[HA]$
- If pH = 5.5 and pK_a = 4.5, then $[A^-]/[HA] = 10$
- If pH = 6.5 and pK_a = 4.5, then $[A^-]/[HA] = 100$

Half-equivalence point:

- Point at which half the amount of titrant required to reach equivalence point has been added
- So half of the unknown solution has been converted into its conjugate
  - Conjugates are present in a 1:1 ratio ($[HA] = [A^-]$) → great buffer!
  - At this point, $pH = pK_a$ of the unknown solution
  - Why? $pH = pK_a + \log [A^-]/[HA]$; $[A^-]/[HA] = 1$ & $\log(1) = 0$

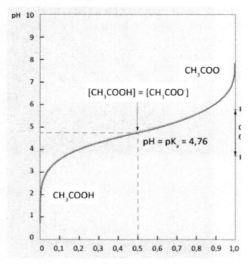

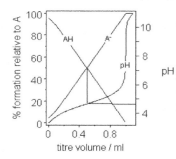

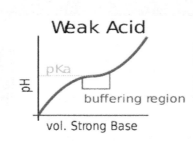

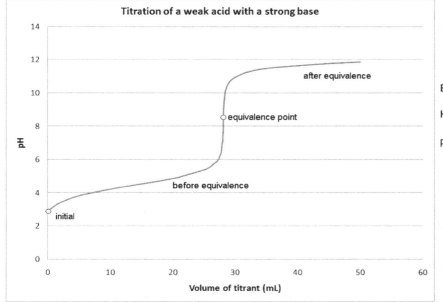

Equivalence point = 30 mL base

Half-equivalence point = 15 mL base

pK_a acid $\approx$ 4.6

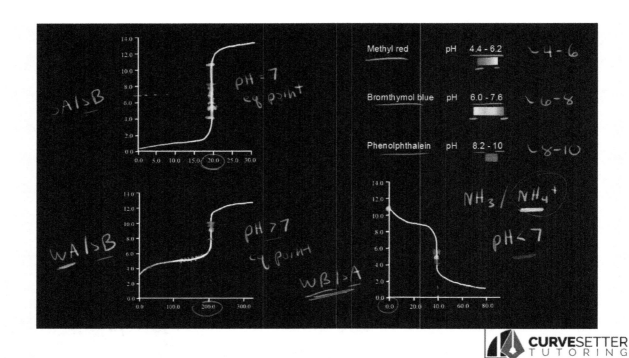

Indicators: used in titrations to indicate when equivalence point has been reached

- pK$_a$ of indicator must be very close to pH of solution at the equivalence point

- Indicators are just a conjugate pair of acids and bases, with each conjugate being a different color in solution
  - H-Ind → H$^+$ + Ind$^-$

- There are many different types of indicators

Phenolphthalein indicator

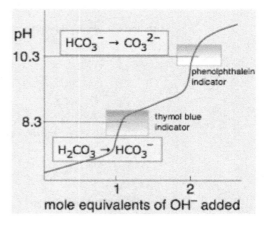

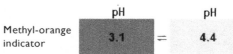

Methyl-orange indicator

Redox titration

- Unlike titrations with Bronsted-Lowry acids and bases, redox titrations involve electron transfers from reducing agent to oxidizing agent

- Often one species acts as indicator because one form (oxidized/reduced) is colored and the other isn't

- Using balanced redox equation you can determine moles of electrons transferred and how many moles of the titrant are required to fully oxidize or reduce the other species

- Instead of measuring pH, cell potential is measured

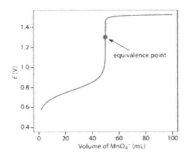

THERMODYNAMICS AND THERMOCHEMISTRY

General Chemistry Lecture 10

OBJECTIVES

- **Thermodynamics basics**
  - Laws of thermodynamics
- **Heat changes**
  - Heat capacity and calorimetry
  - Conduction, convection, and radiation
  - Coefficients of thermal expansion
- **Enthalpy**
  - Endothermic versus exothermic reactions
  - Heat of reaction, heat of formation, BDE (bond dissociation energy)
  - Hess' Law
- **Gibbs Free Energy**
  - Reaction spontaneity and relationship to G, H, S
- **Phase changes**
  - Heats of fusion and vaporization
  - Phase diagrams

Thermodynamics Basics

- **Thermodynamics:** the science of energy transfers
- **State function:** property that doesn't depend on the path taken to get to a certain state
  - Ex. mass, pressure, energy, **enthalpy (H), entropy (S), Gibbs free energy (G)**

Laws of Thermodynamics:

- **Zeroth Law:** If two systems are in thermal equilibrium with a third system then they're also in thermal equilibrium with each other (if temp x = temp z, and temp y = temp z, then temp x = temp y)
- **First Law:** Energy of an isolated system remains constant (energy can't be created or destroyed, just transformed)
  - $\Delta U = Q - W$
  - U = internal energy, Q = heat (+Q = heat put into system, -Q = heat removed) ,W = work (+W = work done on system, -W = system does work on surroundings)
  - Gases: PV diagram depicts various states of a gas at different temperature and pressures; can be used to assess how the internal energy of a system changes, as well as changes in Q and W

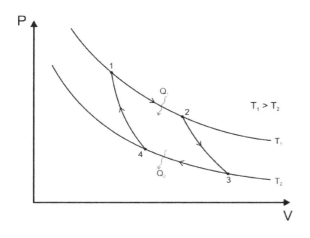

Each point (1, 2, 3, 4 = unique state of the gas)

Work done bay gas = area enclosed by shape on PV graph (or area under curve)

Work = -PΔV
Gas expands = -W = gas did work (lost energy)
Gas contracts = +W = work done on gas

1 → 2 → 3 → 4 → 1 = full cycle (Carnot Cycle)
In full cycle no net change in internal energy
Work done by gas (energy lost) compensated for by heat added (energy gained)

Second Law: the entropy of an isolated system will never decrease over time

- **Entropy (S)** = a measure of the "disorder" of a system

- $S_{gas} > S_{liquid} > S_{solid}$

- Systems naturally evolve towards states of increasing entropy

- The entropy of the universe is constantly increasing

Third Law: a crystal solid at 0 degrees Kelvin has 0 entropy

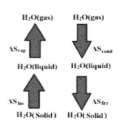

Enthalpy (H): measurement of the energy in a thermodynamic system

- ΔH: measure of the change in heat/energy during a chemical reaction

    - $-\Delta H$ = energy released

    - $+\Delta H$ = energy absorbed

- Overall reactions are either: **exothermic (-ΔH)** or **endothermic (+ΔH)**

- Individual bonds: forming a bond = $-\Delta H$ (energy released);

    breaking a bond = $+\Delta H$ (energy required)

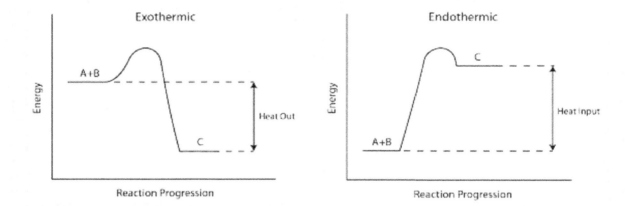

- **Heat capacity:** amount of heat/energy (J) required to raise the temperature of a substance by 1 degree (C or K)
  - $J/°C$ or $J/°K$

- **Specific heat capacity (C):** amount of heat/energy required to raise a certain amount of mass (g, kg, etc.) of a specific substance by 1 degree (C or K)
  - Chemistry often uses $J/g°C$ or $J/g°K$

Q = mCΔT

- Q = heat added, m = mass substance, C = specific heat capacity, ΔT = temp change
  - Make sure units cancel properly!
- Can only use if substance is not changing phase (otherwise the heat would be used to change phase, not temp)
  - Substance that absorbs heat either changes phase or increases in temp, never both
- C is fixed for a specific substance and specific phase
- Larger C = more resistant to changes in temp (strong IMF)
  - Liquid H_2O has a very high heat capacity (4.18 $J/g°K$)

- **Calorimetry:** measuring the amount of heat absorbed or released during a reaction

Types of Heat Transfers

Conduction: heat transferred directly from molecule to molecule (during collisions)
- materials in physical contact for this to occur
- Ex. Your hand touching a hot pan

Convection: heat transfer due to the movement of warm fluids (liquids or gases)
- Ex. Weather and movement of a warm front

Radiation: the transfer of energy in electromagnetic waves that radiate away from the source object
- Ex. The sun

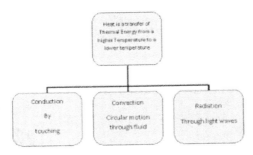

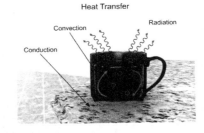

Heat Transfer

Coefficient of Thermal Expansion: Use to describe how the size of an object changes with changes in temperature
- Volumetric, linear, or area change

- Materials almost always expand with increases in temperature
    - As temp increases (increasing average KE of molecules) the molecules move around more and spread out slightly

Enthalpy and Heats of Reaction

Enthalpy/Heat of reaction = ΔH_{rxtn} → net enthalpy change of a reaction

- $\Delta H_{rxtn} > 0$ = endothermic reaction (heat must be put in)
- $\Delta H_{rxtn} < 0$ = exothermic reaction (heat released)

Standard heat of reaction = $\Delta H_{rxtn}°$ → the enthalpy change of a reaction that occurs under standard conditions

To calculate $\Delta H_{rxtn}°$ we must use the standard heat of formation (ΔH_f) values for the product and reactant species

- $\Delta H_f° =$ the change in enthalpy when one mole of that substance is formed from its constituent elements in their standard state (may be - , +, or 0)
- $\Delta H_f°$ of any pure element in its standard form ($C_{graphite}$, $H_{2(g)}$, etc) is 0
- Table of standard heats of formation always given (units are kJ/mol)

$\Delta H_{rxtn}° = \sum \Delta H_f(products) - \sum \Delta H_f(reactamts)$
- Use table of standard heats of reaction, and for each molecule, multiply the value on that table by its stoichiometric coefficient from the balanced chemical equation (n x $\Delta H_f°$)

BDE (bond dissociation energy) = energy required to break bonds
- BDE > 0
- ΔH_{rxtn} = $BDE_{reactants} - BDE_{products}$
- ΔH_{rxtn} = energy needed to break reactant bonds + energy released when forming product bonds
- Multiply each BDE value by the number of that bond type present in the balanced reaction (methane has 4 C-H bonds)

ΔH_f = energy released when bond forms
- $\Delta H_f < 0$ usually
- $\Delta H_{rxtn} = \sum \Delta H_f{}_p - \sum \Delta H_f{}_r$

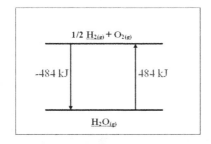

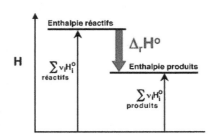

Hess's Law: the total enthalpy change for a multi-step reaction is the sum of all the enthalpy changes of each individual reaction/step

- Because enthalpy is a state function (independent of path) you can calculate the $\Delta H_{rxtn}°$ of a multiple-step reaction in two ways; either breaking it up into each individual step and summing the $\Delta H_{rxtn}°$'s of each step, or just calculating the $\Delta H_{rxtn}°$ using the final and initial states

Ex. A → D actually occurs in three steps, A→B, B→C, and C→D

- You can calculate $\Delta H_{rxtn}°$ using $\Delta H_{rxtn}° = \sum \Delta H_f(D) - \sum \Delta H_f(A)$ OR by adding up $\Delta H_{rxtn1}° + \Delta H_{rxtn2}° + \Delta H_{rxtn3}°$

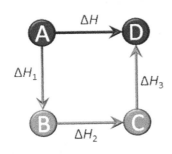

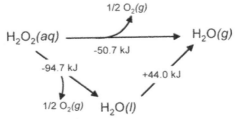

From Kotz, Treichel, and Townsend *Chemistry and Chemical Reactivity*

Problem Suppose you want to know the enthalpy change for the formation of methane, CH_4, from solid carbon (as graphite) and hydrogen gas:

$$C(s) + 2 H_2(g) \rightarrow CH_4(g) \qquad \Delta_f H° = ?$$

Hess's Law

The enthalpy change for this reaction cannot be measured in the laboratory because the reaction is very slow. We can, however, measure enthalpy changes for the combustion of carbon, hydrogen, and methane.

Equation 1: $\quad C(s) + O_2(g) \rightarrow CO_2(g)$ $\qquad \Delta_f H_1° = -393.5$ kJ/mol-rxn

Equation 2: $\quad H_2(g) + \frac{1}{2} O_2(g) \rightarrow H_2O(\ell)$ $\qquad \Delta_f H_2° = -285.8$ kJ/mol-rxn

Equation 3: $\quad CH_4(g) + 2 O_2(g) \rightarrow CO_2(g) + 2 H_2O(\ell)$ $\qquad \Delta_f H_3° = -890.3$ kJ/mol-rxn

Use this information to calculate $\Delta_f H°$ for the formation of methane from its elements.

$CO_2(g) + 2H_2O(\ell) \rightarrow 2O_2(g) + CH_4(g) \qquad \Delta_f H° = 890.3 \frac{kJ}{mol\text{-}rxn}$

$C(s) + O_2(g) \rightarrow CO_2(g) \qquad \Delta_f H_1° = -393.5 \frac{kJ}{mol\text{-}rxn}$

Gibbs Free Energy (G) = the energy a system has available to do work (J/mol or kJ/mol)

- ΔG indicates whether a reaction in spontaneous (proceeds in the forward direction), or non-spontaneous (in which case the reverse direction would be spontaneous)
- At **any point in time** (for a certain temperature and pressure) you can calculate ΔG of a reaction
  - Indicates in which direction the reaction is proceeding at that point
  - Depends on the difference between the energy (stability) of R and P at those conditions

- **$\Delta G = \Delta H - T\Delta S$**
- **$\Delta G < 0$ = exergonic → reaction is spontaneous (proceeds in the forward direction)**
- **$\Delta G > 0$ = endergonic → reaction is non-spontaneous (proceeds in the reverse direction)**
- **$\Delta G = 0$ → reaction is at equilibrium (rate fwd reaction = rate reverse reaction)**

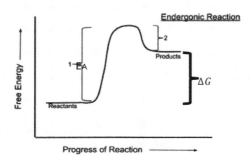 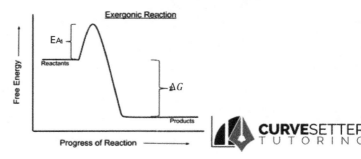

Standard-State Gibbs Free Energy ($\Delta G°$) = the change in Gibbs free energy for a reaction at standard state conditions

- 25° C, 1 atm, all species start at 1M concentration

- There is only ONE $\Delta G°$ for a given reaction (it doesn't change)

- Indicates whether reaction is spontaneous or not at standard conditions (and therefore which direction it will proceed in, in order to reach equilibrium)

$$\Delta G° = \Delta H° - T\Delta S°$$

- To calculate ΔG (non-standard conditions) using $\Delta G°$, use:

$$\Delta G = \Delta G° + RT \ln Q$$

Q =reaction quotient, R = gas consatnt (8.314 J/molK), T = temp in Kelvin

At equilibrium (when Q = K) ΔG = 0, therefore to calculate $\Delta G°$:

$$\Delta G° = -RT \ln K$$

Phase changes

- Melting, freezing, boiling, etc. = physical (not chemical) changes

- Must break or reform intermolecular bonds (not intramolecular)

- As particles go from s → l → g, and as they increase temperature within each phase: KE_{avg} increases, temp increases, entropy increases

- ΔH_{fusion} = energy required to change a substance from solid to liquid (J/mol, J/kg, cal/mol, etc.)
  - Flip the sign and that's heat released when freezing of substance occurs

- $\Delta H_{vaporization}$ = energy required to change substance from liquid to gas

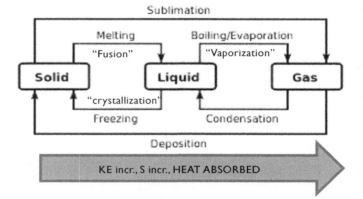

Heating Curve for water:

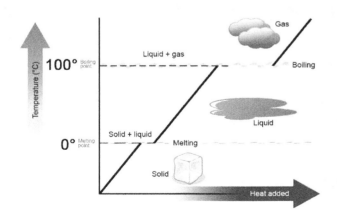

- Phase changes occur at a constant temperature

- Energy put into a substance will either change its phase OR increase its temperature

- $Q = n(\Delta H_{fusion})$ to determine heat required to melt n moles of a substance

- $Q = mC\Delta T$ to determine energy required to change temperature by a certain amount

- Steeper slope on curve = lower C

Phase Diagram:

- Depicts the phase changes of a substance as a function of P and T

- At any point along a curve = 2 phases in equilibrium

- Solid favored at low temp and high pressure (water exception for pressure)

- Gas favored at high temp and low pressure

- Triple point: T and P at which all three phases can exist simultaneously

- Critical point: beyond tis point, you have a supercritical fluid (has properties of both liquid and gas; liquid and gas not distinct phases)

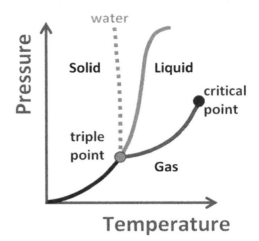

Water: liquid slightly denser than solid

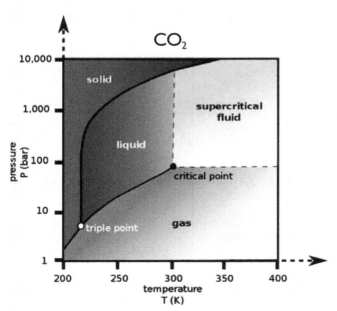

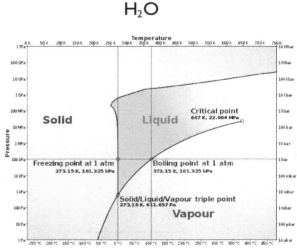

REACTION RATES AND EQUILIBRIUM

General Chemistry Lecture 11

OBJECTIVES

- Rates of chemical reactions
  - Factors that determine reaction rate
  - Rate law and the rate constant, k
  - Complex reaction and elementary steps
  - Rate determining step
- Activation energy
- Arrhenius equation
- Catalysts
  - Mechanism of action
  - Impact on energy profile
- Kinetic control of reaction rate versus thermodynamic control
- Equilibrium
  - Equilibrium constant, K
  - Reaction quotient, Q
  - Relationship between K and ΔG
- Le Chatelier's Principle

Reaction Rate

Reaction rate = the rate of change of the concentration of products or reactants

$$\text{Rate} = \frac{\Delta concentration}{\Delta time} = \frac{M}{sec}$$

$$aA + bB \longleftrightarrow cC + dD$$

$$\text{Rate} = -\frac{1}{a}\frac{\Delta[A]}{\Delta t} = -\frac{1}{b}\frac{\Delta[B]}{\Delta t} = \frac{1}{c}\frac{\Delta[C]}{\Delta t} = \frac{1}{d}\frac{\Delta[D]}{\Delta t}$$

- As reactants disappear and products appear, the rate of the forward reaction will decrease so rate is often discussed with respect to instantaneous rate (d[A]/dt) as opposed to average rate

- In general, reaction rate is determined by: how often the molecules collide, energy of the molecules, activation energy
  - Increased temp, increased [reactants], lower activation energy (catalyst present) = increased rate

Rate Law: equation that relates the rate of a reaction to the concentration of the reactants

$aA + bB \leftrightarrow cC + dD$ Rate = $k[A]^m[B]^n$

- Rate constant, k, is fixed for a given reaction at a certain temperature (and whether in presence of catalyst)
    - Larger k = faster reaction
- **Reaction order** = m + n
- Units of k depend of reaction order
    - 0 order: rate = k $\rightarrow$ k = M/sec
    - 1st order: rate = k[A] $\rightarrow$ k = 1/sec
    - 2nd order: rate = k[A]^2 = k[A][B] $\rightarrow$ k = 1/Msec

How to determine m and n:

1. For reactions composed of one single-step mechanism (also called an "elementary reaction"): m and n are the stoichiometric coefficients for A and B found in the balanced equation

2. For "complex reactions" (composed of more than one elementary steps): the rate law depends only on the rate determining step (RDS), if there is one

- RDS = slowest elementary step of that mechanism
- Each elementary step of a complex reaction has a rate law that can be found using stoichiometric coefficients
    - ($aA + aB \leftrightarrow cC + dD$;   Rate = $k[A]^a[B]^b$)

- So if you know all the elementary steps of complex reaction and which one is the RDS, then the overall rate of the complex reaction is found using the stoichiometric coefficients from the balanced equation for the RDS

     Overall: A + B $\rightarrow$ C + D
     Step 1:   A + 2B $\rightarrow$ C + E   (slow)   *E is an intermediate*
     Step 2:   E $\rightarrow$ B + D   (fast)
     Rate = $k[A][B]^2$,   reaction order = 3

3. If you don't know the RDS or elementary steps of a reaction, you must determine the rate law experimentally:
- Experiment is run multiple times with varying concentrations of reactants, and the initial reaction rate measured

A + B $\rightarrow$ C + D

trial	[A]	[B]	Rate (M/sec)
1	.02	.01	2.03
2	.04	.01	8.17
3	.02	.02	4.01

Order with respect to A:

$$\frac{rate2}{rate1} = \frac{k[A]^m[B]^n}{k[A]^m[B]^n} = \frac{k(.04)^m(.01)^n}{k(.02)^m(.01)^n} = \frac{8.17}{2.03}$$

$$2^m = 4$$
$$m = 2$$

Order with respect to B: n = 1

Rate = $k[A]^2[B]$

Arrhenius Equation: enables you to calculate the rate constant for a given reaction and set of conditions

$$k = Ae^{-\frac{E_A}{RT}}$$

A = constant accounting for the orientation of molecules
R = Universal gas constant
T = Temp in Kelvin
E_A = activation energy

Activation Energy: minimum energy that must be provided to the reactants for a reaction to occur

- E_A is require so that reactants can get over that initial energy "hump" (after that it's "downhill"), which is the highly unstable and high energy **transition state/activated complex**

- **Reactants ------- [T.S.] ‡ -------> Products**

- Lower E_A = increased rate (more of the molecules are able to reach the energy state required to react)

- **Catalysts** increase reaction rate by lowering the E_A

Transition state-activated complex: highest energy/least stable state within the reaction

- Colliding reactant molecules must have enough energy to reach that of the T.S.

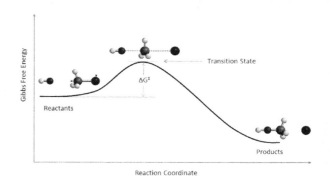

Reaction: $HO^- + CH_3Br \rightarrow [HO\text{---}CH_3\text{---}Br]^{\ddagger} \rightarrow CH_3OH + Br^-$

Reaction Coordinate:

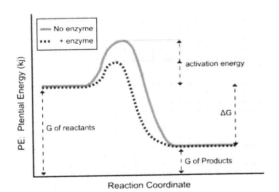

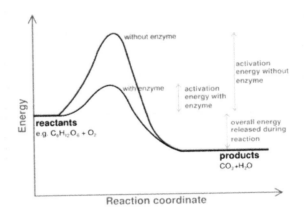

Catalyst: speed up the reaction by lowering the E_A\

- Do NOT get used up in the reaction (come out unchanged)
- Enzyme = biological catalyst
- By lowering E_A, they speed up the forward and the reverse reaction, so catalysts do influence kinetics (enable the reaction rate to increase); increasing k
- They do not influence thermodynamics (the position of equilibrium, which depends only on the enthalpy of reaction, entropy of reaction, and temp); no effect on K_{eq}

Thermodynamic versus kinetic control of reactions:

- Kinetics refers to how quickly a reaction occurs, but how fast it reaches equilibrium will not affect the point at which equilibrium is reached
    - Impacted by both temperature (incr. T always = incr. k) and E_A

- Thermodynamics refers to whether the reaction will occur at all (is it spontaneous or not?)
    - ΔG , which is affected by ΔH, T and ΔS (T may increase or decrease G depending on S)
    - $-\Delta G$ = reaction is spontaneous and will eventually occur (but could be very, very slow)

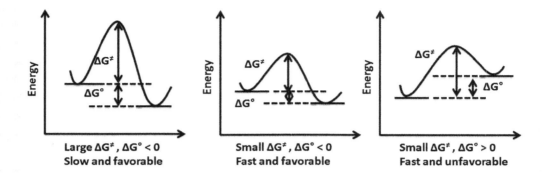

Large $\Delta G^{\ddagger}$, $\Delta G^{\circ} < 0$
Slow and favorable

Small $\Delta G^{\ddagger}$, $\Delta G^{\circ} < 0$
Fast and favorable

Small $\Delta G^{\ddagger}$, $\Delta G^{\circ} > 0$
Fast and unfavorable

Equilibrium Constant

In a closed system for a reversible reaction: When the reaction has reached equilibrium, there are no net changes in the concentrations of reactants or products; fwd and reverse reactions are occurring at the same rate.
$aA + bB \leftarrow \rightarrow cC + dD$

$$K_{eq} = \frac{[C]^c[D]^d}{[A]^a[B]^b}$$

- **K_{eq} = equilibrium constant** → indicates the relative ratio of products to reactants present once the reaction has reached equilibrium
- We have many different K's: K_a, K_b, K_{sp}, etc.
- Depends on the relative stabilities of the R and P
- Use molarity for aqueous substances, partial pressures for gases, and don't include liquids or solids in K_{eq}
- K_{eq} is constant for a reaction at a certain temperature

Law of Mass Action: This says that the rate of a reaction is only dependent on the concentration of the pertinent species (usually just the reactants). It also says that for a reaction in equilibrium, the ratio of products: reactants is constant (i.e. it is the basis for K_{eq})

K_{eq} is also a ratio of the forward rate constant over the reverse rate constant (at standard conditions)

$$K_{eq} = \frac{k_{fwd}}{k_{rev}}$$

K < 1 → more R than P at equilibrium
K = 1 → equivalent ratio of R to P at equilibrium
K > 1 → more P than R at equilibrium

Reaction Quotient (Q): relative ratio of P to R when the reaction is not at equilibrium

$$Q = \frac{[C]^c[D]^d}{[A]^a[B]^b}$$ → just like for K, don't include solids or liquids

Comparing Q to K indicates what direction the reaction will proceed in in order to reach equilibrium:
Q > K: reaction moves in the reverse direction
Q < K: reaction moves in the forward direction

The Relationship Between K_{eq} and Gibbs Free Energy

$\Delta G°_{rxtn}$ and K_{eq} both depend on the difference in stability between reactants and products and indicate how far the reaction proceeds in the forward (or reverse) direction in order to reach equilibrium. In other words, they are closely related.

$\Delta G°_{rxtn} < 0$, $K_{eq} > 1$ → P favored at equilibrium (fwd direction is spontaneous)

$\Delta G°_{rxtn} = 0$, $K_{eq} = 1$ → neither P nor R favored

$\Delta G°_{rxtn} > 0$, $K_{eq} < 1$ → R favored at equilibrium

$\Delta G = \Delta G° + RT\ln Q$

At equilibrium, Q = K, so: $\Delta G° = -RT \ln K$

Le Chatelier's Principle

- If a system is at equilibrium and some change is applied (change in: temp, pressure/volume, concentration), then it will shift in order to reestablish equilibrium

Concentration:

- Concentration of P increased: reaction will shift towards R (move in reverse direction)
- Concentration of R increased: reaction will shift towards P (move in forward direction)

Note: there is no change in K; rather, the system shifts in order to reestablish K

Adding a solid or liquid to the reaction has no effect (they're not included in K)

Pressure/Volume:

- Increase pressure/decrease volume: shifts to side with less moles of gas (trying to reestablish the K_{eq} ratio of the partial pressures)
- Decrease pressure/increase volume: shifts to side with more moles of gas
- Adding an inert gas to a container with constant volume: no shift (because no change in the ratio of species' partial pressures)

Temperature:

- Unlike changes in concentration and pressure, changes in temperature **will** affect K_{eq} AND $\Delta G°_{rxtn}$
- Endothermic reaction ($\Delta H_{rxtn} > 0$): Increasing temperature (like "adding heat") will increase the K value (more products at equilibrium)
- Exothermic reaction ($\Delta H_{rxtn} < 0$): Increasing temperature (like "adding heat") will decrease the K value (more reactants at equilibrium)

Remember that increasing temperature will always cause the reaction rate to increase (kinetic effect), so that the reaction reaches equilibrium sooner

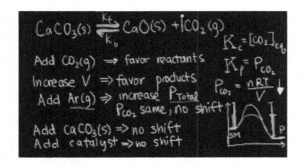

ORGANIC CHEMISTRY INTRO: PROPERTIES AND TRENDS

Organic Chemistry Lecture 1

OBJECTIVES

- Organic hydrocarbons
  - Degrees of unsaturation
  - Ring strain of cyclic hydrocarbons
- Carbocations and Carbanions
  - Stability: charge location, induction, resonance
- Acidity
- Basicity
- Nucleophiles
  - Trend of nucleophilicity
  - Common nucleophiles
- Electrophiles
- Leaving group

- Hydrocarbons: Organic compound containing C and H atoms only
  - Meth- 1 C, eth- 2 C, prop- 3 C, but- 4 C, pent- 5 C, hex- 6 C, hept- 7 C
  - -ane, -ene, -yne → depend on type of bonds present

- **Alkane:** only single bonds between C atom (saturated hydrocarbons)
  - C_nH_{2n+2}
- **Alkene:** contain at least one C=C (carbon to carbon double bond)
  - C_nH_{2n}
- **Alkyne:** contain at least one carbon to carbon triple bond
  - C_nH_{2n-2}
- **Aromatic:** cyclic molecule with resonance (contains benzene-like molecule)

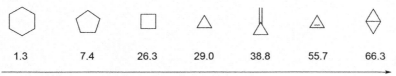

Ring strain of cyclic hydrocarbons:
- Sp³ carbon atoms are tetrahedral therefore prefer to have a bond angle of 109.5
- In a ring structure, the bond angle between attached carbons is often significantly below 109.5 → destabilizing

1.3	7.4	26.3	29.0	38.8	55.7	66.3

strain energy (kcal/mol)

Degrees of Unsaturation (DoU): indicates number of pi bonds and/or rings

- 1 ring = 1 DoU; 1 pi bond = 1 DoU
    - Double bond = 1 DoU; triple bond = 2 DoU; benzene = 4 DoU
- DoU = (2C + 2 – H) / 2
    - C = # carbons, H = # hydrogens and/or halogens
    - If nitrogen present, count as one additional C and one additional H

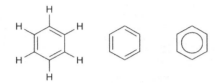

Carbocations and Carbanions

- **Carbocation:** molecule with a carbon atom that has a +1 charge (only has 3 bonds to it)
    - Doesn't have full octet; unstable

- **Carbanion:** molecule with a carbon atom that has a -1 charge (has 3 bonds to it plus a lone pair)
    - Has full octet but unstable because -1 FC on atom with low EN

Induction:

Electron Donating Groups = atoms/group of atoms with low EN (alkyl groups)
- EDGs minimize the effect of a + charge

Electron Withdrawing Groups = atoms/group of atoms with high EN (O, N, F, Br, Cl, etc)
- EWGs minimize the effect of a - charge

Stability of carbocations and carbanions:

Carbocation:

- $3° > 2° > 1° > methyl$
- More EDGs (alkyl groups) = more stable
- More EWGs (EN atoms) = less stable

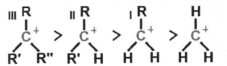

Carbanions:

- $methyl > 1° > 2° > 3°$
- More EWGs = more stable
- More EDGs = less stable

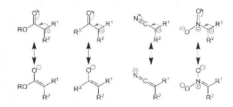

- If a carbocation or carbanion has resonance then the molecule is more stable (the + or − charge is delocalized)

Acidity:
- Molecule with a more stable to conjugate base = more acidic
    - Increasing EN of the atom that loses the H (and gets a − charge as a conjugate base)
    - Increasing resonance of conjugate base (delocalizing the − charge)
    - Increasing size/polarity of the atom that has a − charge (HCl > HF)

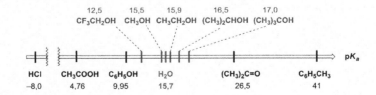

Basicity:
- Molecule with a more stable conjugate acid = more basic
    - Opposite trends as acidity (i.e. Decreasing EN of atom that gains H; Smaller atom that gains the H atom)
    - Less resonance of base ($CH_3CH_2NH_2 > C_6H_5NH_2$)
    - Atomic groups that are poor LGs are in general stronger bases

Nucleophile: donates a pair of electrons to an electrophile, forming a bond (Lewis base)

- Pi bond or atom with a lone pair

- Likes and attacks positively charged species ("nucleo" "phile")

$$E^+ \overset{+}{\frown} + :Nu^- \xrightarrow{\ k\ } E-Nu$$

$$\overset{\ominus}{Nu} + \overset{\delta+ \ \ \delta-}{R-X} \longrightarrow R-Nu + X^{\ominus}$$
$$\mathbf{1} \qquad \mathbf{2} \qquad\qquad \mathbf{3} \qquad \mathbf{4}$$

Nucleophilicity increases with…

- Increasing negative charge of atom that acts as nucleophile (NH_2^- > NH_3)

- Increasing size/polarizability of atom (I^- > Cl^-; SH^- > OH^-)

- Decreasing EN because better at sharing its pair of e-

- Generally, strong bases are good nucleophiles (Brønsted-Lowry base is a nucleophile that attacks and forms a bond with a hydrogen)

- Decreasing steric hindrance

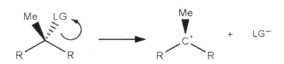

- Common nucleophiles: Halides (I^-, Br^-, etc.), OH^-, RO^-, NH_3, NH_2^-, CN^-

Electrophile: electron deficient species that accepts an electron pair by forming a bond with a nucleophile

- Lewis acid

- Has + or δ^+ charge and/or an incomplete octet

- Common electrophiles: H^+, H_3O^+, BF_3, δ^+C

$$E^+ \overset{+}{\frown} + :Nu^- \xrightarrow{\ k\ } E-Nu$$

Leaving Group:

- Better LG = more stable existing on its own (apart from the molecule that it leaves) and better at holding the e- (and the negative charge) that it receives

- Weak bases (conjugates of strong acids) = good LG

poor leaving group

good leaving group

ABSORPTION SPECTRA AND METHODS OF SPECTROSCOPY

Organic Chemistry Lecture 2

OBJECTIVES

- Classifying the electromagnetic spectrum
- Infrared region
    - IR Spectroscopy
    - Common wavenumbers on IR Spectroscopy

- Visible and Ultraviolet regions of light
    - Absorption and complementary colors
    - Indicators
    - Conjugation
    - Electron transitions
    - Transition metals
    - UV/Vis Spectroscopy
- NMR Spectroscopy
    - Method
    - Equivalent protons, splitting, integration, shielding
- Mass Spectrometry

Classifying the electromagnetic spectrum

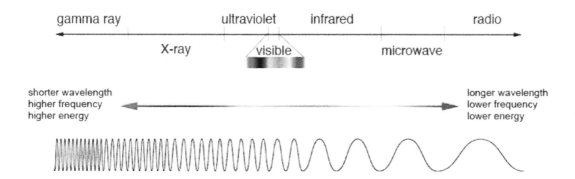

Infrared Region

- Intramolecular bonds stretch and compress (spring-like dynamics) with characteristic frequencies
- These **bond vibration frequencies** are usually in the IR region of light
- These frequencies can be measured and are indicative of the type of bond (between which atoms and within which functional group) that are present

IR Spectroscopy: used to determine which functional groups are present in a molecule

- Shine IR light of varying wavelengths through a substance
- Certain bonds vibrate at certain frequencies and absorb those specific frequencies of light
- Plot the % transmittance versus *wavenumber*

  - Wavenumber $= \nu = \frac{1}{\lambda} = $ cm^{-1}

  - Increased ν = decreased λ = increased energy

  - Downward peak means light of that wavenumber was absorbed

- IR Spectrum usually between 4000 to 600 cm^{-1}
- Approximately 1500 – 500 cm^{-1} = fingerprint region

O-H: 3600-3000 cm^{-1} (strong, broad)

N-H: 3500-3300 cm^{-1} (strong)

sp^{2}C-H: 3100-3000 cm^{-1}

sp^{3}C-H: 3000-2900 cm^{-1}

C≡C: 2260-2100 cm^{-1}

C≡N: 2260-2200 cm^{-1}

C=O: 1780-1650 cm^{-1} (strong, sharp)

C=C: 1680-1600 cm^{-1}

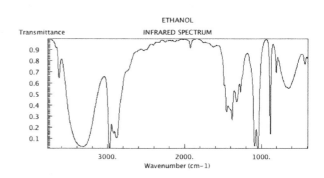

Visible Light

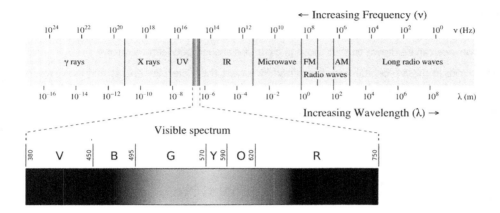

Absorption and complementary colors:

- The color that a substance appears to be is the complementary color to the one that it absorbs
  - "Complementary" = opposite side of color wheel
  - Substance absorbs blue light and reflects all other colors back (into your eye) → it appears to be yellow
  - A compound that appears to be green/turquoise is one that best absorbs _____ light

Indicators:

- Indicator = a pair of conjugates; either both different colors or one colored, one colorless (H-Ind and Ind⁻)
- At a pH below that of the pK_a of the indicator: color of H-Ind dominates; Above its pK_a: color of Ind⁻ dominates

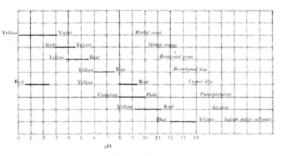

Conjugation

- **Conjugation:** 3 or more connected atoms with pi electrons (electrons in un-conjugated, p-orbitals)
  - Generally looks like: alternating double bonds (may also involve atoms with lone pairs)
  - Resonance can be drawn to shift those pi electrons around between the atoms
- The electrons in these p-orbitals are delocalized → lowers the molecule's energy and increases its stability
- Therefore lower energy (longer wavelength) EM radiation is absorbed by conjugated molecules
- If there's enough conjugation, the light absorbed will be in the visible spectrum
  - More conjugation = increased wavelength of light absorbed = light absorbed closer to red (ROYGBIV)
  - Low amount of conjugation: light absorbed is in the UV spectrum

Beta Carotene (red-orange):

Vitamin B12 (red):

R = 5'-deoxyadenosyl, Me, OH, CN

Chlorophyll (green):

- Complexes with transition metals are also often colored
- Transition metals have partially filled d orbitals
  - Ligands cause them to become different in energy
- When e- jump from one orbital to another they absorb or release energy
- The light absorbed is often in the visible spectrum
- Color it appears is complementary to the color absorbed

UV-Visible Spectroscopy

- Technique used to determine the wavelength of light absorbed by a compound
- Similar procedure to IR Spectroscopy; measuring absorbance of light within the UV and visible spectrums
    - UV light = approximately 200-400 nm
    - Visible light = approximately 400-750 nm
- Absorbance of certain wavelengths of light within UV/visible spectrum causes an electron to transition to an orbital of higher energy
- Output of procedure is a graph of absorbance versus wavelength; may be one or more peaks
- Compounds with extensive conjugation usually absorb within visible spectrum

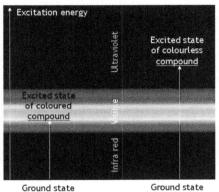

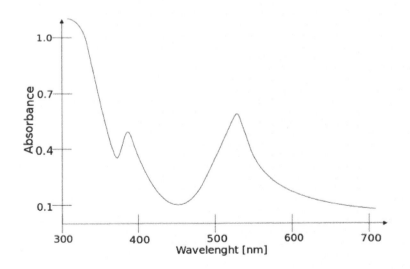

Nuclear Magnetic Resonance (NMR) Spectroscopy

- Technique that assesses the magnetic properties of the nuclei of specific elements (commonly ^1H or ^{13}C)

- H-NMR assesses things about Hydrogen atoms and is used to decipher to structure/identity of organic molecules or the purity of a sample

- Many nuclei have spin (need an odd # of protons to have a NET spin) and act like a magnet with a certain alignment of the poles
    - When an external magnetic field is applied they're excited to a higher energy level then fall back down to ground state, emitting energy of a characteristic frequency (called its **resonant frequency**)

- The resonant frequency depends on the atoms' specific chemical environment
    - Protons with the same exact chemical environment (**equivalent hydrogens/protons**) have the same resonant frequency and will therefore be represented by the same peak on the spectrum

- Spectrum has peaks at various ppm values, with each peak representing a specific "type" of H atom in the molecule

- ppm value is the **chemical shift** of that proton measured relative to a standard molecule, **TMS** (tetramethylsilane) which has a shift of 0 ppm

- Height of the peak is its "relative intensity"

- The more chemically different that two protons groups are, the farther apart they are on spectrum

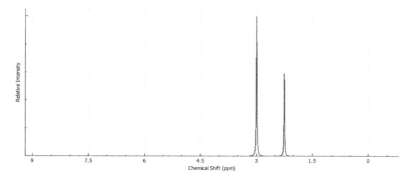

- # of equivalent hydrogen groups = # peaks on spectrum

- **"Integration"** = area under the peak → proportional to the # of hydrogens represented by that signal (# H atoms within that group of equivalent hydrogens)

- **Splitting:** A single signal on spectrum (representing one group of equivalent hydrogens) may be split into multiple different peaks clustered in the same region
  - N = the number of **neighboring hydrogens** (adjacent hydrogens; hydrogens that are three bonds away)
  - N + 1 = number of peaks that the signal is split into

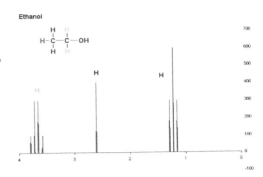

- **Shielding:** a proton is shielded from the magnetic field that is applied during NMR spectroscopy if the nucleus has high e- density
  - Nucleus is shielded if that atom is nearby atoms with low EN, like carbon
  - Nucleus is de-shielded if it is nearby highly EN atoms or pi bonds because the e- of that H are being pulled away so are unable to shield the proton from the externally applied magnetic field
  - DESHIELDED protons are shifted DOWNFIELD (to the LEFT on the spectrum, towards higher ppm values)

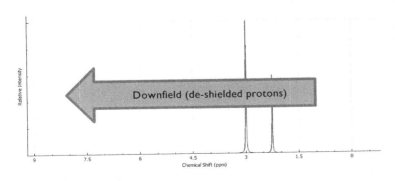

Common chemical shift ranges:

Type of proton		Chemical Shift (ppm)
Primary alkyl	RCH₃	0.8-1.0
Secondary alkyl	R₂C H₂	1.2-1.4
Tertiary alkyl	R₃C H	1.4-1.7
benzylic	ArCH₃	2.2-2.5
Alkyl chloride	RCH₂Cl	3.6-3.8
Alkyl bromide	RCH₂Br	3.4-3.6
Alkyl iodide	RCH₂I	3.1-3.3
Alkyl fluoride	RCH₂F	4.0-4.5
Ether	ROCH₂R	3.3-3.9
Ester	RCOOCH₂R	3.3-3.9
Alcohol	HOCH₂R	3.3-4.0
Ketone	RCCH₃ ‖ O	2.1-2.6
Ester	RCH₂COOR	2.1-2.6
Aldehyde	RCH ‖ O	9.0-10.0
Vinylic	R₂C=CH₂	4.6-5.0
Aromatic	ArH	6.0-9.0
Alcohol Hydroxyl	ROH	0.5-6.0
Carboxylic	RCOOH	10-13
Phenolic	ArOH	4.5-7.7
Amino	RNH₂	1.0-5.0
Amide	RCNHR ‖ O	5.0-9.0

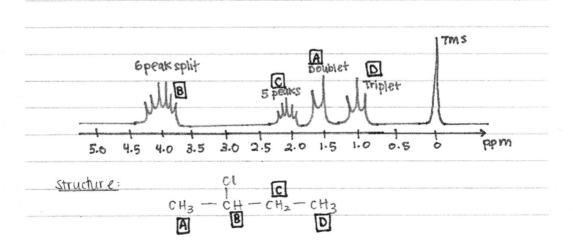

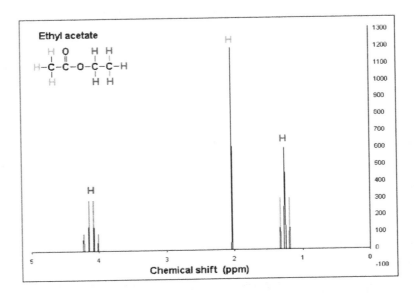

Ethyl acetate

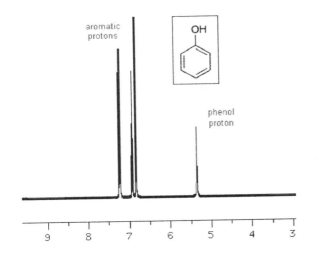

aromatic protons

OH

phenol proton

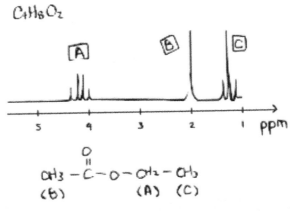

$C_4H_8O_2$

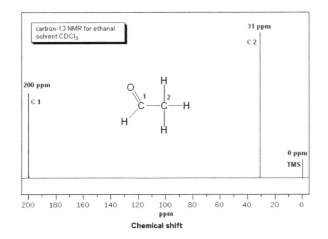

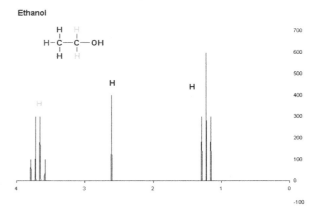

Mass Spectrometry

- Analytical technique that enables one to determine the molecular weight of a molecule and/or identify a molecule based on its fragmentation pattern

- Sample is bombarded with a stream of e- (ionized) and some of the molecules break apart into various fragments of different sizes

- The various ions are then exposed to a magnetic field, deflected and separated by their mass-to-charge (m/z) ratio, then detected, and plotted onto a mass spectrum

Height of peak = abundance of that fragment

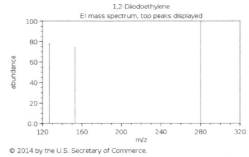

© 2014 by the U.S. Secretary of Commerce.

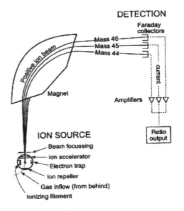

- **Parent peak / molecular ion (M⁺) peak:** the peak that represents the ion of an un-fragmented molecule of the sample (often the peak with the one of the highest m/z ratios and one of the tallest)
  - m/z ratio of parent peak almost always represents the molecular mass of the parent molecule
  - Smaller peaks clustered nearby the parent peak are isotopes of the parent molecule (ex. M+1 peak = isotope of the parent molecule which has a ^{13}C atom instead of ^{12}C)

- **Base peak:** Tallest peak on spectrum which represents the most abundant fragment/species
  - abundance of base peak set to 100%

- Base peak may or may not be the molecular ion peak

- Other likely peaks: M-1 = fragment with loss of 1 H atom; M-2 peak = loss of 2 H atoms; M + 2 peak = isotope of the parent molecule with one ^{37}Cl or one ^{81}Br

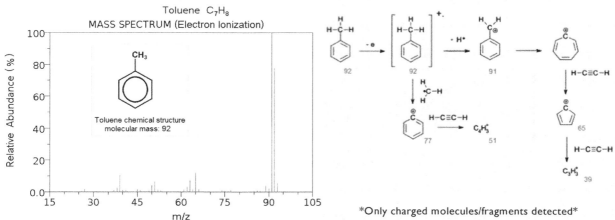

Toluene C_7H_8
MASS SPECTRUM (Electron Ionization)

Toluene chemical structure
molecular mass: 92

NIST Chemistry WebBook (http://webbook.nist.gov/chemistry)

Only charged molecules/fragments detected

METHODS OF SEPARATION AND PURIFICATION

Organic Chemistry Lecture 3

Chromatography

- In general, chromatography is an analytical technique used to separate out components of a mixture based on the affinity of molecules to the stationary or mobile phase

- Stationary and mobile phase differ in polarity, size, and/or same other physical property so that components of mixture interact differently with them and either elute out of the mixture with the mobile phase or stay in the mixture

- Stationary phase stays fixed within column/on paper while mobile phase does not. If component of mixture is attracted to mobile phase and/or repelled by stationary phase it will **elute** out of mixture.

Types:
- Paper and Thin Layer Chromatography (TLC)
- Column Chromatography
- High Pressure Liquid Chromatography (HPLC)
- Gas Chromatography
- Size Exclusion Chromatography
- Ion-Exchange Chromatography
- Affinity Chromatography

Know when each type is used (for separation of what type of substances; mainly to separate or analyze?)

Paper/Thin Layer Chromatography (TLC)

- Usually used to separate out the pigments of a mixture, which have differing polarities (basis of separation = polarity)
  - Mainly analytical (because separated pigments can't be collected/recovered)

- **Procedure:** dot sample of mixture(s) to be analyzed at base of paper/material, often also add controls; place bottom of paper into a shallow bath of volatile solvent; solvent moves up paper quickly by capillary action, some pigments move with it (more attracted to solvent and/or repelled by paper) and some lag behind (more attracted to paper); remove from bath when solvent front reaches near the top of paper; measure distance travelled by solvent front and pigments

- R_f = distance travelled by pigment / distance travelled by solvent front
  - $R_f = 1$ → pigment moved as far as solvent front
  - Lower R_f = pigment travelled less far

- Stationary phase (paper/plate) is often silica gel→ polar
- Mobile phase (solvent) is usually non-polar
  - If so, non-polar compounds move further up along plate, higher R_f

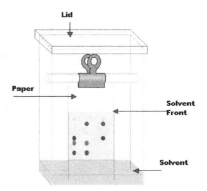

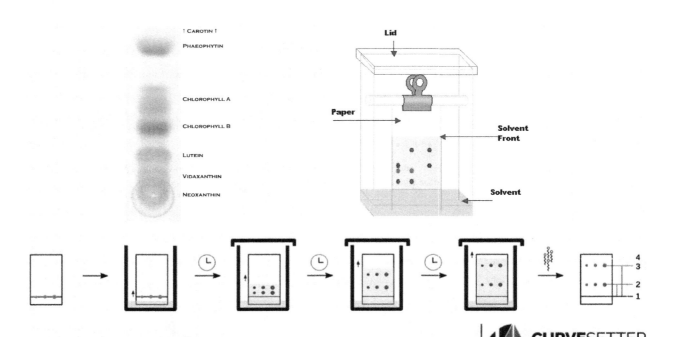

Column Chromatography

- Used to separate out components of a liquid mixture and then collect the components; basis of separation is polarity of mixture components

- **Procedure:** mixture dissolved into solvent (mobile phase) and gradually added to column that is packed with a solid material; components of mixture separate out based on polarity, those that reach bottom of column are then collected as they elute out

- Stationary phase is a solid substance; often it is silica get (polar)
- Mobile phase is a solvent that the mixture is dissolved into
  - If stationary phase polar and mobile phase non-polar, non-polar substances will elute out first

- Often have to add multiple different mobile phases into column in a sequence of increasing (or decreasing) polarity in order to get all components to eventually elute out

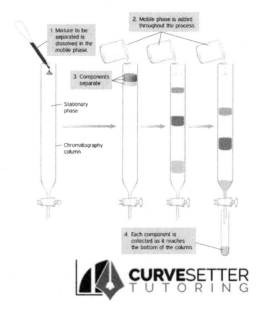

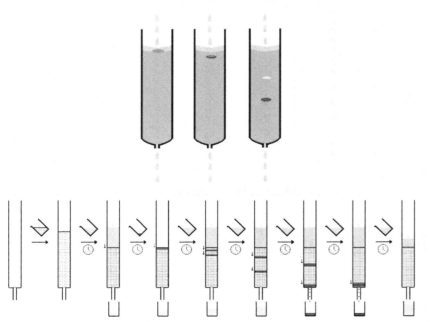

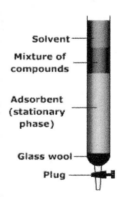

High Pressure/Performance Liquid Chromatography (HPLC)

- Used to separate out, quantify, and often identify the components of a liquid mixture based on different polarity and/or charge; more efficient, exact, and high-tech version of column chromatography
  - Column chromatography relies on gravity to elute out the components; HPLC uses high pressure so that they elute out much more quickly

- Output = graph with series of peaks that shows the exact "**retention time**" (how long it stayed in column) for each component; area under peaks can be used to **quantify the amount of each component** that was present in the mixture
  - Mixture components can also be collected

- **Normal Phase HPLC:** Very similar to column chromatography but high pressure forces mixture through the column; stationary phase is silica particles (polar) and mobile phase is a non-polar solvent such as hexane
  - Longer time spent in column (higher retention time) = more polar component

- **Reverse Phase HPLC:** The more commonly used form; non-polar stationary phase and polar solvent
  - Higher retention time = more non-polar

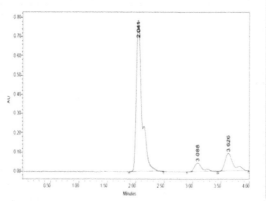

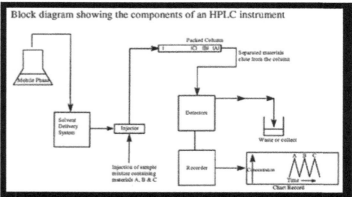

Block diagram showing the components of an HPLC instrument

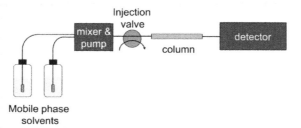

Mobile phase solvents

Gas Chromatography

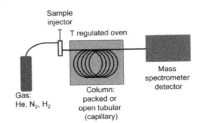

- Used to separate out liquid components of a mixture based on their boiling points; only required a very small amount of the sample

- Mobile phase = inert gas (He, N_2, etc)which carries the liquid mixture through a heated column

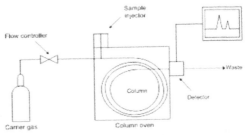

- Stationary phase = wax-like liquid adsorbent packed into column (sometimes not used)

- Detector must be used to give quantitative analysis of the mixture components (and to identify them) as they elute out
  - Many different detector types possible (mass spec, for example)

- As the temperature in the column gradually increases, mixture components will reach their boiling points and their gaseous forms detected

- Higher BP spends more time in apparatus and detected later

Analytical Gas Chromatography

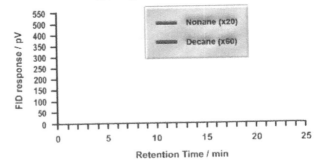

Microcrystalline Cellulose FID Response 300K

Nonane (x20)

Decane (x60)

Distillation

- Separate liquids based on their boiling points; requires more liquid sample than gas chromatography does

- Basic procedure: mixture of 2 or more liquids is heated gradually is one beaker/vessel; the liquid with the lowest BP begins to boil first and turns into vapor, leaving the beaker and entering a condensation tube where it turns back into a liquid and is then collected in a collection flask

- **Simple distillation:** Used to separate components that have > 15 degree difference in their BPs OR to separate a liquid out from other impurities (ex. Boil water and salts remains at bottom at the end)

- **Fractional distillation:** Used to separate components with smaller differences in their BPs; long "fractioning column" above mixture enables better separation of components because more condensation-evaporation cycles

- Compounds with lower boiling points (weaker IMF) evaporate more quickly and are collected first
    - Higher BP of hydrocarbons when… more carbons present, higher molecular weight, less branching (enables more London forces), and less kinks
    - IMF strengths: Ion-dipole > H-bonds > dipole-dipole > dipole-induced dipole > London dispersion forces

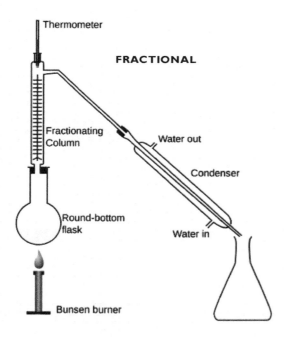

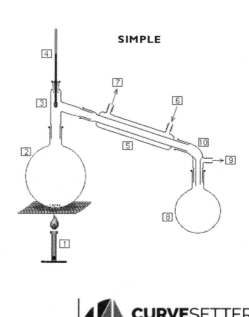

Resolution

- Technique to separate a racemic mixture into its two constituent enantiomers
  - Enantiomers have the same physical/chemical properties but diastereomers don't

- Add a resolving agent (chiral compound that is purely R or S) to the racemic mixture so that it bonds to the two enantiomer molecules. Now you have a mixture of 2 diastereomers that can be separated by their differing physical properties. Once separated remove the resolving agent to turn them back into enantiomers
  - Racemic mixture + resolving agent → mixture of diastereomers → separate diastereomers by physical properties → remove resolving agent and turn each diastereomer back into the original enantiomer

- $(R_1 + S_2)$ $\xrightarrow{\text{Add resolving agent, R}}$ $(R_1\text{-R} + S_2\text{-R})$ $\xrightarrow{\text{separate,then remove R}}$ (R_1) (S_2)

Extraction

- Liquid-liquid extraction: separate a liquid mixture by distributing its components between two immiscible (do not mix) solvents

- Usually uses liquid solvents with differing polarity to create one **aqueous phase (polar)** and one **organic phase (non-polar)**
  - Ionic and polar solute molecules of mixture enter the aqueous phase
  - The two phases differ in densities too; often the aqueous phase is denser and is therefore below the organic phase

- Mixture will separate into its components throughout different rounds of extraction
  - bring one of the components into aqueous/organic phase, then drain it out of **separating funnel**; repeat

- Partition/distribution coefficient= amt. X in one solvent / amt. X in the other

- Acid/base extraction uses acids and bases to protonate/deprotonate one or more components and cause it to become charged so that it enters the aqueous phase

Liquid-liquid Extraction

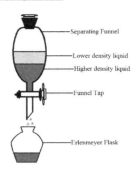

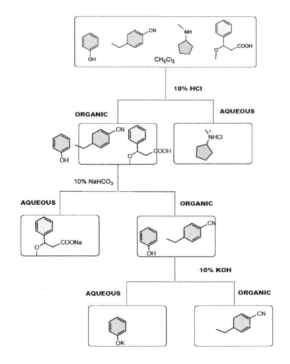

- To extract amines, add strong acid (HCl)

- To extract carboxylic acid, use weak or strong base (HCO3⁻)
  - weak base cannot extract out phenol or other poorly acidic molecules

- To extract phenol, need strong base (NaOH, KOH, etc.)

Separating peptides/proteins

Electrophoresis (SDS-PAGE):

- Polyacrylamide gel with electrical field through it; particles migrate towards end of gel with opposite charge to their own charge
    - One end of gel is negatively charged (**cathode**) and one end is positively charged (**anode**)

- Small pores in gel separate the particles **by size** (smaller ones reach the end first, larger ones lag behind)

- When separating proteins, negative charge must be added to them and they must be denatured so that they're linear
    - Add detergent sodium dodecyl sulfate (**SDS**)

- The denatured negatively charged proteins all migrate towards the anode
    - Longer polypeptide chains lag behind, shorter ones migrate faster

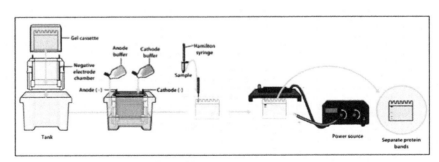

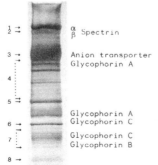

Size Exclusion Chromatography:

- Separate molecules (usually proteins/peptides or other large polymers) based on their size

- Column filled with porous substance (stationary phase) that allows molecules of certain sizes to pass through the tube-like holes

- Molecules dissolved in solvent (mobile phase) that will be poured into the column

- How quickly the molecules/proteins pass through the column and elute out depends on their size

- Larger proteins elute out first and have a shorter retention time because they can't fit into the holes and therefore pass straight through the column

- Smaller proteins enter all the holes/tubes (like taking detours) and therefore take longer to elute out

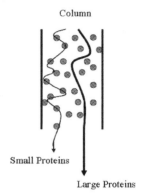

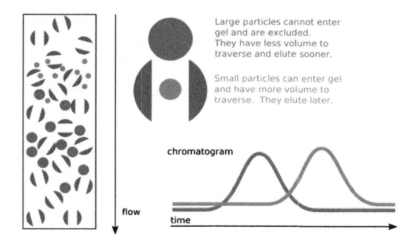

Large particles cannot enter gel and are excluded. They have less volume to traverse and elute sooner.

Small particles can enter gel and have more volume to traverse. They elute later.

Ion Exchange Chromatography:

- Separation of ionic molecules (often proteins) based on their charge and attraction/repulsion to a charged column

- Stationary phase = charged beads within column; mobile phase = aqueous solvent
  - Cation exchanger: negatively charged column traps positively charged molecules in it
  - Anion exchanger: positively charged column traps negatively charged molecules in it

- pH of solvent and PI of proteins determines the charge of the proteins
  - pH = PI → neutral
  - pH > PI → deprotonated; negatively charged
  - pH < PI → protonated; positively charged

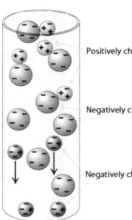

Positively charged proteins

Negatively charged beads

Negatively charged proteins

Affinity Chromatography:

- Separate/isolate specific proteins based on their affinity for other specific molecules/ligands that are bound to the column (stationary phase)

- Based on the attraction between a protein and a specific ligand/substrate (such as an antigen and antibody)

- Procedure: affinity column has a certain molecule bound to it; wash protein mixture through the column; target protein binds to column and other proteins elute out; elute out target protein using a different solvent (called the elution buffer) that interferes with attraction between target protein and column molecules

- Ex. Add a poly-histidine tag (multiple His amino acids at end of protein) to protein of interest by changing DNA sequence of the protein or covalently linking it
  - His has high affinity for Ni^{+2}, affinity column has Ni^{+2} bound to it
  - Elute out protein of interest using imidazole, which binds to Ni^{+2} and replaces protein, or by changing pH

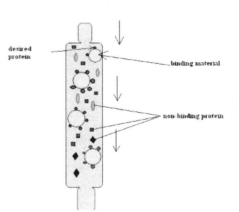

desired protein

binding material

non-binding protein

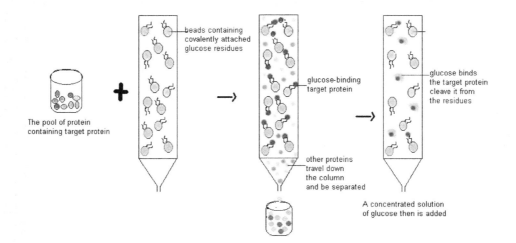

The pool of protein containing target protein

beads containing covalently attached glucose residues

glucose-binding target protein

other proteins travel down the column and be separated

glucose binds the target protein cleave it from the residues

A concentrated solution of glucose then is added

The demonstration of the steps in Affinity Chromatography

THE ORGANIC CHEMISTRY OF BIOLOGICAL MOLECULES

Organic Chemistry Lecture 4

OBJECTIVES

- **Amino Acids**
  - Zwitterion; Acidity and Basicity; Introduction to Isoelectric Point (pI)
  - Absolute Configuration
  - Strecker Synthesis and Gabriel Synthesis
- **Peptide bond**
  - Formation and resonance of the bond
- **Lipids**
  - Saponification reaction
- **Carbohydrates**
  - Nomenclature
  - Stereochemistry; Epimers and Anomers
  - Conformations of hexose
  - Glycosidic Linkage
  - Acetal and Hemiacetals; Reducing sugars

Amino Acids

Amino Acid Backbone:

- Alpha carbon, amine group, carboxyl group, side chain (R group)
- Amino acids are amphoteric (acid and basic)
- At low pH both the amine and carboxylic acid are protonated
  - NH_3^+ pKa = 9.5; COOH pKa = 2
- Above pH of 2 but below 9.5: COO^- and NH_3^+ **(zwitterion)**
- Above pH of 9.5: COO^- and NH_2

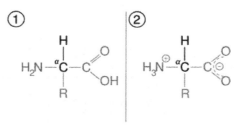

Acidity and Basicity:

- Amino acids are characterized as acidic or basic based on the pKa of their side chain (R group)
- When the pH of solution = pKa of the side chain, half of the a.a. that R group protonated, and half have it deprotonated; as pH rises, the amount of a.a. with the R group deprotonated increases towards 100%
- pKa's to know: Asp (approx. 4), Glu (approx. 4), His (6.5), Lys (10), Arg (12)

Isoelectric Point: pH at which molecule is net neutral

- For basic a.a.: pI = (pKa(R group) + pKa(amine))/2
- For acidic a.a.: pI = (pKa(R group) + pKa(COOH))/2
- For neither acidic nor basic a.a.: pI = (pKa(COOH) + pKa(amine))/2

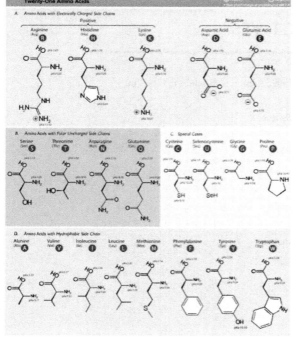

Note: all a.a. are amphoteric because they have an acidic group and a basic group

Abbreviations for the amino acids		
Ala	Alanine	A
Arg	Arginine	R
Asn	Asparagine	N
Asp	Aspartic acid	D
Asx	Asparagine or aspartic acid	B
Cys	Cysteine	C
Gln	Glutamine	Q
Glu	Glutamic acid	E
Gly	Glycine	G
Glx	Glutamine or glutamic acid	Z
His	Histidine	H
Ile	Isoleucine	I
Leu	Leucine	L
Lys	Lysine	K
Met	Methionine	M
Phe	Phenylalanine	F
Pro	Proline	P
Ser	Serine	S
Thr	Threonine	T
Trp	Tryptophan	W
Tyr	Tyrosine	Y
Val	Valine	V

Absolute Configuration at αC:

- The αC is a chiral center

- The designations "L" and "D" are used for the absolute configuration of biological molecules

    - L and D forms are enantiomers (L = S and D = R; except for cystine)

- All amino acids can exist as either L or D except for glycine (no chiral center because it has two H atoms attached)

- In Fischer projection (COOH at top), the amino group is on the LEFT for L-a.a.

- Only L-a.a. are made in the body and incorporated into proteins

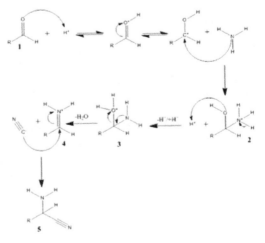

Strecker Synthesis of Amino Acids

- Forming a.a. from an aldehyde
- Create both L and D a.a. (non-stereospecific)

Gabriel-Malonic Ester Synthesis of Amino Acids

- Forming a.a. from primary alkyl halide and phthalimide
- Also non-stereospecific

- **Peptide bond:** amide linkage between amino acids

- Formation of the peptide bond is a **condensation reaction** (remove H₂O) and is facilitated by tRNA molecules during translation
    - Addition-elimination reaction between carboxylic acid and primary amine (amine attacks the carbonyl)
    - Reaction is non-spontaneous (ΔG > 0) and requires catalysis and ATP

- Peptide bond has resonance

  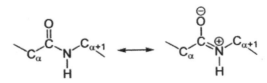

  - Very stable bond; difficult to break

  - Breaking peptide bond = hydrolysis reaction (requires the addition of water and a strong base)

  - Partial double bond character makes this region of the peptide planar and rigid (planes themselves can rotate relative to each other)

  - 6 atoms are within this rigid plane

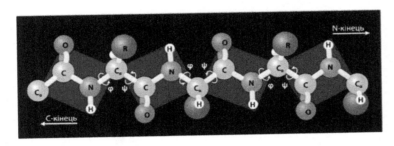

Lipids: Saponification Reaction

- Triglyceride = glycerol backbone plus 3 long chain fatty acids
  - Glycerol linked to hydrocarbon chain by carboxylic acid of the fatty acid (ester bond)

- Soap = potassium or sodium salts of fatty acids

- Saponification = reaction in which triglycerides react with strong base (NaOH or KOH) to form soap
  - Ester bond cleaved (ester hydrolysis) and fatty acids liberated→ form a salt with cation (Na$^+$ or K$^+$) → SOAP

Carbohydrates

- Monosaccharide = 1 sugar unit; Disaccharide = 2 units; Polysaccharaide = multiple units

Carbohydrate Nomenclature
- aldose = sugars with aldehyde; ketose = sugars with ketone
- triose = 3C sugar; tetrose = 4C; pentose = 5 C; hexose = 6 C
  - Glucose is an aldohexose; fructose is a ketohexose

- pyranose = sugars in 6 membered ring structure
- furanose = sugars in 5 membered ring structure
  - Glucopyranose = cyclic glucose; fructofuranose = cyclic fructose

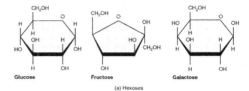

(a) Hexoses

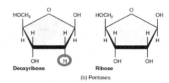

(b) Pentoses

"deoxy" = H instead of OH

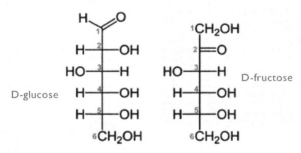

D-glucose

D-fructose

- Sugars are also classified as D/L based on configuration at penultimate carbon (second to last carbon in linear form; last chiral center)

  - D sugars have an R configuration at penultimate carbon → Fischer projection of glucose has OH group on the right of penultimate carbon

  - L sugars have an S configuration; L sugars rarely found in nature

  - L and D sugars are enantiomers of each other (every chiral center flips)

- Cyclic sugars are designated as α or β depending on the configuration of the anomeric carbon (Carbon #1; only becomes a stereocenter once molecule is cyclic)

- α sugar: OH of anomeric C and CH2OH groups on OPPOSITE sides of the ring

- β sugar: OH of anomeric C and CH2OH groups on SAME sides of the ring

- α and β sugars are **epimers** (differ at only 1 chiral center); more specifically referred to as **anomers** (epimers that differ at the anomeric C)

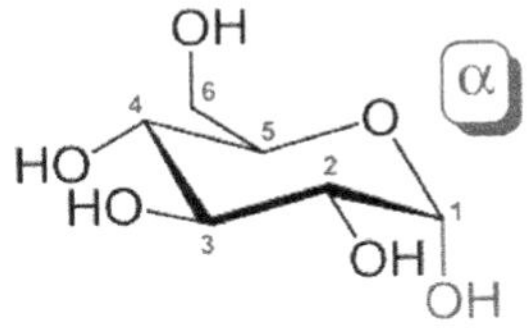

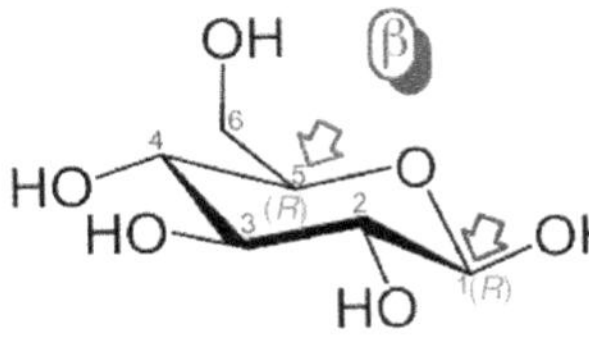

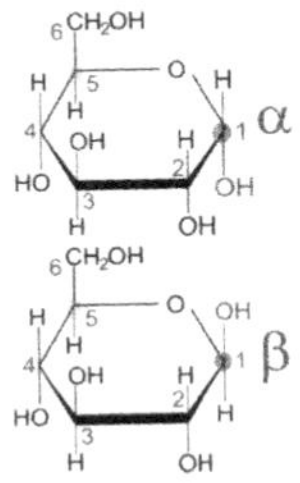

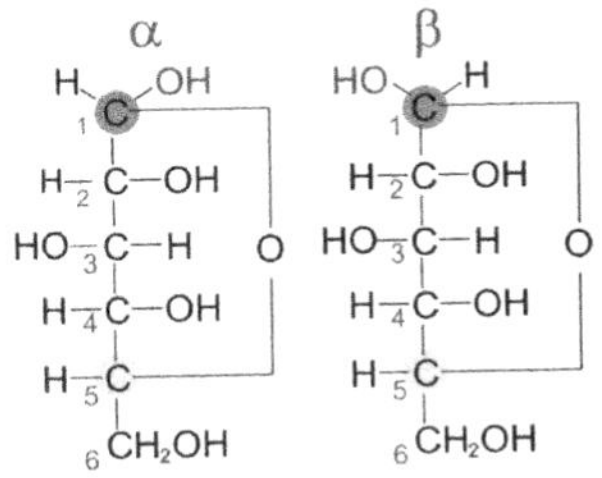

α-D-glucopyranose   ⇌   β-D-glucopyranose

Mutarotation: the spontaneous conversion between the two anomeric forms of a sugar; an equilibrium exists between the two forms

alpha ↔ linear ↔ beta

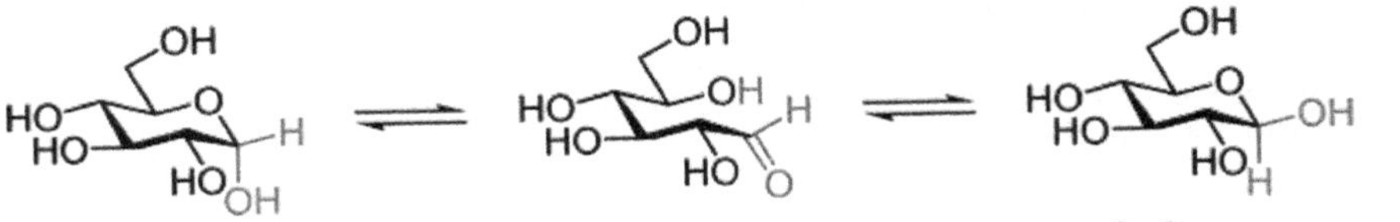

α-glucose   ⇌   β-glucose

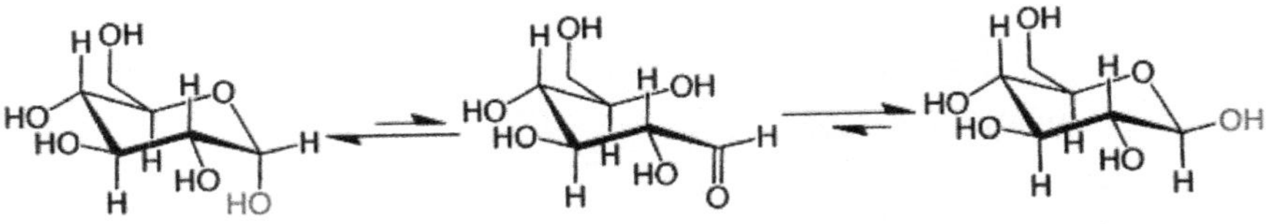

36 %   0,02 %   64 %

Hexose Conformations:

- Chair is most stable (all groups staggered)

- Steric hindrance for all other conformations decreases their stability

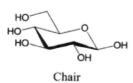

Chair

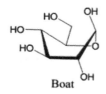

Boat

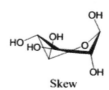

Skew

Chair

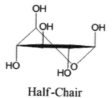

Half-Chair

Envelope

Glycosidic Linkage: Covalent bond between carbohydrate and some other molecule, which may or may not be another sugar (most common: between two sugars or between sugar and nitrogenous base in nucleotides)

- Forms between hemiacetal of a sugar and alcohol of some other molecule
- Classified as alpha or beta by conformation of anomeric carbon and labelled by which carbons it joins (β-1,4)

β – position

Cellulose

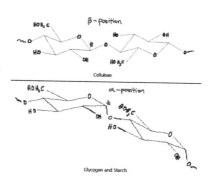

α – position

Glycogen and Starch

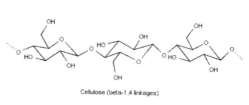

Cellulose (beta-1,4 linkages)

CH$_2$OH   CH$_2$OH

OH   OH

HO CH$_2$ |α-1,6

CH$_2$OH   CH$_2$OH   CH$_2$

OH |α-1,4   OH   OH

OH   OH   OH

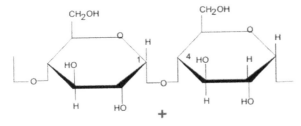

Hydrolysis of glycosidic linkage is the hydrolysis of an acetal group

- Requires an enzyme and water
- Ex. Amylase breaks down starch into monosaccharides

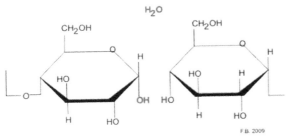

F.B. 2009

Hydrolysis of 1:4α Linkage

- **Acetal** = "non-reducing sugar"
  - Cannot act as reducing agent

- **Hemiacetal** = "reducing sugar" because it can act as a reducing agent when it opens to linear form
  - Undergo mutarotation (in equilibrium with linear form and both anomers)
  - Positive Tollen's test or Benedict's test indicates reducing sugar because aldehyde present
  - Shows a red precipitate on Benedict's test experiment: hemiacetal gets oxidized at anomeric carbon and reduces Cu^{+2} to Cu^+ (red)

"ketal" and "hemiketal" terms have been dropped

(acetal)   (ketal)

acetal

Hemiacetal

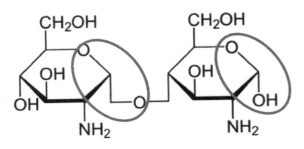

- Addition of alcohol to carbonyls (ketone or aldehyde)
  - Aldehyde/ketone reacts with 1 equivalent alcohol to produce hemiacetals, then another equivalent of alcohol to form an acetal
  - Alcohol is a poor nucleophile, so must catalyze with acid (H⁺) which protonates the carbonyl
- Reverse reaction requires acid and water

ALDEHYDES AND KETONES

Organic Chemistry Lecture 5

OBJECTIVES

- Overview of aldehydes and ketones
  - Nomenclature and general properties
  - Reactivity of carbonyl
  - Acidity of α H
- Redox reactions involving aldehydes and ketones
- Nucleophilic addition to carbonyls
  - Acetals and hemiacetals
  - Imines and enamines
  - Hydride reduction of carbonyls
  - Reaction with cyanohydrin
- Keto-enol tautomerization
- Aldol condensation reaction
  - Retro-aldol
- Kinetic and thermodynamic enolates

Aldehydes and Ketones Nomenclature:

- Note that molecule has aldehyde in it when ends with "–al" (acetal)

    - Methanal (formaldehyde): $H_2C=O$

- Note the presence of ketone from "keto-" or "-one"

General properties

- The carbonyl C=O bond is very polar, O is δ^- and C is δ^+

    - C is electrophilic and susceptible to nucleophilic attack

    - Reactivity of carbonyl carbon decreases if it is surrounded by large atoms/groups (steric hindrance)

- In general, aldehydes are more susceptible to nucleophilic attack than ketones

    - Less steric hinderance

    - Alkyl groups that surround carbonyl carbon on either side in the ketones are electron generous (slightly reduce the δ^+ charge

- Intermolecular interactions between molecules with carbonyls are strong (dipole-dipole) but not as strong as alcohols or carboxylic acids (which have intermolecular H-bond)

Acidity of α-H

- The α-H of aldehydes and ketones is any hydrogen that is on the carbon next door to the carbonyl carbon

- These hydrogens are slightly acidic

    - They can be removed by a strong base such as OH^- or RO^-

- Once H^+ is removed, the carbanion created (**enolate ion**) has resonance, which stabilizes it slightly

    - **Enolate ion:**

    - Enolate ion is nucleophilic

- If the enolate ion is protonated, an enol is formed:

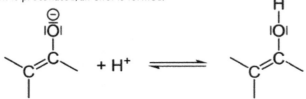

- Overall, a ketone may be converted into an enol

- The ketone form is more stable than the enolate and the enol form

Redox reactions involving aldehydes and ketones

- Alcohols can be oxidized to form aldehydes and ketones (more in next lecture)
    - Primary alcohol + weak oxidizing agent → aldehyde
    - Secondary alcohol + oxidizing agent → ketone

primary or
secondary alcohol

aldehyde
or ketone

[O]= chromium-based reagent, activated DMSO, hypervalent iodide compound, TPAP or TEMPO

R^1= alkyl or aryl substituent
R^2= hydrogen, alkyl or aryl substituent

- Aldehydes are much easier to oxidize than ketones (have the H attached to the C of the carbonyl)
- Under acidic conditions, the oxidation of aldehyde forms a carboxylic acid (COOH)
- Under basic conditions a salt of carboxylic acid forms (COONa)

Nucleophilic addition to carbonyls

- Carbonyl carbon is slightly positive and therefore electrophilic
  → can be attacked by nucleophiles
- Nucleophilic addition results in the breaking of a pi bond and
  the addition of the nucleophile (new sigma bond)

Acetals and Hemiacetals (see previous lecture):

- Hemiacetal formed by reacting an aldehyde or ketone with one equivalent alcohol plus acid
- Acetal formed by reacting an aldehyde or ketone with two equivalents alcohol plus acid; or by reacting a hemiacetal
  with one equivalent alcohol plus acid

Imines and Enamines

- Imine: C=N

Enamine: R=C-N

Imine Formation:
- Aldehyde/ketone reacted with **primary amine** at low pH

Enamine Formation:
- Aldehyde/ketone reacted with **secondary amine** (plus acid catalyst)

*Tertiary amines
are not reactive!

Hydride Reduction of Carbonyls

- Reduction of a ketone forms a secondary alcohol

- Reduction of an aldehyde forms a primary alcohol

- The reduction of aldehydes and ketones is most readily and commonly performed using a hydride ion (H⁻)
  - Source of hydride ion commonly: NaBH₄ or LiAlH₄
  - Both can reduce aldehydes and ketones to alcohols but LiAlH₄ is more reactive (stronger reducing agent)

Cyanohydrin Formation

- Cyanohydrin:

- importance: precursor to some amino acids

- Cyanohydrin can be formed through a nucleophilic addition reaction in which the cyanide ion is added to an aldehyde or ketone
    - CN^- is nucleophilic and attacks the carbonyl carbon
    - Source of cyanide ion is usually a salt (KCN, NaCN) or HCN
    - Often acid catalyzed

Keto-enol Tautomerization

- Enol and keto forms of a molecule are structural isomers and tautomers
    - Tautomers = isomers that differ in the position of H atoms and/or electrons
    - The keto form is much more stable than the enol form
- Tautomerization = the interconversion between tautomers
- Keto and enol forms undergo tautomerization
- A chemical equilibrium exists between this interconversion
    - At equilibrium, there is much of the keto form present versus the enol form because of the increased stability of the keto form

Overall reaction:

Reaction mechanism

Acid catalyzed enolization

Base catalyzed enolization

Aldol Condensation

- The reaction of an enol or enolate ion (created from a carbonyl) with the another carbonyl (aldehyde or ketone) to form a β-hydroxy-aldehyde/ketone (aldol addition product)
  - β-hydroxy-aldehyde/ketone = aldehyde/ketone with a hydroxyl group on the beta carbon

- Often the β-hydroxy-aldehyde/ketone product is then **dehydrated** (heat added & water removed) to form a conjugated enone (α- β-unsaturated carbonyl)

aldol

CH₃O:

(lost H shown for clarity)

enolate of aldol
(shown as carbanion)

loses OH

α,β-unsaturated
aldehyde

ENOL mode

catalytic H⁺

enol

(reacts in protonated form)

aldol addition product

- H₂O

aldol condensation
product

ENOLATE mode

base

enolate

- Enolate ion has a nucleophilic C (one resonance contributor has lone pair on the carbon!)
  - This δ^- C of enolate ion attacks the δ^+ C of the other carbonyl

- Reaction must be **acid or base catalyzed**

- Reaction mechanism:

Acid catalyzed aldol reaction

Protonated carbonyl (electrophilic)

Enol (nucleophilic)

Aldol

Acid catalyzed dehydration

Aldol
(Lost H shown for clarity)

α,β-unsaturated aldehyde

Base catalyzed aldol reaction (shown using OCH$_3$ as base)

(Lost H shown for clarity)

enolate

Aldol

Base catalyzed dehydration (sometimes written as a single step)

Aldol

CH$_3$O:

(Lost H shown for clarity)

Enolate of aldol (shown as carbanion)

loses OH

α,β-unsaturated aldehyde

ketone enolate (nucleophile)   +   aldehyde (electrophile)   — aldol addition →   product "aldol" carbon–carbon bond formed

C-α   C-β

— aldol condensation lose H$_2$O →   + H$_2$O

1   +   2   →   [3]   — H$_2$O →   4

+   →   OH⁻ →   — H$_2$O →

Retro-aldol Reaction

- Essentially the reverse of the aldol reaction

- Overall a β-hydroxy-aldehyde/ketone breaks down into two carbonyl products

- Also requires acid or base catalysis

- Bond between alpha and beta carbons of the carbonyl is broken

Kinetic versus Thermodynamic Enolate

- A ketone has 2 sets of alpha hydrogens; if they are different (asymetrical) then two different enolates can form
  - Which one forms depends on the conditions (temperature, bulkiness of base that removes the H, etc.)

- The one that is more stable but also usually more difficult/slower to form = **thermodynamic enolate** (reaction is under **thermodynamic control**)
  - Higher activation energy but more stable product

- The one that forms more rapidly but is likely less stable = **kinetic enolate** (reaction under **kinetic control**)
  - Lower activation energy but less stable product

Kinetic Enolate:

- H removed from the less substituted alpha carbon (H ismore sterically accessible → easier access for base)

- The enolate ion that forms is less stable because less substituted alkene *

- Favored under condition of: lower temperature; sterically hindered base used (LDA)

    * Zaitsev's rule says that reactions favor the production of
       more substituted alkene

Thermodynamic Enolate:

- H removed from more sterically hindered alpha carbon

- Enolate ion that forms is more stable because more substituted alkene

- Favored under conditions of: higher temperature; non-bulky base (OH⁻)

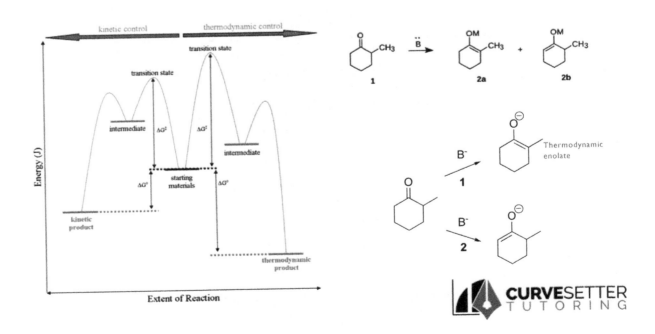

ALCOHOLS AND CARBOXYLIC ACIDS

Organic Chemistry Lecture 6

OBJECTIVES

- Overview of **alcohols**
  - Acidity
  - Hydrogen bonding
- Redox reactions involving alcohols
- S_N1 reaction: mechanism, characteristics, conditions
- S_N2 reaction: mechanism, characteristics, conditions
- Protection of alcohols
  - Protecting groups: Mesylates and tosylates
- Overview of **carboxylic acids**
- Nucleophilic attack reactions
- Forming amides, esters, and acid anhydrides
- Redox reactions involving carboxylic acids
- Decarboxylation of carboxylic acids
- Reactions at alpha carbon: halogenation and substitution

Alcohols Overview

- Alcohol: hydroxyl (–OH) group bound to a saturated carbon

- Alcohol group in a molecule indicated by prefix "hydroxy-" or by suffix "-ol"

- Molecules with alcohols have intermolecular hydrogen bonding (O has two lone pairs therefore two H-bond acceptors; H is an H-bond donor)

- **Acidity:** alcohols are generally weakly acidic (pKa usually between 15 and 20)

  - Alcohols with more nearby alkyl groups are weaker acids because alkyl groups are e- donating, so the resultant conjugate base is destabilized

  - Phenol is one of the more acidic alcohols because the negative charge of the conjugate base is delocalized by resonance

Primary alcohol   Secondary alcohol

Redox Reactions Involving Alcohols

- Oxidation: Alcohol → aldehyde/ketone → carboxylic acid

ethanol   acetaldehyde   acetic acid

Primary alcohol + weak oxidizing agent → aldehyde

Secondary alcohol + any oxidizing agent → ketone

[O]= chromium-based reagent, activated DMSO, hypervalent iodide compound, TPAP or TEMPO

R^1= alkyl or aryl substituent
R^2= hydrogen, alkyl or aryl substituent

Primary alcohol + strong oxidizing agent → carboxylic acid

$$R-CH_2-OH \xrightarrow{[O]} R-C \overset{O}{\underset{OH}{}}$$

primary alcohol   carboxylic acid

Tertiary alcohol + oxidizing agent = no reaction)

[O]= KMnO$_4$, Jones oxidation, PDC in DMF, Heyns oxidation, RuO$_4$ or TEMPO

Strong Oxidizing Agents	Weak Oxidizing Agents
Salts or acids of: MnO_4^- $Cr_2O_7^-$ CrO_4^{-2} (transition metals with oxygen)	PCC PDC DMP

Sɴ1 Reaction

- **Sɴ1 = unimolecular nucleophilic substitution**
  - Unimolecular = reaction rate only dependent on one species

- Overall mechanism: LG leaves molecule, forming a carbocation → carbocation attacked by nucleophile
  - R-LG → R⁺ + LG⁻ + Nuc → R-Nuc
  - Carbocation is an intermediate

- Rate = k[electrophile]; electrophile = R-LG
  - That means that the rate of Sɴ1 reaction depends only on the molecule with the leaving group; that's because the mechanism's slowest step (RDS) is the step in which the leaving group leaves the molecule and a carbocation is formed

Carbocation formed:

- Planar geometry (120 degree bond angles)
- Can rearrange to become more stable via a hydride shift (H atom moves) if the adjacent carbon is more substituted and would therefore be more stable

- Stability of the carbocation determines the rate of the reaction
  - $3° > 2° > 1° >> $ methyl
- Can be attacked from nucleophile on both sides, so both R and S forms of the product are made (racemic mixture)

Conditions under which SN1 preferred:

- If the carbocation formed is tertiary: SN1 always preferred over SN2; if it is methyl or primary: SN2 will occur; if it is secondary, either can occur
  - If secondary, a weaker nucleophile will favor SN1 (such as H_2O, ROH, NH_3)
- Polar, protic solvents preferred because they stabilize the carbocation
  - H_2O, ROH, etc.

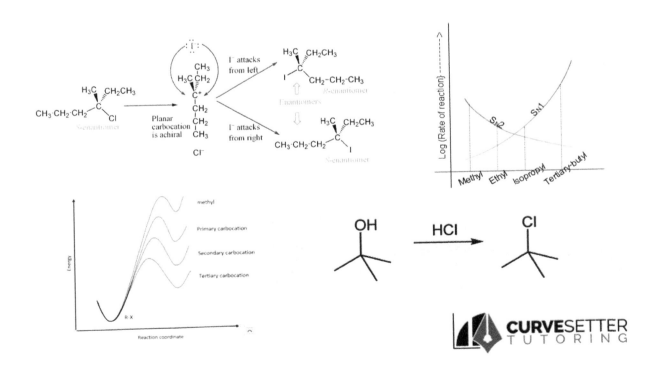

SN2 Reaction

- **SN2 = bimolecular nucleophilic substitution**
  - Bimolecular = reaction rate dependent on two species

- Overall mechanism is **single step**
  - Nucleophile attacks R-LG as LG leaves molecule ---- (pentavalent T.S.) ----→ Nucleophile bound to carbon
  - NO carbocation intermediate

- Rate = k[electrophile][nucleophile] = k[R-LG][Nuc]
  - Depends on both species because it's a single step mechanism!

- Electrophilic carbon is attacked from the backside by the nucleophile ("backside attack") which results in an inversion of the configuration at that carbon from reactant to product (R → S or S → R)

- Rate depends on how sterically hindered the carbon atom is (how easy is it for the nucleophile to attack it?)
  - Methyl > 1° > 2° >> 3°

- Nucleophile attacks at the same time as the LG leaves
  - Pentavalent transition state

Conditions under which SN2 preferred:

- If carbocation formed is methyl or 1°: SN2 occurs; if carbocation is 3° : SN1 occurs
- Favored by polar, aprotic solvents (can't hydrogen bond)
- Favored by good LG
- Favored by strong and small/not bulky nucleophile
  - commonly halides (I⁻ > Br⁻ > Cl⁻)

S$_N$1 Mechanism:

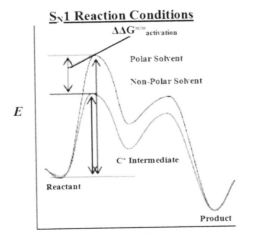

S$_N$2 Mechanism:

S$_N$1 or S$_N$2? → First look at carbon- if tertiary (3 alkyl groups attached) it will be S$_N$1; if methyl or primary it will be S$_N$2. If it is secondary, look at solvent, nucleophile strength and LG.

S$_N$1 Reaction Conditions

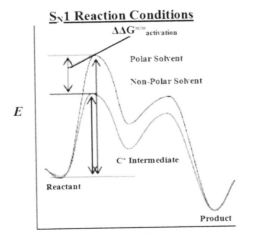

$\Delta\Delta G^{\ddagger}_{activation}$

Polar Solvent

Non-Polar Solvent

E

C$^+$ Intermediate

Reactant

Product

Reaction Coordinate

S$_N$2 Reaction Conditions

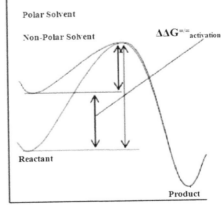

Polar Solvent

Non-Polar Solvent

$\Delta\Delta G^{\ddagger}_{activation}$

E

Reactant

Product

Reaction Coordinate

Protection of Alcohols

- **"Protecting group":** group added to reactant molecule in order to prevent a certain region from reacting
    - Ex. Protection of a ketone:

- Alcohols can be protonated, deprotonated, substituted or eliminated, so to prevent those from happening a protecting group is often added to the alcohol and then removed at the end of the reaction so that the alcohol comes out un-changed

- **Mesylates (OMs)** and **tosylates (OTs)** are most commonly used to protect alcohols (as well as amines)
    - They are also good LGs, so once reaction is over they can quite easily be removed

Mesylate:

Tosylate:

- Mesylates and tosylates don't react with oxidizing agents that would normally oxidize alcohols to carbonyls

Preparation of mesylates and tosylates:

- Alcohol + tosylchloride → tosylate
    - OH + TsCl → OTs
- Alcohol + mesylchloride → mesylate
- The mesyl or tosyl group's bond with chlorine is replaced by a bond with the O of the alcohol

Carboxylic Acids

- Carboxylic acid = organic compound with carboxyl functional group (-COOH)
  - Contain carbonyl and alcohol
- Often indicated by the suffix "-oic acid"
- Extensive hydrogen bonding results in strong IMF → high boiling point
- Polar and protic

Acidity

- Carboxylic acids are weakly acidic (still, stronger than alcohols)
  - pKa generally around 4
- The conjugate base (-COO⁻) is stabilized by resonance, which makes them stronger acids
- The strength of these acids depends on what atoms/groups are present in the rest of the molecule (inductive effects, resonance, etc.) *

*see next lecture

Nucleophilic Attack Reactions with Carboxylic Acids

- The carbon of the carboxyl group is δ^+ and therefore electrophilic → susceptible to nucleophilic attack

- Nucleophilic substitution reaction: If the alcohol gets protonated by a strong acid, it become a good leaving group so a substitution reaction occurs whereby the OH_2^+ is a leaving group and the nucleophile forms a new bond with the carbon

- Pi bond or oxygen of alcohol can act as a nucleophile:

Amides

- **Amide:**  (tertiary amide)

- Amides are carboxylic acid derivatives in which the OH group is replaced by an amine
  - $O=C-NH_2$ → primary amide
  - $O=C-NRH$ → secondary amide

- Lactam = cyclic amide

α-lactam β-lactam

γ-lactam δ-lactam

- Amides can be formed by reacting a carboxylic acid (or other carboxylic acid derivation) with an amine

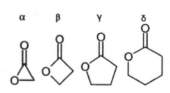

Esters

Ester:

Lactone: cyclic ester

α β γ δ

- **Esterification:** Reaction of an acid and alcohol to produce an ester and water

  - Esterification involved in making **triglycerides** (ester bonds between the fatty **acid** and **glycer**ol)
  - [Carboxylic acid + alcohol → ester]   required acid catalysis
  - Mechanism (addition-elimination reaction): Carbonyl of COOH protonated → ROH attacks carbonyl carbon → OH protonated to make a better LG → H of ROH leaves → OH of COOH protonated to make better LG and leaves as water → another deprotonation

Acid Anhydride Formation

- **Acid anhydride:**

- Formed from the addition of two carboxylic acids and the removal of H2O

  - "anhydride" = without water

$$\Delta, \; -H_2O$$

- Can also be formed from other carboxylic acid derivatives

$$+ \; NaCl$$

Reduction and Decarboxylation

- Carboxylic acids can be reduced by a strong reducing agent to **primary alcohols**
    - **LiAlH4** usually used as reducing agent
    - Two hydrides added to carbon of carboxylic acid
    - LiAlH4 + RCOOH → H2RCOH + H2O

- **Decarboxylation:** the removal of a carboxyl group from a molecule:
    - Occurs for **β-keto acids** (carboxylic acid with ketone on β-C)

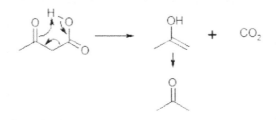

Reactions at α-C of Carboxylic Acids

Alpha Substitution:

- Another atom (from an electrophile) replaces the H atom at the alpha carbon
- Enol or enolate intermediate is part of the reaction mechanism

Halogenation of Carboxylic Acid at α-C:

- Called the "Hell-Volhard-Zelinskii Reaction"
- Substitution in which a halogen replaces the alpha H
- **Mechanism:** first the COOH is converted into an acid halide (ex.COOH → COBr) → alpha H is removed and tautomerization occurs (enol form present) → halogen attacked by pi bond of enol form → halogen added to alpha C → acyl halide converted back to carboxylic acid

CARBOXYLIC ACID DERIVATIVES, PHENOLS, AND AROMATICS

Organic Chemistry Lecture 7

OBJECTIVES

- Overview of carboxylic acid derivatives
  - Types
  - Properties
  - Reactivity
  - Steric effects, ring strain, and electronic effects
- Nucleophilic substitution of acid derivatives
- Transesterification
- Ester hydrolysis
- Amide hydrolysis
- Phenols
  - Involvement in biological redox reactions
- Biological aromatic compounds

Carboxylic Acid Derivatives Overview

Acid/Acyl Halide:

R—C(=O)—X

Acid/Acyl Chloride:

R—C(=O)—Cl

Amide:

R—C(=O)—N(R")(R')

Ester:

"-oate"

R—C(=O)—OR'

Thioester:

R—C(=O)—SR^1

Acid Anhydride:

R—C(=O)—O—C(=O)—R'

Properties:

- Polar carbonyl bond and nucleophilic carbon of carbonyl

- All have dipole-dipole interactions

- Only H bonding for amides → amides have stronger IMF than the other derivatives (all else equal)

Reactivity:

- Reactivity of acid derivatives can be assessed by looking at the strength of the LG

  - Better LG = more reactive acid derivative

  - Less basic LG = better LG = more reactive acid derivative

- Halides such as Cl- are great LGs (very poor bases) → acid halides the most reactive

- RCOO- also a good LG (resonance stabilized)

- RO- and NHR- /NR2- are poor LG (basic groups!);

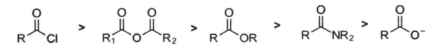

Steric Effects:
- If large atoms/groups are attached to or are nearby the carbonyl carbon, then they decrease the carbonyl carbon's susceptibility to nucleophilic attack (decrease reactivity)

Ring Strain:
- Smaller rings have high ring strain
  - Forced to have a bond angle less than what is most favorable
  - IF there is partial pi bond character in these bonds they cannot rotate and are therefore prevented from achieving the most stable ring conformation
  - β-lactam = 4 membered lactam (amide ring) → high ring strain

Electronic Effects:
- Reactivity of acid derivative can be assessed by strength of LG
- LG must take on a lone pair of e- and usually a negative charge
- Better LGs are those that can better take on those e- due to high EN (halogens of acid halides) or resonance stabilization (RCOO- of acid anhydride)

Nucleophilic substitution of acid derivatives

- Exchange original acyl group for incoming nucleophile (substitution)

- Nucleophilic attack on carbonyl carbon → LG is group of acid derivative (Cl⁻ for acyl chloride, etc.)

- Reactivity depends on LG:

- Tetrahedral intermediate follows nucleophile attack; LG rapidly exits and carbonyl reforms

- If nucleophile is H_2O then we have acyl hydrolysis
    - Ester hydrolysis, amine hydrolysis, etc.

- Reactions of acid derivatives that we discuss are just specific nucleophilic substitution reactions
    - Transesterification
    - Amide hydrolysis
    - Ester hydrolysis

Nucleophilic substitution with
DMAP catalyst:

1   **3**   **4**

Amide formation:

acyl halide   primary or
            secondary
            amine

amide

Transesterification

- Ester added to alcohol and original OR group of ester exchanged for incoming OR₁ group of alcohol
    - Acid catalysis required
    - These two esters exist in equilibrium
- Nucleophilic attack by O of alcohol on δ^+C of carbonyl

$$R'OH + R''O{-}\overset{O}{C}{-}R \longrightarrow R''OH + R'O{-}\overset{O}{C}{-}R$$

Ester Hydrolysis

- Ester → carboxylic acid + alcohol
  - Reverse reaction to esterification (making ester from carboxylic acid plus alcohol)
- Addition-elimination reaction
- Biological application: triglyceride → fatty acid + glycerol
- Requires an acid or base catalyst (and water)

Forward Direction: Acid-catalyzed hydrolysis

Reverse Direction: Fischer esterification

Amide Hydrolysis

- Amide hydrolyzed into carboxylic acid and amine
- Acid or base catalyzed
- N protonated so that NH2R is the leaving group (much better LG than NRH⁻)

Phenols

- **Phenol:** C_6H_5OH

- **Quinone:** (1,4)-benzoquinone

- **Hydroxyquinone:**

- Quinones and hydroxyquinones represent a class of compounds
  - Quinones: any number of –CH= groups into –C(=O)– groups
  - Hydroxyquinone: derivative of benzoquinone formed by replacing one or more hydrogens with hydroxyl groups

- Phenols are oxidized to quinones

- Quinones are oxidized to hydroxyquinones

Ubiquinone:

- Coenzyme that is present in animals and bacteria

- Also called Coenzyme Q, Coenzyme Q10

- Exists in mitochondria of cells that do aerobic respiration
  - Part of the electron transport chain which is necessary to produce ATP

- Can be oxidized, reduced or fully reduced → therefore can be a 1 or 2 e- carrier in the ETC

Biological aromatic compounds

- **Polycyclic aromatic compound:** hydrocarbons that consist of multiple aromatic rings without other substituents
  - Number of rings varies
  - Non-polar and not charged
  - Released due to burning of organic substances (coal, wood, gas, etc.)
  - Many are carcinogenic

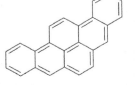

- **Heterocyclic aromatic compound:** molecules with multiple aromatic rings and one or more elements other than carbon (often S, O, or N)
  - Furan and pyrrole

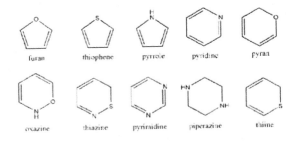

furan   thiophene   pyrrole   pyridine   pyran

oxazine   thiazine   pyrimidine   piperazine   thiine

SENSORY PROCESSING AND PERCEPTION

Psychology/Sociology Lecture 1

OBJECTIVES

- Concepts and Theories of Sensation and Perception
  - Types of sensory receptors
  - Psychophysics: Threshold , Weber's Law, and Signal Detection Theory
  - Sensory adaptation
  - Gestalt Psychology
  - Bottom-up/Top-down and Parallel Processing
- Vision
  - Structure of the eye; Rods and cones
  - Visual processing pathway
  - Feature detection
- Hearing
  - Structure of the ear
  - Hair cells
  - Auditory processing pathway
- Vestibular Sense
- Somatosensation
- Taste (gustation)
- Smell (olfaction)
- Kinesthetic Sense and proprioception

Sensation: Concepts and Theories

Types of Sensory Receptors:

Electromagnetic Receptor – sense EM waves (such as light)

- Photoreceptors in the eye

Thermoreceptor – sense temperature (cold or hot)

- Found in the skin

Mechanoreceptor – sense a mechanical disturbance, such as stretching or compression

- Pacinian corpuscles, Ruffini endings/corpuscles, and Meissner's corpuscles in skin; auditory and vestibular hair cells

Chemoreceptor – detect chemicals and their levels

- Taste buds and olfactory nerves
- Also sense changes inside the body such as fluid osmolarity, pH levels, CO_2 levels, etc.

Nociceptor – sense pain

- Found in the skin and throughout most body tissues

Baroreceptor – sense pressure

- Found in the aortic arch and sense arterial pressure

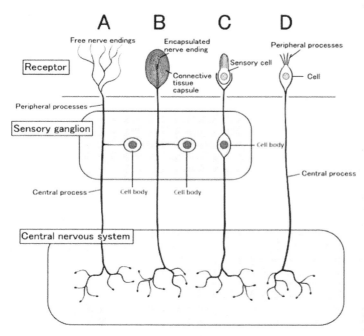

Sensory Pathways

- Sensory information sent from the PNS, where it is detected, to the CNS
- In the CNS, interpretation of the stimulus occurs based on… which neurons sent the impulse/where they synapse (information about sensory modality), frequency of the action potentials (codes for signal intensity), and the duration of continuous firing (duration of stimulus exposure)

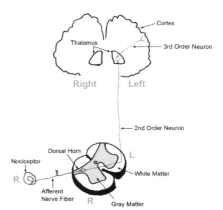

- Most senses are **contralateral,** meaning that the information is received and interpreted in the opposite brain hemisphere to the side of the body that detected the sensory input
    - **Hearing** is both ipsilateral (same side) and contralateral
- **PNS → spinal cord → thalamus → cerebral cortex**
    - sensory information enters consciousness
    - Olfcatory information doesn't go through the thalamus
- **PNS → spinal cord → cerebellum**
    - sensory information doesn't enter consciousness; "subconscious perception"

Psychophysics – looks at the relationship between physical stimuli and the resultant sensations and perceptions

- **Absolute threshold:** the level of a stimulus at which it will be detected 50% of the time

- **Difference threshold:** how different two stimuli need to be for an individual to be able to recognize that they aren't the same (at least 50% of the time)
    - Also called the **Just Noticeable Difference (JND)**

- **Weber's Law:** the size of the JND is a constant proportion of the original stimulus value
    - The value of the proportion varies across sensory modalities, stimuli, and tasks
    - Perceived weight differences – if the JND for a 10 kg weight is 1 kg, then could one detect the difference between a 100 kg and a 108 kg weight? (the JND for a 100 kg weight is …?)

- **Signal Detection Theory:** attempts to assess/quantify when an individual will detect the presence of a stimuli against all other background "noise"

	Signal present	Signal absent
Responds "yes"	HIT	FALSE ALARM (type I error, false +)
Responds "no"	MISS	CORRECT REJECTION (type II error, false -)

Sensory Adaptation: change in the responsiveness of one's sensory system to a constant stimulus

- Ex. Walk into a sushi store and it smells very fishy at first but within minutes you can no longer smell the fish

- Ex. Adaptation to the dark; the longer you're in a dark room, the better you're able to see

- Usually a *decrease* in the AP firing rate over time

- Not the same as habituation, which is a type of "learning" and involves changes in the physiological, emotional, or behavioral response to a stimulus

- Receptors may be **fast-adapting**, **slow-adapting**, or **non-adapting** (nociceptors)

Perception: the process of becoming aware of, organizing, and interpreting sensory information
- Dependent not only on the sensory information but also the individual's memory, past experiences, expectations, and attention

Bottom-up processing: using the sensory information to compile a cohesive understanding of the whole
- "data-driven"

Top-down processing: applying one's knowledge, experiences, and expectations in interpreting and understanding the sensory information
- Applying higher level information to lower level (more basic) information
- Often occurs when the sensory information is vague or incomplete
- Ex. Reading the title of a book that's very washed out; we may recognize the cover of the book or be able to understand the title despite washed out letter due to our understanding of language

Parallel processing
- The ability of the brain to simultaneously process different streams of sensory information

Gestalt Principles:
- Different rules that describe how people tend to organize, group, and perceive sensory stimuli (usually visual)
- "the whole exceeds the sum of its parts" → what we perceive is based not only on the sensory input but also on the innate tendency of our brain to organize the stimuli in a certain way

Figure/ground – we tend to pick out and focus on one figure/object, perceiving it as separate from the background of an image

Gestalt Laws of Grouping:

Law of Proximity-   **Law of Closure-**

Law of Similarity-   **Law of Connectedness-**

Law of Continuity-

Vision

The structure of the eye-

Cornea – clear tissue in front of eye that acts like a lens to focus & refract light

Iris – changes the size of the pupil the control how much light gets into the eye
- Colored part of the eye

Pupil – region through which light enters the eye

Lens – focuses light onto the retina; biconvex shape refracts light
- Curvature of the lens is constantly changing (**accommodation**) due to **ciliary muscles** → enables one to focus on objects at different distances
- Ciliary muscles are under parasympathetic control

Sclera – white and protective outer layer of eye

Retina – layer of the eye onto which light is projected and detected by photosensitive cells (rods and cones)

Fovea – region of the retina with the highest visual acuity; high concentration of cones
- **Visual acuity** is the clarity and sharpness of vision

Optic Nerve – a bundle of the axons of ganglion cells
- Exits the back of the eye at the optic disk (blind spot because no photoreceptors)

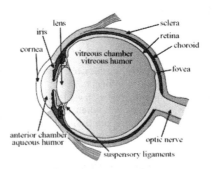

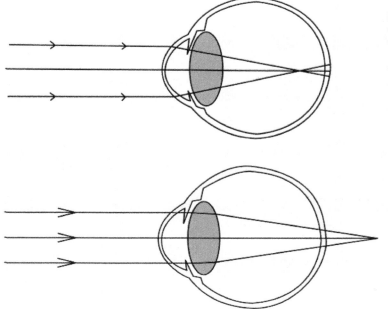

Myopia
- Near-sightedness
- Lens too curved so too much refraction of light
- Correct with concave lens

Hyperopia
- Far-sightedness
- Lens not curved enough so too little refraction of light
- Correct with convex lens

Photoreceptor cells-

Rods
- Detect light at low levels and motion
  - Responsible for vision in the dark
- Only black and white; don't detect color
- Low spatial acuity

Cones
- Detect bright light and responsible for color vision
- High spatial acuity
- 3 types of cones – "green", "red", and "blue" → named based on the range of frequencies that they detect

- Both rods and cones have **opsin proteins**
- Opsin proteins enable the photon to be converted into a chemical signal
- Opsin is bound to **retinal** molecule which undergoes isomerization from 11-cis retinal to all-trans retinal → opsin GPCR changes conformation → signal transduction cascade

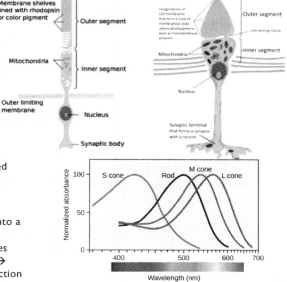

Phototransduction Pathway

Light present:
Photon converts 11-cis retinal into all-trans retinal → conformational change of opsin GPCR → PDE activated and breaks down cGMP → Na^+ channels close → rods and cones hyperpolarize and stop releasing glutamate → bipolar cells depolarize → ganglion cells depolarize → action potential sent along optic nerve to the brain

No light:
cGMP levels are high → Na^+ channels kept open → rod/cone cells are depolarized → glutamate released to bipolar cells → glutamate inhibits (hyperpolarizes) bipolar cells

Cells involved and conduction pathway
- Light penetrates through the cells of the retina to reach the rods and cones, where the EM waves are detected
- Signal sent from rods/cones → bipolar cells → ganglion cells → optic nerve

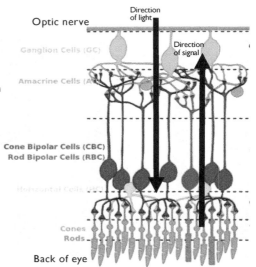

- At the **optic chiasm**, axons of the optic nerve arrange themselves so that axons that originated in left visual field of both retinas end up in the right brain hemisphere and vice versa

- Axons synapse in the LGN of the thalamus

- Signal sent from LGN to the primary visual cortex of the occipital lobe

- Information sent from primary visual cortex to higher visual processing in other regions of the occipital cortex

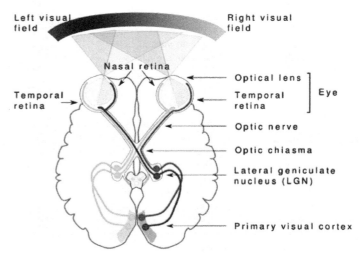

Feature Detection: attempts to understand how the various and diverse features of an image are extracted and compiled to form a cohesive and useful understanding
- "Feature detectors" are neurons that selectively fire in response to specific features of an image (color, brightness, edges, movement, angles, etc.)
- The proposed idea was that these different features of the image are processed in parallel, and eventually these details are compiled in the occipital cortex to form a cohesive image
    - Uses **parallel processing** and is an example of **bottom-up processing**

Motion Perception
- Retinal ganglion cells can encode motion
- Some ganglion cells fire preferentially to movement in a certain direction
    - They can detect this because 1 ganglion cell receives into from multiple bipolar cells which recieved info from many rods/cones (can only signal light or no light and color)

Depth Perception
- We must be able to extract depth using various cues in order to perceive a 3D image when the information from the retina is in a 2D image
- We use binocular cues (information from both eyes) and monocular cues (information from one eye)

Binocular Cues-
- Retinal disparity: compare images from the right and left retinas → the more different they are, the closer an object is to you
- Convergence: how much your eyes must converge towards the midline of your face to focus on an image

Monocular Cues-
- Relative size – one adult much smaller than another is farther away
- Relative motion – closer objects move faster
- Motion parallax – as you move, if the image move a lot in your visual field then its farther
- Perspective – parallel lines converge at a distance
- Accommodation of ciliary muscles
- Interposition – one object that blocks another is closer
- Texture gradient – texture more clear on closer objects
- Light and shadows
- Etc…

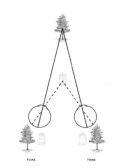

Hearing

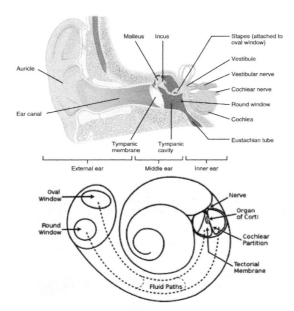

Outer ear = auricle/pinna + auditory canal
- Captures sound waves and directs them into the ear

Middle ear = tympanic membrane (eardrum) + ossicles
- Tympanic membrane vibrates when sound waves arrive
- Ossicles are the smallest bones of the body; there are 3 – malleus, incus, stapes
    - Vibrations from the tympanic membrane are passed from the malleus → incus → stapes → inner ear

Inner ear = oval window, cochlea filled with fluid (endolymph), organ of Corti, hair cells, tectorial membrane, and basilar membrane (plus the vestibular system)
- Stapes transmits the vibrations to the oval window, which transmits them through the endolymph
- Pressure waves in the endolymph transmitted to hair cells (auditory sensory receptors)

Pressure waves in endolymph cause the basilar membrane (where hair cells are located) to vibrate → hair cells move while the tectorial membrane doesn't → stereocilia are dragged across the tectorial membrane and bend relative to the hair cells → mechanically-gated ion channels open (K^+ and Ca^{+2} enter) → hair cells **depolarize** (no AP) and release neurotransmitters onto fibers of the auditory nerve → AP fired in **auditory nerve** fibers → impulse sent to **auditory cortex** in **temporal lobe** (by way of the thalamus)

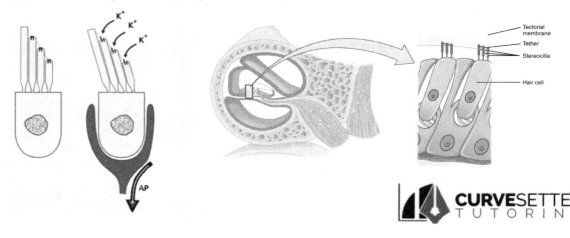

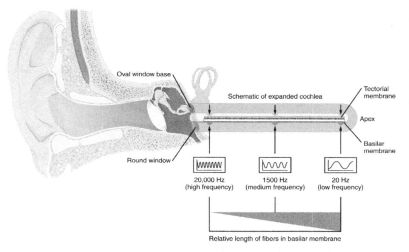

- Frequency of sound encoded by region of the cochlea where hair cells are firing

- Closer to apex = lower frequency

- Loudness of sound encoded by frequency of AP firing

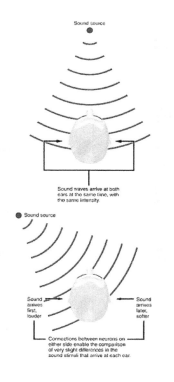

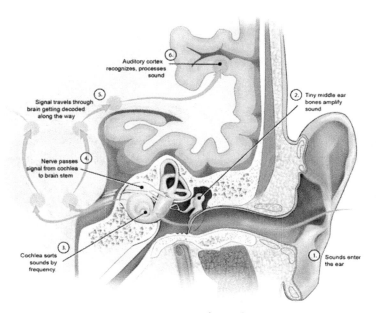

Vestibular Sense

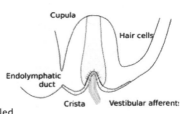

- Part of the inner ear that senses motion, balance, and spatial orientation
  - The orientation of our body with respect to gravity
  - Contributes to our kinesthetic sense

Semi-circular canals

- 3 round interconnected tubes that are oriented at right angles to each other; filled with endolymph
- Each canal contains a bundle of hair cells, which have their cilia embedded in a gelatinous cupula
- Certain body movements result in movement of the endolymph in a given direction, deflecting the cupula and bending the cilia within → impulse is sent to the brain
- These detect rotational movement and acceleration of the head

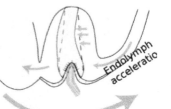

Otolithic organs

- Comprised of 2 chambers, the utricle and saccule
- Each has hair cells with their cilia embedded in a gelatinous membrane
- Membrane is weighted down with $CaCO_3$ crystals – changes in acceleration of the head results in these crystals bearing down more on the membrane → cilia bend and an impulse is sent to the brain
- Sense linear acceleration

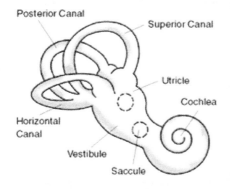

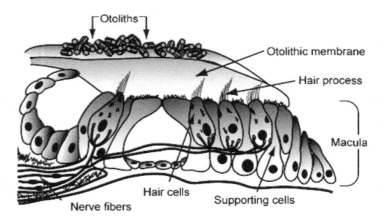

Somatosensation

Somatosensation = the sense of touch, pain, and temperature at the surface of the body
- Information about touch is sent to the somatosensory cortex in the brain

Temperature:
- Sensed by thermoreceptors in the skin

Pain:
- Sensed by free nerve endings (nociceptors) in the skin

Touch:
- **Pacinian corpuscles –** pressure and vibration
- **Meissner's corpuscles –** texture and vibration
- **Merkel's disks –** touch and pressure
- **Ruffini's corpuscles –** stretching of skin
- Touch receptors differ in their speed of adaptation, size of the receptive field, and location (depth) in the skin

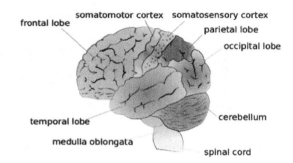

Taste (Gustation)

- **Taste buds** on the tongue contain many **taste receptor cells**

- **Taste receptors** are chemoreceptors that bind to chemicals from food
    - Receptors detect a specific taste: sour, sweet, salty, bitter, or umami
    - Ex. Sweet receptors bind to various sugars and sugar substitutes

- Bitter, sweet, and umami receptors use a **GPCR signal transduction mechanism** – ligand (food chemical indicative of that specific taste) binds to receptor → secondary messenger cascade → cell depolarizes and send AP

- Salty and sour receptors have **ion channels**

- Info is sent via **cranial nerves** to the **temporal and parietal lobes**

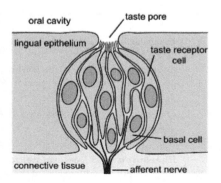

Smell (Olfaction)

1. **Olfactory bulb**
2. **Mitral cells** – receive information from olfactory receptor neurons; axons of mitral cell form the olfactory tract → brings information to many different brain regions including the entorhinal cortex and the amygdala
3. Bone
4. **Nasal epithelium** – lines the roof of the nasal cavity
5. **Olfactory glomerulus** – cluster of nerve endings
6. **Olfactory receptor neurons** – chemoreceptors embedded in nasal epithelium; detect chemicals (odorants) that bind to receptors

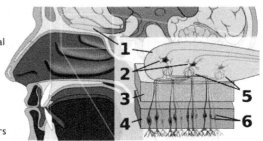

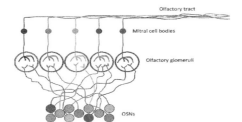

- Olfaction and gustation interact – the combined information gives of our full sense of taste and smell

- Olfaction is the only sense that isn't routed through the thalamus

- Olfactory bulb is part of the **limbic system**
  - Smell tightly linked to memory and emotion

- Olfactory information is mainly processed by the **temporal lobe**

- **Pheromones-** chemical messengers that trigger a social response in members of the same species
  - Humans- many pheromones involved in sexual behavior

Bipolar neuron
(a)

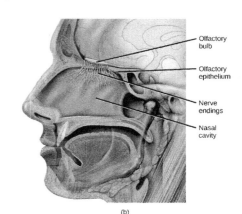

Olfactory bulb

Olfactory epithelium

Nerve endings

Nasal cavity

(b)

Kinesthetic Sense

Kinesthetic Sense: awareness of and ability to control our own bodies' **movements**; relies on information from the vestibular sense and proprioception

- Enables us to coordinate movement and control physical activities
- Component of muscle memory

Proprioception: awareness of the position of one's body in space

- **Golgi tendon organs –** detect muscle tension; located in tendons

- **Muscle spindle fibers –** detect muscle stretch (length); located in muscles

- **Joint capsule receptors –** located in synovial joints and contain a collection of different sensory receptors that convey information about joint strain, position, and movement
  - Free nerve endings, Ruffini endings, Golgi type endings, etc.

ATTENTION, COGNITION, AND INTELLIGENCE

Psychology/Sociology Lecture 2

OBJECTIVES

- Selective Attention
  - Broadbent's Filter Model
  - Treisman's Attenuation Model and the Cocktail Party Effect
  - Visual Attention: Spotlight Model
- Divided Attention
  - Kahneman's Resource Model
  - Multitasking
- Cognition
  - Information-Processing Model
  - Cognitive Development: Piaget's Stages; changes in the elderly; the role of culture, genetics, and the environment
  - Biological factors
  - Problem solving: approaches and barriers to problem solving
  - Heuristics and biases
- Intelligence
  - Theories of intelligence
  - Role of genes and the environment

Attention

Attention: attending to an input of information; allocating processing and cognitive resources towards the information/stimuli

Selective Attention: focusing on a single input while filtering out all other inputs

Divided Attention: attending to multiple tasks or inputs simultaneously; "multitasking"

- Attention is often studied using a **dichotic listening test –** person has headphones on with a different auditory input in each ear → asked to attend to one or both → how much information gets through from the unattended ear? Can person listen to both at the same time?

Selective Attention

Broadbent's Filter Model of Selective Attention:

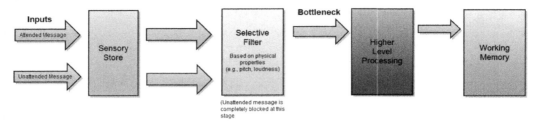

Broadbent's Filter Model

- Theory proposes that the inputs are filtered at a very early stage of processing → only the attended ear passes the selective filter, others blocked

- Only the attended input makes it to higher level processing (interpreting the meaning)

- Can't explain the **Cocktail Party Effect** or **priming**

Cocktail Party Effect:
- At a loud party, one can filter through all the surrounding conversations, choose one of interest, and focus on it, while filtering out the others
- But, while focusing on one input, the listener can still catch words or phrases of particular importance/significance from unattended inputs
    - Therefore the unattended inputs must be processed at some level (not completely blocked)

Treisman's Attenuation Model:

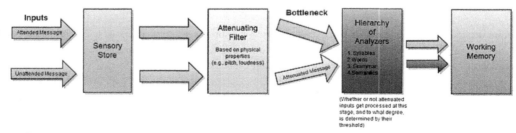

Treisman's Attenuation Model

- Theory proposes that, the unattended input(s) are not fully eliminated from higher level processing but are attenuated ("turned down")
    - It is assigned less attentional/cognitive resources but still processed at some level
    - Can explain the cocktail party effect – some key words/phrases only need a small amount of processing to be picked up as important and consciously noticed

Visual Attention-
- Attentional **Spotlight**: we focus our visual attention on a specific area, like shining a spotlight on it
- Visual stimuli in areas directly surrounding the spotlight are slightly attended to, but are at lower resolution

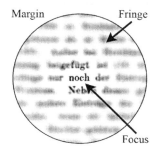

Divided Attention

Kahneman's Resource Model:
- This model proposes that attention requires cognitive/processing effort, which is a limited resource (he called it "attentional capacity")
    - Total attentional capacity is dependent on the level of arousal
- This resource is allocated to different tasks, which require differing levels of attentional resources

Multitasking Performance
How well someone can multitask depends on…
- Training/practice → practice results in a task requiring less attentional resources → one can allocate the excess resources to other tasks
- Complexity → tasks that are more complex and difficult require a greater share of the attentional resources
- Task similarity → similar tasks are difficult to complete simultaneously because they require the same types of processing
    - Better to listen to music while doing math homework versus while writing/reading

Cognition

Information Processing Model: likens our cognitive processing to the functioning of a computer - both have an input device, a processing device, and storage; information can be moved into and out of storage

- Sensory input taken in and briefly held in **sensory memory** (less than a second)
- If input is given **attention**, then it enters **working memory**; if not it decays
- Information can be held in working memory for a few seconds
- If information is **rehearsed,** then it will be transferred to **long term memory,** where it is stored (encoding)
    - Can be later retrieved from LTM (retrieval)

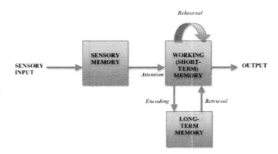

Piaget's Theory of Development-

- Cognitive development is a process consisting of 4 main stages that each child will go through (at his/her own pace)
    - Highlights the universality of cognitive development
- Nature and nurture – cognitive development dependent on biology/genetics and on the child's interactions with his/her environment
- Key tenet is that children are actively engaging with and trying to make sense of the world
- Children develop **schemas,** or mental frameworks, to help them organize and assess the environment
- Schemas change over time as children acquire new information; new information is assimilated or accommodated
    - **Assimilation-** new information is fit into existing schema (schema informs the new experience)
    - **Accommodation-** new information results in changing an existing schema or creating a new one (new information informs the schema)

Piaget's Stages of Cognitive Development:

Sensorimotor Stage (ages 0-2)
- Infants experience the world directly through their **senses and actions**
- May express **separation anxiety**
- Develop: **Object permanence** → objects continue to exist even if they can't be seen

Preoperational Stage (2-7)
- Children use symbols (words and images) to think about the world → **language development**
- Lack logical reasoning
- **Pretend play** (playing "house")
- **Egocentric** – have difficulty understanding any perspective other than their own

Concrete Operational Stage (7-11)
- Can think logically about concrete objects (learn basic addition/subtraction; can do inductive logic); have difficulty with the abstract/hypothetical
- Loss of egocentrism
- Develop: **Principle of Conservation** → if nothing has been added to or subtracted from a substance, even if it changes form, it still has the same amount of substance

Formal Operational Stage (11 or 12 →)
- Can think abstractly and hypothetically
- Develop more mature moral reasoning

Kohlberg's Stages of Moral Development:

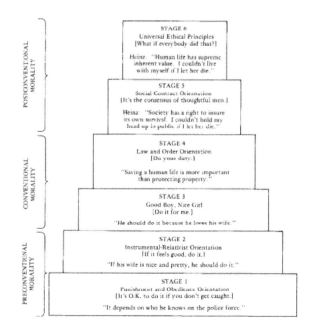

Cognitive changes in the elderly (60+); referring to individuals without dementia or Alzheimer's:

Don't decline-
- "Crystalized intelligence" – general knowledge/information
- Semantic memory – facts; often improves with age
- Implicit memory – memory of behaviors/actions that you don't consciously think about
- Emotional reasoning
- Verbal skills

Decline-
- Recall – bringing memories from LTM into conscious processing
- Episodic memory – memory of autobiographical events
- Working memory – where information is temporarily held for processing
- Processing speed and reaction time
- The ability to multitask (capacity for divided attention)

Cognitive development is affected by...

Culture:
- Cognitive development is inseparable from the culture one is raised in
- Language plays a critical role in the development of higher cognitive functions and how we see the world
- The relationships we have, interactions with individuals in our community, and learning (both in and out of school)
- **Vygotsky** had a different view of cognitive development from Piaget
    - Rather than seeing development as largely universal, he saw it as varying immensely based on one's cultural and social upbringing (cognitive development is a **sociocultural process**; cultures vary widely)
    - He also highlighted the important role of language (inner speech, social speech) in modulating our thoughts and intellectual functions

Genetics:
- Numerous genetically based intellectual defects can delay cognitive development
- Genetics contributes to intellectual abilities, social functioning, and the rate at which children develop

Environment:
- Socioeconomic status
- Housing, nutrition, parental contribution
- Chronic stressors can delay cognitive development
- Environmental enrichment – access to books, toys, etc.

Biological factors affecting cognition:

- Mirror neurons → facilitate social functioning; enable us to learn from watching others and to empathize
- Hippocampus and memory → hippocampus enables us to perform encoding; moving thoughts from STM/working memory into LTM
- Brain damage → the cases of "HM" and Phineas Gage demonstrate how certain brain lesions can dramatically affect our cognitive abilities and personality
  - HM – hippocampus removed; extreme and specific memory defects (retrograde amnesia and couldn't form new memories)
  - Phineas Gage – iron rod through frontal lobe → extreme personality and behavior changes; minimal change in cognitive functioning
- Memory dysfunctions such as Alzheimer's and Korsakoff's Syndrome

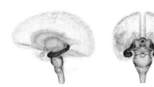

Problem Solving

Types of problems-

Ill-defined problem: don't have clear goals/expected solutions
Well-defined problem: have clear goals/expected solutions
- Enable more specific planning from the start

Approaches to problem solving-

Algorithms: a methodical step-by-step procedure
- Usually lead to correct answers but time consuming
Heuristics: using mental short-cuts ("rules of thumb")
- Less time consuming but often leads to incorrect answer
Trail and Error: keep trying out different solutions until one is correct
- Not useful to use alone if there are many different possibilities

Insight: solution appears suddenly in the mind
- Usually occurs if similar problem has been encountered before; often outside conscious awareness

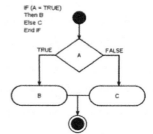

Barriers to Problem Solving

- **Functional fixedness-** fixate on viewing the functions of a certain object as fixed and failing to explore other options
- **Mental set-** fixate on using a problem solving method that has worked in the past
- **Irrelevant information-** using information that is irrelevant or misleading

Heuristics and Biases:

Bias = strong inclination to hold a specific opinion about someone or something; often result from using heuristics

- **Overconfidence-** overconfidence can impair judgement and overestimate the likelihood of success of a specific solution while ignoring other possibilities
- **Confirmation bias-** tendency to look for and use only the information/data that confirms your existing beliefs
- **Anchoring-** giving additional weight to the first information that you were provided with

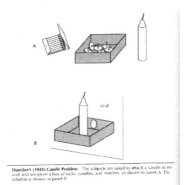

Duncker's (1945) Candle Problem The subjects are asked to attach a candle to the wall and are given a box of tacks, candles, and matches, as shown in panel A. The solution is shown in panel B.

- **Belief perseverance-** tendency to cling to one's initial beliefs, even if evidence is provided that refutes them

- **Availability heuristic-** using examples that are most readily recalled to you in order to evaluate a situation or solve a problem

- **Representativeness heuristic-** when looking a specific situation/problem we tend to compare new situations/problems to a prototype that exists in our mind and assess their similarity; then we extrapolate about causality and probability of a specific outcome based on this comparison

- **Framing-** the manner in which a situation is presented affects the decision
  - Especially involved in risk-taking – situation may be framed to highlight the benefits (positive framing) or the risks (negative framing)
  - Ex. Choice between food labelled "with 10% fat" or "90% fat free"

- **Hindsight bias-** tendency to retrospectively overestimate their ability to have predicted a situation ("I knew it all along")

Theories of Intelligence

Cattell
- Proposed that 2 different forms of intelligence existed
- Fluid intelligence = reasoning capabilities and solving new problems
- Crystalized intelligence = general knowledge; shown by previous intellectual achievements

Spearman: General Intelligence
- Suggested that there was a single general intelligence (which he termed the "g factor"), that could be quantified
  - Found that subjects performed similarly across different cognitive tests

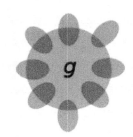

Gardner: Theory of Multiple Intelligences
- Suggested that there are around 8 different types of intelligences that are largely independent from one another; people vary in their strengths
  - Nature, intrapersonal, interpersonal, spatial, musical, logical, verbal-linguistic, bodily-kinesthetic
  - Intelligence should not be numerically quantified by tests or a summarized by a single factor

Thurstone: Primary Mental Abilities
- Suggested that 7 different "primary mental abilities" exist (reasoning, numerical, spatial, etc.)
- Similar to Gardner

Sternberg: Triarchic Theory of Intelligence
- Intelligence is more broad than a single factor, but Gardner included a little too much (some of which Sternberg viewed more as hobbies and activities)
- Three main aspects of intelligence: practical, experiential/creative, componential/analytic

Factors affecting intelligence:
- Heritability/genetics- many studies have looked at the relationship between IQ (used as a quantifiable measure of intelligence) and genetic relatedness, as well as estimated the amount of variation in IQ that can be attributed to gene variance
  - Results very, but estimates suggest that the heritability of intelligence/IQ for adults is **greater than 50%** (likely between 60-80%); ethical debate about the importance of exploring this topic and searching for specific genes
  - Heritability increases as individuals reach adulthood
- Environment and culture
  - Malnutrition, severe environmental or familial stressors, access to education, SES, etc.

Variations in intellectual functioning-

IQ = "intelligence quotient" → score from a set of standardized tests that is used to quantify intelligence
* Follows a normal distribution- centered at 100, SD = 15

Mental retardation (intellectual disability):
* IQ score of below 70 is considered mental retardation
    * 55-70 = mild; 35-55 = moderate, etc.
* Below average intelligence and poor basic living skills
* May be caused by genetic conditions (down syndrome), severe illness (such as brain infections), exposure to toxins (such as lead), severe abuse or neglect, or issues during pregnancy

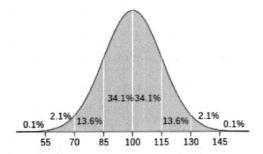

CONSCIOUSNESS, SLEEP, AND MEMORY

Psychology/Sociology Lecture 3

OBJECTIVES

- Consciousness
  - Definition; states of consciousness
- Sleep
  - Sleep stages and cycles
  - Circadian rhythms
  - Dreaming
  - Sleep disorders
- Drugs and altered states of consciousness
  - Drug types and their affects
  - Drug addiction
- Memory
  - Encoding; processes that facilitate encoding
  - Types of memory: sensory, short-term, working, long term
  - Semantic networks; spreading activation
  - Retrieval: processes of retrieval, retrieval cues, and the role of emotion
  - The Serial Position Effect
  - Forgetting: memory dysfunctions, decay, proactive and retroactive interference
  - Memory construction
  - Biological basis of memory

Consciousness

Consciousness: being aware of one's surroundings and of oneself
- Reticular activating system – region of the brainstem that mediates alertness and arousal
- Can be assessed by looking at an individuals' brain waves using an EEG

States of consciousness:

- **Alertness/wakefulness-** the "normal" state of consciousness

- **Sleep and dreaming**

- **Altered states of consciousness**
  - **Meditation:** acquiring a state of heightened awareness, inner calm, and peace; quieting or tuning out specific trains of thought
  - **Hypnosis:** individual appears to lose voluntary control of their behavior and become highly suggestible
  - **Drug-induced** altered state: **psychoactive drugs** alter perception, mood, and awareness
  - **Pathological:** vegetative state, coma, locked-in syndrome, etc.

Sleep

- Physiological changes during sleep can be measured by an EEG (brain waves), and EOG (eye movements), and an EMG (muscle activity)

- There are 5 different stages of sleep, all of which have characteristic patterns of brain and muscle activity
  - **REM sleep –** where the majority of dreaming occurs
  - **Non-REM (NREM) sleep** = stages 1 – 4

- Individuals cycle through these stages in cycles that last approximately 90 minutes each
  - Increased amount of REM (more frequent and for longer) later in the night

- People generally require less sleep as they age

- **Purpose of sleep**:
  - Restoring, repair, and rejuvenate tissues; clear metabolites from the brain
  - Consolidate and organize memories
  - Save energy and stay away from danger (evolutionary explanation)

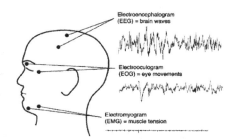

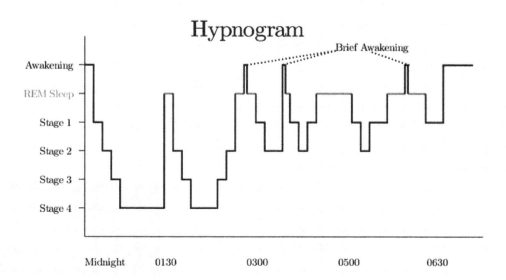

Awake
- **Beta waves** when alert
- **Alpha waves** when awake but relaxed
- Both alpha and beta waves have high frequency and low voltage

Stage 1:
- Very light sleep; can be easily awoken (like a "cat nap")
- **Theta waves**

Stage 2:
- Light sleep
- **Theta waves** with "sleep spindles" and "K complexes"

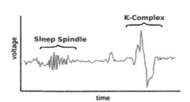

Stage 3/4:
- Deep sleep
- **Delta waves;** low frequency and high voltage

REM sleep:
- Brain becomes more active, HR and BP increase slightly, dreams occurring
- Brain waves look similar to beta waves; low voltage and high frequency

Dreaming:
- Most dreaming occurs in REM sleep, but it can occur in other stages
- Brain is highly active while dreaming; eye movement also high but overall muscle activity is very low
- Some suggest that dreaming facilitates memory formation/consolidation and problem solving; others suggest it is random brain activity
- **Freud** – dreams are "the royal road to the unconscious" - reveal unconscious and suppressed desires; ego's defenses are lowered so repressed thoughts are revealed
  - **Manifest content-** the actual events/plot of the dream
  - **Latent content-** the dream's symbolic meaning

Circadian Rhythm:
- Circadian rhythm is an internal 24-hour biological clock
- Responsible for setting our sleep/wake cycle
- Many physiological processes fluctuate regularly with the circadian rhythm – body temperature, hormone production, wakefulness, etc.
- Adjusted by external cues such as light
- Controlled by **suprachiasmatic nucleus** in the brain

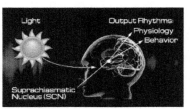

Sleep Disorders (somnipathy)-

Parasomnia- group of disorders involving abnormal sleeping patterns
- Somnambulism (sleepwalking)
- Night terrors
- Bruxism (teeth grinding)

Insomnia- difficulty falling asleep and staying asleep

Sleep apnea- sudden pause in breathing during sleep

Narcolepsy- falling asleep excessively and at inappropriate times

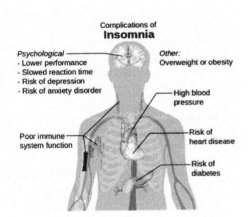

Complications of
Insomnia

Psychological
- Lower performance
- Slowed reaction time
- Risk of depression
- Risk of anxiety disorder

Other:
Overweight or obesity

High blood pressure

Poor immune system function

Risk of heart disease

Risk of diabetes

Altered States of Consciousness: Drugs

Hallucinogens
- Result in hallucinations, changes in sensory perception, mood, thoughts
- Ex. LSD, psilocybin (psychedelic mushrooms), marijuana, PCP, ketamine

Depressants
- Result in reduced levels of arousal and mental/physical functioning
- Generally stimulate GABA (inhibitory) or inhibit glutamine (excitatory)
- Ex. Alcohol, barbiturates, benzodiazepines, cannabis (both a depressant and a hallucinogen), opioids

Opioids
- Drugs that act on opioid receptors, resulting in pain relief, feelings of euphoria, sedation, and respiratory depression
- Ex. Codeine, morphine, heroin, fentanyl

Stimulants
- Stimulate the sympathetic NS
- Often increase catecholamine levels in the synapse (dopamine, epinephrine, norepinephrine)
- Ex. Caffeine, nicotine, cocaine, amphetamine

Drug Addiction-

Dependence: body adapts to constant administration of the drug so that once an individual stops taking it, many dangerous physiological changes occur (**withdrawal**)

Tolerance: individual needs higher dose of the drug to produce the same effect; occurs with prolonged use

In the brain:
- Drugs of abuse target the **reward circuit** in the brain (dopaminergic) → activation by flooding it with dopamine → trains the brain to seek out this highly rewarding activity
- Activation of the reward circuit by drugs is at far greater levels than produced by normal stimuli (food, sex, etc.); individual seeks out the drug despite the detrimental consequences
- Reward circuit involves the **nucleus accumbens**, **VTA**, and **frontal cortex**

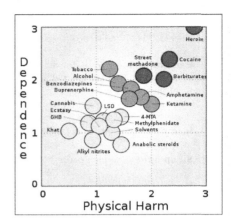

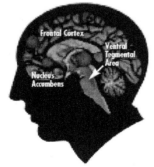

DRUGS OF ABUSE TARGET THE BRAIN'S PLEASURE CENTER

Brain reward (dopamine) pathways

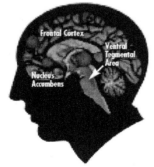

These brain circuits are important for natural rewards such as food, music, and sex.

Drugs of abuse increase dopamine

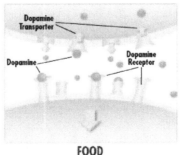

FOOD

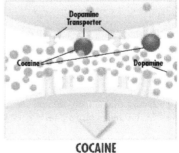

COCAINE

Typically, dopamine increases in response to natural rewards such as food.
When cocaine is taken, dopamine increases are exaggerated, and communication is altered.

Memory

Memory: encoding → storage → retrieval

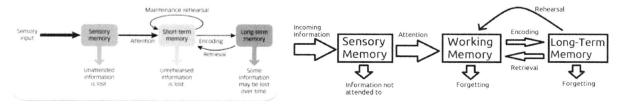

Encoding

- Information from sensory memory is transferred to short term memory (STM) or to long term memory (LTM) in order to be retained in the brain
    - Information in converted into a form that can later be retrieved

- Hippocampus plays a central role → receives information from sensory cortex areas and other association regions, combines the inputs, and commits the information to memory

- There is **acoustic** encoding (sound), **visual** encoding (images), and **semantic** encoding (meaning)
    - Encoding into STM relies heavily on acoustic encoding; encoding into LTM relies heavily on semantics

Processes that facilitate encoding:

- **Mnemonics**- any method of organizing and linking information to help you remember it
    - Acronyms – "ROY G BIV"
    - Method of loci – imagine walking through a familiar place; link items to be remembered to specific regions in that place (such as rooms in a house)
    - Peg-word system – link the items to be remembered to already known items/phrases or numbers

- **Chunking-** break up long lists/groups of information into more manageable chunks

- **Spacing-** space out your studying/encoding sessions; 1 hour 3x/week > 3 hours 1x/week

- **Self-referencing-** relating the information to oneself makes it easier to remember

- **Depth/Levels of processing-** if the information is processed at a deeper level (semantically), it will be more strongly encoded

- **Sleep**

- **Dual-Coding Theory**:

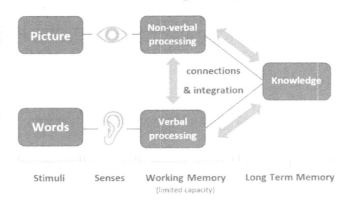

Memory Storage

Types of Memory-

Sensory memory: very limited duration (less than a few seconds); brief snapshot of sensory information that rapidly decays unless encoded to be transferred to STM or LTM
- Iconic memory- brief memory of visual info
- Echoic memory- brief memory of auditory info; lasts a bit longer than iconic

Short-term memory: limited duration memory (a few seconds); information must be **rehearsed and processed** in order to be transferred to LTM
- Proposed capacity of STM is **7±2** chunks of information

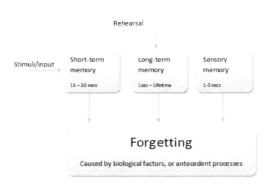

Working memory: system in which information is held temporarily for processing and/or manipulation

- Important for problem solving, decision making, and reasoning
- Some see it as a more accurate representation of STM; some see it as a separate cognitive system
- **Baddeley's Model of Working Memory**
    - **Phonological loop** deals with auditory information and rehearsal
    - **Visuospatial sketchpad** deals with visual and spatial information
    - **Central executive** coordinates and regulates all processes of working memory
    - **Episodic buffer** links different sensory inputs; deals with chronology and semantics

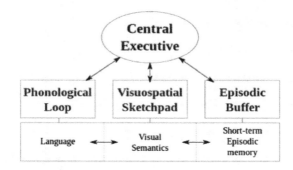

Long-term memory: unlimited capacity and long-term storage of information

- **Explicit/Declarative Memory-** memories that can consciously recalled; facts and events
    - Largely relies on the hippocampus, temporal lobe, and the amygdala (emotionally charged episodic memories)
    - **Episodic-** personal experiences and autobiographical events
    - **Semantic-** facts, concepts, general knowledge

- **Implicit/Procedural Memory-** memories without conscious recall
    - Largely relies on the cerebellum, motor cortex, and basal ganglia
    - **Procedural-** skills and muscle memory
    - **Priming**
    - **Conditioning**

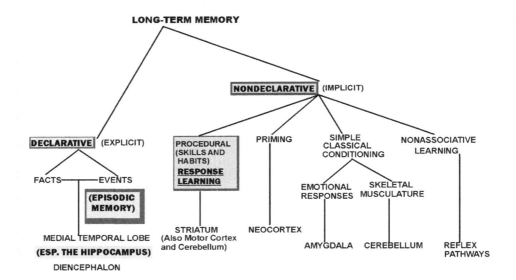

LONG-TERM MEMORY

NONDECLARATIVE (IMPLICIT)

DECLARATIVE (EXPLICIT)

FACTS — EVENTS

(EPISODIC MEMORY)

MEDIAL TEMPORAL LOBE
(ESP. THE HIPPOCAMPUS)
DIENCEPHALON

PROCEDURAL
(SKILLS AND
HABITS)
**RESPONSE
LEARNING**

STRIATUM
(Also Motor Cortex
and Cerebellum)

PRIMING

NEOCORTEX

SIMPLE
CLASSICAL
CONDITIONING

EMOTIONAL
RESPONSES

SKELETAL
MUSCULATURE

AMYGDALA   CEREBELLUM

NONASSOCIATIVE
LEARNING

REFLEX
PATHWAYS

Semantic Networks and Spreading Activation:

- **Semantic network:** information in LTM is stored in a network with nodes (key concepts) that are linked and associated with each other
  - More semantically related items are more strongly connected in the network

- When one node becomes activated, it activates nodes that it is connected to; this propagation of activation between related ideas is called **spreading activation**

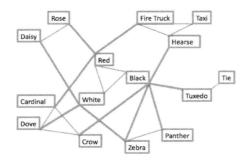

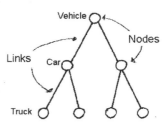

Retrieval

- **Retrieval** – bringing information out of storage (a.k.a. "remembering")
  - Two main types: recall and recognition

- **Recognition:** associating an event, fact, or object with some piece of information stored in memory
  - Involves comparison of the new information with what's in your memory; "recognizing" something familiar
  - Ex. Recognize someone walking down the street as a celebrity; multiple choice tests

- **Recall:** bring the piece of information about an event, fact, or object, out of storage
  - Ex. Free response test, fill-in-the-blank, remembering someone's phone number
  - Recall generally more difficult than recognition
  - Free recall versus cued recall

- **Relearning:** upon relearning information, each successive trial is quicker/requires less cognitive resources

Retrieval cues- Stimuli that facilitate the retrieval of a memory

Priming: previous exposure to a stimulus results in easier/quicker subsequent retrieval of the same or a closely related concept

Encoding Specificity Principle: explains how the conditions present at encoding influence memory retrieval
- **State-dependent learning-** recall is better if individual is in the same internal state as when the memory was formed (usually referring to states of consciousness, such as caffeine versus no caffeine)
- **Context-dependent memory-** recall is better if the individual is in the same context as they were when memory was encoded (ex. location)

Emotion and retrieval:
- There is usually enhanced retrieval of emotional material (such emotional-charged words and experiences)
  - Evolutionary basis
  - Emotion is thought to affect the processes of encoding, storage, and retrieval
- Retrieval is usually enhanced if the emotional state at the time of encoding and retrieval are the same (state-dependence of memory)

The Serial Position Effect:

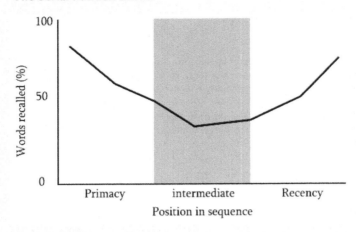

- Items in a list that appeared at the beginning and end are more efficiently recalled

- **Primacy effect:** these items had more time to encode

- **Recency effect:** these items are more "fresh in your memory"; still exist in the working memory

Forgetting

Forgetting – loss of information from LTM (no longer able to be retrieved)

Amnesia – memory deficit caused by disease or brain damage
- **Anterograde amnesia:** cannot form new memories
- **Retrograde amnesia:** cannot retrieve previously-encoded memories

Aging–
- Recall generally declines
- Prospective memory (remembering to do something in the future) declines
- Recognition generally stable

Decay – memories fade over time
- Can counteract decay with active rehearsal
- The neurochemical pathways encoding the memory becomes weaker
- **Ebbinghaus Forgetting Curve:** decay is most pronounced at the beginning, then levels off

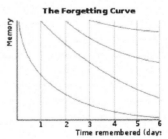

Interference – interaction between new information and previously-encoded memories
- **Proactive Interference:** previously learned information (in memory) interferes with one's ability to encode new information
- **Retroactive Interference:** new information interferes with memory for/ability to recall old information

Dementia – general loss of memory and other cognitive abilities
- Not a "normal" part of aging - more severe than the decline expected due to aging; associated with various brain diseases
- Alzheimer's diseases accounts for over half

Alzheimer's Disease – progressively worsening brain disease involving memory loss and eventual loss of all cognitive abilities; severity and rate of progression varies but eventually fatal
- 6th leading cause of death in the US
- Tau and beta-amyloid protein plaques build up around neurons, slowing them down and killing them

Korsakoff's Syndrome – chronic memory disorder usually caused by severe and prolonged alcohol abuse
- Directly caused by deficiency of thiamine (vitamin B-1) → brain cannot produce energy
- Results in: issues learning new information, short-term and long-term memory loss, confabulation
  - Confabulation = making up information to fill memory gaps

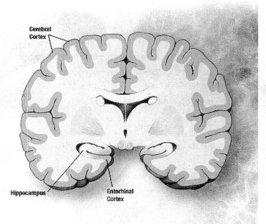

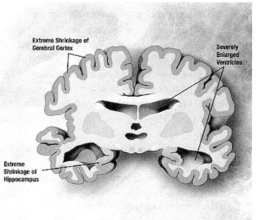

Memory Construction-
- Memories are not infallible snapshots of the past; they are reconstructions, and are subject to changes upon each retrieval (depend on environment, mood, social setting, etc.)
- Errors in retrieval often occur; memory may "feel" extremely real and accurate even when it's not
- Ongoing debate about "**recovered memories**", which are usually associated with child sex abuse and thought by some to have been forgotten/repressed as a coping mechanism
    - Others argue that these memories were "implanted" by the line of questioning and/or suggestions made by a therapist (**false/implanted memories**)

- **Misinformation effect:** exposure to misleading information after an event can alter the memory and lead to errors in recall
    - Ex. After watching a video of an accident, subject is asked "how fast were the cars going when they smashed/bumped into each other?"
    - Retroactive interference

- **Source monitoring error:** individuals often make an error in identifying where a memory originated
    - Ex. Being upset with somebody and not knowing if it is from a dream or an actual disagreement; hearing a news story from a friend and thinking you read it in the newspaper

- **Flashbulb memories:** memory of an extremely salient and emotionally-charged event
    - Usually "feel" very vivid and accurate upon recall but often full of errors
    - Involvement of the amygdala

Biological Basis of Memory

Neural Plasticity: the brain is extremely malleable and dynamic; changes throughout one's life as a function of experience, environment, emotion, behavior, learning, and memory
- Refutes the idea of a single "critical period" follow by a static brain
- After brain injury (or surgical removal of region) neurons adapt and reorganize to compensate → different brain region can take over some of the lost functions, other processes/sensory capabilities strengthen
- Senses develop over time with experience; one can develop a more "refined palate" or sense of smell
- Rehabilitation following stroke and other brain injuries takes advantage of neuroplasticity
- Some neurogenesis occurs; especially in the hippocampus

Long-term Potentiation (LTP): strengthening of synapses between neurons that have fired together from recent experience
- Pre-synaptic neuron will cause a stronger and longer-lasting EPSP → stronger response from post-synaptic neuron
- "Neurons that fire together wire together"
- Extensive LTP in the hippocampus
- LTP underlies learning and memory
    - More interconnectivity between neurons

LANGUAGE, EMOTION, AND STRESS

Psychology/Sociology Lecture 4

OBJECTIVES

- Language
  - Theories of language development
  - Language and cognition
  - Language and speech in the brain
- Emotion
  - Components of emotion
  - The universal emotions
  - Signatures of emotion
  - The adaptive role of emotion
  - The three theories of emotion: Cannon-Bard, James-Lange, Singer-Schachter
  - Perceiving emotion: involvement of brain regions, the limbic system, and the ANS
- Stress
  - Types of stressors
  - Appraisal of stressors
  - Impacts of and responses to stress: physiological, emotional, behavioral
  - How people manage stress

Language

Theories of Language Development-

Nativist Perspective (Chomsky)
- Proposed that humans have biologically-programmed, *innate ability to grasp language*
  - Due to a feature of our brain called the **language acquisition device** (LAD)
    - Enables children to understand the basic structure/rules of language ("**universal grammar**") early on
- Exposure to language in early development (must occur during a "critical period") activates the LAD
- Vocabulary largely acquired through experience

Behaviorist/Learning Perspective (Skinner)
- Language is learned through a *child's experiences with the environment* and interactions with others – involves trial and error learning (operant conditioning), mimicry, and classical conditioning
- *Reinforcement principles* – correct pairing of word with meaning and correct grammar usage are rewarded ("Good job Jimmy! Yes, that's a bike"; child asks for juice and mother gives it); incorrect language usage is punished ("Not correct, Jimmy")

Social Interactionist Theory (Vygotsky)
- Social communication and interactions with others enable children to develop language skills and significantly impacts cognitive development
- Cognitive development is a sociocultural process, with language acquisition playing a central role

Language and Cognition-

Sapir-Whorf Hypothesis (Whorfianism)
- We understand and interpret the world through language (our language shapes how we see the world)
- Ex. our perception of colors differs based on how our language categorizes them
- **Linguistic Determinism:** a stronger form of the theory; says that language entirely determines thought
- **Linguistic Relativity:** a weaker and more flexible form of the theory; says that language shapes our thoughts/perceptions, but the process is not deterministic and is influenced by other factors too
  - Whorfianism largely refers to linguistic relativity; this form (relativity as opposed to determinism) is embraced by more psychologists

Language and speech in the brain-

Broca's area:
- Located in the frontal lobe of the individual's dominant hemisphere (usually the left; "left → language")
- Controls the production of speech
- **Broca's aphasia** (expressive aphasia) → individual has telegraphic speech; has more issues with language production than with language comprehension
  - Telegraphic speech = broken speech; uses some of the correct words to express the content but lacks the proper grammar to link them together and has trouble getting the words out

Wernicke's area:
- Located in the temporal lobe of the dominant hemisphere (usually the left); along the lateral sulcus
- Controls comprehension of speech and written language
- **Wernicke's aphasia** (receptive aphasia) → individual speaks with the correct rhythm (and general syntax) of normal speech, but the speech is largely meaningless; comprised of random words strung together in severe cases (word salad)

- The **arcuate fasciculus** is a band of axons that connects these two areas
- **Global aphasia:** all aspects of language use are impaired

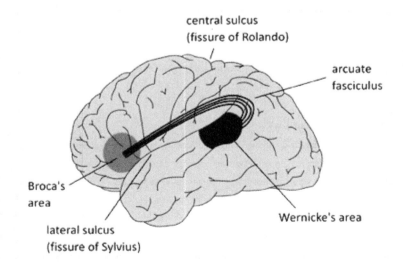

Emotion

- **Cognitive** – the awareness of the specific emotion that we feel
- **Physiological** – the changes inside our bodies (usually arousal) resulting from the emotion; such as heightened HR during fear, surprise, or anger
  - Other physiological responses: face flushed red, sweating, BP changes, crying, etc.
- **Behavioral** – how we express the emotions; how the emotions impact our behaviors

Universal emotions (7) and their signatures:
- **Fear, anger, contempt, disgust, sadness, happiness/joy, surprise**
- Anger = eyebrows lowered and scrunched together; lips tightened; wide eyes → expression meant to make us look more intimidating in conflict
- Fear = eyebrows lifted and often scrunched together; wide eyes
- Contempt = one lip corner raised
- Disgust = nose scrunched up; upper lip pulled and and corners turned down; eyebrows scrunched together
- Sadness = lips turned down; brows pulled slightly together
- Happiness = corners of mouth raised; "smiling with your eyes" shown by wrinkles around outer corners
- Surprise = eyebrows pulled up; eyes wide with pupils dilated; mouth wide open

The adaptive role of emotion-

- **Darwin** noticed that emotions are adaptive
  - Fear will result in an individual taking action to escape the stimulus/situation that triggered that fear
  - Anger will portray an individual's dominance in their response to conflict
  - Emotions facilitate social bonding and convey ones' needs to others in society
    - Ex. crying elicits response from the mother or father; a sad individual will contribute less in society and likely attract attention and care from others;

Yerkes-Dodson Law:
- Performance is optimum at a medium level of arousal; too much or too little will impair performance
  - Arousal resulting from slight fear, stress, or excitement while completing a task
  - Ex. Don't want to be aloof, passive or inattentive while taking a test; also don't want to be so afraid/stressed that your reasoning and logic are clouded

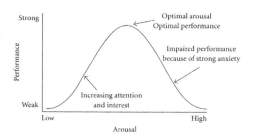

The Three Theories of Emotion

James-Lange:

- Stimulus causes physiological changes such as increased HR and sweating
- Physiological changes (ANS arousal) are interpreted, resulting in conscious awareness of the emotion ("I am afraid")
- Physiological changes → cognitive awareness

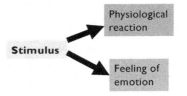

Cannon-Bard:

- Stimulus simultaneously triggers the physiological and cognitive responses
- Physiological changes and conscious awareness of the emotion occur at the same time and are independent of one another (neither causes the other)

Singer-Schachter:

- Stimulus causes physiological changes
- Cognitive interpretation of these physiological changes occurs, using the context of the situation to come up with a logical explanation
- This interpretation results in the experience of emotion

Perceiving Emotion

Brain regions involved-

- **The limbic system** mediates emotional responses, basic drives, memory, and the maintenance of homeostasis
  - Limbic system = thalamus, hypothalamus, amygdala, olfactory bulb, hippocampus, cingulate gyrus
  - **Amygdala:** coordinates our emotional responses; especially fear, anger, aggression, and anxiety
  - **Hypothalamus:** involved in maintaining homeostasis and controlling the ANS; physiological responses to emotion are under control of the ANS
- **Reward circuit (VTA and nucleus accumbens)** involved in the positive, pleasurable responses to rewarding activities such as eating, sex, listening to music, etc.

The autonomic nervous system (ANS):

- The ANS carries out the physiological responses to emotion-provoking stimuli
- ANS = sympathetic NS and parasympathetic NS
- The sympathetic NS mediates responses to shocking, fear-provoking, and stress-inducing stimuli
  - Sweating, increases in HR and BP, pupil dilation, deep breathing

The Limbic System

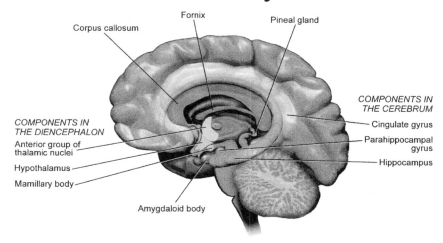

Fornix

Pineal gland

Corpus callosum

COMPONENTS IN THE CEREBRUM

COMPONENTS IN THE DIENCEPHALON

Cingulate gyrus

Anterior group of thalamic nuclei

Parahippocampal gyrus

Hypothalamus

Hippocampus

Mamillary body

Amygdaloid body

Stress

Eustress = stress perceived as positive

Distress = stress perceived as negative

Types of Stressors-

Cataclysmic event: large-scale, unpredictable, and sudden events that affect many individuals; usually referring to natural disasters
- Ex. Hurricane, plane crash, flood, violent political uprising

Significant life change: individual's life changes in some dramatic way that significantly affects them
- Ex. Divorce, death of a child/spouse, losing a job

Daily hassle/micro-stressor: small stressors or hassles that result from one's daily activities or encounters
- Ex. Traffic jam on your way to a meeting, long line at the DAV, work drama, child is sick

Ambient stressor: chronic, low-level stressors that result from one's background environment
- Ex. Global warming, pollution

Appraisal

Appraisal is the assessment/evaluation of an event → appraisal process results in different emotions depending on ones' conclusion of their ability to handle the stressor

Lazarus' Theory of Cognitive Appraisal-

- Lazarus proposed that the appraisal of stress involves two stages:

    - **Primary appraisal** – initial interpretation of the nature of the stressor and the potential threat/danger it poses

    - **Secondary appraisal** – assessment of one's ability to cope with the stressor; presence of available resources

- One's conclusions from the secondary appraisal determines their emotional response

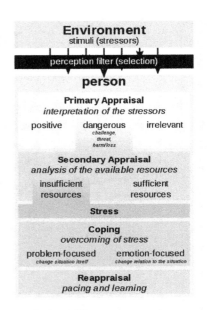

Physiological responses to and impacts of stress-

- **Acute stress** involves activation of the sympathetic nervous system and the HPA axis → heightened levels of epinephrine, norepinephrine, and cortisol in the body

- **Cortisol** is the "stress hormone" – is especially heightened when individual is experiencing chronic stress
  - Glucocorticoid released by the adrenal cortex
  - Raises BGL by triggering fat metabolism and gluconeogenesis; suppresses the immune system

- **Chronic stress** can result in: decreased immune system functioning (increased susceptibility to illness), poor sleep quality, decreased cognitive capabilities, fatigue, trouble concentrating, mood disorders, excessive muscle tension, high BP, increased risk of diabetes, weight gain, digestive problems, breathing problems, increased risk of stroke and heart disease, decreased sex drive, etc.

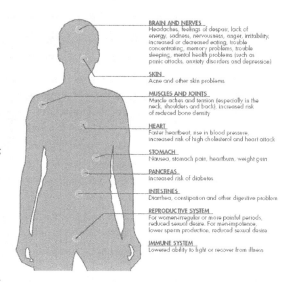

Selye's General Adaptive Syndrome

- Selye proposed that the physiological response to stress involves three stages:

1. **Alarm stage:** initial recognition of the stressor; body accumulates resources to deal with it; hormones levels (cortisol and epinephrine) begins to rise

2. **Resistance stage:** body uses up all of its resources trying to manage the stressor; over time the defenses become weaker

3. **Exhaustion stage:** body has exhausted all of its resources and can no longer try to resist the stressor or its negative impacts; body only reaches this stage if the stressor is chronic and has not yet been eradicated

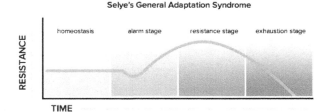

Selye's General Adaptation Syndrome

Managing Stress

- **Behavioral** response to stress may be adaptive or maladaptive
  - Maladaptive – altered eating habits (eating too little or too much), using drugs/alcohol, engaging in risky behavior, avoiding responsibilities, or failing to cope with the problem
  - Adaptive – dealing with the problem head-on, seeking out social support or professional help, or engaging in a number of **adaptive coping mechanisms** (see below)
- **Social support** can protect against or minimize the detrimental effects of stress
- **Resilience:** the process of adapting to and "bouncing back from" adversity, tragedy, or stress → can be developed over time by using adaptive coping mechanisms
- **Exercise** → endorphins released; aerobic activity counteracts some of the health-related and psychological consequences of stress
- **Meditation**, **spirituality**, and organized **religion** (added benefit of social support)
- **"Bio-feedback"** – recognizing and controlling one's physiological response to stress
  - Such as controlling heart rate and breathing

THE BIOLOGICAL BASIS OF BEHAVIOR

Psychology/Sociology Lecture 5

OBJECTIVES

- The Nervous System
  - The neuron, neuronal communication, action potentials, and synaptic activity
  - Structure of the nervous system
- The Brain
  - Forebrain, midbrain, and hindbrain
  - Brain regions and their functions
  - Methods used to study the brain
- Neurotransmitters
  - Types of neurotransmitters and their key influences/roles
  - Parkinson's disease, schizophrenia, and Huntington's disease
- Behavioral Genetics
  - Genes, temperament, and heredity
  - Genes and environment interaction
  - Genetic and environmental influences on behavior development
- Human Development
  - Prenatal and adolescent development
  - Motor development

Neurons

Neuron (nerve cell): specialized cell of the nervous system that can receive and send messages via electrical impulses
- **Afferent neuron –** send information from the body to the brain/spinal cord (CNS)
- **Efferent neuron –** send information from the CNS to the rest of the body
- **Interneuron –** form connections between neurons (reflex arc)

Function: neurons send and receive signals and interact with each other in neural networks to coordinate how the body functions (movement, consciousness, memory, sensation, reflexes, etc.)

Structure:
- **Soma/cell body-** contains the nucleus and organelles
- **Axon hillock-** region of the soma where the action potential is initiated
- **Dendrite-** extensions from the soma that receive input
- **Axon-** action potential is propagated down the axon
- **Myelin sheath-** fatty substance that covers the axon intermittently (gaps between = **Nodes of Ranvier**); insulates the axon to speed up conduction
- **Axon terminal-** release neurotransmitter into the synapse when action potential reaches the end of the axon
- **Synapse-** junction between neurons; small gap across which neurotransmitters are sent

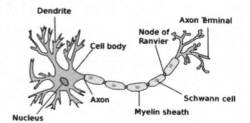

Action Potential

- **Resting potential:** Na^+/K^+ ATPase pumps working to achieve high $[K^+]$ inside the neuron and low $[Na^+]$ inside the neuron → ~ -70 mV

- **Depolarization:** depolarizing inputs from other (presynaptic) neurons lead to the opening of *some* voltage-gated Na^+ channels → Na^+ comes into the cell and membrane potential rises to the threshold → ~ -55 mV

- Once the threshold voltage is reached, all of the voltage-gated Na^+ channels open (via positive feedback loop) and an **action potential** will fire down the length of the axon, starting at the axon hillock

- After a region of the axon depolarizes to ~40 mV, the sodium channels close while voltage-gated K^+ are activated → K^+ flows out of the cell and the cell potential drops back down

- **Undershoot** (after-hyperpolarization): K^+ channels stay open too long and the membrane potential drops below resting potential → referred to as a **refractory period** because it is much more difficult for a cell to initiate a new action potential at this time

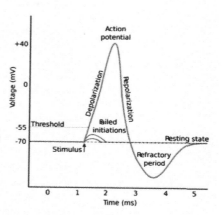

Overall:

- Stimuli (chemical, electrical, or mechanical) are received at the dendrites of a neuron and result in either excitation (EPSP) or inhibition (IPSP)

- The effects of multiple concurrent inputs are summed together in the soma (axon hillock) and result in a net depolarization or hyperpolarization that determines the cell's response → cell responds by firing an action potential if threshold is reached or is temporarily inhibited from firing

- AP is an all-or-none event; intensity of the signal coded by frequency of AP firing

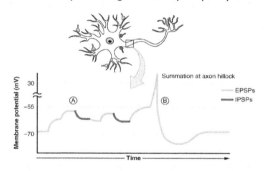

Synaptic Activity

- Once an action potential reaches the end of the axon, it causes voltage-gated Ca^{+2} channels to open → Ca^{+2} rushes into the axon terminal

- **Ca^{+2} influx** triggers neurotransmitter-containing vesicles to fuse with the membrane of the axon terminal → neurotransmitters (NT) are released into the **synaptic cleft**

- NT binds to receptors on the membrane of the postsynaptic cell

- Some of the NT diffuses away or remains in the cleft until it is cleared away by **reuptake** mechanisms

- NT receptor on postsynaptic cell is usually a ligand-gated ion channel (or linked to an ion channel) → binding of the NT results in ion influx or efflux → **EPSP** or **IPSP**

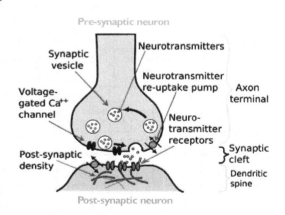

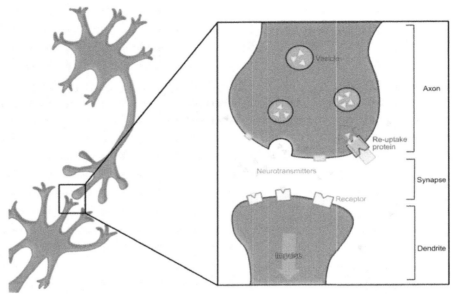

The Vertebrate Nervous System

Organization:

CNS = brain + spinal cord
- Control centers and integration
- Bundles of CNS axons = **tracts**
- White matter = myelinated axons; grey matter = neuronal cell bodies

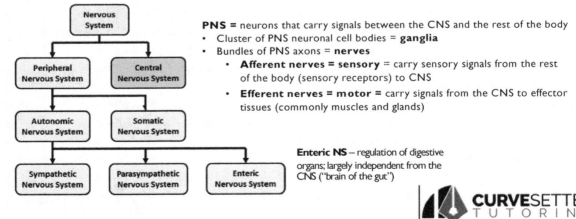

PNS = neurons that carry signals between the CNS and the rest of the body
- Cluster of PNS neuronal cell bodies = **ganglia**
- Bundles of PNS axons = **nerves**
  - **Afferent nerves = sensory** = carry sensory signals from the rest of the body (sensory receptors) to CNS
  - **Efferent nerves = motor =** carry signals from the CNS to effector tissues (commonly muscles and glands)

Enteric NS – regulation of digestive organs; largely independent from the CNS ("brain of the gut")

Peripheral Nervous System Divisions-

Somatic Nervous System:
- Voluntary control of the skeletal muscles of the body
- Acetylcholine used as the neurotransmitter

Autonomic Nervous System:
- Involuntary control of visceral motor functions; regulation of the internal environment (homeostasis)
  - Sends information to effectors; effectors = muscles and glands
- 2 major subdivisions (plus the enteric NS)-
    Sympathetic Nervous System: "fight-or-flight"
    - Response to stress and dangerous situations → arouses the body and prepares it for action
    - Increases blood flow to skeletal muscles and decreases flow to GI tract
    - Increases HR, BP, and breathing rate; dilates pupils; mobilizes fuel (glycogenolysis)
    Parasympathetic Nervous System: "rest and digest"
    - Conserves energy during restful state and promotes "house-keeping" activities
    - Increase blood flow to digestive and excretory systems
    - Decreases HR, BP, and breathing rate

Reflexes

Reflex Arc: nerve pathway controlling a reflex (no conscious control of the response to a specific stimulus)
- Stimulus registered by a sensory receptor in the body → afferent nerve synapses in spinal cord or brain stem
- Interneuron may or may not be involved
- Efferent nerve fiber carries signal to an effector, where the response is carried out
  - **Monosynaptic reflex:** sensory neuron → motor neuron
  - **Polysynaptic reflex:** sensory neuron → interneuron(s) → motor neuron

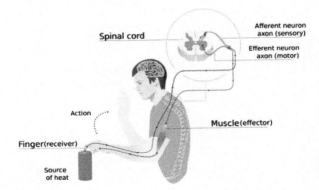

The Brain

Forebrain (prosencephalon) = diencephalon (thalamus and hypothalamus) + telencephalon (cortex)
- **Thalamus:** relay center (and some processing) of sensory information; attention
- **Hypothalamus:** homeostasis; control of emotions, autonomic functions, and basic drives ("The Four F's"); control and regulation of the endocrine system
- **Cerebral cortex:** conscious thought processes and cognitive functions; processing and integration of sensory input; memory and emotion; control of skeletal muscle (motor cortex)

Midbrain + hindbrain = "brain stem"
Midbrain (mesencephalon)
- Some processing of auditory and visual input
- Contains the **substantia nigra** and the **ventral tegmental area** (VTA); both have many dopaminergic neurons and are important in the reward circuit and movement (communicate with the basal ganglia)

Hindbrain (rhombencephalon) = cerebellum, pons, medulla → responsible for controlling vital bodily functions
- **Cerebellum:** controls and adjusts movement and balance; coordination
- **Pons:** relay center for information; many nuclei that deal with vital visceral motor functions (sleep, breathing, swallowing, equilibrium, posture)
- **Medulla:** relays sensory information; control of vital visceral motor functions

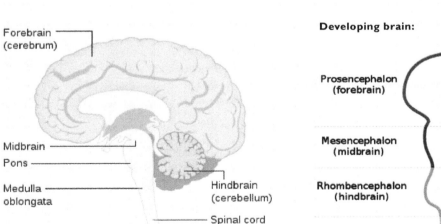

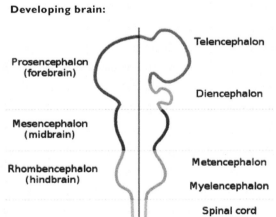

Frontal Lobe: conscious thought, planning, behavioral control, decision making, reasoning, personality, expressive language (Broca's), and movement

- **Motor cortex:** voluntary motor activity
- **Prefrontal cortex:** "executive functions" – concentration, judgement, decision-making, planning, personality

Parietal Lobe: kinesthetic sense, spatial perception, spelling and arithmetic, general perception, object recognition, sensory discrimination

- **Somatosensory cortex:** processing somatosensory input

Occipital Lobe: visual processing

Temporal Lobe: auditory input, receptive speech (Wernicke's) and understanding language, memory, expressive behavior

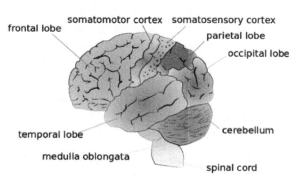

Lateralization of functions-

- Most senses (except smell and hearing, which are both) and motor functions are contralateral

- **Left** = logic, language, math, positive emotions, detail-oriented

- **Right** = creativity, art, music, intuition, negative emotions, holistic

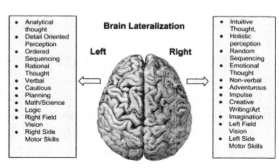

Methods used to study the brain-

- **CAT/CT Scan:** Uses x-rays to produce cross-sectional images of the brain or some region of the body; shows differing densities of tissue and provides *structural* information
  - Exposure to ionizing radiation
  - MRI generally superior for imaging the brain, but CT is quicker and cheaper than MRI

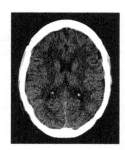

- **MRI:** magnetic resonance imaging → applies a strong magnetic field to the tissue and creates image using principles of NMR (molecules excited then fall back to ground state, emitting radio frequency energy)
  - Provides *structural* information and indicates tissue properties (ischemia, edema, tumors, etc.)

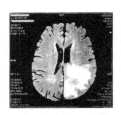

- **fMRI:** provides real-time information about brain *activity and functioning* by measuring changes in blood flow

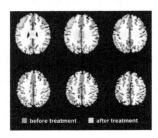

- **PET scan:** uses radioactive tracer (such as a glucose analogue) to assess metabolic activity of tissue; provides information and tissue *activity and functioning*

before treatment   after treatment

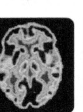
PET Scan of Normal Brain

PET Scan of Alzheimer's Disease Brain

Neurotransmitters

Electrical Synapse: gap junction connects the cytoplasm of adjacent neurons, enabling direct transmission of the impulse
Chemical Synapse: neurotransmitters used for signaling; diffuse across a synapse

Neurotransmitters-
Catecholamines: dopamine, epinephrine, norepinephrine
- Derivatives of tyrosine ("**cat**s are **tir**ed so they sleep in the **DEN**")

- **Dopamine:** made in the VTA
  - Plays in important role in the reward pathway, mood, and in the control of movement
  - Conveys feelings of pleasure
  - Involved in addiction behaviors
  - **Parkinson's disease** = low levels of dopamine; **schizophrenia** = high levels of dopamine; **Huntington's disease** = changes in dopamine levels due to major cell death in the striatum (largely dopaminergic)

- **Epinephrine/Norepinephrine:** released by adrenal medulla as a hormone and nervous system as a NT
  - Fight or flight hormones; activate the sympathetic nervous system; released under stress
  - Norepinephrine more used as a neurotransmitter and involved in alertness, memory, mood, and attention

- **Serotonin**
  - Involved in mood, hunger, sleep, and digestion
  - Contributes to feeling happy; too little serotonin linked to depression
  - Synthesized from tryptophan

- **Acetylcholine**
  - Involved in muscle activity (released at the NMJ), learning, memory, and attention

- **GABA**
  - Main inhibitory neurotransmitter in the brain
  - Many sedatives and tranquilizers act by mimicking or enhancing the effects of GABA

- **Glutamate**
  - Main excitatory (except in vision) neurotransmitter in the brain
  - Can overstimulate the brain and lead to excitotoxicity

- **Endorphins**
  - Neurotransmitter involved in feelings of euphoria and well-being; analgesic effects
  - Released after exercise

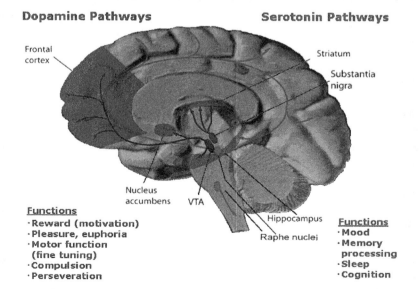

Behavioral Genetics

Behavioral genetics = studying the role of genetics in behavioral traits

- Personality and behavior are influenced by both genes and the environment
  - Some behaviors, personality traits, and features of development are influenced more by inheritance than others
- Personality and behavioral traits are more similar in more related individuals, depicting the influence of heredity; also true for shared (versus non-shared) environment, depicting the influence of environment

Twin studies and **adoption studies** can be used to assess the relative contributions of heredity and the environment to personality, behavioral tendencies, cognitive functioning, disease, etc.

- "How much of the variance in phenotype can attributed to variance in environment/genetics?"
- **Twin studies:** monozygotic twins share 100% of their DNA; dizygotic twins share 50%
  - If the rate of concordance for a trait is greater in MZ twins than DZ twins → genetics plays a role; more of a difference between MZ and DZ = larger role played by genetics
- **Adoption studies:** compare adopted individual to his/her genetic relatives and to others who share his/her environment → assess similarities and differences

- **Genetic predisposition**: increased likelihood of developing a certain trait or disease based on one's genotype
  - Despite this predisposition, an individual needs to also be exposed to specific environmental conditions for the trait to manifest; genetic predisposition + correct environment → trait expressed
  - **Stress-diathesis model:** genetic vulnerability towards a psychological disorder plus environmental stressors results in development of the disorder (must have both facets for disorder to develop)
- **Temperament:** an individual's underlying general nature
  - Ex. easy going versus temperamental and irritable
- **Personality:** an individual's characteristic patterns of behavior, thought, and emotion
  - Personality is influenced by temperament in addition to other environmental elements
  - Temperament considered more innate/biologically-based and less malleable than personality
- Adoption and twin studies: temperament usually found to more similar to genetic relatives (relatively high degree of heredity); attitudes, values, political beliefs, and faith found to be more similar to those the subject shares an environment with (relatively high degree of environmental influence)
- Overall, **genes and the environment interact to produce to phenotype**

Physiological Development

General brain development

- At birth, the brain has its maximum number of neurons but very few connections
- Extensive **synaptic pruning** (programmed, healthy loss of unneeded synapses and neurons) occurs throughout development and continues throughout one's life → dependent on experience and learning; "use it or lose it"
  - Pruning is indicative of learning; older, unnecessary connections are lost to make room for new, stronger ones
- Extensive **growth of synaptic connections** and **formation of neural networks** occurs throughout development → dependent on experience and learning
  - Brain **grows in size** due to growth of synaptic connections and myelination of neurons; number of neurons does not change (decreases slightly, in fact)

Motor development

Basic infant reflexes-

- **Moro (startle) reflex:** loud sound or sudden motion → baby will scream and cry and extend limbs out, then pull them back in
- **Rooting reflex:** stroke/touch babies mouth → baby will turn towards object
  - Helps infant find nipple to breast feed

Rooting Reflex

- **Palmar reflex:** object touches infant's hand → infant grasps the object
- **Babinski reflex:** sole of foot stroked → big toe curls up and other toes splay outward
- **Tonic neck reflex:** infant's head turned to one side → arm on same side extends out, other arm curls inward
- **Stepping reflex:** infant held upright and feet touch ground → infant moves as if walking

Asymmetrical Tonic
Neck Reflex
(ATNR)

Stages of Motor Development-

- **Reflexive movement (0 – 1):** infant engages in innate reflexive movements
- **Rudimentary movement (0 – 2):** basic voluntary motor skills such as sitting, grasping, walking, and standing
- **Fundamental movement (2 – 7):** increased motor control, coordination, and manipulation; fine motor skills such as running, jumping, playing catch, etc.
- **Specialized movement (7 – 14):** combining fundamental movements and applying fine motor control to specialized tasks
- **Application of movement (14 +):** continue to expand on, fine-tune, and apply movements

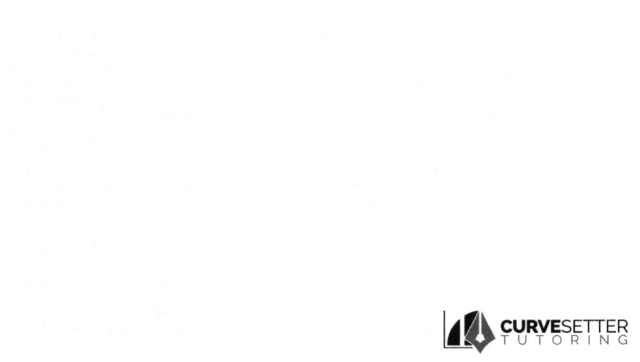

PERSONALITY AND PSYCHOLOGICAL DISORDERS

Psychology/Sociology Lecture 6

OBJECTIVES

- Personality: Theories
  - The "Big 5"
  - Psychoanalytic perspective
  - Humanistic perspective
  - Behaviorist perspective
  - Trait perspective
  - Social-cognitive perspective
  - Biological perspective
- Psychological disorders
  - Introduction to psychological disorders: approaches to understanding and classifying
  - Anxiety disorders
  - Obsessive compulsive and related disorders
  - Trauma/stressor-related disorders
  - Somatic symptom and related disorders
  - Bipolar and related disorders
  - Depressive disorders
  - Schizophrenia
  - Dissociative disorders
  - Personality disorders

Theories of Personality

The "Big 5" (The Five Factor Model)
- Proposes that there are 5 main personality descriptors, all of which lie on a spectrum; people vary in each dimension and the sum of these factors can describe their personality

"OCEAN"
- **Openness (to experience)** – involves differing degrees of curiosity, adventurousness, creativity, and risk-taking; cautious, closed-minded and pragmatic are at the other end of the spectrum
- **Conscientiousness** – involves reliability, ambition, and discipline
- **Extraversion** – involves sociability, tendency to like/dislike social settings, talkativeness; other end of spectrum is reserved, introverted, etc.
- **Agreeableness** – involves ability to work in teams, helpfulness, trustworthiness, competitiveness, etc.
- **Neuroticism** – involves how prone one is to stress/worrying; involves degree of emotional stability

Psychoanalytic perspective (Freud)
- Personality shaped by unconscious thoughts, desires and feelings, as well as repressed childhood memories

- Dreams reveal these unconscious desires because the ego's defenses are lowered

- Mental illness results from unconscious conflicts

- 3 parts of our personality:
  - **Id:** unconscious part of the brain that contains primitive drives/desires and suppressed childhood memories; goal: avoid pain and seek pleasure (pleasure principle); kept in check by ego and super-ego
  - **Ego:** mediates between the id and superego to achieve pragmatic goals and suppress unrealistic ones; operates by the reality principle
  - **Super-ego:** moral conscience; concerned with social norms and right versus wrong; strives for higher purpose
- Personality is formed by the interactions between these three parts

- **Psychoanalytic therapy** → goal is to make those unconscious desires and repressed memories known through talk therapy and dream analysis; therapist lets patient talk freely (**free association**), then does the interpreting/uncovering

- **Freudian slip:** unintentional error in speech that was though to reveal unconscious thoughts/desires

- **Libido:** part of the id that is the "life instinct" → sexual drive and pleasure principle

- Freud thought that all children develop through **5 psychosexual stages**

- If child does not develop through a stage (by resolving the fixation), then the fixation will last into adulthood and certain residual tendencies/behaviors from that stage will be seen in the adult

Oral (0 – 1): focus of libido is the mouth → infant chews, sucks, bites
- Resolved when weaning from breast feeding
- Fixation: smoking, thumb-sucking, overeating, etc.

Anal (1 – 3): focus of libido is the anus → infant earning to develop control over bowel and bladder movements
- Resolved through "potty training"
- Fixation = "anal retentive" (overly neat/neurotic)

Criticism: minimal scientific basis; Freud based his theories on his own anecdotal evidence

Phallic (3 - 6): focus of libido is the genitals → masturbation, Oedipus and Electra complex
- Resolution is overcoming the Oedipus complex for boys and the Electra complex for girls (hostile to same sex parent because sees them as a rival)
- Fixation = problems with relationships or sexual dysfunction

Latency (6 – 12): no focus of libido, sexual feelings are dormant
- Resolution is engaging in meaningful social interactions and asexual activities to reduce the residual tension of the phallic stage

Genital (12+): focus of libido is on reproduction; interest in the opposite sex
- Resolved when reaching sexual maturity and through having meaningful relationships

Humanistic perspective (Carl Rogers)

- Believed that humans are inherently good
- We have free will and are driven towards **self-actualization**
  - Rogers rejected the deterministic beliefs of the psychoanalytic theory and the field of behaviorism
  - Self actualization requires **congruence** between one's ideal self and their real self (self-image)
- Children develop their own **"self concept"**
  - **Incongruence** occurs if self concept (based on actual behavior and experience) contradicts ideal self → results in psychological distress
- **Humanistic/person-centered therapy:**
  - Each person treated as unique and special; unconditional positive regard for individual
  - Therapist must create open and trusting environment for the individual to be able to accept themselves
  - "Client" and therapist on an equal level → form a genuine, trusting, supportive relationship
  - Client grows through self-insight and self-trust

Trait perspective

- Personality is determine through an accumulation of personality traits
  - Traits are stable dispositions that vary across individuals
- Different psychologists have come up with various lists of traits or ways of classifying personality traits
- Includes the "Five Factor Model"

Cattell: organized 16 personality factors ("surface traits") into 5 global factors ("source traits")
- **Surface traits** are very obvious and can be quickly identified
- **Source traits** are less obvious, take a while to uncover, and underlie all surface traits
- Surface traits: warmth, intellect, emotional stability, tension, perfectionism, aggressiveness, paranoia, sensitivity, dutifulness, liveliness, social assertiveness, abstractness, anxiety, independence, open-mindedness, introversion

Allport: developed a list of thousands of trait words; grouped these words into three main categories
- Cardinal traits: dominate people's personality; rare and develop later; based on central theme(s) of person's life
- Central traits: general building blocks of one's personality; all people largely posses these to some degree (ex. kind)
- Secondary traits: situational traits that are only seen in specific circumstances

- Personality formed through our environment, social experiences, and cognitions
  - Involves mimicking and observational learning based on those we interact with
  - When we see someone rewarded for a behavior, we are likely to mimic that behavior in the future

Bandura: our environment, cognitions, and observational learning largely determine our behavior

- **Bobo doll** – Bandura had children watch a video of someone acting aggressively to a toy doll; afterwards, the children were also more likely to be aggressive towards the toy (mimicking)

Biological perspective

- We have innate biological differences in personality; there is a high degree of heritability of personality traits

Eysenck: personality is largely genetic, along with some learning

- Individuals fall somewhere along a spectrum of 2 dimensions - **introversion vs. extroversion** and **emotional stability vs. neuroticism** → variations across spectrum give rise to distinct personalities
- Pointed to the activity of the limbic system activity as a source of neuroticism and to the activity of the reticular formation as a determinant of introversion (already at a higher baseline arousal → need less social arousal)

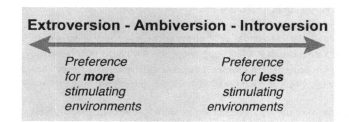

- Behaviorists study only observable behavior (shunned the 'unscientific theories' of Freud and others)
- Personality is the sum of our behavioral tendencies; behaviors are learned through our environment
  - We begin as a **blank slate** → personality acquired over time through learning from our environment
  - Process is deterministic because based entirely on the environment we are exposed to

B. F. Skinner: Patterns of behavior are acquired through observational learning and operant conditioning

- Operant conditioning involves the principle of **reinforcement**
  - Good behavior is rewarded → perform more of that behavior in the future
  - Bad behavior is punished → perform less of that behavior in the future

Behavioral therapy: involves the use of conditioning to shape the client's behavior from maladaptive towards more adaptive patterns (ex. systematic desensitization)

Operant Conditioning

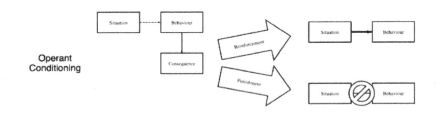

Psychological Disorders

Biomedical approach:
- Looking at psychological disorders from an entirely biological perspective → illness due to some malfunctioning physiological or neurological process or chemical abnormality (such as unbalanced neurotransmitter levels)

Biopsychosocial approach:
- Looking at psychological disorders by integrating biological, psychological, and social factors, and their interactions; more of a holistic and integrated approach → embraced by the majority of health professionals

Classifying psychological disorders-
- In order to diagnose a mental illness, the **DSM-V** (5th edition) is used
  - DSM = Diagnostic and Statistical Manual of Mental Disorders
  - Produced by the APA; updated regularly to incorporate the newest research on these disorders
- DSM has specific categories of mental disorders and under each disorder, there are very specific criteria for each disorder (ex. Individual must have had 5 or more of the following symptoms within the past month)
- Key diagnostic criteria: symptom type, symptom severity, symptom frequency, and *interference with daily functioning*
  - Presence of symptoms aren't enough; only considered a disorder if it negatively impacts a person's daily functioning
  - Person may not have insight (unaware of the disorder; think that nothing is wrong) → use objective assessment as well as sources close to the individual for information

Rates:

- Rates vary across the world → higher in the US than almost all other countries
  - Lower elsewhere due under-diagnosis and stigma (?)
- In the US, approximately **25% of people** suffer from mental illness at some point in their lives
  - Many researchers still consider this an underestimate
  - Despite these rates, not nearly enough people get professional help (over half don't receive treatment)
  - Anxiety disorders are the most common, followed by mood disorders
- For different disorders, the rates differ across gender and ethnicity
  - Ex. Men have much higher rates of alcohol abuse; women have higher rates of mood disorders
  - African Americans, Hispanics, and Asian Americans have reportedly used mental health services at a much lower rate than Caucasians

Anxiety disorders

- Characterized by frequent and excessive fear, worrying, or dread
- Occur more often in females than in males
- The most common psychological disorder

- **Phobia:** strong and persistent fear of a specific object or situation
  - **Agoraphobia:** fear of situations in which individual thinks that he/she would have trouble escaping (ex. crowded subway, airplane)

- **Generalized Anxiety Disorder (GAD):** excessive, persistent, and irrational worry; physical symptoms including fatigue, trouble sleeping, etc.

- **Panic Disorder:** recurrent panic attacks and fear/excessive worrying about having another panic attack
  - **Panic attack** involves severe fear/dread (feeling like you're going to die) and extreme physiological changes such as rapid heart rate, shaking, shortness of breath, etc.

- **Separation Anxiety Disorder:** anxiety when separated from caregiver/loved one
  - Usually occurs in children and infants

- **Social Anxiety Disorder:** anxiety in social situations

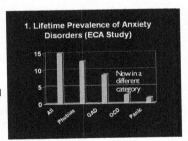

Obsessive-compulsive and related disorders

- Patterns of obsessive thoughts/urges and maladaptive compulsions
  - Compulsion: repeated physical or mental behaviors that must be performed to reduce the dread/discomfort produced by the obsessive thoughts

- **Obsessive-compulsive disorder**
  - Common obsession and compulsions: obsession with germs/cleanliness → repeated and excessive cleaning; obsession with safety → checking and relocking locks; obsession with symmetry/order → arranging
  - Obsession (unwanted and persistent thought) produces anxiety → compulsion performed to relieve the anxiety → behavior continues in a cycle and is reinforced

- **Body dysmorphic disorder**
  - Obsessive thoughts and anxiety about perceived flaws in their appearance

- **Hoarding disorder**
  - Excessive accumulation of items and extreme dread at the idea of having to get rid of them

- **Trichotillomania:** hair-picking disorder

Trauma and stressor-related disorders

- Involve extreme and prolonged mental disturbance following exposure to a traumatic event
- Individuals with more environmental stressors and from lower SES are more susceptible

- **Posttraumatic stress disorder (PTSD)**
  - Symptoms include: flashbacks to the trauma, depressed mood, anhedonia (inability to derive pleasure from things the individual once used to), anger, difficulty sleeping, feeling detached/dissociating, and irritability

- **Acute stress disorder**
  - Similar to PTSD but shorter duration

- **Adjustment disorder**
  - Shorter duration and less severe than PTSD and acute stress disorder

Signs & Symptoms: PTSD	
• Efforts to avoid thoughts	• Difficulty with sleep
• Avoids activities	• Irritability
• Poor memory	• Outbursts of anger
• Anhedonia	• Hypervigilance
• Feeling detached	• Difficulty concentrating
• Feeling 'flat'	• Exaggerated startle response
• Sense of a foreshortened future	• Intrusive thoughts
• Flash-backs	

Adapted from DSM-IV-TR (2009) p.468.

Somatic symptom and related disorders

- Physical symptoms that cause extreme distress but can't be explained by some medical condition
  - Symptoms cause individual to have intense thoughts, emotions, and/or behaviors

- **Somatic symptom disorder:** distressing somatic symptoms (such as pain, fatigue, etc.) that have no medical explanation

- **Illness anxiety disorder:** extreme preoccupation with the idea of being physically sick with some unrecognized illness; concern over normal bodily sensations or mild/benign symptoms

- **Conversion disorder:** change in neurological functioning (sensory, motor, or other) that can't be explained by some medical condition; thought to be affected by extreme emotion or anxiety

- **Factitious disorder:** individual fabricates an illness, even to the extent of fabricating evidence through self-harm or other extreme measures, *without* external incentives; purely to obtain the "patient/sick role"
  - Not malingering; malingering motive involves some external benefit such as financial gain, escaping work, receiving drugs, etc.

Bipolar and related disorders

- Involve symptoms of mania and of depression to differing extents

- **Manic episode:** elevated, dramatic, and often irritable mood; inflated self-esteem; decreased appetite and need for sleep; increased energy and rapid speech; increase in goal-directed behavior
  - **Hypomanic:** less severe version of manic episode; doesn't significantly impact person's daily functioning

- **Depressive episode:** depressed mood; anhedonia (loss of pleasure); feelings of worthlessness, guilt, and hopelessness; changes in sleeping patterns (too much or too little) and appetite; difficulty concentrating, thinking, and remembering
  - May be considered mild (**dysthymia**) or severe (major depressive episode)

- **Bipolar I disorder:** presence of one or more manic episodes (or mixed episodes); individual may or may not have depressive episodes

- **Bipolar II disorder:** presence of at least one hypomanic episode and at least one depressive (or dysthymic) episode; no manic episodes

Depressive disorders

- Involve depressed mood; anhedonia (loss of pleasure); feelings of worthlessness, guilt, and hopelessness; changes in sleeping patterns (too much or too little) and appetite; difficulty concentrating, thinking, and remembering

- **Biological basis-**
  - Abnormal neurotransmitter levels (catecholamines and serotonin)
  - SSRI's increase the amount of serotonin; but this serotonin hypothesis has been oversimplified by the public and is not nearly so simple (for example, serotonin depletion in health individuals doesn't cause depression)
  - Decreased hippocampal size and neurogenesis
  - Huge contribution of genetics (high degree of heritability)
- **Risk factors:** family history, substance abuse, chronic health problems, major life stressors (stress diathesis model)

- **Treatment:** Medications (commonly SSRIs), counseling, CBT, TMS (transcranial magnetic stimulation), and ECT (electroconvulsive therapy); later two used for severely depressed patients

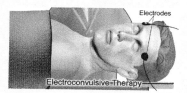

- **Major depressive disorder**

- **Persistent depressive disorder (formerly "dysthymia"):** chronically depressed mood and decreased pleasure; not quite a severe as major depression; but more chronic (not in discrete episodes)

- **Premenstrual dysphoric disorder:** pattern of depressive symptoms that cycle with one's menstrual cycle

- **Postpartum depression:** following birth in new mothers

- **Seasonal affective disorder:** seasonal depression (present in fall and winter but resolves afterwards)
  - Bright light therapy often used

Beck's cognitive triad: proposes that there are three key belief systems involved in depression; negative views about the self, the world, and the future
- CBT (cognitive behavioral therapy) aims to target and change these maladaptive beliefs and the associated behaviors

Cyclic nature of the cognitions and behaviors involved in depression:

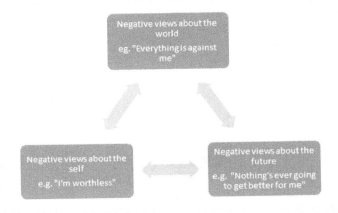

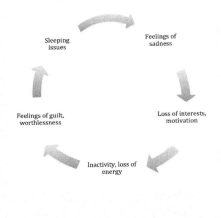

Schizophrenia
- Disorder involving a seeming loss of tough with reality; abnormal thoughts, behavioral patterns, emotions, and sensory perceptions; presence of positive and negative symptoms
  - Symptoms cannot be induced by a substance or by withdrawal from a substance

- **Positive symptoms:** presence of abnormal behaviors
  - Hallucination: abnormal sensory perception
  - Delusion: abnormal false beliefs
  - Disorganized speech, thought, and behavior
  - Catatonic behavior: not moving and non-responsive

- **Negative symptoms:** loss of normal behaviors
  - Flat affect, avolition (decreased motivation), apathy, alogia (decreased speech), decreased social functioning

- **Antipsychotics:** medications often used to treat schizophrenia (and sometimes bipolar disorder)
  - **First-generation "typical" antipsychotics:** block a type of dopamine receptor; often result in extrapyramidal side effects – movement issues such as muscle spasms, restlessness, tremors, rigidity; Parkinsonian-like movement)
  - **Second-generation "atypical" antipsychotics:** different mechanisms of action; less motor side effects; often result in weight gain and metabolic changes; much more commonly used

Biological basis of schizophrenia:
- Strong genetic basis (highly heritable) → stress-diathesis model applies

- **Traditional dopamine hypothesis**: positive symptoms associated with an overabundance of dopamine and/or hyperactive dopamine receptors
  - Evidence: dopamine antagonists can improve these symptoms

- **Newer glutamate hypothesis**: abnormal glutamate signaling and NMDA activation

- Less activation of the frontal lobe associated with negative symptoms

- Abnormal sensory perceptions associated with abnormal activity in the occipital lobe and auditory cortex

- Brain abnormalities: **enlarged ventricles** seen

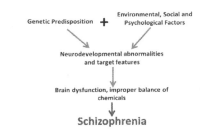

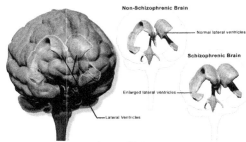

Dissociative disorders
- Involve dissociation: involuntary loss of touch with reality
- Feelings of detachment or being outside one's own body; memory loss or loss of touch with one's identity; disconnect between thoughts and reality
  - Commonly associated with previous traumatic experiences

- **Dissociative identity disorder (DID)**
  - Formerly called "multiple personality disorder"
  - Individual has 2 or more distinct identities/personality states that intermittently 'take control' over the person
  - Different personalities shown through individual's behavior and their ability to remember certain things
  - Commonly associated with childhood trauma (especially abuse)
  - Much more common in females
  - Number of MPD/DID cases rose signficantly following entrance of this disorder into pop culture

- **Dissociative amnesia**
  - Gaps in memory and involuntary loss of personal information/parts of one's identity
  - Memory still exists in one's brain but cannot be recalled
  - Often due to the individual involuntarily blocking out stressful or traumatic events

Personality disorders

- Persistent, maladaptive thoughts, emotions, and behaviors; characterized by a specific disordered 'personality type'

Cluster A – odd or eccentric behaviors
- **Paranoid:** suspicious of people; paranoid; hypersensitive
- **Schizoid:** detached, reclusive and indifferent; little interest in relationships
- **Schizotypal:** odd and bizarre thoughts and behavior; limited affect; magical thinking

Cluster B – dramatic, emotional, or impulsive behaviors
- **Antisocial:** serious behavior issues; no remorse or guilt; poor impulse control; disregard of others (limited empathy)
- **Borderline:** unstable mood; extreme vacillations in emotion; self destructive, impulsive, and reactive; often self-harm
- **Histrionic:** dramatic, impulsive, and needs to be the center of attention
- **Narcissistic:** grandiose self-image; unable to apologize; egocentric

Cluster C – anxious fearful, or obsessive behaviors
- **Avoidant:** feeling inadequate, inferior, and ashamed of oneself; extremely sensitive to rejection
- **Dependent:** must be taken care of; submissive and clinging behavior
- **Obsessive-Compulsive:** perfectionistic and rigid behavior; stubborn

MOTIVATION, ATTITUDE, AND BEHAVIOR

Psychology/Sociology Lecture 7

- Motivation and Theories of Motivation
  - Instinct, arousal, drives, and needs
  - Incentive Theory
  - Arousal Theory
  - Drive Reduction Theory
  - Maslow's Hierarchy of Needs
  - Biological and sociocultural motivators of behavior
- Attitude and Behavior Change
  - Components of attitude
  - Behavior influencing attitude
  - Stanford Prison Experiment
  - Attitude influencing behavior
  - Cognitive Dissonance Theory
  - Persuasion: Elaboration Likelihood Model
  - Factors that affect attitude change
- Other explanations of behavior
  - Freudian defense mechanisms
  - Attraction
  - Aggression

Motivation

Motivation: the desire/willingness for one to do something
- Four interrelated factors influence motivation:

1. **Instinct:** unlearned and innate behaviors that are due to our biological programming
   - We are motivated to behave in certain ways due to evolutionary and biological influences
   - Characteristic of a certain species; relatively uniform across members of the species
   - Ex. Humans have an innate fear of snakes and large predators; throughout human history this fear has developed due to dangerous/threatening experiences with these stimuli

2. **Drive:** we are motivated to reduce internal tension/discomfort that results from unmet physiological needs such as hunger, fatigue, etc.

3. **Needs:** basic physiological needs that must be met, as well as higher-level needs such as love and belonging

4. **Arousal:** we are motivated to perform certain actions in order to reach an optimum state of arousal (not too high or too low)

Incentive Theory: we are motivated by the presence of extrinsic motivators
- As opposed to most other theories of motivation, this theory focuses on extrinsic (outside) incentives as opposed to intrinsic ones; may be tangible (money) or intangible (recognition, love, respect, etc.)
- Embraces principles of operant conditioning
- Positive reinforcement – behavior that results in some reward will be more likely to occur in the future

Arousal Theory: every person has their own optimum level of arousal; at this level they perform optimally (Yerkes-Dodson Law) → behavior occurs in order to achieve this level of arousal
- Too aroused → relaxing behavior performed; under aroused → stimulating behavior performed

Drive Reduction Theory: unmet need(s) → state of tension/discomfort and drive to reduce the feeling → actions are performed that meet the need(s)
- Ex. Haven't eaten → feel hungry and driven to acquire food → cook and eat a meal
- An example of a negative feedback system

Maslow's Hierarchy of Needs:
- We are motivated to behave in certain ways in order to take care of our needs
- Some needs are more pressing and take precedence over – needs at the base of the pyramid must be fulfilled first
  - Ex. Person must have fulfilled physiological and safety needs before they begin seeking fulfillment for love/meaningful relationships
- Once all lower level needs are set, the individual can seek fulfillment at the highest level – self-actualization; any sudden lack of fulfillment at a lower level will result in disruption of progress at this level
- Fulfillment of self-actualization needs = personal development

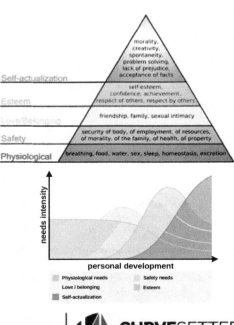

Biological and sociocultural motivators of behavior:

- Hunger, thirst, need for sleep, sex drive - extensive neuronal and hormonal control over fulfillment of these biological needs
- Substance addiction
- Culture and tradition
- Learned needs such as power, recognition/status, materialistic desires, etc.

- Many behaviors simultaneously fulfill a physiological need as well as a social/cultural need (see diagram) →

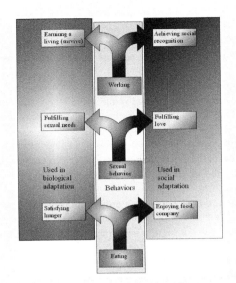

Attitude

Components of attitude ("ABC"):

Affective component: feelings/emotions about an object/person/situation influence our attitudes towards it
- Ex. Feel disgust for a person → attitude towards them will be negative, dismissive, mean, etc.

Behavioral component: behavior and attitude influence each other
- Ex. Optimistic and motivated attitude towards a subject ← → individual works hard and performs well

Cognitive component: involves one's beliefs, thoughts, and knowledge about the object
- Ex. Know a particular person is mean/devious → attitude towards them will be one of distrust, avoidance, disapproval, etc.

Behavior influencing attitude

- Numerous techniques of persuasion/acquiring compliance capitalize on the fact that previous behavior shapes one's attitude towards the request (or requester), often altering their subsequent behavior

Foot-in-the-door phenomenon: if someone is first asked for a small request and they comply, then they are more likely to agree to a larger request that follows (as opposed to being asked only the larger request)
- Ex. Ask your mother to drive you to the supermarket, then ask her to also go through McDonald's drive through

Door-in-the-face phenomenon: if someone is asked for a large request and they say no, then asked for a smaller request afterwards, they are more likely to comply to the small request
- Ex. Ask your parents for a car for Christmas, then once they shut it down, ask if you can "at least have a new phone"

Low ball technique (for convincing): get someone to agree to something at a low cost (cost may be time, money, effort, etc.), then increase the cost once they agree
- Ex. First ask someone to donate a small sum to charity and, once they agree, ask if they can make monthly donations

Norm of reciprocity: an individual is more likely to comply with a request from someone who has accepted their request (or done them a favor) in the past

Role-playing effects:

- When individuals take on a role that requires specific behaviors/actions, there is usually a shift in their attitude as a result (attitude shifts to align with the newly acquired role)

Zimbardo's Stanford Prison Experiment –

- Zimbardo set up an experiment at Stanford to assess whether prisoner-guard hostility and reported guard brutality was a result of the personalities of the guards (abusive, hostile, etc.) or of the prison environment
- Some students randomly assigned to take on the role of being prisoners, and others took on the role of bring prison guards; study took place in a mock prison environment
- "Prisoners" were treated exactly as prisoners would have been (handcuffed, taken from home without warning, locked up in small cells, stripped and assigned a uniform, etc.); guards performed any behaviors necessary to keep order and ensure prisoners followed all directions
- Result: "prisoners" began to adopt the attitudes of real prisoners – hopeless, depressed, submissive; "guards" adopted attitudes were abusive, authoritative, and malicious (psychological torture to prisoners)
- Experiment was prematurely ended due to severe psychological disturbance of some participants and abusive behavior of some of the guards towards prisoners

Attitude influencing behavior

- Our attitude towards a particular person, object, or situation often underlies how we behave
- Ex. Political attitudes often compel people to attend marches, rallies, and to vote for particular candidates
- Ex. Having a 'negative attitude' may result in an individual behaving poorly towards others, ignoring responsibilities, being reclusive, or not performing optimally

Cognitive Dissonance Theory

- Cognitive dissonance occurs when an individual holds concurrent contradictory beliefs/attitudes, when their beliefs and behaviors are contradictory, or when they are confronted with new information that contradicts their existing beliefs
  - Ex. A doctor tells his patients not to smoke cigarettes and knows all the associated health consequences, but still regularly smokes
- This dissonance results in discomfort, and the individual strives to re-achieve consistency by changing his/her belief, behavior, attitude, or perception of the behavior
  - Ex. Doctor quits smoking himself, stops suggesting that his patients quit smoking, or convinces himself that he values a short, indulgent life over a long, healthy life
- Often results in attitude changing to match behavior or behavior changing to match attitude

From: Reeve, J. (2009). *Understanding motivation and emotion* (5th Ed). USA: John Wiley & Sons. Pages 275-277.

Persuasion: Elaboration Likelihood Model

- Theory to describe how attitudes are formed, how attitude change occurs, and how persuasion can be effectively used to influence how other think and/or behave

3 key elements of persuasion –
1. **Message characteristics:** logic, content of the argument, structure and organization of the argument, etc.
2. **Source characteristics:** qualities of the source of the message; such as expertise, knowledge, credibility, attractiveness, power, etc.
3. **Target characteristics:** qualities of the individual receiving the message; mood, intelligence, age, etc.
   - More intelligent people are more resistant to persuasion

Routes of information processing –
Central route: people are largely persuaded by the content of the argument
- Careful thought about the content and soundness of the argument (high elaboration)
- Occurs when individual has high interest in the topic, motivation to listen to the message, and ability to understand the message
- Attitude change that results is enduring, and highly predictive of future behavior

Peripheral route: people largely persuaded by superficial aspects of the message or speaker (flashiness/attractiveness of the presentation, or source characteristics such as attractiveness of the speaker)
- Shallow processing of the message (low elaboration)
- Occurs when individual has low interest in the topic, low motivation to listen to the message, or is unable to understand the message
- Attitude change that results is temporary and not highly predictive of future behavior

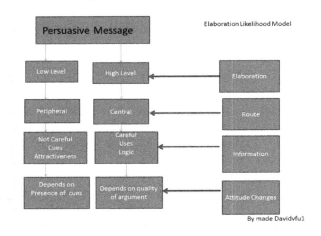

By made Davidvfu1

Factors that affect attitude change

- **Cognitive dissonance** – motivation to obtain consistency in one's thoughts, attitudes, or behaviors
- Behavior changes often result in subsequent attitude changes that align with the newly adopted behaviors
- Characteristics of the message, source, and target (**elaboration likelihood model**)
- Extrinsic motivators – **rewards and punishments** often result in changes in behavioral tendencies as well as changes in attitude
- **Emotion** – affect is a major component of our attitudes
- **Experience**
- **Sociocultural influences** – religion, culture, education, social interactions, media, role models, etc.
- **Identification:** attitude change occurs in efforts to resemble (identify with) a group or individual
- **Internalization:** one adopts a rewarding attitude and integrates it into their sense of self

Social Cognitive Theory (Albert Bandura)

- The environment, social interactions, and how we process our interactions with others and with the world (our cognitions) shape our personality and attitude

- **Reciprocal Determinism:** there are reciprocal interactions between environmental/social factors, personal factors (cognitive processes), and behavior; behavior is determined by personal and environmental factors, but also shapes them

  - Behavioral component is largely shaped by observational learning, operant conditioning (reinforcement and punishment), and classical conditioning

  - Personal component includes attitudes, beliefs, self-efficacy, goals, attributions, etc.

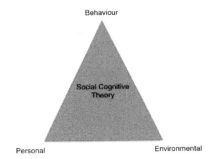

Sublimation	• Transforming a socially unacceptable anxiety into a source of energy that produces no adverse consequences and is socially acceptable
Humor	• Capacity to not take oneself too seriously, as in accepting ones shortcoming and talking about it in a socially acceptable way
Anticipation	• Forcasting future danger in small steps to cope with the danger gradually
Rationalisation	• Justifying a disturbing or unacceptable thought or feeling by selecting a logical reason to think or feel that way
Reaction Formation	• Adopting or expressing the oposite of ones true feelings or motives
Regression	• Returning to an earlier stage of development
Identification	• Taking on the characteristics of someone viewed as successful
Displacement	• Releasing one's anxiety out on a substitute as releasing on the source of the true source could be harmful
Projection	• Attributing ones own unacceptable behaviour onto someone else
Fantasy	• Gratifying frustrated desires by imaginary achievements
Denial	• Unpleasant external realities are ignored

Note: Adapted from "*Understanding motivation and emotion,*" by J. Reeve, 2009, United States of America: Wiley

Other explanations of behavior –

Freudian Defense Mechanisms:
- In order to deal with discomfort due to subconscious desires, thoughts, or memories, the ego employs a variety of different defense mechanisms

- Mechanisms operate at a subconscious level so the individual isn't aware of why they are behaving in this way

- According to Freud, expressing defense mechanisms is normal behavior; but, if they get out of hand (become way to frequent and negatively impact the individual's life), the individual experiences mental illness (**neurosis**)

Attraction –
There are 4 main elements that foster attraction between individuals:

1. Proximity
   - We tend to like people who are closer to us
   - Why? More opportunities for interaction, and likely to have more things in common (same hometown, work, schooling, culture, etc.)
   - **Mere Exposure Effect:** we tend to have a preference for things that we're familiar with

2. Physical attractiveness
   - Romantic attraction is influenced largely by physical attraction; more important in the early stages of attraction/interest

3. Similarity
   - People tend to feel attraction towards those they share things in common with; such as: age, religion, culture, SES, scholarly pursuits, political beliefs, etc.

4. Reciprocity
   - People tend to be more interested in an individual who shows interest in them

Aggression –

- Aggression is a type of behavior that is centered around harming or intimidating another person, physically or mentally; results in harm to oneself and to the other individual(s)

- **Freud** thought that aggression often resulted from defense mechanisms such as projection, displacement, or reaction formation

- Aggression is influenced by the **limbic system** (role of the hypothalamus and the amygdala), **neurotransmitters** (such as serotonin), and **hormones** (such as testosterone and cortisol)
    - Ex. Charles Whitman – went on a killing spree after telling doctors about his sudden aggressive urges; autopsy following his death found a small tumor pressing down on his amygdala
    - Ex. Castrated animals show less aggression; one study showed higher testosterone levels in prisoners who had committed violent crimes
    - Ex. Cats who have their amygdala stimulated act more aggressively towards mice and other cats

- Role of the **frontal lobe** in planning behavior, assessing consequences, and self-restraint
    - Ex. Phineas Gage

- Evolutionary biologists/psychologists focus on the **adaptive role** of aggression; securing individual survival/increasing fitness in competition for limited resources

- Bandura showed that aggression can be **learned** from others
    - Bobo doll experiment – children who observed others being aggressive to the bobo doll were then more likely to be aggressive towards it

- Aggression is also influenced by **culture**
    - Media consumption → violence in media may encourage aggressive behavior
    - Some cultures encourage violence in males by framing it as honorable and masculine

Hostile aggression:
- Goal is to harm the other person
- Strong emotions involved and often an act of retaliation
- Behavior is usually impulsive, uncontrolled, and reactive

Instrumental aggression:
- Purpose is to achieve/obtain some other goal (other than causing harm to the other person)
- Behavior is planned, controlled, and sometimes described as "cold-blooded"

LEARNING

Psychology/Sociology Lecture 8

OBJECTIVES

- Non-associative learning: Habituation, dishabituation, and sensitization
- Associative learning: types; cognitive and biological processes involved
- Classical conditioning
  - Stimuli and responses involved
  - Acquisition and extinction
  - Spontaneous recovery
  - Generalization vs discrimination
- Operant conditioning
  - Process of operant conditioning
  - Types of reinforcement and punishment
  - Shaping and extinction
  - Escape and avoidance learning
  - Reinforcement schedules
- Observational learning
  - Modelling
  - The biological and cognitive processes involved

Non-associative Leaning

- Habituation, dishabituation, sensitization, and desensitization are types of **non-associative learning** that largely take place in the CNS
  - Not the same as sensory adaptation which occurs at the level of the sensory receptors in the PNS

Habituation: decrease in responsiveness to a repeated stimulus
- Habituation is not the same as fatigue or sensory adaptation; these two processes must be ruled out when exploring habituation as a learning process
- Ex. Constant construction outside your house every morning; over time you become less annoyed/distracted by it

Dishabituation: after a repeated stimulus is removed for a period of time then reintroduced, there is enhanced responsiveness to it
- Usually: habituation → stimulus removed → stimulus reintroduced → dishabituation
- Ex. Construction ceases for a month then comes back; response of annoyance/distraction is heightened

Sensitization: increase in responsiveness to a repeated stimulus
- Often happens with repeated stimuli that cause increasing physical pain or some emotional response (such as aggression and fear)
- Also occurs with some drugs of addiction; generally stimulants
- Ex. Stewie and Lois: "mom, mommy, mum, mom, mummy…mum, ma" … "STOP!!"

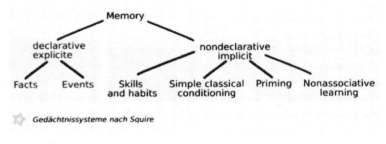

Gedächtnissysteme nach Squire

Associative Learning

- **Associative learning** occurs when a stimulus becomes associated with a certain response or with another stimulus; largely includes all learning except for habituation, dishabituation, and sensitization

Types –
- Classical conditioning, operant conditioning, observational learning
- **Imprinting:** learning in animals that must occur during a particular "critical period"
- Learning about new facts, ideas, experiences (episodic learning), cultural and social expectations, etc.

Biological and cognitive processes involved –
- **Insight learning:** having a sudden realization due to a flash of inspiration; an "ah-hah!" moment
- **Latent learning:** learning that occur passively, without obvious reinforcement of behavior; learned behavior is not expressed immediately, but when the behavior is required
- Innate/instinctive behaviors: fixed pattern of behavior found across a species; biological predisposition
- **Instinctive/instinctual drift:** tendency of an animal to revert back to instinctive behaviors during the process of conditioning

Classical Conditioning

Classical conditioning: repeatedly pairing a stimulus that produces an innate/reflexive response with a neutral stimulus until the neutral stimulus also evokes that response on its own

- **Pavlov** is the psychologist associated with classical conditioning ("Pavlov's dog")

- **Unconditioned stimulus** (food) produces a reflexive **unconditioned response** (salivation)

- **Neutral stimulus** (bell) produces no response

- **During conditioning:** neutral stimulus is repeatedly paired with unconditioned stimulus, resulting in the unconditioned response

- Over time, the neutral stimulus becomes associated with (and is predictive of) the unconditioned stimulus

- **After conditioning:** neutral stimulus has become a **conditioned stimulus** once it can elicit the reflexive response, now called a **conditioned response**, when presented alone

Processes involved –

Acquisition: the process of pairing the unconditioned stimulus (US) and neutral/conditioned stimulus (NS/CS) together; subject learns that the presence of the CS signals arrival of the US

Extinction: the conditioned response (CR) decreases over time as the CS is presented alone (without the US)

Spontaneous recovery: the sudden reappearance of a previously-conditioned response that had gone extinct
- Conditioning occurs → extinction → rest period → spontaneous recovery

Now he fears even Santa Claus

Generalization: when a stimulus that is similar to the CS can also elicit the CR
- Ex. Pavlov's dog – if a doorbell or chime could also elicit salivation
- "Little Albert" experiment by Watson – baby (Albert) learned to associate a furry white rat with a loud frightening noise; CS = white rate, CR = crying; generalization occurred and Albert began to scream and cry at other white furry objects

Discrimination: when only a particular CS can elicit the CR; similar stimuli won't be able to elicit the same response
- Ex. Pavlov's dog – if a doorbell or chime could not elicit the the CR, and only a particular doorbell could

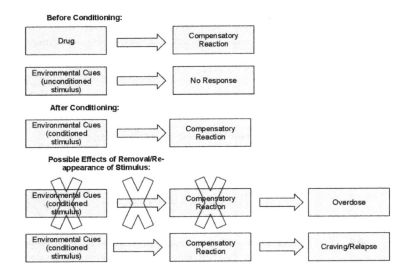

Conditioned Stimulus: Context of Apparatus Side   Unconditioned Stimulus: Drug

Procedure

1. Habituation: Let them Explore

2. Conditioning: CS (Black Context) is paired with US (Drug)

3. Testing: Let them explore both sides and measure
how much time is spent in either compartments

Operant Conditioning

- Occurs when the frequency of a behavior is increased or decreased due to the presentation of a consequence that follows it (reinforcement or punishment)
  - Most strongly associated with **B.F. Skinner**
  - "Skinner box" – apparatus used to train animals with operant conditioning

Loudspeaker
Lights
Response lever
Food dispenser
Electrified grid

Terms –
- Positive: stimulus added
- Negative: stimulus removed
- Reinforcement: results in an increase in the frequency of behavior
- Punishment: results in a decrease in the frequency of behavior

Possible Consequences –
- **Positive reinforcement:** add appetitive/desirable stimulus to increase a correct behavior
- **Negative reinforcement:** remove undesired/noxious stimulus to increase a correct behavior
- **Positive punishment:** add undesired/noxious stimulus to decrease incorrect behavior
- **Negative punishment:** remove appetitive/desirable stimulus to decrease incorrect behavior

CURVESETTER
TUTORING

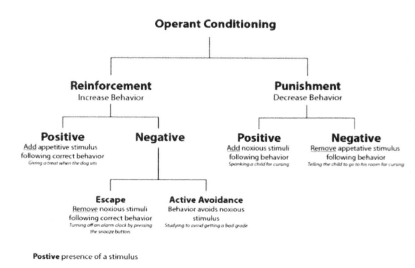

Operant Conditioning

Reinforcement
Increase Behavior

Positive
Add appetitive stimulus following correct behavior
Giving a treat when the dog sits

Negative

Escape
Remove noxious stimuli following correct behavior
Turning off an alarm clock by pressing the snooze button.

Active Avoidance
Behavior avoids noxious stimulus
Studying to avoid getting a bad grade

Punishment
Decrease Behavior

Positive
Add noxious stimuli following behavior
Spanking a child for cursing

Negative
Remove appetative stimulus following behavior
Telling the child to go to his room for cursing

Postive presence of a stimulus

Negative absense of a stimulus

Reinforcement increases behavior

Punishment decreases behavior

Escape removes a stimulus

Avoidance prevents a stimulus

Avoidance learning: learning to avoid an unwanted stimulus that would arrive after the correct behavior is not performed
- Avoid impending stimulus

Escape learning: learning occurs to get rid of an ongoing and unwanted stimulus
- Stop ongoing stimulus

Law of Effect – underlies the principles of operant conditioning; says that behaviors that result in a desirable outcome will increase in frequency and behaviors that result in an undesirable outcome will decrease in frequency

Author Curtis Nicen

CURVESETTER
TUTORING

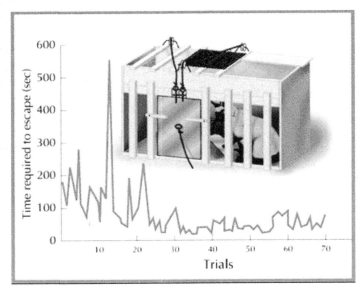

Primary reinforcement: biologically (innately) appetitive stimuli
- Ex. food, water, sex, addictive drugs

Secondary (conditioned) reinforcement: stimuli that must have been conditioned at some point to be seen as desirable to the learner
- Ex. money, text message notification, good grades, school-bell ringing, etc.

Processes –

Shaping: gradually teach a complex behavior by breaking it down and reinforcing it progessively in steps
- Ex. Teach dog to listen to your voice → teach dog to sit when you ask → teach dog to lay down once sitting → teach dog to rollover once laying down

Extinction: occurs when the conditioned behavior stops once the reinforcement or punishment has been removed

Schedules of Reinforcement –

Variable ratio (VR): reward given after a randomly changing number of instances of the correct behavior
- Ex. Food pellet given after 8 lever presses, then after 10, then after 2, then after 4, etc.
- Best and quickest way to reinforce new behavior

Fixed ratio (FR): reward given after a certain fixed number of instances of the correct behavior
- Ex. Food pellet given after every 6 lever presses
- Frequency of behavior increases as learner reaches the end of each block of behavior (gets closer to the instance of behavior that is rewarded)

Fixed interval (FI): reward given after a fixed interval of time
- Ex. Food pellet given after every 20 seconds, as long as at least 1 lever press occurred during that time
- Frequency of behavior increases as learner reaches the end of each time interval

Variable interval (VI): reward given after a variable interval of time
- Ex. Food pellet given after 8 seconds, then after 15, then after 2, then after 23

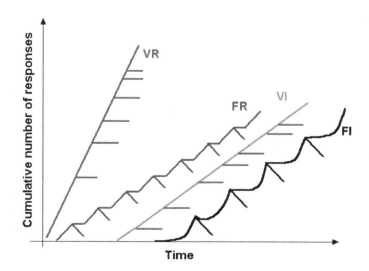

Observational Learning

- **Modeling:** learning by observing and imitating others

- **Mirror neurons:** group of specialized neurons in the cortex that fire when we perform a certain action and when we observe other performing that action (vicarious motor activation)
    - A vital component of social functioning; enable us to learn from watching others (imitation) and to understand the behavior of other individuals
    - The social difficulties seen in individuals with autism theorized to be some issue with the mirror neuron system

- **The brain and vicarious emotion:** a vicarious emotional response (empathy) often occurs when a brain region is activated both by our own emotions and by observing other experience those same emotions
    - Mirror neurons thought to be involved
    - Brain activity has been seen to vary in individuals displaying differing degrees of empathy → potential neural basis for the lack of empathy seen in individuals who are said to be "sociopaths" or "psychopaths"

- Observational learning underlies our identity – we learn right versus wrong from others; we mimic the behavior of those we spend extensive time with; the environment we are raised in (loving, chaotic, judgmental, etc.) shapes our values, attitude, and personality

THE SELF, IDENTITY, AND SOCIAL THINKING

Psychology/Sociology Lecture 9

OBJECTIVES

- Self-concept and self-identity
    - Self-esteem, self-efficacy, and locus of control; learned helplessness
    - Types/aspects of identity
    - Looking glass self (Cooley)
- Identity formation
    - Theories of identity development
    - Social and cultural influences
- Attribution
    - Self-perception, environmental perception, and our perception of others
    - Attributional biases
- Prejudice, Bias, and Stereotypes
    - Definitions
    - Contributions to prejudice: power, prestige, class, emotion, and cognition
    - Stereotypes
    - Processes involved with stereotypes
    - Stigma
    - Ethnocentrism and cultural relativism

The Self

Self-concept = self-identity: collection of beliefs/ideas that you have about who you are
- **Existential self:** the awareness of having a constant self that is separate from others
- **Categorical self:** the awareness of our existence in the world along with all others; can assess our characteristics and compare ourselves to others
- **Self schema:** set of memories and categorizations that guide our self identity/concept

Social identity: based on affiliation with certain groups and socially defined attributes of our identity
- Includes occupation, SES, religion, culture, etc.

Contributions to our sense of self –
Self-esteem: personal evaluation of our worth
Self-efficacy: our evaluations of how well we can do something; may be low or high depending on the task
- People with higher overall self-efficacy recover better from set-backs

Different types of identities

- **Race:** based on physical characteristics such as skin color
  - White, Black, Asian, Pacific Islander, etc.

- **Ethnicity:** based on cultural characteristics/affiliations
  - According to the US Census, "Hispanic or Latino" is considered an ethnicity but not a race

- **Gender:** Male, female, non-binary, etc.; gender is fluid, like sexuality
  - Note: biological sex = male, female, or intersex - based on genital structures (biological factors only)

- **Sexual orientation:** heterosexual, homosexual, bisexual, asexual, or many different non-binary identifications

- **Class/SES; Age**

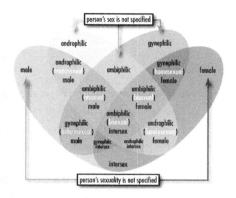

Locus of Control

Internal locus: individual believes that he/she has control over what happens; believes that events arise largely from one's disposition/actions (as opposed to external forces)
- Take responsibility for actions; blames oneself for failures or praises oneself for successes
- Tend to be happier/less stressed

External locus: individual believes that he/she doesn't have control over what happens; external forces are at work (good luck/bad luck, someone else's fault, etc.)
- Tend to be more stressed and more prone to depression; often feel helpless

Seligman's Learned Helplessness
- Occurs when an animals cannot escape some noxious stimulus (shock) → they eventually stop trying; "give up"
- There is a perceived lack of control over the situation
- Also occurs in humans, especially in traumatic event/high stress situations; thought to contribute to depression
- People with low self-efficacy and external locus of control more prone to learned helplessness

Cooley's Looking Glass Self

The Looking Glass Self

- Cooley proposed that our self identity is determined largely by our interactions with others and how we think others perceive us
- We are extremely influenced by what we *imagine* others' opinions to be, but we may or may not be correct in our assumptions
- Often times we end up adopting others' opinions (that may/may not be accurate) and then confirming them → self-fulfilling prophecy
    - Positive feedback between expectations and behavior
- People with stigmatized conditions are likely to internalize the stigma and become negatively affected by it

Identity Development

Kohlberg: Stages of moral development
- 6 stages of moral reasoning through which we develop; not all reach the top stages, most only reach stage 4 or 5
- Pre-conventional morality → conventional morality → post-conventional morality

Vygotsky: Zone of Proximal Development (ZPD)
- When learning something, the ZPD is the region in between what we can and cannot do alone; having experiences in the ZPD encourages development

Zone of proximal development (Learner can do with guidance)

Learner can do unaided

Learner cannot do

Cooley: Looking glass self

Freud: Psychosexual stages of development
- Sexuality (driven by libido of id) and unconscious desires/thoughts largely determine our personal development
- Oral → anal → phallic → latent → genital
- Failing to overcome any stage results in behaviors of fixation (seen in adults)

Erickson: Psychosocial stages of development
- Sexuality and social interactions largely determine our development
- 8 stages – each stage has a conflict that must be overcome

Erickson's Stages of Psychosocial Development:

Trust vs. Mistrust (0 – 1.5)

- Must develop a sense of trust from interactions with loved ones and caregivers

Autonomy vs. Shame and doubt (1.5 – 3)

- Must develop a sense of autonomy over actions and independence

Initiative vs. Guilt (3 – 6)

- Must take initiative and learn to exert control over the environment; exploratory

Industry vs. Inferiority (6 – 12)

- Develop competence in school and cope with new demands in the academic setting

Identity vs. Role confusion (adolescence)

- Develop a sense of identity in social settings

Intimacy vs. Isolation (early adult)

- Develop intimate and meaningful relationships

Generativity vs. Stagnation (adult)

- Care for others and contribute positively to things or people that will outlive them

Integrity vs. Despair (old age)

- Look back on life and feel fulfilled; have a strong sense of identity and wisdom

Other influences on identity formation:

Culture and socialization

- Others' perceptions influence how we see ourselves (looking glass self)
- We form our social identity by interactions with individuals, social groups, and institutions; assess our place in the world and identify with others

Imitation

- We identify others as role models and mimic their behavior; observational learning occurs throughout development

Role-taking

- We take on different roles throughout our development (friend, student, "mom" while playing house, etc.); some more serious and enduring, some more playful and experimental; helps us formulate a stable sense of identity

Reference group

- A group that we compare ourselves to and aspire to relate to
- We use this group to evaluate our identity, our progress, and our behavior (point of reference during self evaluation)
- Ex. Reference group at this time may be current medical students and/or doctors

Attribution

Attribution: how we understand our own behavior and the behavior of others; given a certain situation, we will attribute someone's (or our own) behavior to the situation or the person's disposition

- **Dispositional attribution** → attribute behavior to internal causes (factors related to the individual/oneself – their character, identity, etc.)
  - Ex. "She failed the test because she's not smart and doesn't work hard"

- **Situational attribution** → attribute behavior to external causes (factors of the environment)
  - Ex. "She failed the test because the teacher made it too difficult; because other students were talking"

- Our self perceptions influence our perceptions of others
  - When assessing other people we often compare them/their behavior to ourselves; if we are paying attention in class and studying hard we may judge others more harshly for not doing so
- Our perceptions of the environment influence our perceptions of others
  - Certain environments are conducive to certain behaviors and not to others (yelling at others' on the soccer field is okay, but not in the classroom; dancing sexually in a club is okay, but not at a restaurant)
  - Influenced by expectations, manners, values, culture, etc.

Attributional Biases –

Fundamental attribution error: tendency to explain others people's behavior as caused by their personality (internal causes) as opposed to the environment; often place undue emphasis on internal factors as the cause of a situation

- Ex. Blame an individual for being homeless by saying that they're lazy and unintelligent (as opposed to assessing the contributions of poverty, gentrification, poor social nets in place, lack of mental health services, etc.)
- More common in individualistic societies such as the US

Actor/observer bias: tendency to attribute our own behavior to the situation (external causes), and other people's behavior to their disposition/personality (internal causes)

- Ex. Blame another person for being obese by calling them lazy; attribute your obesity to genetics, living in a food desert etc.
- We tend to assume that we are victims/innocent observers of a situation, whereas other are actors who willfully cause the outcome

Self serving bias: when we succeed we attribute the situation to ourselves (internal causes such as personal qualities), but when we fail we attribute the situation/outcome to the environment or to other people

- Ex. "I failed the test because my teacher explained the concepts poorly"; "I aced the test because I'm smart and hardworking")
- Enables us to achieve high self-esteem
- More common in individualistic societies like the US

Just-world fallacy: the tendency to believe that the world is fair and people will get what they deserve

- Often results in victim blaming in an attempt to rationalize a tragedy

Optimism bias: the assumption that we have a lesser chance of experiencing something bad than other people or that we have a greater chance of experiencing something good than other people do

- "Bad things happen to other people, but not to me"
- Often a component in the choice to engage in risky behavior (such as smoking, unprotected sex, sky diving, etc.)
- Mechanism of self-preservation and decreased worry/neuroticism

Halo effect: tendency to let a certain dominant impression of an individual influence our perception of their character and behavior

- "Well she's top of our class, I'm sure her relationship with her boyfriend is just perfect"

Prejudice

Prejudice: preconceived judgments or opinions of a person or group that aren't based on actual evidence/experience but on social characteristics (age, gender, race, SES, sexual orientation, etc.)
- People usually exhibit favoritism towards groups that they identify with (in-group) and prejudice towards others (out-group) → fundamental attribution error plays a role

Factors that contribute to prejudice –
- Power, prestige, and class: our perceived status in society influences how we view others relative to ourselves (tendency to look down on those perceived to be less influential/successful)
  - The American "bootstrap" ideology → especially embraced by those in high SES/favorable economic situations

- Emotion → emotional experiences often establish or further cement prejudice
  - Ex. Assaulted by someone of a particular race → harbor negative feelings about all individuals of that race

- Cognition → stereotypes and judgements of certain groups are stored in memory and influence how we interact with those individuals and how we process situations involving them

Stigma: disapproval of a person or group based on their social characteristics
- Groups with a stigma attached to them are often treated poorly, and made to feel shameful or dishonorable
- Stigmas exist against mental illness, homosexuality, homelessness, etc.

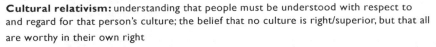

Ethnocentrism: evaluation of people from other cultures based on the values and beliefs of your own culture; assume that your way of doing things is the "right way" and is superior to other cultures

Cultural relativism: understanding that people must be understood with respect to and regard for that person's culture; the belief that no culture is right/superior, but that all are worthy in their own right

Stereotype: widely-held generalization of a particular group of people
- Often occur without conscious awareness; can immensely impact how we view and treat people
- Stereotypes often lead to racial prejudice and discrimination

Stereotype threat: when an individual is in a situation in which they think they are at risk of conforming to a particular stereotype that has been assigned to them (often results in vicious cycle – self-fulfilling prophecy)
- Racial and gender differences in test performance

Self-fulfilling prophecy: false perception of a situation (often a stereotype) becomes internalized and affects the behavior of that person, ultimately resulting in manifestation of that perception
- Positive feedback between belief and behavior
- Negative stereotype → individual gets nervous about whether they can perform/succeed → performance drops → stereotype internalized more → …

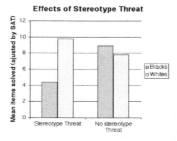

SOCIAL PROCESSES AND INDIVIDUAL BEHAVIOR

Psychology/Sociology Lecture 10

OBJECTIVES

- Social/group processes that impact individual behavior
  - Social facilitation
  - Deindividuation
  - Bystander effect
  - Social loafing
  - Social control and peer pressure
  - Conformity; Asch's experiment
  - Obedience; Milgram's experiment
  - Group polarization and group-think
- Norms and deviance
  - Social norms
  - Folkways, mores, and taboos
  - Sanctions and anomy
  - Deviance
  - Labelling theory and strain theory
  - Collective behavior
- Agents of socialization
- Elements of social interaction: status, role, and group

Social/group processes that impact individual behavior:

Social facilitation: people tend to perform some tasks better when in the presence of others
- Occurs with simple and/or well-practiced tasks
- I.e. running with a group of people; performing a well-rehearsed dance

Deindividuation: in groups, individuals often experience a loss of self awareness and are often exhibit a loss of restraint; "mob mentality"
- Large groups facilitate high arousal and a low degree of personal responsibility (anonymity)
- Zimbardo prison experiment

Bystander effect: people are less likely to help a victim when they are one of many bystanders
- "It's okay, somebody else will call 9-1-1" → diffusion of responsibility
- The NY murder of Kitty Genovese

Social loafing: people tend to put in less effort when in they are in a group than they would if they were doing the project/task alone

Social control: means of controlling the behavior of an individual/group
- Informal social control – the norms and values of a society (learned and internalized by the individual during socialization) dictate what is right and wrong
- Formal social control – external sanctions are put in place to prevent chaos/anarchy (formal laws and rules that result in consequences of illegal/wrong behavior)
    - Ex. Suspension, ticket, jail sentence

Peer pressure: the influence of peers on an individual → coerces the individual to behave like his/her peers in order to fit in (ex. Peer pressure to do drugs, to ignore bullying, etc.)

Conformity: the act of complying with group standards, rules, and expectations
- **Normative social influence –** people conform because they want to be liked/accepted by others
  - Peer pressure
- **Informational social influence (social proof) –** people conform because they want to be right and assume that others are correct

- **Asch's experiment:** participant (told he was doing a vision test) in a room with other confederates is shown one line and then asked which line it resembles out of 3 options; individual in room asked one by one - all confederates responded out loud with the incorrect answer and participant answered last → most participants also answered incorrectly with the same answer as confederates
  - Afterwards, Asch asked why they conformed and most responded that they did so to "fit in" → normative social influence

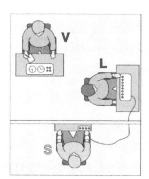

Obedience: complying with law and order; following the requirements of authority
- **Milgram's experiment:** assessed whether individuals obey the commands of an authority figure or follow their conscience when the commands are unethical
- Subject was instructed by study director to administer shocks of varying intensity to an individual (confederate) in another room
- Participants often administered extreme levels of shock (obeying the authority figure), even if they could hear the confederate screaming in pain and knew that the shock would have been extremely damaging

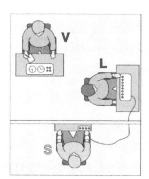

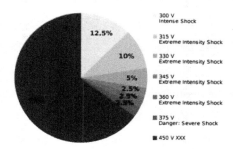

Group polarization: the tendency of groups to make decisions that are more extreme than would have been if each individual answered alone

- Occurs when group members start with generally similar opinions on the matter, and then engage in dialogue
- Ex. Jury members who all initially favor some punishment are likely to decide on a harsher punishment than initially inclined once dialogue ensues
- Can occur whether group is physically together or not (conversing via computer/media)

Group think: group decision making tends to occur in a way that minimizes dissent (conformity of group members)
→ results in less creativity and less analysis of all the possibilities

- Decision made is often irrational and less likely to be successful
- Group wants harmony and to reach consensus, so dissenting opinions are not entertained **(mindgaurding)**
- More common in more cohesive groups

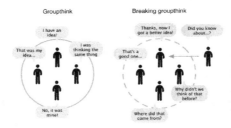

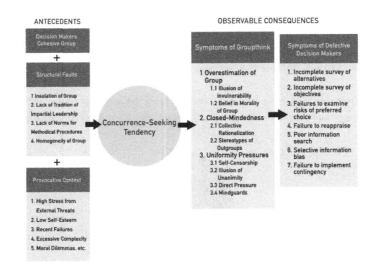

Social Norms

Social Norm: understandings that guide appropriate behavior in a society
* Norms guide behavior for specific instances (shake hands when you meet someone, refraining from talking in a movie theatre, etc.)

* **Folkway:** traditional behavior for casual day-to-day interactions; not following them is considered rude
    * Ex. Saying thank you when one does a favor for you, not burping at the dinner table

* **Mores:** social norms that are morally significant; prescribe right vs. wrong
    * Ex. Don't cheat in a game or on a spouse

* **Taboos:** behaviors that are strongly prohibited and even seen as wrong to discuss
    * Ex. Cannibalism, incest
    * Differ across cultures, religions, etc.

Anomie: society in which there is little moral/ethical guidance of behavior; individuals feel disconnected from society

Sanction: consequences in society that reinforce behavior
* Sanctions may be negative (punishment/penalty for disobeying a rule, law, or other social norm) or positive (reward)

* **Formal sanction –** formally enforced by an institution (such as government) or organization
    * Ex. Jail sentence, speeding ticket, suspension, etc.

* **Informal sanction –** enforced informally by others in society
    * Shame, ridicule, ostracizing the individual, etc.

Theories of Deviance
Deviance: violating social norms

Differential association theory: deviant and criminal behavior is learned in the environment through interactions with others (learning the motives, techniques, attitudes, etc.)
* The more that we associate with deviant individuals, the more likely we are to engage in deviant behavior
* Fails to account for the contribution of genetics and other biological factors that influence one's behavior (such as mental illness)

Labelling theory: society largely creates deviance by arbitrarily labelling certain behaviors as such and by negatively labelling and stereotyping minority groups
- The majority group in society contributes to stereotyping, stigmatizing and self-fulfilling prophecies in individuals from the minority groups

Strain theory: the way society is set up results in strain between the culturally defined norms and the acceptable methods to achieve certain goals
- Ex. The cultural definition of success is largely based on wealth, but many individuals are extremely limited in their ability to achieve monetary wealth (due to institutional injustices, structural limitations, etc.) and resort to deviant behavior

Collective Behavior –
Mass hysteria: illusion of some threat spread throughout society and results in collective panic, fear, and stress
- Ex. Salem witch trials

Fad: temporary trend (Ex. Pokémon, hula hoop, paleo diet)

Riot: group revolts against society in a violent public demonstration

Socialization

Socialization: learning the values, norms, and ideology of one's society

Agents of socialization –
- The majority of socialization occurs during the formative years of our childhood. At this time there are four main agents that facilitate the process of socialization:
    - Family
    - School
    - Peers
    - Mass media

- Later in life, the workplace also becomes a central agent of socialization

Elements of Social Interaction

Status

- **Achieved status –** earned by the person; ex. Doctor, athlete, criminal
- **Ascribed status –** one that you are born with/is beyond your control; ex. Male/female, race, SES
- **Master status –** the status that the individual feels is most important/influential to them
  - Ex. "Above all, I am a father"

Role

- **Role conflict –** conflict between multiple statuses held by one person
  - Ex. Conflict between the responsibilities and expectations of being a mother, a wife, and a working physician
- **Role strain –** a single role that requires conflicting responsibilities/expectations
- **Role exit –** occurs when an individual disengages from a particular role

Groups

- **In-group:** group with a shared identity/interest to which an individual identifies (ex. Students at your school, church you attend, culture you identify with, etc.)

- **Out-group:** group to which an individual does not identify

- **Primary group:** small group comprised of intimate and long-lasting relationships; constantly interact with each other (a core social group)
  - Ex. Your family, your hometown best friends, etc.
  - Usually a key part of the individual's identity

- **Secondary group:** larger group comprised of less personal and more temporary relationships; often formed in a more formal setting
  - Ex. Coworkers, classmates

- **Group size:**
  - **Dyad:** 2 people
  - **Triad:** 3 people

SOCIAL BEHAVIOR AND SELF PRESENTATION

Psychology/Sociology Lecture 11

OBJECTIVES

- Networks and organizations
  - Networks
  - Formal organizations
  - Bureaucracy: Characteristics of ideal bureaucracy
  - McDonaldization and the Iron Law of Oligarchy
- Expressing and detecting emotion
  - The role of culture and gender
- Presentation of self
  - Impression management
  - Dramaturgical approach; front stage vs. back stage self
- Communication: verbal and non-verbal
- Attachment
- Altruism
- Social support
- Social behavior in animals
  - Foraging; mating and mate choice
  - Game Theory
  - Altruism and inclusive fitness

Networks

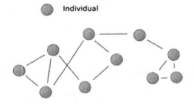

Networks: social ties and relationships between people

Social Network Theory:

- Map of a social network contains nodes (individuals) linked by social ties
- Ties differ in strength → weak versus strong ties
- Weak ties can, in some ways, be more impactful/valuable than strong ties → weak ties are more numerous and enable the sharing of resources and ideas to a vast network

Organizations

Organization: a group of people organized together for a certain purpose
- **Formal organization:** have a fixed set of rules and operation procedures
  - Clear responsibilities and authority of individuals; hierarchical organization and division of labor

Types of formal organizations –

- **Utilitarian organization:** members are rewarded and/or compensated for their contributions and membership
  - Shared purpose of productivity
  - Ex. Businesses, university
- **Normative organization:** members organized together voluntarily due to shared goals and sense of purpose
  - Ex. Religious organizations, charities, sorority/fraternity
- **Coercive organization:** membership is not voluntary; members must conform to strict rules and obey authority
  - Extremely structured and strict; use of force to ensure conformity; loss of individuality
  - Ex. Prison, the military

Bureaucracy

Bureaucracy: organization with a hierarchical structure that is governed by extensive amount of rules/policies, and has detailed procedures for operation

- Purpose is to maximize efficiency and order of the organization
- Typically associated with governmental organizations, but can be non-governmental

Characteristics of an ideal bureaucracy –

- Formal structure comprised of a hierarchy
- Governed by written rules and regulations
    - Goal displacement → following rules may become more important than goals
- Division of labor into specialized units
- Impersonality – all matters conducted in an unbiased manner
- Impartial employment based on qualifications/merit
    - Can lead to the Peter Principle → people keep getting promoted based on their current performance and not on the responsibilities of the higher position; results in people getting ultimately promoted to a level of incompetence where they cannot perform

Iron Law of Oligarchy: all organizations, even ones that start out democratic, eventually turn into oligarchies

- **Oligarchy:** group governed by a select few ("the elite")
- Occurs because certain leading individuals get power and become resistant to giving up that power → entire organizations eventually lead entirely by "leadership class"

McDonaldization: tendency of society to shift towards and adopt the operating principles of a fast-food restaurant → embracing efficiency, calculability (quantification), standardized and predictable services, replacement of human labor with technology

Interaction and Self-presentation

Role of gender and culture in expressing and detecting emotion –

- **Gender:** certain societal/cultural expectations surrounding masculinity vs. femininity in the expression of emotion
  - Women expected to be more emotional → have often been assumed to be unable to take on certain leadership roles (e.g. CEO, president) due to stereotype of being ruled by emotion as opposed to logic
  - Men expected to withhold their emotions (sadness in particular) but express aggression
- **Culture:** Individualistic cultures (like the US and other Western cultures) promote feelings of autonomy, pride, and independence; collectivistic cultures (mainly Eastern cultures) promote the interconnectedness of individuals

Impression Management –

- The process of managing our self image by attempting to influence others' perceptions
  - We do so by controlling the information presented in social interactions
  - Conscious and unconscious process
- Often used synonymously with "**self-presentation**" → presenting ourselves in a certain way to control how others perceive us

Dramaturgical Approach –

- Analogy of life as a stage/theatrical performance; we imagine ourselves as actors playing different roles in life
- Our ultimate goal is to present ourselves in the most acceptable and presentable way to others (the audience)
- Our performance/role depends on where we are (the set of the play) and whether we on the front stage or the back stage

Front stage

- Where we play particular roles in front of the audience and follow all societal norms/conventions
- Use impression management to regulate how people perceive us
- When we are in a social setting we express the "front stage self"

Back stage

- Where we can "let our guard down"; no audience so we can drop the front and fully be ourselves
- When we are in an intimate/private setting with a small number of our closest family members or friends

Communication

Verbal communication: involves words; speaking, writing, television, radio, email, etc.

Non-verbal communication: doesn't involve words; eye contact, body language, posture, facial expressions, etc.

Animal signals and communication –

- **Pheromones** → species-specific chemicals that affect the behavior the receiving organism
    - Pheromones are involved in aggression, alarm, signaling the presence of food/resources, territorial behavior, mate choice and mating, nursing, aggregation, etc.
- Aggression – teeth-baring, growling, back arching, fur-raising, etc.
- Mating – certain dances/performances often performed to attract the attention of and win a mate
    - Ex. Insect and bird mating dances
- Auditory: bird songs, dog barking, growling, purring, etc.
- **Intraspecific communication:** between individuals of the same species
- **Interspecific communication:** between individuals of different species
    - Ex. Predator-prey relationship

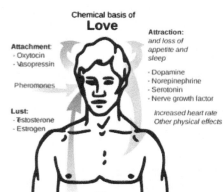

Fig. 7.—Half-bred Shepherd Dog in the same state as in Fig. 5. By Mr. A. May.

Attachment

Attachment theory: forming strong attachment to a primary caregiver is a crucial part of personal development
- Attachment has emotional, physical, and cognitive components

Harlow –
- Experiments using monkeys to study attachment and distress
- Harlow suspected that the infant-mother connection was not a learned behavior for the purpose of obtaining food, as behaviorists had suggested, but was an innate need for comfort
- Monkeys raised in isolation (no mother or social contact) had extreme social issues, aggression towards other monkeys, and numerous psychological issues (such as self-mutilation and compulsive rocking)
- Monkeys separated from actual mother and raised with a wire 'mother' that provided food as well as a cloth mother → monkeys only went to wire mother when hungry and spent much time clutching to cloth mother
- Harlow demonstrated that infant monkeys had an innate need for tactile bonding with mother; attachment not solely for food/nourishment purposes

Ainsworth –
- "Strange situation experiments": infants (ages 1 – 1.5) in a room and observed covertly by experimenter while infant's mother and stranger enter and leave room in certain schedule
- Infant left alone with mother → stranger enters room → mother leaves room → mother returns then stranger leaves → mother then leaves → ...
    - Behavior was scored and Ainsworth came up with 4 main attachment styles based on the findings

Attachment Styles:

Secure attachment –
- Infant happily explores surroundings when mother present; cries when she leaves, but can be quickly consoled when she returns
- Infant wary of stranger when mother gone but more friendly when mother present
- Children with attentive, loving, and sensitive caregivers
- The majority of infants exhibit this style of attachment

- The following three attachment styles are examples of **insecure attachment** → generally these children have insensitive, inattentive, or inconsistent caregivers

Ambivalent attachment –
- Infants cry when mother leaves and remain upset after she returns (difficult to console them); inconsistent response to mother – may cling to her anxiously or display aggression/anger (hit and push mother)

Avoidant attachment –
- Infants are not very exploratory and are emotionally distant; show indifference to mother leaving and returning
- Mainly friendly to stranger

Disorganized attachment –
- Infant's response is unpredictable, extreme and erratic; shows both ambivalent and avoidant attachment
- Infant may appear to be passive, angry, and/or confused

Altruism (biological definition): an action that increases the fitness of another organism while decreasing the fitness of the acting organism
- Seen extensively in kin relationships (closely related organisms) as well as in social groups
- Ex. Worker bees sacrificing their own fitness to work for the colony; organisms caring for sick/wounded members of their social group; fighting off predators for the colony; sharing food and other resources

- **Inclusive Fitness** – includes fitness gained from helping to protect/raise/support organisms that have some relatedness to the organism
    - Ex. Sibling, nieces, nephews, cousins, etc. all share some proportion of their DNA with you; by supporting kin, an organism can increase it's genetic representation in the subsequent generations (**kin selection**)

Social support:
- Three main types – emotional (love, companionship, trust), instrumental (tangible support), and informational (advice and suggestions)
- Extremely important for health and well-being (both physical and psychological); promotes resistance to and recovery from psychological disorders; helps reduce stress levels
    - People with lower levels of social support have higher rates of psychological disorders

Reciprocal altruism:

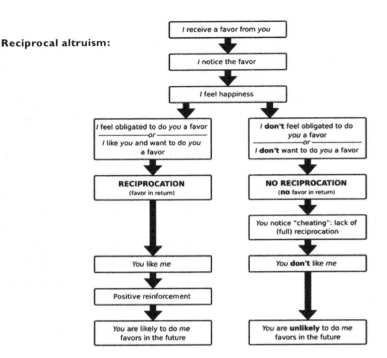

Social Behavior in Animals

Foraging Behavior

- Foraging = seeking out food
- According to behavioral ecology, animals forage in a way that will maximize energy gained per unit of time
- Foraging is partially genetic and partially learned
  - Primates observe elders in their social group and mimic their foraging behavior (observational learning)
- Animals are at risk of predation while foraging; must balance their need for energy with this risk

Mating and mate choice

- Mate choice = **intersexual selection**
- Generally, an individual attempts to choose a mate who is most genetically fit → may be assessed based on sexually dimorphic traits, physical appearance, behavior (mating dances), competition, etc.
- Within one species, usually one sex is choosy and members of the other sex compete with each other for access to mates (**intrasexual selection**)
  - Usually females are choosy and males compete amongst themselves for the females

Applying game theory

- Game theory – using models to study choice, cooperation, and conflict in rational decision-makers
- Choices involve a cost-benefit analysis; rational choice theory proposes that individuals make choices to maximize gains and minimize losses
- "Zero-sum game" → loss for one person results in a gain for the other individual

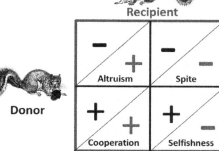
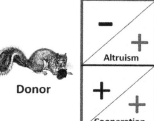

APPROACHES TO SOCIOLOGY AND DEMOGRAPHICS

Psychology/Sociology Lecture 12

OBJECTIVES

- Theoretical Approaches to Sociology
  - Macrosociology vs. Microsociology
  - Functionalism
  - Conflict Theory
  - Feminist Theory
  - Symbolic Interactionism
  - Social Constructionism
  - Exchange/Rational Choice Theory
- Demographics
  - Age: life course, age cohorts, and social significance
  - Gender: sex vs. gender; the social construction of gender
  - Gender segregation
  - Race and ethnicity: the social construction of race
  - Racialization and racial formation
  - Immigration status
  - Sexual orientation

Macrosociology vs. Microsociology

Macrosociology:
- Focuses on large-scale structures/institutions and social processes; looking at society as a whole
  - Observes overall processes, trends, and wide-scale changes in society
  - Society analyzed as an entity that is greater than the sum of all the individuals
- Can use macro sociology to assesses how these structures and processes affect humans and how an individual's position within these structures influences his/her behavior
- Theories: Functionalism, conflict theory

Microsociology:
- Focuses on small-scale interactions and considerations of the individual
  - Individual interactions (such as a conversation) and group dynamics
- Can use to assess how individuals can can affect the social structure and collectively make a difference
- Theories: Symbolic interactionism, rational choice/exchange theory

BOTH macro and micro: feminist theory and social constructionism

MACROSCOPIC

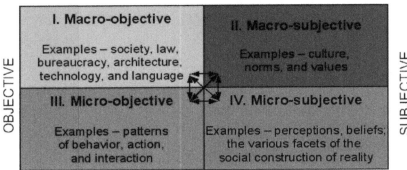

MICROSCOPIC

Functionalism

- **Emile Durkheim**, considered the father of sociology, ascribed to the functionalist perspective
  - Durkheim founded the field of sociology alongside Karl Marx and Max Weber

- Views society as a system of many interdependent components that work together to achieve **dynamic equilibrium** and social stability
  - All parts interact with and rely on each other; these elements (not the individuals) shape society as a whole
  - Main structures = family, education, religion, crime, economy
  - Each structure achieves crucial main function(s) for society

- Element of society may be functional (contribute to stability/equilibrium), dysfunctional, or both
  - Crime is both → functional because contributes to the enforcement and public awareness of laws, norms, and mores; dysfunctional because creates conflict, people removed from the workplace/social institutions
  - Social dysfunctions must be corrected or society must readjust in order to reachieve equilibrium

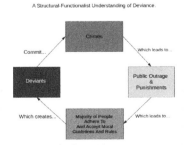

- **Social facts**: elements of society that serve some function in enforcing social control
  - Ex. Values, norms, morals, traditions, etc.

- Socialization = passing down the norms and values to the next generation; facilitates the overall functioning and homeostasis of society

- Social structures have manifest and latent functions –
  - **Manifest functions**: the obvious and intended functions of a structure (ex. School → Transmission of knowledge, skills, and occupational training; socialization)
  - **Latent functions**: the unintended and less recognizable functions of a structure (ex. School → care-giving services, meeting a mate, sorting of students based on potential, etc.)

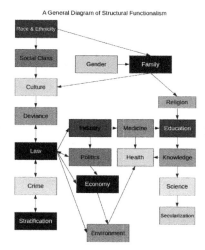

A General Diagram of Structural Functionalism

Conflict Theory

- Focuses on conflict over resources, values, and interests, as well as differences in power
  - Society as a constant struggle for social, political, economic, and material resources
  - These struggles and power differentials are inherent and maintain order in society

- Social structures and institutions have inherent inequality → tension and discrepancies between advantaged and disadvantaged groups
  - Ex. Oppression of minorities; racial and gender inequalities
  - Largely takes the perspective of those who lack power (minorities and disadvantaged groups)

- Key theorists: Karl Marx and Max Weber
  - **Marx** – focus on class struggle between those who control production (bourgeoisie) and the working class; thought that this was the predominant and most influential ongoing conflict in society
    - Marx though that capitalism caused so much tension, exploitation, and crisis that it would eventually collapse
  - **Weber** – thought that there was more than one source of ongoing conflict (not just the owners vs. the workers) and assessed the diversity of reactions to inequality; did not think that capitalism was doomed to collapse

Feminist Theory

- Feminist theory is a branch of conflict theory that focuses on the different experiences of men and women as a result of gender-based inequality and power differences
  - Can be studied at a macro level and micro level

- Assesses sources and outcomes of gender inequality (gender roles, stereotyping, discrimination, objectification, the wage gap, etc.)
  - **Glass ceiling:** barrier that prevents women from advancing in the corporate world

- **Intersectionality:** looking at various social aspects (gender, race, SES, religion, etc.) and how they interact to shape the unique experiences of individuals; especially oppression and discrimination

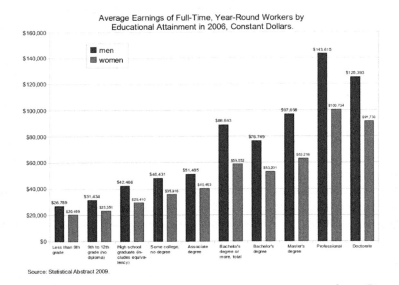

Source: Statistical Abstract 2009.

Symbolic Interactionism

- Micro sociological perspective that views society as the accumulation of everyday interactions and individual perceptions

- Analyzes the subjective meaning that people assign to objects, interactions, and behaviors → these subjective meanings influence how people think, behave, and interact with others in society

- Society and culture constructed through these symbolic interpretations, which are negotiated, modified, and transmitted (the meaning/significance of something in society is fluid and actively shaped)
  - Language and communication used to generate and transmit these interpretations
  - Ex. Two fingers and the dove are symbols that are associated with peace; race and gender are largely social constructs upon which we place a lot of significance and rely on to guide behavior (but the interpretations, significance, and implications of gender and race are constantly shifting)

- **George Herbert Mead**: sociologist who is largely credited with symbolic interactionism
  - Formulated the dramaturgical approach
  - Argues that the "self" is a social product

Social Constructionism

- Proposes that our perceptions of reality are actively shaped by social interactions and are comprised of meaningful social constructs → studies the social process of constructing shared assumptions/understandings about the world and social institutions

- **Social construct**: meaning, significance, and concepts associated with a particular object/event → created and modified by individuals in society
  - Ex. Gender, romance, marriage, occupation, social class/SES

- Assesses how individuals and groups contribute to this dynamic and ongoing process of social construction

Exchange/Rational Choice Theory

- Individuals make decisions (for social interactions or other courses of actions) based on earning the greatest reward at the lowest cost
  - Proposes that opportunities for profit, both tangible and intangible, motivate us to behave and interact with others in certain ways

- A crucial aspect of decision making is **cost-benefit analysis**; profit = (reward of behavior) − (cost of behavior)
  - Looking at behavior from an economic perspective
  - Costs and benefits are often subjective

- "Rational choice theory" focuses on measurable resources/profits/costs

- "Social exchange theory" focuses on decisions regarding interaction and costs/benefits that can be tangible, or intangible

Demographics

Age:
- Average lifespan in the US in approximately 78 years
- Age cohort = group of people around the same age and therefore share some common social/cultural experiences
  - Baby Boomers → Generation X → Millennials → Generation Z
- Ageism = discrimination based on age
- Baby boomer cohort is aging – need to prepare the funds, programs, medical resources, and working force to support them and eventually replace them in the economy (as the retire and pass away)

Gender: Male, female, transgender, non-binary, etc.; gender is fluid, like sexuality
- Gender is a social construct – we view it as a binary concept in which people conform to one or the other but in reality individuals can lie anywhere along a spectrum; gender roles are a construct of culture that attempt to prescribe appropriate/expected behavior for each gender
- Note: biological sex = male, female, or intersex - based on genital structures (biological factors only)
- Gender segregation: many activities, institutions, and traditions are segregated
  - Ex. Some sports teams, schools, bathrooms, etc.

Sexual orientation: heterosexual, homosexual, bisexual, asexual, and many other identifications
- Sexual orientation is along a spectrum (not binary)

Race and ethnicity
- **Race:** based on physical characteristics such as skin color
    - White, Black, Asian, Pacific Islander, etc.

- **Racialization:** ascribing a racial identity to someone who doesn't identify with that label
    - People behave differently around an individual depending on how they have chosen to classify his/her race

- **Racial formation theory:** racial categories seen as a social construct; each category has been defined by economic and political powers (individuals in power create and define these categories to serve their best interests)

- **Ethnicity:** based on cultural characteristics/affiliations

Immigration status
- Patterns of immigration –
    - Almost all individuals in the US are immigrants or descendants of immigrants
    - Overall, immigration into the US has been increasing over the past few decades
    - Majority of immigrants today are from Mexico, Central America, India, and China
    - Immigration from European countries into the US has dropped significantly over the last 300 years (in terms of percent of US immigrants)

- Intersectionality of immigration status, race, and ethnicity – an individual's identity is dependent on the interaction of many elements; individuals of a given race likely have very different cultures, beliefs, values, and experiences depending on their ethnicity and immigration status
    - The social barriers, prejudice, and discrimination of minorities is highly dependent on the intersection of these elements

SOCIAL INSTITUTIONS AND CULTURE

Psychology/Sociology Lecture 13

OBJECTIVES

- Education
  - Teacher expectancy and the hidden curriculum; segregation and stratification in education
- Family
  - Kinship, diversity of families, and parenting styles
  - Marriage and divorce; violence in the family
- Religion
  - Religiosity and types of religious organizations
  - Social change and religion
- Government/economy
  - Power and authority
  - Different political and economic systems
- Health and medicine
  - Medicalization, the sick role, and the illness experience
  - Healthcare delivery
  - Social epidemiology
- Culture
  - Elements of culture; material vs. symbolic culture
  - Culture lag and culture shock; assimilation and multiculturalism
  - Subcultures and counterculture; mass media and pop culture
  - Evolution; transmission and diffusion of culture

Education

- Education provides a way to pass down values, norms, ideas, and other aspects of the dominant culture; it also promotes critical thinking and the formation of new ideas, as well as helps maintain discipline/obedience in young individuals

- Education may also increase inequality as a result of the hidden curriculum, teacher expectancy, and educational segregation/stratification

- **Hidden Curriculum**: refers to any unintended results of education (such as passing down norms and value of the dominant culture)
  - Education can enforce and perpetuate existing inequalities by teaching kids according to their class/social status; resources, expectations, rigor and quality of the education correlated with class/SES of the students

- **Teacher expectancy:** teacher expects certain behavior from certain students based on their social class, race, SES, gender, etc. → affects how teachers treat those children → alters how those students perform; students begin to conform to the expectations
    - Self-fulfilling prophecy - positive feedback loop
    - Expectations may be high (impact student positively) or low
    - Generally rooted in stereotypes associated with certain characteristics of the student
    - Perpetuates inequalities and class differences

- **Educational stratification/segregation:** the academic achievement of students depends extensively on their social background (largely their SES)
    - There is a widening disparity in achievement of students from high versus low income areas
    - Children from poorer areas generally attend schools with less funding, receive poorer education, are less likely to pursue higher education, and receive lower wages once out of school
    - This further reinforces class differences and social inequalities

Percentage of students that take advanced courses in mathematics and physics, by sex, Grade 12

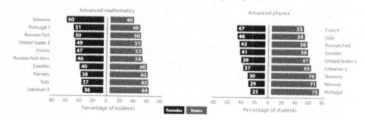

More boys than girls take advanced courses in mathematics and physics in secondary education in Grade 12.
Note: † Met guidelines for sample participation rates only after replacement schools were included, ‡ Did not satisfy guidelines for sample participation rates. The Russian Federation 6hr+ results are for a subset of the Russian Federation students. This subset of students are in an intensive stream that have at least 6 hours of mathematics lessons per week.
9 countries.   Data source: TIMSS Advanced 2015

Family

- **Important functions -** reproduction and child rearing, socialization, formation of identity, religious and cultural transmission, affection, love/belonging, defining social status

- **Nuclear family**: includes a couple and their children
- **Extended family**: includes grandparents, cousins, nieces, nephews, etc.
- **Kinship**: relationships due to marriage, adoption, or blood ties; helps define relationships between people in society
    - **Primary kinship**: found in the nuclear family (your parents and siblings)
    - **Secondary kinship**: includes those who are directly related to anyone in your nuclear family (a.k.a. primary kin of your primary kin)

Marriage – forms a primary kinship and a new nuclear family
- Monogamy: marriage to a single person
- Polygamy: marriage to multiple people at one time
    - Polyandry: woman married to multiple men
    - Polygyny: man married to multiple women
- **Divorce** – termination of marriage
    - Divorce rates have increased significantly since the mid 20th century
    - Stigma surrounding divorce has also decreased

- Violence in the family – includes elder abuse, spousal abuse, and child abuse
    - Generally has severe psychological impacts on the abused; especially significant impact on children

- Power in the family –
    - **Matriarchy**: women is head of the family
    - **Patriarchy**: man is head of the family

Parenting styles –
- **Authoritative:** parent is respectful and supportive of child but sets clear rules/limits and disciplines the child
    - Best style of parenting
- **Authoritarian:** parent is extremely strict, controlling, and shows little warmth/support
- **Permissive:** parent is inconsistent, often gives in to the child, and lacks the ability to discipline the child
- **Uninvolved/Neglectful:** parent is uninvolved, emotionally detached, indifferent to child, and doesn't set rules

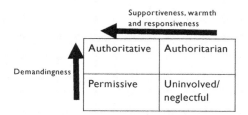

Religion

- **Functions** (functionalist perspective) – provides social support, creates social cohesion and sometimes dissent, serves as a form of social control, and provides an important form of socialization

Types of religious organizations –

- **Ecclesia:** large and dominant religious organization that includes majority of members from that society; generally recognized as a national religion and allied with government/the state
    - Many of the state churches in Europe (Ex. The Church of England)
- **Church:** mainstream and well-integrated religion; may be affiliated with the state or not
    - Ex. The Christian Church and the Catholic Church in the U.S.
- **Sect:** religious organization that is not part of mainstream society/culture; usually formed by breaking away from a large existing church to promote a more orthodox or distinct version of the religion; exclusive membership
    - Ex. Methodists, the Amish, Baptists
- **Cult:** non-traditional and socially deviant beliefs and practices (strays far from societal norms)
    - Often a new religious movement; includes politically-oriented cults, doomsday cults, racist cults (the KKK), etc.
    - Ex. Scientology

- **Religiosity:** quality of being devoted to one's religions ("devoutness")

Religion and social change

- **Secularization** - movement towards embracing attitudes and beliefs that do not have a religious basis → religion losing its significance in society
    - Secularization occurs as societies progress/modernize; religion plays less of a role in social life, government, and the culture of a society

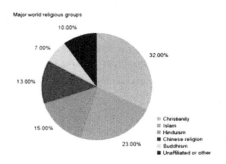

- **Modernization** - religions can promote social changes or are forced to respond to social changes that occur alongside modernization
    - Modernization and secularization go hand in hand

- **Fundamentalism** – religion with a strict set of beliefs and practices that are well-integrated into the followers' daily lives; generally embraces a literal interpretations of the scripture

Government and economy

- **Functions** – Government makes and enforces rules of society, maintains social order, dictates operation of the economy, maintains relationships with other nations. Economy provides a means for production/consumption, distribution of goods and services, and earning of wages.
- **Power and authority** – derived from laws, rules, and regulations, designated customs/traditions and norms of society, and authority figure (such as the mayor, governor, president, etc.)

Distribution of power (government systems) –

Autocracy: rule by one person
- Dictatorship: rule by a single person (dictator) who seized control

Democracy: rule by the people
- Representative democracy: citizens directly choose leaders to represent their interest
- Direct democracy: citizens have more direct control/contribution; much more rare

Oligarchy: rule by a small select group of people
- Aristocracy: rule by people born into a 'ruling class'
- Meritocracy: rule by people selected on the basis of merit

Monarchy: one family at the head of the government (kings and queens)

Authoritarian/ Totalitarian: strong central power enforces strict control over the people; limited freedom

Division of labor: different facets of a manufacturing process split up and assigned to different people/systems
- Improves efficiency and accountability of production

Forms of economy –

Market economy: individuals own and operate the means of production (such as a free enterprise economy and capitalist economy)

Command economy: the government owns and operates the means of production
- **Communism:** public (not private) ownership of the means of production; often results in dictatorship, and acute scarcity (i.e. famine and widespread poverty)
- **Socialism:** the society owns and operates the economy as a whole; attempt to equalize the wealth amongst citizens → many social welfare programs

Mixed economy: features of market and command economy (like the US)

Traditional economy: traditional economic system based on customs/traditions (agriculture, hunting and gathering)

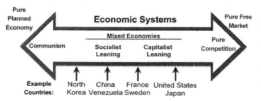

Health and Medicine

Delivery of healthcare –
- Primary care: first-line of care involving preventative medicine and ongoing care in the form of check-ups, etc.
  - GP/PCP and ER triage
- Secondary care: referrals to specialty care
- Tertiary care: very specialized form of care; often with an entire institution dedicated to that (ex. Cancer center)

Medicalization: the conceptualization of human conditions as physiological issues and diagnosable diseases
- Condition viewed from a scientific/medical standpoint in attempts to understand causes, diagnosis, prevention and treatment
  - Ex. The medicalization of addiction, mental illness, and deviance
- Positive impacts - increased awareness, treatment, prevention, development of medications, etc.
- Negative impacts - stigma and labelling, may impact an individual's identity and/or self-efficacy, may lead to over-diagnosis, may result in overlooking the social contributions to a condition, etc.

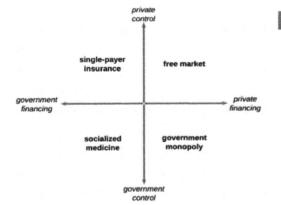

The sick role: a role that individuals take on when sick; includes certain rights and obligations

Rights –
- Person is not held responsible for his/her illness
- Person is excused from carrying out normal social duties (work, caring for family, etc.)

Obligations –
- Person must try to get better
- Person should seek out and comply with medical care

Illness experience: the overall subjective experience of being in a state of poor health; how people perceive and adjust to changes in their health

Social epidemiology: studies the impact of social, cultural, and economic factors on one's health
- Understanding origins of health disparities, assessing social determinants of health, and attempting to combat these disparities
- Applying an understanding of social phenomena (social) to the study of health outcomes and disease distributions (epidemiology)

Culture

Elements of culture: beliefs and values, language, rituals/traditions/customs, norms, media, religion, arts/literature, political and economic system, etc.
- Elements of a culture are passed down the next generation via socialization

- **Material culture:** concrete, tangible, and visible elements of the culture
  - Ex. Clothing, architecture, cars, etc.
- **Symbolic culture:** intangible elements of a culture; shared ideas, values, and beliefs
  - Language, norms, religious beliefs, etc.
  - Language → Sapir-Whorf Hypothesis

- **Popular culture:** shared by the masses
- **High culture:** participated in by the elite
- **Cultural universals:** beliefs, traits, or behaviors common to all cultures
  - Ex. Marriage, music, art/dance, etc.

Culture lag: norms and rules within a culture take time to catch up with technological innovations and rapid societal advances → results in conflict within the society
- Material culture evolves more quickly than non-material/symbolic culture

Culture shock: the feeling of shock or disorientation when an individual experiences a foreign culture (due to travel or moving to a new area)

Assimilation: an individual or group adopts the culture of another group; usually occurs when small group (such as foreign immigrants) assimilates into the dominant culture
- Assimilated group/individual gives up most elements of their previous cultural identity

Multiculturalism (ethnic pluralism): the existence of many different cultures within one society; the various cultures are all respected and individuals do not have to give up their cultural identity to live in the society
- America as a "melting pot"

Subculture: group with a different cultural identity than the dominant culture (i.e. a culture within a dominant culture)

Counterculture: group with a culture that opposed the dominant culture ("anti-establishment")
- Ex. The counterculture "hippie" movement of the 1960's

Mass media and "pop culture" –
- Mass media = media that reaches a large amount of people (TV, radio, internet, newspaper, ads, etc.) → has a powerful influence on culture
- Pop culture = dominant and well-recognized images, ideas, beliefs, and practices in a culture; i.e. the mainstream culture
  - Pop culture is ubiquitous and permeates our lives, shaping culture and our identity (both collective and personal)

Cultural transmission: transfer of the elements of a culture from one generation to the next; culture is passed down through socialization

Cultural diffusion: the spread of elements of a culture from one group to another (i.e. cross-cultural communication and exchange) → occurs increasingly with modernization

SOCIETAL AND DEMOGRAPHIC SHIFTS

Psychology/Sociology Lecture 14

OBJECTIVES

- Demographic shifts
  - Malthusian theory
  - Demographic transition
- Populations
  - Population pyramids; growth and decline
- Birth, death, and migration
  - Fertility and mortality rates and patterns
  - Migration: push and pull factors
- Social movements
  - Relative depravation
  - Organization, strategies, and tactics
- Globalization
  - Contributing factors
  - Globalization perspectives; social changes
- Urbanization
  - Industrialization and suburbanization
  - Urban growth and urban decline
  - Gentrification
  - Urban renewal

Demographic shifts

Malthusian Theory

- **Malthus** proposed that the human population grows exponentially but that resources (mainly food) grows at an arithmetic rate → population will exceed its capacity → result is a **Malthusian catastrophe**

- Malthus urged that we must avoid this catastrophe and that 2 types of measures can keep the population in check:

  1. **Positive checks:** anything that shortens human life therefore increasing the death rate (i.e. poor living conditions, disease, etc.)

  2. **Preventative checks:** decreasing the birth rate by exercising 'moral restraint'/birth control measures

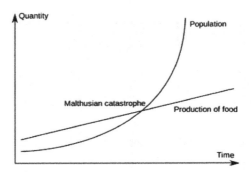

Demographic Transition:

- Shift from high birth rate (BR) and high death rate (DR) → low BR and low DR; occurs as a **society industrializes**

- Population increases throughout the transition then eventually stabilizes and decreases slightly in the last stage

- 5 stages:
    1. high BR and DR
    2. high BR, dropping DR → population increases rapidly
    3. dropping BR, dropping DR → slower population increase
    4. low BR and DR → population stabilizes
    5. very low BR, low DR → population drops slightly

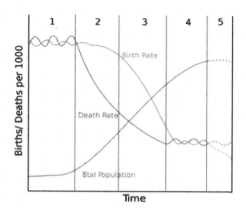

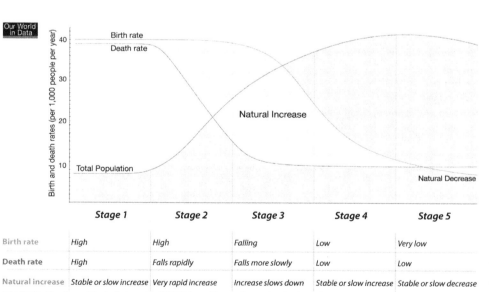

	Stage 1	Stage 2	Stage 3	Stage 4	Stage 5
Birth rate	High	High	Falling	Low	Very low
Death rate	High	Falls rapidly	Falls more slowly	Low	Low
Natural increase	Stable or slow increase	Very rapid increase	Increase slows down	Stable or slow increase	Stable or slow decrease

Source: http://ourworldindata.org/data/population-growth-vital-statistics/world-population-growth

Populations

- **Population**: the inhabitants in a particular area
  - Growth occurs when birth rate is greater than death rate, as long as immigration exceeds emigration
    - Population change = (births + immigration) – (deaths + emigration)
    - Population growth rate = (BR + immigration rate) – (DR + emigration rate)

- Crude birth rate = total births/1000 people   (in a certain defined time period)
- Crude death rate = total deaths/1000 people   (in a certain defined time period)
- Age specific rates are the BR and DR for individuals within a certain age range
- Fertility rate = number of births/1000 women; if all those women were to pass through their childbearing years

- Migration **push factors** (push people to want to leave an area): unemployment, poverty, fear, feeling unsafe, political unrest, war, disasters, drought, etc.
- Migration **pull factors** (push people to want to enter a foreign area): employment, opportunity, safety, stability, political security, fertile land, etc.

- Expected population shifts and growth rates can be projected using models
- **Population pyramid** shows the % of people within each each range and gender category
  - Shape of population pyramid indicates whether population is expending, stable, or decreasing

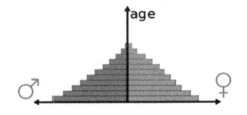

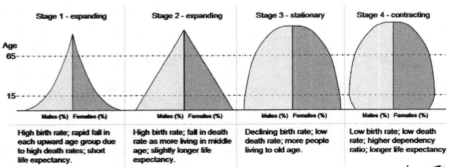

Stage 1 - expanding	Stage 2 - expanding	Stage 3 - stationary	Stage 4 - contracting
High birth rate; rapid fall in each upward age group due to high death rates; short life expectancy.	High birth rate; fall in death rate as more living in middle age; slightly longer life expectancy.	Declining birth rate; low death rate; more people living to old age.	Low birth rate; low death rate; higher dependency ratio; longer life expectancy

Social Movements

Relative Deprivation –

- Individuals compare what they have (resources, amenities, activities, employment, etc.) to what others have, and are discontent when they feel deprived of certain things; relative deprivation may involve political, economic or social resources
- Relative deprivation can cause individuals to engage in deviant behavior, and may cause social unrest or trigger the organization of a social movement

Organization, strategies, and tactics of social movements:

- Social movements involve a collective effort to promote or prevent certain changes in society
- Must involve some strong, charismatic leader figures, such as MLK, that possess *charismatic authority* (command attention due to their personality/charisma)
- Organization of individuals and planned, highly visible efforts, such as marches, riots, and protests
- Generally sparked by one of a few initiating events
- Free rider problem → people are resistant to actually join/contribute to the movement because they will likely benefit from its results whether or not they join (and there may be consequences to joining)

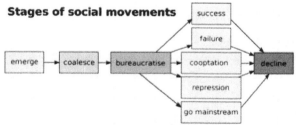

Adapted from Blumer (1969), Mauss (1975), and Tilly (1978)

Sit-ins of the 1960s:

Trayvon Martin shooting protest:

Globalization

Globalization: increasing global connections and interdependence of societies; growth of a global consciousness and a global economy

- Connections are economic, social, cultural, and political → sharing and integration of ideas, values, belief systems, and ways of life

- **Contributing factors:** technological advancement - especially communication technology and mass media; expanded global trade; rapid global transport; development of multinational companies; mobility of labor and outsourcing; increasing economic interdependence (development of a global economy); expanded role of NGOs, such as the UN

- **Civil changes:** globalization can result in increasing inequality, which may trigger civil unrest and terrorism; may also result in colonialism (one country exerts power/control over and takes advantage of another country)

Urbanization

Urbanization: shift in a area from being rural to becoming more urban
- Population of the area increases and it becomes a hub for people to live, work, shop, and hang out
- In addition to changes in the built environment (more crowded, high-rise building and other efficient uses of space, more traffic, etc.), many social and cultural changes occur in the area
    - Urban culture replaces rural culture
- The world is becoming increasingly urbanized, and more of the world's population is moving into urban areas

Trends in Urbanization by Region, 2003.

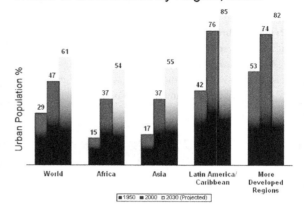

Source: United Nations, World Urbanization Prospects

CURVESETTER
T U T O R I N G

Industrialization: when an area transitions (economically and socially) from an agrarian society to an industrial society

- Mechanization of manufacturing and mass production; expanding reliance on and development of technology; concentration of labor into factories
- Urbanization and industrialization generally occur simultaneously
- First and second industrial revolutions occurred in the US and Europe in the 18th and 19th centuries; other area of the world are gradually industrializing

Suburbanization: people begin moving out of urban areas (cities) and into suburban areas surrounding the city; formation of "urban sprawl"

- Can lead to urban decay

CURVESETTER
T U T O R I N G

Urban growth: growth of urban areas
- Industrialization and urbanization → urban growth

Urban decline/decay: urban area deteriorates and falls into disrepair
- Suburbanization often leads to urban decline as people move out of the cities, leaving many areas of the city abandoned and drawing money/business and investments out of the area

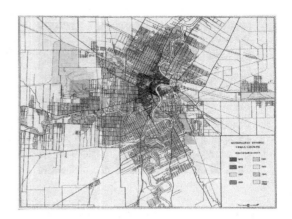

Urban renewal: the process of renovating and improving an urban area that has fallen into disrepair as a result of previous urban decline
- Replacing old buildings; bringing money, business, and investment back into the area; improving safety
- Often leads to gentrification
- **Gentrification** – the influx of more affluent residents, increase in the price of housing and goods, and displacement of the original residents who can no longer afford to live there
    - Disproportionately affects minorities and those from lower social class/SES

CURVESETTER
TUTORING

SOCIAL CLASS, INEQUALITY, AND DISPARITIES

Psychology/Sociology Lecture 15

OBJECTIVES

- Inequality in the built environment
  - Neighborhood safety and residential segregation
  - Environmental justice
- Social class and inequality
  - Social stratification, social class, and SES
  - Class consciousness; cultural and social capital
  - Social reproduction
  - Power, privilege, and prestige
  - Socioeconomic gradient in health
  - Global inequality
- Social mobility
  - Intergenerational and intragenerational; vertical and horizontal
- Poverty
  - Absolute poverty vs. relative poverty
  - Social exclusion
- Health and healthcare disparities
- Discrimination
  - Individual and institutional discrimination
  - Prejudice and discrimination
  - Role of power, prestige, and class

Inequality

Neighborhood safety and residential segregation

- Lower income neighborhoods have more violence
  - More exposure to deviant behavior during development; less opportunity; increases stress levels in residents

- Residential segregation – segregation of groups into different neighborhoods ("groups" mainly categorized by race/ethnicity, income, and SES)
  - The majority of low income families are racial minorities → housing records show that these groups are often segregated into poorer and less safe neighborhoods
  - Produces negative socioeconomic outcomes for minorities
  - Direct segregation is illegal now but the effects of Jim Crow laws and other discrimination tactics persist; current neighborhood segregation related to suburbanization, discrimination, and income/SES

- **Environmental justice** – poorer neighborhoods suffer more detrimental environmental impacts → negatively impacts the health of its residents
  - Low income neighborhood have more pollution, poorer air quality, less sanitary conditions, overcrowding, etc.
  - Ex. Air pollution exacerbates asthma and increases cancer risk

- **Food desert**: low-income urban area with a lack of healthy, fresh food options → residents surrounded by fast food, dried and processed foods, and other unhealthy options → increased risk of diabetes, obesity, etc.

Food Deserts in the United States

STAND WITH FRONTLINE COMMUNITIES IN OUR FIGHT FOR ENVIRONMENTAL JUSTICE, AGAINST THE RAVAGES OF TOXIC CHEMICALS AND CLIMATE CHANGE.

Social class and social stratification

Social Stratification: the way in which individuals are categorized into different strata of a social hierarchy based on social characteristics such as race, income, education, political power, etc.
- Highly dependent on social class and SES
- Social class more dependent on one's background (where they are from, education level, wealth/power of their relatives and ancestors); social status is largely dependent on one's current financial, occupational, and overall current social situation
- Lower class → working class → middle class → upper class

- **Class consciousness:** awareness an individual has regarding his/her social and economic status, and the social class that they are in
- **False consciousness:** inability to perceive/understand one's true status in society

- **Cultural capital:** non-financial social elements that promote social mobility
  - Education, knowledge, skills, language, manners
- **Social capital:** non-financial resources in the forms of relationships, social support, and connections to social networks that promote upward mobility

- **Social reproduction:** structures, activities, and customs in society that result in inequality being reinforced and transmitted from one generation to the next (due to our education system, economy, social class system, unequal access to opportunity, discrimination/prejudice, etc.)

Power, privilege, and prestige –
- **Power** refers to ability to control situation and other people; **prestige** refers to the respect/reverence others have for an individual based on that person's achievements, social class, and reputation → both result in an individual having a lot of **privilege** (perks and special rights/advantages)

Socioeconomic gradient in health –
- Wealthier individuals are generally healthier than poorer individuals
- Gradient determined by differences in environmental conditions, stress levels (related to locus of control), healthcare access and quality, access to health-promoting resources (yoga classes, fitness center, healthy food options, etc.), and education level

Global inequalities –

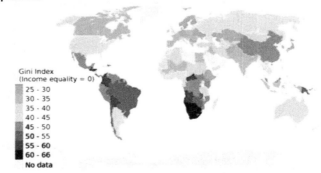

Gini Index
(Income equality = 0)
- 25 - 30
- 30 - 35
- 35 - 40
- 40 - 45
- 45 - 50
- 50 - 55
- 55 - 60
- 60 - 66
- No data

Patterns of social mobility

- **Caste system:** form of hierarchal social stratification with extremely limit social mobility; individual is born into a certain class and remains in that class throughout life

- **Class system:** upper, middle, and lower class divisions; affected by individual's social characteristics/background as well as individual efforts/achievements → some social mobility

- **Meritocracy:** class system in which individual merit defines one's status → idealized system with extensive degree of mobility

- **Intergenerational mobility:** change in social class from generation to the next
- **Intragenerational mobility:** change in social class within a single generation
- **Vertical mobility:** movement to a higher or lower social class (upward or downward)
- **Horizontal mobility:** movement within the same social class (such as changing occupations or social groups)

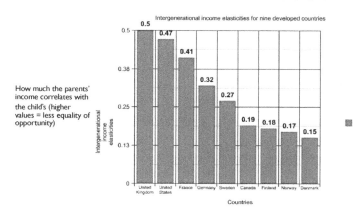

"The Great Gatsby Curve"

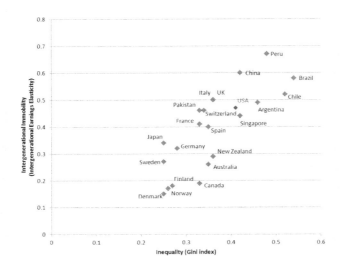

Poverty

Relative poverty: inability to meet a certain living standard as defined by the society
- Differs extensively across regions (relative poverty in Manhattan would be very different from relative poverty in Sudan; could also differ within various neighborhoods of one city)
- Ex. Living on less than a certain % of average income in an area

Absolute poverty: inability to meet basic needs and obtain necessities due to lack of money
- Also differs across regions, but not as extensively
- Inability to access food, clean water, shelter, education, etc.

Social exclusion: occurs when specific people/groups are systematically prevented from accessing certain resources, opportunities, and rights that the majority has access to
- Jim Crow laws resulted in an extensive amount of social exclusion of African American individuals

Disparities in health and healthcare

Income/Social status –
- Lower income individuals have poorer health outcomes
- SES gradient in health
- Wealthier individuals have better access to healthcare and higher quality healthcare

Gender –
- Historically, a majority of studies have been conducted on men and outcomes have been assumed to be the same for women
- Men less likely to seek out care for health concerns and less compliant

Race/Ethnicity –
- Health outcomes are generally worse for minority groups
- Minorities have higher rates of HIV/AIDS
  - African Americans represent about 13% of the US population but almost half of all new HIV cases
- African Americans have higher rates of heart disease, stroke, and diabetes; also higher infant mortality
- Caucasians more likely to have health coverage and/or receive higher quality care

2011 & 2012 Maternal Death Cohorts, Six Most Prevalent Causes of Death by Race/Ethnicity

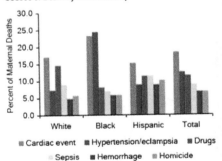

Source: Linked Death-Birth Files, 2011 & 2012 Maternal Death Cohorts
Prepared by Office of Program Decision Support, FCHS, DSHS, 2014

African Americans with HIV are least likely to receive consistent medical care

Retention in care declines across racial/ethnic groups within first three years

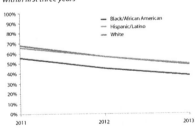

Percentage of people diagnosed with HIV in 2010 who remained in care in 2011, 2012, and 2013.

Source: U.S. Centers for Disease Control and Prevention

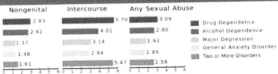

Discrimination

Discrimination: unfair and unjust treatment of an individual on the basis of social characteristics such as race/ethnicity, gender, religion, SES, disability, etc.
- Discrimination is acting on prejudiced beliefs; prejudice = belief/judgement, discrimination = behavior
- Power, prestige and class are both causes of and manifestations of the stratification of society; those in lower strata are more likely to be discriminated against
- Discrimination commonly based on one's race/ethnicity, sexual orientation, gender, SES, and/or religion

Individual discrimination: an individual makes a conscious choice to discriminate against another person

Institutional(ized) discrimination: discrimination of a group by institutions of society; intentional or unintentional
- Due to widely held prejudiced beliefs and biases that become integrated into the procedures, policies, and operations of an institution
- May involve unequal access to opportunities (ex. housing discrimination), selection criteria (ex. job selection), treatment of individuals by the institution (ex. wage gap), etc.

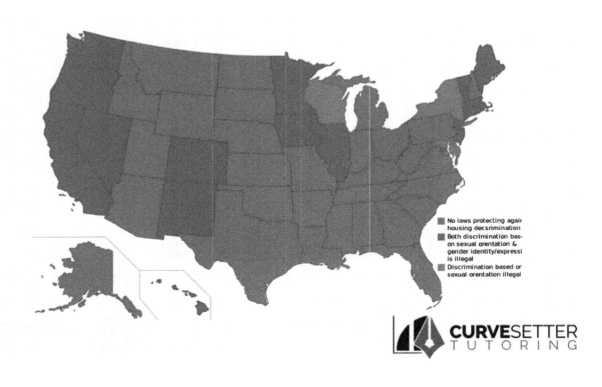

No laws protecting agai[n]
housing decsrimination
Both discrimination bas[ed]
on sexual orentation &
gender identity/expressi[on]
is illegal
Discrimination based o[n]
sexual orentation illegal

EXPERIMENTAL DESIGN

Psychology/Sociology Supplementary Slides

- Types of variables
  - Independent, dependent, moderator, mediator, confounding
- Experimental versus non-experimental research design
  - Causation and correlation
  - Experimental design: random assignment and blinding
- Common study designs
- Null hypothesis
  - Statistical significance
  - P-value
- Validity and reliability
  - Internal validity and external validity

Types of Variables

Independent variable: variable that isn't affected by other variables in the experiment
- Study will determine if/how levels of the IV affect the DV
- In an experiment, you will manipulate the IV and look at resulting changes in the DV (Ex. "How does the amount of water (IV) affect plant growth (DV)?")

Dependent variable: variable that is affected by other variables (namely, the IV)
- DV changes as a function of the IV

Confounding variable: another factor that is correlated with the IV and the DV and may mistakenly cause the experimenters the claim that the IV manipulation resulted in changes in the DV
- Ex. A prescribing to a vegan diet versus standard diet may appear to result in increased longevity; but income level could be a confound → people on a vegan diet are wealthier (better access to quality resources, healthcare, fitness, etc.), which is the true cause of increased longevity
- Potential confounds should be controlled for in every study

Confounding variable →

Commonly: age, race, gender, income, etc.

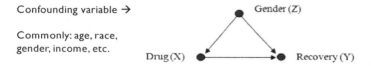

Mediator variable: explains the relationship between two variables

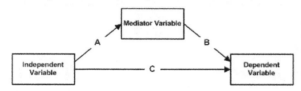

Moderator variable: affects the strength of a relationship between two variables (i.e. makes the relationship stronger or weaker)

Experimental versus Non-Experimental

Experimental Design

- IV is manipulated by the experimenter (often treatment versus placebo) and DV measured
- Participants randomly assigned to the levels of the IV
  - Some IVs and research questions render this impossible/unethical → use non-experimental design
- Control group required
- Enables us to **infer causality** if a statistically significant result is found
  - Never say "*proves*"

Non-Experimental Design

- Lack manipulations of the IV, random assignment, and controls
- Assessing correlations between observed values of variables
- Does not enable us to infer causation; can **infer correlation**
  - correlation ≠ causation

Random assignment – participants randomly assigned to levels of the IV (usually treatment versus placebo)
- Use random number generator or other method to ensure that every participant has an equally likely chance of being in any group
- Crucial element of an experiment
- Goal is to prevent systematic differences between the groups and bolster the internal validity

Blinding – controls for different types of bias
- **Single Blind:** participant doesn't know certain things about the experiment, such as the group they have been placed in (i.e. doesn't know if they're taking a placebo pill or true treatment pill)
- **Double Blind:** participant and experimenter don't know certain things about experiment, such as which group the participants are placed into

Negative Control: group that is not exposed to any treatment (expect no effect)

Positive Control: group that is exposed to treatment with a certain expected effect

Common Study Designs

Non-Experimental –

Cross-Sectional Study: assessing data from many different people in a population at a single moment in time (like taking a "snap shot" of the population)

Longitudinal Study: assessing data that has been collected over a prolonged period of time; can track changes and progress of individuals
- Cohort studies and case-control studies

Cohort Study: cohort (group with a common characteristic) studied over time to see which group will have a certain outcome (**prospective** cohort) or have had a certain outcome (**retrospective** cohort)
- Cohort may be individuals born in a certain year, people exposed to a certain event, people with a certain risk factor, etc; control/comparison group does not share that characteristic

Case-Control Study: comparing group with a certain outcome, such as a disease, to those without that outcome in an attempt to identify some factor that led to the outcome seen
- case = those with the outcome; control = those without it

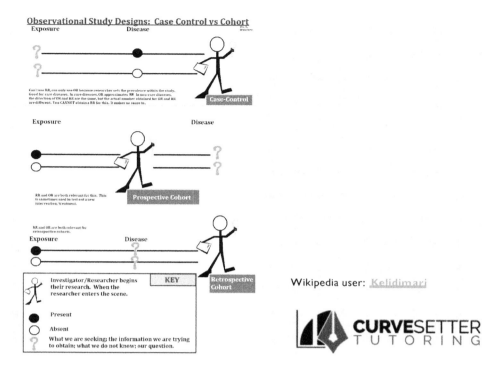

Observational Study Designs: Case Control vs Cohort

Wikipedia user: Kelidimari

Case Study: in-depth analysis of a single case

- Case is a single person, situation, or population; most commonly the case is one patient and his/her affliction
- Low external validity (shouldn't try to generalize from a single case) but give a very detailed picture of that case and may spur subsequent research questions

Meta-Analysis: statistical analysis of the results from multiple studies on the same topic

- Used to make an overall conclusion/summary of multiple (often conflicting) findings

Observational Study: observing a certain behavior/phenomenon without intruding or exerting any manipulation

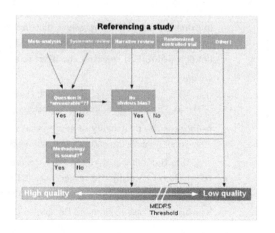

Experimental –

Randomized Control Trial (RCT): "true experiment" in which participants are randomly assigned to groups (levels of the IV) and a control group is present; enables us to infer causality

- **Between groups:** 2 different groups of participants are compared to each other; commonly treatment group and placebo group
- **Within groups:** participants are compared to themselves after some manipulation/change - learning, taking medication, etc. → groups are 'pre' and 'post'

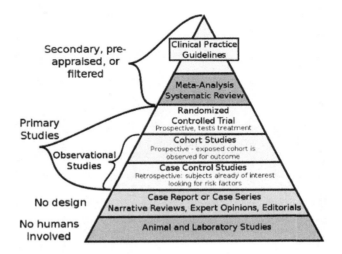

Null Hypothesis: default assumption that there is 'no effect' (no difference between experimental group and control group)

- In other words, null hypothesis is that the experimental group and control group are from the same population and that differences between them are simply due to chance, not the experimental manipulation
- If null hypothesis is rejected, the **alternative hypothesis** is supported (there is an effect/difference between groups)

Statistical Significance: use for hypothesis testing; to determine if a certain relationship exists

- **p-value** is the probability of getting that result, or one more extreme, if the null hypothesis was true
  - Small p-value indicates that it would be unlikely to get that result had the null been true, which suggests that the null is not an accurate depiction of reality → supports the alternative hypothesis
- **Alpha level** is set by the researchers (usually .05 or less)
  - *If p-value < alpha then result is statistically significant*
- Researchers hope to find and be able to publish statistically significant findings
  - More likely to find a statistically significant result when ... large sample size, controlling for potential confounds, more dramatic manipulation of IV, etc.

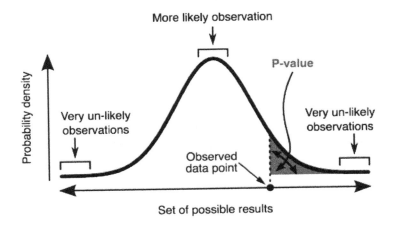

A **p-value** (shaded green area) is the probability of an observed
(or more extreme) result assuming that the null hypothesis is true.

Validity

Validity: measure of the ability to draw _true_ conclusions from a given study

Internal Validity: the extent to which changes in the DV are a result of changes in the IV
- High internal validity – highly controlled and monitored experiment (potentially in a lab environment) with a relatively homogenous subject pool (controlling for confounds)
- Threats to internal validity: experimental mortality/attrition (subjects drop out from the groups differentially), maturation (subjects change due to the passing of time, not experimental conditions), poor measurement tools and instrumental error, secular drift (cultural changes), regression to the mean, etc.

External Validity: the extent to which the study results can be generalized to "real-world" populations
- Generally studies with high external validity are those that are closer to "real-world" conditions (outside of the lab, less tightly controlled/monitored), and have more heterogeneous subject pools
  - Often internal and external validity have a "trade-off" relationship
- Threats to external validity: Hawthorne effect (subjects' behavior changes when being observed), too restrictive selection of participants, over-controlled lab set-up, etc.

Construct validity: how much a test actually measures the construct that it claims to measure

- Ex. Does a certain questionnaire actually measure depression? Does your teacher's biology test actually measure your knowledge of the biology material? Does an IQ test measure intelligence?

Content validity: how much the content of the test is related to (and is a good measure of) the construct it is meant to measure; to what extent the test questions cover *all elements* of that construct

- Ex. Does a well-being test measure all facets of health such as an individual's eating habits, fitness, cardiovascular health, etc.? Does a depression test include measures of apathy, sleeping/eating patterns, mood, and motivation?
  - If the test questions only cover one/a few of those elements, then it has low content validity

Criterion validity: the extent to which a test result is correlated with the behavioral outcome; includes predictive and concurrent validity

- **Predictive validity:** the extent to which the test accurately predicts a later outcome
  - Ex. Does the SAT accurately predict performance in college?

- **Concurrent validity:** the extent to which the results of one measure are related to the scores on another (already established) measure taken at the same time
  - Ex. Do the results of a newly developed depression test correlate with the established Beck Depression Inventory?

Reliability

Unreliable & Unvalid

Unreliable, But Valid

Reliable, Not Valid

Both Reliable & Valid

- Reliability is the <u>consistency</u> or <u>repeatability</u> of a measure

- Reliability does not depend on validity and vice versa

- If a study is done multiple times and yields similar results every time, then it is reliable; however, the results may or may not be valid

3 KEY STUDY GUIDELINES

Core Strategy Video 1

Tip 1: Have multiple passes through the same material

- Revisit concepts, terms, and formulas more than once
  - "Spiraling" – evidence-based and used in medical school curriculums
  - Otherwise what you learned earlier will be a faint memory when test comes around
  - Especially important for people with extended study timelines

- Account for this in your study plan to ensure that you actually do it!

- Committing high yield content to memory is crucial
  - "High-yield" material = concepts that resurface frequently
  - On test day you are frantic and under extreme time constraints; the info that's most retrievable is what has been committed to long term memory
  - Don't just watch the videos; actively engage with rehearsing and memorizing the information

- If flashcards usually work for you, then use them
  - But ensure you have a thorough conceptual ("big picture") understanding
  - Best to make your own flashcards based on your content weaknesses
  - If not flashcards, be sure to test yourself in some way (ex. jot down concepts/terms during video and quiz yourself later)

- Get creative and be persistent: sticky notes and/or diagrams around your house/room; use the app whenever you can

- Making your own study guides, equation sheets, and lecture summaries is very effective
  - The act of writing down the material, putting it in your own words, and targeting what you need to review is very important for committing that information to memory

Tip 2: Master the art of remaining calm under pressure

- Timed practice material will help you master this skill
    - Additional practice – time yourself reading dense scientific literature that you find online and try to summarize it when finished

- Don't shy away from extremely challenging practice passages--embrace them
    - Teach you to remain collected, not get derailed, and answer the questions knowing whatever info you gathered

- Develop a strategy to recollect yourself

- Don't let one dense and challenging passage hog your time and tank your section
    - No single question or passage is worth more than the others; do what you can within the time constraints and don't agonize over it

Tip 3: Keep moving forward from question to question & passage to passage

- Pick an answer and move on
    - Don't let yourself think about the previous ones (it will derail you)

- Feigning some confidence in your abilities and answer choices - fake it till you make it
    - You are in charge of the passage, not the reverse
    - MCAT is a mental test requiring stamina and **confidence**

- Don't change your answer unless you're quite sure that you misread the question/passage, or you see a clear calculation/interpretation error you made
    - "Go with your gut" is true and scientifically proven for performance on MC tests

MAKING THE MOST OUT OF PRACTICE MATERIALS

Core Strategy Video 2

Effective Practice Materials

- The AAMC materials are your holy grail
  - o Learn them inside and out; try to get inside the test writer's heads
  - o By far the most representative

- Avoid hard-copy tests and practice passages

- Single passages can be helpful, but more so at the start of your practice

- Material from other companies – differ in format and style from real AAMC tests
  - o Free sample tests can be found!
  - o Use if you feel that you need more than AAMC (not scoring where you want to be and having trouble with test-taking strategies, timing, complex passages)
  - o Scoring is not as accurate – often deflated – so don't read into it too much

Tips on Taking Practice Tests

- You want to mimic the environment you will experience on test day as closely as possible
  - Complete practice materials in a quiet but unfamiliar environment if possible
  - There will be some minor distractions on test day (sneezing, note scribbling, etc.)
  - If possible, start test in (early) morning

- Do majority of your practice material at the end of your content review; especially tests
  - May or may not want to do a diagnostic
  - If totally new to the MCAT, maybe do diagnostic test to get an idea of the way the test is structured (but do not use AAMC test if possible)
  - You want to have a solid foundation in content in order to make the most of practice exams

- Start doing practice material untimed
  - Untimed - develop your critical reading and interpretation skills
  - Generally start untimed practice with distinct passages

- Once you feel more comfortable, begin timing yourself
  - Develop constant awareness of time and the ability to stay on track
  - Ex. Am I approximately halfway through when 45 minutes are left in this section?
  - CARS timing – no more than 10 mins total per passage (no more than 4-5 mins reading passage)

- Try very hard to never pause a practice test, even if totally overwhelmed (unless there's a huge noise interruption/distraction)

- Develop ability to stay calm when faced with very challenging passages/questions

- On full tests, try not to do "show solutions" unless doing it as untimed practice

- Take all of your breaks; especially on test day!
  - Eat a snack, recollect yourself, BREATHE

Reviewing Your Tests and Practice Materials

- Learn these practice materials inside and out
  - Learn common questions types, how the test-makers try to lead you astray from the correct answer (answer decoys), common passage types, etc.
  - Yes you won't see that exact passage/question again, but you will likely see something similar
  - Try to get inside the test-makers heads

- Spend more time reviewing the tests/practice materials than actually taking them
  - Taking the practice test/passage is only half the battle!
  - Important process is independently deciphering your strengths/weaknesses, common mistakes, etc.
  - Pinpoint the strategies that are working for you

- If possible, review CARS on the same day as the day you took the test
  - Especially helpful for CARS if the passage, your interpretation of it, and your thought processes for the questions are fresh in your head
  - For this section, the absolute best way for you to study is to **practice and review**

- Look at questions you answered incorrectly *and correctly*
  - We often get an answer right for the wrong reasons

- Write down content you are shaky on (even if you got the answer correct) and review it; and compile notes on the practice materials

BASIC TEST-TAKING AND PASSAGE ANALYSIS STRATEGY

Core Strategy Video 3

Highlighting: to do or not to do?

Should I highlight?
- Majority of students find that highlighting is beneficial
- When you read a textbook/article for school, do you highlight/underline/take notes? If so, this type of learning if beneficial to you and most likely will be on the MCAT

Why highlight?
- The act of highlighting requires you to process which information is central to the passage, pick up the main ideas, and note the location of certain key terms/phrases
- Visual anchors: enable you to efficiently scan passage and locate key points, names, dates, terms, etc. when answering the questions
- Scanning highlights can be a good way to get a quick refresher on the main ideas and development of the passage

Caution - do NOT over-do it! → over-highlighting wastes time, can break up your flow of reading the passage, overwhelming to look back at; HIGHLIGHT SPARINGLY
- Shouldn't have more than about 20% of the passage in yellow

What to highlight

CARS

- Main ideas
  - When author summarizes an argument, a situation, a person, etc.
  - "Thesis" statement, if present
- Shifts
  - Shifts in tone, opinion, perspective, timeframe
  - "However", "On the other hand", "Despite this"
- Author's point of view
  - Pay attention when the author dictates his/her opinion, provides support for or against something, or provides their overall subjective perspective
  - Distinguish author's perspective from that of other people/ideas referenced
- Words that indicate tone/"mood"
  - Is the tone critical, curious, somber, nostalgic, optimistic, pessimistic, etc.

Non-CARS

- In general, students tend to highlight less in non-CARS sections (especially C/P and B/B)

- Experimental objectives
  - "An experiment was conducted to determine …"

- Clinical relevance
  - "Bacterial species X, Y, and Z are found in the human microbiome … the presence of X has been implicated in the development of IBS and stomach ulcers.

- Experimental findings, data trends, correlations
  - "It was found that monozygotic twins were more likely than dizygotic twins to …"

- Unfamiliar acronyms, chemical species, key molecules

Note-taking

- Avoid taking notes for CARS
  - Significantly interrupts the flow of your reading and comprehension
  - Instead - mental summary after reading each paragraph (helpful for all sections)

- Necessary for physics passages – **diagrams**, equations, formulas, etc.

- When doing quick math, writing it down can help to prevent avoidable errors

- Biology/biochemistry – jot down molecular interactions (signaling, activation/repression, etc.)
  - Can then quickly refer back to notes/diagram rather than having to reread in passage
  - Helps you cement the role of certain molecules/enzymes/cells as you read

Tips for passage-based questions

- Read the question **very carefully** and rephrase it if complex
  - Misreading the question is a common cause of mistakes
  - Ex. "Which of the following, if true, would least undermine the author's argument?" → which answer choice is most in line with author's argument → cross out anything that weakens author's argument

- ALWAYS look back at the passage
  - When question is referring to a specific part of the passage, read a few lines above and below that part

- For "big picture" CARS questions, rapidly skim the entirety of the passage for the main idea, overall tone, purpose of the passage, etc.

- For science passages, the first paragraph often indicates the clinical relevance of the study
  - "Big picture" info that gives the experimental/scientific details some context
  - Often mentions content that is related to but not part of the main study

- After you read the question, briefly think about the answer in your head and refer back to passage BEFORE looking at answer choices
    - Answer choices are meant to look attractive and lead you astray
    - When question asks about graph/figure, look at back at it and try to interpret it briefly yourself before looking through answer choices

- In CARS, the answer choice must fulfill 2 main criteria: 1. Directly relevant to (and answers) the question; 2. Supported by the passage
    - Avoiding using outside knowledge to inform your answer on CARS

- Non-CARS: as you read, pay attention to places in the passage that mention concepts/terms you're familiar with → you will likely be tested on this in the questions
    - Experiment and specific details may be very complex, dense, and overwhelming – don't get bogged down by this and pay attention to content that you know
    - Don't spend too much time analyzing graphs/charts until a question requires you to; passages occasionally include a figure that is never referred to in the questions

DON'Ts

- Read questions before reading passage

- Skip around from one passage to another (not in order)

- Leave questions blank (even if you plan on going back to them later)

- Skip entire "challenge" passages

- Avoid looking at the clock

- Spend too much time on any one passage

Made in the USA
Las Vegas, NV
28 March 2023

69786021R00345